ON LABOUR

The Development of Industrial Society Series

William T. Thornton

ON LABOUR

Its Wrongful Claims and Rightful Dues

Its Actual Present and Possible Future

IRISH UNIVERSITY PRESS
Shannon   Ireland

First edition London 1869

Second edition London 1870

This I U P reprint is a photolithographic facsimile of
the second edition and is unabridged, retaining the
original printer's imprint.

© *1971 Irish University Press Shannon Ireland*

All forms of micropublishing
© *Irish University Microforms Shannon Ireland*

ISBN 0 7165 1788 4

T M MacGlinchey Publisher

Irish University Press Shannon Ireland

PRINTED IN THE REPUBLIC OF IRELAND BY
ROBERT HOGG PRINTER TO IRISH UNIVERSITY PRESS

The Development of Industrial Society Series

This series comprises reprints of contemporary documents and commentaries on the social, political and economic upheavals in nineteenth-century England.

England, as the first industrial nation, was also the first country to experience the tremendous social and cultural impact consequent on the alienation of people in industrialized countries from their rural ancestry. The Industrial Revolution which had begun to intensify in the mid-eighteenth century, spread swiftly from England to Europe and America. Its effects have been far-reaching: the growth of cities with their urgent social and physical problems; greater social mobility; mass education; increasingly complex administration requirements in both local and central government; the growth of democracy and the development of new theories in economics; agricultural reform and the transformation of a way of life.

While it would be pretentious to claim for a series such as this an in-depth coverage of all these aspects of the new society, the works selected range in content from *The Hungry Forties* (1904), a collection of letters by ordinary working people describing their living conditions and the effects of mechanization on their day-to-day lives, to such analytical studies as Leone Levi's *History of British Commerce* (1880) and *Wages and Earnings of the Working Classes* (1885); M. T. Sadler's *The Law of Population* (1830); John Wade's radical documentation of government corruption, *The Extraordinary Black Book* (1831); C. Edward Lester's trenchant social investigation, *The Glory and Shame of England* (1866); and many other influential books and pamphlets.

The editor's intention has been to make available important contemporary accounts, studies and records, written or compiled by men and women of integrity and scholarship whose reactions to the growth of a new kind of society are valid touchstones for today's reader. Each title (and the particular edition used) has been chosen on a twofold basis (1) its intrinsic worth as a record or commentary, and (2) its contribution to the development of an industrial society. It is hoped that this collection will help to increase our understanding of a people and an epoch.

The Editor
Irish University Press

ON

LABOUR

ON LABOUR

ITS WRONGFUL CLAIMS AND RIGHTFUL DUES

ITS ACTUAL PRESENT AND POSSIBLE FUTURE

BY

WILLIAM THOMAS THORNTON

AUTHOR OF 'A PLEA FOR PEASANT PROPRIETORS'

ETC.

'La grandeur du problème ne nous doit point accabler. Seulement il convient de l'aborder avec frayeur et modestie. Le résoudre, personne en particulier ne le pourrait ; en combinant leurs efforts, tous le peuvent. Dans l'œuvre du progrès universel, que sont, considérés l'un après l'autre, les meilleurs ouvriers? Et néanmoins l'ouvrage avance, la besogne du genre humain va s'accomplissant d'une manière irrésistible, et chaque homme qui étudie travaille, même en se trompant, à l'œuvre de la vérité'

LOUIS BLANC, *Organisation du Travail*

SECOND EDITION

LONDON
MACMILLAN AND CO.
1870

LONDON: PRINTED BY
SPOTTISWOODE AND CO., NEW-STREET SQUARE
AND PARLIAMENT STREET

PREFACE

THE SECOND EDITION.

THIS edition has been carefully revised throughout, but the greater part of the new matter introduced will be found in the Chapter on Supply and Demand, and in the Book treating of Labour and Capital in Antagonism. In the first of these, which has been completely recast and almost completely rewritten, certain peculiar notions of mine are resubmitted, with explanations and amplifications, in a form in which I am quite content that final judgment should be passed upon them. The other, to which one whole chapter has been added, and several minor additions have been made, presents a certainly sincere and, as I hope, a fairly comprehensive view of the facts and principles of industrial cooperation. During the process of revision, I have received considerable aid from critics both friendly and hostile. Among the former I have the satisfaction of being able to name the 'Fortnightly,' in which Mr. Mill has honoured my book by making it the subject of two separate articles—the 'Westminster,' and

'British Quarterly Reviews,' the 'Times,' and the 'Journal des Économistes.' Among the latter I have been a good deal disappointed to meet the 'Spectator,' but not at all surprised to encounter the 'Edinburgh Review.' To one and all, however, with the single exception of the last named, I am indebted for more or less of comment of that salutary kind which at once induces and assists a writer to re-examine his previous opinions.

To the 'Edinburgh Review,' some of whose maunderings I had quizzed, perhaps a little too unmercifully, in my former edition, my obligations are of a different order. The contributor to that journal who has taken me in hand, commences indeed with a shout of *Io triumphe!* and in his fourth sentence announces himself as a conqueror about to drive me from an indefensible position, but he nevertheless pays me the compliment of thenceforward systematically garbling my statements, thereby plainly evincing his inability to grapple with them. Of which piece of politeness I at one time proposed to make fitting acknowledgment, by printing here and there beneath my own words, my reviewer's versions or interpretations of them. On second thoughts, however, I felt that this would not be worth while. Even those who have no means of knowing anything of me but what the reviewer tells them, must at once perceive the utter incompatibility of the monstrosities which he attempts to father on me, with the 'cultivated intelligence' for which he is, at the same time, pleased to give me credit; while no one can read ten consecutive pages of my work without seeing that its aim and tenor are the direct opposites of what the reviewer asserts them to be. Although, therefore, wherever the reviewer has made any pretence at argument, I have not withheld the few words necessary to show that it is only a pretence, I have uniformly passed over in silence his stolid misconceptions and studied misrepresentations. As for the misrepresentations, remembering as I do what the 'Edinburgh Review' was in its palmy days, it is simply painful to me to see it in the decrepitude of old age descending to such paltry shifts. Those who have neither the wit to answer, nor the candour to assent, should for their own sakes keep their ill-will to themselves, for by any strictures they may indulge in, they will merely betray their impotence and meanness. Whatever they may say, there can be no doubt of their being at heart convinced of the truth of that which, in order to oppose, they are constrained to falsify.

The reader is requested to bear in mind that through almost the whole of the volume, with the exception of the last few pages, by 'present time' is meant the end of 1868. The supplementary and now concluding chapter, however, and also some newly-added notes, are to be understood as bearing a date more than a twelvemonth later, viz. that of this supplementary preface.

LONDON : *February* 1870.

PREFACE

TO

THE FIRST EDITION.

'WHEN I was about five-and-twenty,' said the late
Mr. Nassau Senior, 'I determined that I would reform the condition of the poor of England.' When
I was myself about the same age, I conceived, not
indeed the same ambitious design, but much the
same desire as that which it implies. More than
five-and-twenty years have passed since then, and
it is somewhat sadly now, with sexagenarianism at
no great distance, that I contrast the insignificance
of performance with the magnificence of youthful
projects. But the passion of a life is not to be
extinguished by any failures that do not extinguish
life itself, and so long as any strength is vouchsafed
to me, so long shall it be cheerfully devoted to continued search after a cure for human destitution.
Vast as the problem is, 'its magnitude need not
overwhelm us. Only it requires to be approached
with caution and modesty. Though no one singly
can expect to solve it, by combining their efforts all
may. In the work of universal progress, what indi-

vidually are the ablest of workers ? And yet the work advances : mankind's great business tends irresistibly towards accomplishment, and every one who investigates, labours, even while erring, in the cause of truth.'

Words, in substance the same as these, have already served for motto on the title-page, and might by themselves have sufficed likewise for preface, for they explain fully the motives for my present appearance in print. An additional reason for their being repeated here is, that besides being those of one of my most valued friends, they are taken from a treatise of his containing but few other passages to which I am prepared to accord an equally unqualified assent.

LONDON : *December* 31, 1868.

CONTENTS.

BOOK IV.

LABOUR AND CAPITAL IN ALLIANCE.

Book I.

INTRODUCTORY.

LABOUR'S CAUSES OF DISCONTENT.

Book I.

INTRODUCTORY.

LABOUR'S CAUSES OF DISCONTENT.

IF self-glorification were ever permissible, the present age might be excused for so incessantly proclaiming itself to be pre-eminently one of progress. In certain directions, greater advances have undoubtedly been. made during the last sixty-eight years than during the previous six hundred. It is within the briefer and more recent period that man has made a printing machine of the sun, and a postal messenger of lightning, and has put steam into harness, now yoking it beside the winds to his sea chariot, now urging it to whirlwind speed along novel highways of iron. Since the beginning of a century which has still a third of its course to run, the growth of population has in this country been far greater than it had previously been since the Norman Conquest, and the growth of national wealth has been greater still. For every individual living in Great Britain in 1801, there are now more than two; for every one who then enjoyed an income of a hundred pounds a year, there are now three. That modest annuity, moreover, notwithstanding the depreciating influence of Californian and Australian gold discoveries, is now worth a great deal more than it was two generations back—will procure for its recipient a much larger quantity of the necessaries and conveniences of life. Provisions of all sorts, except meat, are now much cheaper; so, too, are fuel, artificial light, aids to locomotion, all articles of furniture and clothing, and most literary and artistic products. Wheat, which, during the wars of the first French Revolution, rose repeatedly to a hundred, and once to a hundred and twenty shillings a quarter, now scarcely ever reaches to much above half the latter price. Of coal, what was then commonly paid in the metropolis for a ton, will now purchase nearly as much again. Hats, boots and shoes, and every intermediate article of attire, may now, with a little management, be had at prices from one half to two thirds of what would then have been charged for habiliments of similar description and quality. At less than the cost of the wax candles used to light a single entertainment of the Prince of Wales' last predecessor, many a London gin palace is now illuminated nightly, throughout the year, with a brilliance never equalled in Carlton House, reflected by mirrors of greater size and beauty than Louis the Magnificent was fain to content himself with for wainscoting the Salle des Glaces in his palace of Versailles. By properly regulating his movements, a man may now make an excursion from London to Brighton, at less expense of time and money, than his grandfather must have incurred in order to ride outside the coach from the Bank to Hampstead. At an average rate of half a crown a volume, he may fit up his library with books which not very long ago would have been thought cheap at half a guinea ; for sixpence a week he may supply himself with a square yard of 'Illustrated News,' adorned with wood engravings that Bewick might have been proud of; while he may, at his choice, have either a wonderful pennyworth of 'Daily News' entirely to himself, or, at the same price, an hour or two's daily reading of the marvellously Brobdignagian sheet into which, since some of us were children, has gradually expanded the Liliputian 'Times' of an era ignorant of steam presses.

That intellectual has kept pace with material progress, might be too much to affirm, but in the extent to which it has fallen short of the latter, there is nothing to be ashamed of. The absolute number of readers cannot now be less than twenty times, nor the number relatively to population less than ten times, what they were when living sexagenarians were learning their alphabet. No doubt there are very many who read little but novels and newspapers, but provided these be good of their kind, there is no very great deal of much more instructive reading. He who reads nothing now but his newspaper, would, sixty years ago, have read nothing whatever; and whoever, even though he seek no other aid, avails himself fully of the light of the ' Morning Star,' or the communicativeness of the ' Daily Telegraph,' will not be ill supplied with materials wherewith to store his mind, and to exercise his judgment and fancy. Hard students besides have been multiplying at the same time with superficial smatterers. There are many more of them, both absolutely and relatively, than there ever were before. If not, such books as Mr. Mill's ' Logic ' and ' Political Economy ' would not be annually bought by the thousand, nor would the scientific works of Sir John Herschel, Sir Charles Lyell, and Dr. Tyndall be in such large, nor the metaphysical works of Professor Bain and of Mr. Herbert Spencer, in such increasing demand. In every period the average quality of readers may be judged of from that of the writers, and what period was ever much better off than our own for philosophers, historians, poets, or novelists? What needs John Stuart Mill but to have been long enough dead in order to have his name bracketed with those of Bacon and Locke? Had we not lately amongst us in Macaulay an English Livy more glowingly pictorial than his Roman prototype? Have we not still in Grote a Thucydides without his occasional harshness, and a Tacitus without his constant affectation? And in Carlyle one whose characteristic excellences, in spite of equally characteristic faults, assign to him a place apart, without parallel among ancient or modern historians? Is there not in single couplets, and triplets, and quatrains of Tennyson more of the true poetic essence than, but for Gray's elegy, could be squeezed out

of the whole body of eighteenth century versification?
Is it not enough simply to mention Thackeray or George
Eliot, to prevent any but a parrot from attempting to revive
the antiquated claims to supremacy in fiction of Fielding,
or Smollet, or of Scott?

On the subject of morals it behoves us, no doubt, to
speak less confidently.   Earnestness and enthusiasm are
now out of date.   To display much emotion about anything, is now almost a mark of imperfect breeding.   Airs
of imperturbable indifference are now the most approved
wear of common sense.   Nor, alas! is it in externals only
that fashion has altered for the worse.   Commercial
honesty has ceased to be one of our national characteristics.   'National eccentricity in money matters' is the
mildest phrase now used by foreigners to indicate the sad
change that has taken place since an Englishman's word
was universally held to be as good as his bond.   As for
political honour or consistency, most of what little of that
remains among our leading statesmen, seems to me to be
concentrated in the single person of Lord Salisbury.   So
is it with the seniors.   Of the boy and girl of the period,
their seniors are not perhaps the fairest judges.   It is
scarcely for these to decide how far the examples of frivolity
and heartlessness themselves have set, have been outdone
by their juniors.   At any rate, it suits my temper better to
suggest excuses for our misguided young people.   They
may be perhaps in a transition state.   It may be because
they have seen so many objects of traditional veneration
dragged down from their pedestals, and denounced as
shams and humbugs, that they have come to believe
nothing really worthy of reverence.   It may be reaction
from ancestral slowness that has made them so fast.   If so,
another reaction is certainly coming on.   Any how, the
unnaturally accelerated pace is sure to tire at last, and it
may, let us hope, be succeeded by another midway between
the previous extremes of speed.   Whether our children
are or are not as yet our inferiors, it is quite on the cards

that they may hereafter grow up into superiors of either their parents or grandparents. Not that the contrast between the latter and ourselves is by any means wholly to our disadvantage. On the contrary, there is not the smallest boast in asserting that a balance fairly struck between our moral backslidings and our moral advances, would show that the latter greatly exceeded. Taking moral gains and moral losses together, we are undoubtedly much ahead of our forefathers. Among our gains is not to be overlooked that increased refinement which has utterly banished drunkenness and ribald language from amongst educated men. Neither should the spirit of enlarged benevolence, now so generally diffused, disgusting as is the cant often talked in its name, for the cant would not be talked if the spirit were not prevalent. What, however, is most noticeable, is perhaps the habitual reference to acknowledged principle—the habitual testing, by a recognised standard, of acts done or to be done—the principles, too, being more enlightened, and the standard more elevated. Doctrines for which ethical teachers were not long since half-despairingly pleading, goals to which they were pointing with faint hope of ever seeing them reached, are now accepted as truisms, and taken as starting points for fresh departures. What use can there be in sanctimoniously shutting one's eyes to facts like these? Why not rather exult in them as proofs that God's kingdom on earth is not receding but advancing? Why not gratefully rejoice that much as iniquity may abound, grace doth yet more abound ; that though the ratio of saints to sinners be still lamentably low, it is at any rate in these latter days higher than it had ever previously been?

Yes, verily, let *laudatores temporis acti* say what they please, there never before was a time like the present : never was there a more advanced or more rapidly-advancing age than that in which we live ! Happy ye, oh youngsters ! did ye but know your luck, whose career is beginning in it instead of ending ; and all such of us as belong to any of

the upper ten thousands of society, or have even contrived
to lay hold on their skirts, may fairly congratulate each
other on progress in which we all participate.   Our position
is decidedly preferable to that of corresponding classes at
any former period.   But is there equal, or is there any,
reason for congratulating the inferior millions by whose
ceaseless exertions the superior myriads are upheld ?   Has
there been like improvement in *their* condition ?   Have
their lines likewise fallen in pleasanter places than any ever
occupied by their forefathers ?   The question is not to be
answered monosyllabically.   Some benefit assuredly, and
that by no means inconsiderable, is derived by the poorest
amongst us from the victories of ' science, and the long
results of time;' but there is nevertheless considerable room
for apprehension, that while enjoying these new spoils of
conquest, they may in many cases have lost, or loosened,
their hold on former acquisitions.

No reader of Lord Macaulay's History can have forgotten the descriptive catalogue there drawn up of the
blessings which philosophy and civilisation have conferred
upon those who hold the plough or tend the oxen, or
weave at the loom, or quarry or square the stone.   We are
there reminded that a rustic can now drive his cart in
a single hour over a distance which, in a premacadamite age,
no vehicle could have traversed in less than twelve : that
an artisan may now, however late he leaves his work, walk
homeward through secure, convenient, and brilliantly lighted
streets which, a hundred and eighty years ago, would have
been so dark after sunset, that he could not have seen his
hand, and so ill-paved and watched, that he might think
himself lucky if he reached his own door without stumbling
and breaking his neck, or being knocked on the head by a
footpad : that every bricklayer who falls from a scaffold,
every sweeper of a crossing who is run over by a carriage,
may now have his wounds dressed and his limbs set with
a skill such as formerly all the wealth of a great lord
like Ormond, or of a merchant prince like Clayton, could

not have purchased: that bull-baiting and cock-fighting, or the sight of wretches in the pillory pelted with rotten eggs and brickbats, or howling at the cart's tail beneath the lash, are no longer permitted to blunt the sensibilities of the populace: that many things—products of tropical countries being specially mentioned—which at no very remote date were costly rarities, reserved for the exclusive use of the opulent, are now within everybody's reach.*

So far Macaulay proceeds upon tolerably firm ground, but presently his footing becomes less secure. Discovering that the summer rate of agricultural wages was, in 1685, 4s. a week in part of Warwickshire, and 5s. a week in part of Devonshire, that in 1682 it was 6s. a week in part of Suffolk, and in 1661, 7s. a week in part of Essex, he at once adopts the lowest of these rates as that which prevailed throughout the southern kingdom during the reigns of the last two Stuarts, and assumes that an English peasant's weekly wages did not then ordinarily exceed 4s.; whereas a district in which they should be as low as 7s., would now be 'thought to be in a state shocking to humanity.' Next, upon the strength of a ballad which appears to have been sung during the same reigns about the streets of Norwich and other clothing towns, he assumes that workmen, in what was then the great staple manufacture of the country, thought themselves well paid if they gained 6s. a week. Then, referring to the register of prices which, since 1729, has been kept in Greenwich Hospital, he finds that the daily earnings of the bricklayers, masons, and carpenters employed in the repair of that building, have risen from 2s. 6d. to 4s. 10d., 5s. 3d., and 5s. 5d. respectively, and those of plumbers from 3s. 6d. to 5s. 6d. Further, he remarks that in 1685, when the pay of a private foot soldier was only 4s. 8d. a week, no difficulty was experienced in obtaining many thousands of English recruits at very short notice, whereas the present weekly stipend of a private, although raised to

* Hist. of England, vol. i. pp. 423–5.

7*s.* 7*d.*, is found to be an ' insufficient attraction for English youth, insomuch that it has become necessary to enlist largely among the poorer population of Munster and Connaught.' From these data he considers it to be clear that the money wages of labour were, in the generation preceding the revolution of 1688, not more than half what they now are ; and seeing that none of the necessaries of life have since doubled in price, while many articles of universal use have become decidedly cheaper, he concludes that labouring men were in that age worse off than at present in all material respects—that they were worse lodged, worse clothed, and worse fed. That any one should think differently, he attributes to that impatience of their actual condition which makes mankind, ' while constantly moving forward with eager speed, constantly look backward with tender regret.' He cannot otherwise understand how it can be doubted that the career of the working class, like that of all other classes of English society, has in every stage been one uninterrupted ' progress from poverty and barbarism towards the highest degrees of opulence and civilisation.'*

Confidently put forward as they are, these are nevertheless but hastily formed conclusions, as will presently appear when the evidence on which they rest has been supplemented by some additional testimony—testimony of which Macaulay fully recognised the authority, and which, indeed, he exhorted his readers to consult, but which he himself somewhat inconsistently neglected to apply. Throughout the particular period which he contrasts with our own, lived Daniel Defoe, that most minute, careful, and comprehensive of enquirers. One subject which he investigated with peculiar interest was the condition of his poorer countrymen, and the following are some of his notes upon it. It is curious to observe how item by item, as if of malice aforethought, he disproves the whole of Lord Macaulay's proofs.

* Macaulay, *ut supra*, pp. 415–427.

'Although in Yorkshire, and generally in the Bishoprick
of Durham, a labourer's weekly wages might,' he says, 'be
only 4s., in Kent, and in several of the southern and
western provinces, they were 7s., 9s., or 10s.' Often when
he (Defoe) had wanted a man for work, and had offered 9s.
a week to sturdy varlets at his door, he had been told to
his face that they could get more by begging, and 'once,'
says he, 'I put a lusty fellow in the stocks for making the
experiment.' Again, he represents himself as habitually
paying six or seven men together on a Saturday night, the
least 10s., and some 30s., for work, and he mentions one
man who for several years gained of him from 16s. to 20s.
a week by his handiwork at the 'mean, scoundrel employment of tilemaking.' Turning to manufactures, he says
nothing was more common than for journeymen weavers
to earn from 15s. to 30s. a week ; and he appeals to silk
throwsters, whether they were not in the habit of giving 8s.,
9s., and 10s. 'to blind men and cripples to turn wheels.'
Then he speaks of 'the difficulty of raising soldiers, the vast
charge the kingdom was at to officers to procure men, the
many little and *not over honest* methods used to entice them
into the service ;' and all this he explains by the ease and
plenty in which Englishmen lived. If, he argues, they had
'wanted employment and consequently bread, they would
have carried a musket rather than starve, and have worn
the queen's cloth or anybody's cloth rather than go naked
and live in rags and want ;' but he that could 'earn 20s. at
an easy, steady employment, must be mad or drunk when
he lists for a soldier to be knocked on the head for 3s. 6d.
a week.' True, the high wages that prevailed were not
always turned to the best account. They were higher here
than in any other country in the world, but whereas a
Dutchman, with 20s. a week, would be sure to grow rich
and to leave his children in very good condition, an
Englishman 'could often but just live, as it was called,'
might perhaps 'hardly have a pair of shoes to his feet, or
clothes to cover his nakedness, and might have his wife and

children kept by the parish.' But then this was caused entirely by the extravagant humour of our poor people in eating and drinking, for they 'ate and drank, but especially the latter, three times as much in value as any sort of foreigners of the same dimensions in the world.' If it had not been for the alehouse, every one might have lived comfortably, for it was incontestable that there was 'more labour than hands to perform it,' and that the 'meanest labour in the nation afforded the workman sufficient to provide for himself and his family.'*

Not even Macaulay's eloquence and ingenuity can countervail these sturdy affirmations of Defoe, which place beyond dispute, that there has not, since the earlier writer lived, been any such marked or general rise of money wages as the other imagined. Besides, money wages, a century or two ago, were very far from representing so accurately as at present the sum total of their recipient's resources. Among the proceedings, legal or other, which, with whatever motive instituted, have, together with many beneficial results, had the baneful one of utterly divorcing the English labourer from the soil, the most efficacious have been Inclosure Bills, which did not come much into fashion until the middle of George II.'s reign. Previously, whoever wished to build himself a cottage, might, without much objection, squat himself down on one of the many tracts of neglected land which, scattered about on every side, then made up a full fourth of the whole area of the kingdom; while the ease with which rent-free dwellings were thus obtainable, necessarily lowered the rent of other dwellings of a similar class. Labourers, consequently, in rural districts had to pay little or nothing for lodgings, and no small portion of their board also was procurable on equally easy terms. The peasant's garden, cribbed probably, like the site of his cottage, from the waste, supplied him with roots and herbs; on the adjoining common he

---

* 'Giving alms no charity,' *passim.*

had grazing for a cow and a few sheep, as well as for
pigs and poultry : some neighbouring wood or heath furnished him with fuel for the gathering, and he was lucky if
he lived too far from a meer or marsh to allow of his catching an occasional eel or mallard, as well as the ague. It
may be that where ' he once fed a flock of geese, is now an
orchard rich with apple blossoms; that the fen in which he
snared wild fowl has long since been drained and divided
into corn-fields and turnip-fields ; that the moor where he
cut turf among the furze bushes is now a meadow bright
with clover, and renowned for butter and cheese.' But of
whatever advantage such transformations may be to the
country at large, to the poor countryman they have been
of less than no advantage at all. His share of the gain
resulting from them is a miserable set-off against his concomitant loss, for what he has gained is simply access to
shops and markets stocked more abundantly than before
from the augmented produce of the improved land, while,
what he has lost, is all that the same land would have
yielded if left in a state of nature. It was by supplemental
aids derived from lands in that state, that the Yorkshire
hind, when earning no more than 5s. a week in money, was
nevertheless enabled, as we are expressly told he was, ' to
live much better' than working men ' in any of the manufacturing countries of Germany, France, or Italy.' When
this was the case in Yorkshire, ' where labour was cheapest,' it is very certain that in Kent and Sussex, and in
the southern counties generally, where agricultural wages
were on an average twice as high as in the north, and
were supplemented in the same manner, the condition of
labourers in husbandry cannot have been one which their
successors have any reason to look back to with contempt.
Nor if the condition of manufacturing labour be considered,
will the result of the comparison be more unfavourable to
the past. In days gone by a large portion of the manufacturing business of the country was done by rural cottagers,
while such operatives as, being in populous cities pent, were

shut off from rights of common, appear, from what Defoe
tells us, to have been in general quite as highly paid in his
time as in ours.   If in some few places there were weavers
earning only 6s. a week or less, so likewise are there now,
and the explanation is the same in both cases, and is to be
sought in the local decay or in the migration of particular
employments.   Thus the invention of the knitting frame had
caused stocking making to be 'transposed' from Norwich
to Spitalfields, insomuch that 'whereas the hose trade from
Norfolk had once returned at least 5,000s. a week,' it had,
in the course of twenty years, become 'not worth the naming.'   The effects of a similar transposition were visible at
Canterbury, where, a few years before, there had been 200
broadcloth looms, but where there were no longer more
than 50, the others having gone with their owners to
London.   From Sudbury, too, and Farnham, many of the
principal tradesmen had removed with their stocks to the
metropolis, where they gave work to a new set of hands,
while their old hands were left behind to bid against each
other for what little work remained with them.*   The
internecine competition and struggle for existence that then
set in, might speedily bring down wages to the point indicated in the song on which Macaulay lays so much stress,
but it is plain that such exceptional reductions did not
sensibly affect the ordinary price of manufacturing labour.
Where the woollen trade was declining, the wages of hand-
loom weavers might well be as low as are at this moment
those of the ribbon makers of Coventry; but wherever
business was thriving, the earnings of textile operatives
generally seem to have been quite as considerable as they
have ever been, unless very temporarily, since.   It cannot
be said to be usual now for journeymen weavers to gain
more than from 15s. to 30s. a week, and we might look in
vain now for silk throwsters who 'pay 8s., 9s., and 10s. a
week to blind men and cripples for only turning wheels.'

* 'Giving alms no charity.'

If, instead of stopping short at the Stuart period, we were to carry our retrospect as far back as to the Tudors and Plantagenets, we might find warrant for asserting that, until accelerated in certain quarters by trades' unionism, the movement of English labourers along the road that leads to the 'highest degrees of opulence and civilisation' has, on the whole, been rather retrograde than progressive. We should arrive at a period when their wages were twice or thrice* as high as their rulers, in the abundance of their solicitude, conceived to be good for them, and when sumptuary laws were deemed by the legislature to be necessary to check their self-indulgent propensities, and to restrain their transgressions in diet and dress: when, accordingly, carters, ploughmen, and other servants in husbandry, were gravely admonished by Act of Parliament against eating or drinking excessively,† and special statutes were passed to prevent their using materials of clothing of higher price than (allowance being made for the difference in the value of money) might now suffice for the purchase of silks and satins, and the finest of linen and broadcloth.‡ But we

* See Statute of Labourers, 23 Edw. III. cap. i. and 25 Edw. III. cap. I.

† 37 Edw. III. cap. 8 and 14. What Parliament in those days understood by excess in eating may be partly estimated from a passage in the earlier of these statutes, which declares domestic servants, whether of gentlemen, tradesmen, or artificers, to be entitled to only one meal a day of flesh or fish, and directs them to content themselves at other meals with milk, butter, cheese, and other such victuals. Alas! for poor Hodge, as, sitting under a hedge, he washes down with cold tea his noon-day repast of bread, cheese, and an onion; what a feast he would think it, if his meagre fare could be so far expanded as to reach even the restrictive limits of the olden time.

‡ As servants in husbandry no doubt furnished the largest quota of those who drew bow or pushed pike at Cressy and Poictiers, it is not probable that their excesses had had much effect in enervating them. At any rate, if fitness for military service be any test, whatever physical deterioration may previously have set in among the labouring population, has not been checked since their luxurious habits have been exchanged for enforced abstemiousness. According to the returns for 1862, more than half the persons who offered themselves at

must not permit ourselves to be led farther into an enquiry which, whatever be its historical or antiquarian interest, may in these pages be not improperly regarded as a digression. The question which here concerns us is not so much whether the condition of our working classes was formerly better or worse than it now is, as whether the actual condition is satisfactory; and to that question no one surely will be hardy enough to venture on an affirmative reply.

But though all must admit the present state of labour to be such as it is impossible to contemplate with approving eyes, there are perhaps few who correctly appreciate the extent to which it falls short of a suitable standard. To elucidate this matter, it is quite unnecessary to produce any darkly coloured pictures of exceptional wretchedness, to paint gloomy interiors of rickety hovels or noisome city cellars, with human beings huddled together like swine, two or three families in one room, and four or five individuals of different sexes on one straw pallet; to exhibit scenes in dreary workhouses, where an old age of quasi-solitary imprisonment concludes a life of unremitting toil; to point to girls, in Welsh iron works, harnessed like cattle to ballast trucks, and straining painfully up hill; to sketch

the headquarters of the recruiting districts in the United Kingdom were labourers, husbandmen, and servants. Of these, 364 in 1,000 were rejected on inspection; of mechanics engaged in occupations favourable to physical development, such as carpenters, smiths, masons, 396 in 1,000 were rejected; of manufacturing artisans, as clothworkers, weavers, lacemakers, 455; of shopmen and clerks, 445. These figures show the relative proportions, but the absolute number of rejections was larger, as more than a fourth of the men had been previously passed by army or civilian surgeons, and were therefore picked men before the inspection. Considerably more than half (6co per 1,000) of the recruits of the year were English, nearly a third Irish, and about a seventh Scotch. The largest proportion of rejections was among the Irish; the least among the Scotch. The proportion of 'tall' men, six feet or upwards, among those examined was a trifle more than one per cent. It was 104 per 10,000 in the English districts, 194 in the Scotch, 91 in the Irish. The differences in favour of Scotland are noteworthy, and suggestive in more than one respect.

the gaunt spectres of the tailor's sweating shop, or those spectral sisters of theirs, whose inarticulate moan has by a master hand been translated into the woeful words, and set to the melancholy music, of the 'Song of the Shirt.'

On the contrary, we can afford to imagine some of the worst evils of our social system removed, some of its darkest stains effaced, some of its foulest ulcers cleansed. Those 'wretched, uncared for, untaught' clowns 'who raise the crops on which we live,'* we may imagine them from being what anyone who stands outside a village beershop on a Saturday evening may perceive them to be, transformed into all that 'the curate and the young ladies who have undertaken the task of guiding them to heaven' are trying to make them. We may imagine them working hard twelve hours a day, for 12s. a week, and ' managing to bring up a large family respectably on the money;' going regularly to church, 'doing their best there to make out something from the service,' and touching their hats to the gentlefolk whom they pass on their way out—living, in a word, manifestly in the fear of God and the squire; spending, too, all their evenings at home, and listening attentively ' while their children read them Bible stories out of good books brought from the Sunday School,' without ever casting a longing look from their own quiet ingle to the blazing fire and uproarious orgies of the public house. Among the manufacturing and mining population, and the whole body of mechanics, artisans, and handicraftsmen, an equal or greater change may be imagined : every individual getting 'a fair day's wage for a fair day's work,' and finding it, or making it sufficient : every family, either in its own snug, self-contained tenement, or in its own set of rooms in a model lodging-house, with water laid on and all suitable appliances for drainage and ventilation, free access allowed

* The words between inverted commas in this paragraph are quotations from memory from a clever article on Agricultural Labourers that appeared in the 'Saturday Review' some years ago.

to the district visitor and city missionary, and a church and national school close at hand.

Let us suppose, then, all these suppositions realised, and indulge ourselves for a moment by dwelling on the pleasing picture they suggest. Mendicancy would then be without excuse. Dives might issue from his sumptuous mansion without his present certainty of finding Lazarus waiting outside the gate, and might return to it without compunction on account of the many poor he had met with in his walks abroad. At present, which of us in tolerably easy circumstances, and not quite steeled by habit, can sit down regularly to the manifold comforts and luxuries inside his home, without having first, as regularly, to argue down the reproachful appeal made by his inward sympathies on behalf of the multitudinous destitution out-side? How we have to appeal, in our turn, to certain very sound and just, but withal somewhat case-hardening maxims! How continually we have to assure ourselves that ' charity creates more distress than it relieves, and does not relieve all that it creates;' and to reflect that even though we gave up all our goods to feed and clothe the poor, the total of hunger and nakedness would not be at all diminished. The necessity for such self-indurating pro-cesses would then have ceased. All bellies being filled, and all backs covered, competence and wealth might be-take themselves, without self-reproach, to the enjoyment of their abundance or superabundance. Poverty would no longer be constantly at hand to offend their sight and hearing with its haggard looks and plaintive whine. Yet immense as would be the relief to poor as well as rich, would the improved position of the former be such as the industrious children of labour ought in reason to be satisfied with? If called upon to answer this question, the curate to whom we were a while ago referring might probably answer, yes. His rector almost certainly would, and many of their coadjutant young ladies, out of respect for their spiritual advisers, and in spite of their own truer instincts,

might not improbably join in chorus. Similar replies
would assuredly be given by the landlord and cotton lord,
the iron-master, and master manufacturer of every denomination, by the merchant and well-to-do shopkeeper ; if,
indeed, by the mass of English respectability, any notice of
the question were vouchsafed, beyond a murmur of indig-
nant surprise at its having been asked. For among what
we are accustomed to designate as 'respectable' people,
the social ideal even of philanthropists commonly rests on
the assumption that the majority must work hard enough
with their hands to relieve a privileged minority from the
necessity of working—if they work at all, except with their
heads. By all means, as much alleviation of the hardships
of the majority as is compatible with this condition, but this
is a _sine quâ non._ And there is in the world such an immensity of work to be done, that unless very many are constantly working, there can be little or no leisure for the few.
The multitudes, therefore, whose vocation is manual labour,
must needs be kept hard at it. Is not labour the appointed
lot of man ? Has it not been ordained that he shall eat
bread with the sweat of his brow ? that after refreshing
himself with sleep, he shall go forth and pursue his work
until the even? If, then, his toil be adequately remunerated—if he receive sufficient provision of bread in exchange for equivalent sweat, and possess in his home all
requisites for shelter and repose, together with fitting changes
of raiment, what more can he rightly claim ? Is it not
incumbent upon him, not simply to do his duty in his
appointed station, but to do it cheerfully? Although no
doubt at liberty, if he have the skill, to raise himself to a
higher position, is he not bound, as long as he remains
where he is, to remain there contentedly ?

If our theme were not our own ' lower orders,' as we are
in the habit of calling them, but some lower order of brutes,
language like this might not be out of place. Provided the
ox be well housed and tended, and not tasked beyond his
strength, his master may perhaps, without forfeiting the

character of a merciful man, merciful to his beast, get as
much work out of him as he can. For the ox of a kind
master, being really better off than if left to take his
chance with the other beasts of the field, in a promiscuous
struggle for existence, may perhaps be fairly required to
make the utmost return in his power for his keep. He is
troubled with no aspirations, moral or intellectual; he has
no mind to improve, nor affections to exercise, nor any
wants but what are gross and carnal. When these are
satisfied, his cup of happiness is full, and all the work
which he is equal to may not be too much to pay for the
filling of it. But with the ox's human fellow-labourer, the
case, whatever his employer may think, is really somewhat
different. How nearly soever to the level of the ox, he may
have been bowed down by burdens too heavy for man to
bear, he is never without some faint reminiscences of a loftier
origin, some yearnings after a higher state. The ethereal
spark is never quite extinct within him. Plenty of meat and
drink, although very likely what he most esteems, are not
absolutely the only things he desires. He has some taste for
recreation and diversion ; and if he have none for anything
but what is low and sordid, it is because the deadening
influences to which he has been subjected have extinguished the germs of his higher capacities. But was not
the development of such germs the one great purpose for
which he was sent upon the earth ? Is not this the theory
of moralists of every sect, how diversely soever they may
word their creeds ? Is not this, or something like this,
implied, whether we speak of the imperative obligation of
self-culture, and of bringing the body under subjection,
and asserting the supremacy of mind, or whether we speak
of life as a journey towards heaven or hell, and declare
man's chief business in this world to be that of preparing
for another ? But though this be the universal theory, how
universally is it ignored in practice ! How calmly, how
approvingly, do we not acquiesce in any degradation and
debasement of our fellow-creatures, which we perceive

or believe to be subservient to our own exaltation and refinement.

At the very commencement of society, as soon as materials for its construction were brought together, its living constituents proceeded forthwith to arrange themselves in layers, the stronger, nimbler, and cunninger climbing up on their brethren's shoulders and occupying the higher places, and leaving to those below only the office of upholding them in their elevation. As the pyramid was originally built, so has it ever since subsisted in general design. It is an animated mass, heaving with multitudinous life, whose movements are continually raising up individual atoms and pushing down others, but without destroying, however much disturbing, the primitive distribution into layers. These are still, as ever, disposed one above another in gradually diminishing series, the lowest and largest having to bear the weight of all the rest. It is so natural to think that what is and always has been is right and ought always to endure, that to most of us, it never occurs to question the propriety of a division of labour which devolves upon two-thirds of the community the whole duty of supporting, and leaves the other third with comparatively little to do but to be supported.* You, my more fortunate

---

* This passage a very able writer in the 'Times' pronounces 'a striking illustration of the danger of metaphors.' 'The assertion that two-thirds of the community support the remaining third,' is declared by him, 'not to have so much truth in it, as the statement that the third sustains the existence of two-thirds.' 'If called upon to picture the conditions of society,' he 'would rather liken it to a crowd borne on a raft floating over a bottomless sea, the planks of which are supplied by a class of capitalists, to whose exertions it is entirely due that the platform has been framed, enabling the mass of mankind to emerge from an abyss of nothingness. If,' he adds, 'universal madness, seizing on mankind, were to take the form of destruction of all capital, the result would be instant and universal starvation, and society would disappear.' I don't know that I admire my critic's metaphor more than he does mine ; but the views which it is adduced to illustrate are quite as much mine as his, nor have they, I believe, ever been more strongly expressed than they may be found to have been at the beginning of the chapter on the ' Origin of Trades Unions,' and in other portions of this work. But there is no inconsistency between them

reader, have haply been nursed in the lap of luxury, or of
one of her upper handmaidens, 'nuzzled,' as an old dra-
matist has it, 'twixt the breasts of happiness.' From your
birth you have been used to have all your rougher work
done for you. Your food and clothes have been provided
without your ever being called upon to soil your hands or
tire your fingers. Whatever occupation you have had, has
left you time enough for your books and your own thoughts,
for study, for meditation, for chewing the cud of fancies,
sweet or bitter. If you have duly profited by these advantages, you have been enabled to lead a life not unworthy of
a rational being, and having been to the manner born,
it has not occurred to you to criticise a constitution of
society which has rendered such a life possible for you and
others equally favoured, although at the expense of many
more not less naturally qualified. Even if you had thought
on the matter, you might have plausibly argued that it
would be far worse for mankind at large if some portion
of the species were not exempt from the coarser business
of life, and your point of view is too exalted to allow of
your duly appreciating the additional burdens of those who
have to take your share of toil as well as their own. It
may be good for you, however, to descend for awhile from
your pinnacle of superiority and to mix with the common
herd below. Imagine yourself to be one of them. Select
for yourself one of their choicest situations. Place yourself
in the position of a journeyman of any sort you please, in
full employment at high wages, only obliged to stick closely
to his trade from dawn till dusk. Could you reconcile your-

and what is said above in the text. Capital, like most other things,
presents different aspects, when regarded from different points, and
recognition of its indispensableness for the subsistence of labour need
not blind us to the subjection in which it holds labour. But, in order
that a smaller number of men may be exempted from drudgery, a
larger number must be subjected to it, is no rhetorical 'misrepresentation of the order of society,' but a plain prosaic matter of fact, which,
to whatever 'deplorable consequences it may have given rise,' there is
no use in protesting against, for no protest, however energetic, can
upset it.

self to such an existence? You are supposed, observe, to be abundantly supplied with all materials requisite, to be comfortably lodged, warmly clad, unstinted in beef and beer. The only thing denied is leisure. But consider what an infinity is implied in that single want. What, without leisure and its uses, would the whole world profit you if it were yours? As it is, you are clothed in fine linen, and if not in purple also, only because that colour is no longer in fashion for male apparel, and you fare sumptuously every day. You are not of course indifferent to the pleasures of the table. So much, remembering Charles Lamb's warning, you will in prudence admit, lest your taste in higher matters be suspected. Still you seldom bestow a thought on your dinner till half-an-hour before you sit down to it ; and admirably as Poole's coat fits, you surely do not stand long before the glass admiring yourself in it after you have got it on. Your delight, apart from those connected with the affections, no doubt consists rather in some favourite and congenial pursuit—active sports, may be, and bodily exercise ; in the conduct of business official, commercial, or industrial ; in conversation, reading, contemplation, and speculation ; in flights of fancy more or less discursive ; possibly in literary composition or the prosecution of some art or science. Without some interests like these, what good would your life do you ? But if without these all that wealth can give would not seem to you to be worth living for, how can you suppose that those to whom wealth has given nothing can be content, or ought to be content, entirely to forego them ? Every country clown, every city cad, every one of those human units whom we pass in a crowd with as little thought of them as individual existences as if they were so many bushes in a thicket—is nevertheless just as much the centre of his own universe as you or I of ours. His life is to him, as ours to us, the most interesting of epics—the one in which he is himself the leading figure. He cannot, any more than we, help regarding all things primarily in their relations to himself; his own cares, his own duties, his own wishes and aims holding the first place in his estimation, and those of all others, excepting of the few who are to him as parts of himself, only a second.   His first desire, like ours, is to live himself; but his ill luck has made him our servant instead of our master; so his whole life must be given up to helping us to live.   Consider what is the proportion of our fellow-men condemned to fates like this.   In this favoured England of ours there is at least as much of culture and refinement as in any other equal space on the globe's surface; there are at least as many persons in it whose circumstances are such as to allow of their following to a considerable extent the bent of their own inclinations, and whose inclinations take occasionally the direction of self-examination and self-improvement : yet even here, for every one such person there also are two,* more than three hundred days of whose every year, and from ten to sixteen hours of whose every working day, are engrossed by the drudgery of the farm, the factory, the mine, the foundry, or the shop.   Two at least are subjected to this drudgery in order that a third may be exempt from it.

Not, indeed, merely on account of their having drudgery to do, are they to be pitied.   There is no man who has to earn his bread, in however liberal a profession, who has not more or less of drudgery imposed upon him, nor who would not disgrace himself by murmuring thereat, however great and well-founded be his consciousness of ability for superior service.   Man's first duty—often directly to his neighbour, and always through his neighbour to himself and to his God—is to take his due share in the common business of mankind.   The meanest and most ignominious part he can play is that of the lazy drone feasting on

---

* It may be proper to mention here, that the statistical estimates of this chapter, though not put forward as minutely accurate, are very far from being conjectural.   In the present instance, the statement in the text is founded on calculations, the materials for which were obtained from the Census Reports for 1861, particularly the one treating of the Occupations of the People in England and Wales

sweets which busy workers have collected. Neither does it behove him to complain if not privileged to choose his work. What right has he to choose more than another? Whatever it be that his hands find to do, let him do it with all his might, thereby best establishing his claim to higher employment. If his work be of much account in the world's eye, let him be thankful; if of little, let him accept it cheerfully. He may console himself by reflecting that there is no drudgery so brainless and mechanical, so dull or disgusting, but that, if undertaken in a proper spirit, it dignifies human nature. 'Better is it to break stones or turn a mangle, than to do nothing. Good roads and clean linen are products of human industry which we need not be ashamed of having had a hand in creating.'* Adam Bede, we are told, had no theories about setting the world to rights, but he saw that there was a great deal of damage done by building with ill-seasoned timber and by slovenly joiner's work, and knowing that one can never see the end of the mischief a bit of bad workmanship may do, he resolved, for his part, to set his face against such doings. He felt that, carpenter as he was, it was quite in his power to leave the world better than he found it ; so he determined always to make the best job he could of every job that fell into his hands ; and he had his reward in the delight derived from the consciousness that he was labouring, though only in a small way, in one of the greatest of causes.

Not therefore does the fact of drudgery being the lot of two-thirds of our brethren suffice to constitute a grievance. In that respect, indeed, no change is possible, for of drudgery must always consist the greater part of the work to be done in this sublunary world. Neither would it at all conduce to the greatest happiness of the greatest number that the drudgery should be equally distributed, instead of

* 'Cornhill Magazine' for November 1860; Article 'Work.' I cannot deny myself the gratification of mentioning that the writer of this noble essay, as well as of a kindred one on 'Holidays' in an earlier number of the same magazine, is my excellent friend and official colleague, John William Kaye.

being, as it is, heaped up in very uneven measure on particular classes, while other classes are comparatively exempt. On this one point, at any rate, Political Economy is decisive, as for the sake of its own continued existence it has need to be, for otherwise it would have nothing to subsist upon. There would never have been any ' Wealth of Nations' for Adam Smith to discourse about, if individuals, instead of betaking themselves to distinct occupations, had been required to take each in turn a spell at every kind of work. It is not merely that we should be badly off for poems and pictures if our Tennysons and Landseers had continually to lay aside the pen or pencil for the plough or shuttle ; we should be quite as badly off for corn and cloth, and for every other material necessary, if there were no ploughmen except weavers, no weavers except ploughmen, and if everyone being Jack of all trades were consequently master of none.

What, however, is really a subject for commiseration, and ought powerfully to appeal to our fellow-feeling, is that so many of our fellow-men are not merely drudges, but are nothing else but drudges—that they have to give up their whole time to drudgery. Nor would there be less, but on the contrary much more cause for pity, if they were quite unconscious of possessing on that account any claim to sympathy. That affectionate submissiveness to a lord's behests —in other words, that spaniel-like servility—for which Scotch Highlanders used to be noted, and which is held up to admiration in the Waverley novels, may be a very laudable quality for dogs, but is very unworthy of human beings, debasing in truth both those who manifest and those who tolerate it. There is a picture in our National Gallery which I fancy may have been designed to exhibit this servility in the most favourable light. The scene is laid in Holland. On one side of a canal that creeps lazily along in the sunshine, a lady is sitting with a pet dog at her feet, on a bench backed by the garden paling of a quaint, gable-ended, country-house. At her side are two gaily-dressed men – her husband and brother perhaps—examining the game-bag of a companion just returned from the chase. To the canal bank in front is moored a barge that has just discharged its cargo of necessaries brought for the use of the household. A little way off trips a milkmaid, with a pair of buckets slung across her shoulders. Opposite, a ploughman jocundly drives his ox a-field. Altogether, rather a choice bit of a pleasing land of drowsyhead, to which extremest revulsion from early prejudice scarcely prevents one from looking back with something like regret. Clearly nobody was in much of a hurry in those days, and everybody apparently being allowed to take things quietly, was well enough satisfied to take them as they were. The lucky group of idlers in the foreground were, one feels sure, looked upon with anything but unkindly eyes by their retainers. The nearest approach to envy which the sight of them produced, was the thought how nice it would be to have, like them, nothing to do but to amuse oneself. The milkmaid who has just passed them does not seem to be singing just now, but she most likely will, as soon as she has put her pails down. The ploughman evidently has no more of care or thought to trouble him than the ox has. And that old fellow on the bridge, basking in the sun—one fancies him a former servant in the manor-house, one of those whose 'service sweat for duty, not for meed,' past work now, but permitted to have the run of the kitchen. Ask him about the family, and instead of complaining of his 'unregarded age in corners thrown,' you will probably find him as garrulous about his dear masters, old and young, as Shakespeare's Adam was about Sir Rowland and Orlando. Not, may be, a very exhilarating peep this into the 'constant service of the antique world,' when one comes to reflect upon its revelations. Yet may not labour have been happier then in accepting, as a matter of course, the situation it was born to—not so much resolving to make the best of it as not dreaming that it much needed to be bettered—than now,

when rich and poor are so often regarding each other
askance, the rich only not scorning the poor, because they
have begun to fear them, the poor not hating the rich the
less because finding themselves no longer so completely
in their power? Was not the former estate, with all its
deficiencies, better than the latter? Why could it not then
last? Well, for one reason, because those even who ask
the question would not let it last, if it were to return. Few
of us are so sordidly selfish but that when adequately provided for the indulgence of our tastes and appetites, we
do not desire to indulge our sympathies also. Of course
the first duty of labourers is to labour. With that of
course nothing must be permitted to interfere. But provided they show themselves duly mindful of their primary
calling to grow our food, and make our clothing, and build
and furnish our habitations, we in turn show ourselves not
unmindful that they have, in common with ourselves, a
higher, though for them a secondary calling, for which it is
a pleasure to us to assist them in preparing. So we establish
National and Sunday Schools, and Societies for the Diffusion
of Useful Knowledge, and urge the passing of Factory Acts,
and Acts for the regulation of Agricultural Gangs, our hearts
glowing the while, and our cheeks flushing in self-approval
of all the disinterested good we are doing. But while
thus taking credit for our exemplary conduct, we must be
prepared to put up with its inevitable consequences. The
poor cannot be given to eat of the fruit of the tree of knowledge, and made thereby to distinguish between good and
evil, without longing to eat likewise of the tree of life, and
to be able to live more nearly as they see their betters living. So our working classes have been taught to long, and
unsatisfied longings, turning within them into heart-burn-
ings, seem completely to have dried up at their sources the
antique gratitude and fidelity which very scant patronage
used at one time so copiously to elicit. They are now far
indeed from supposing themselves to have been created for
no other purpose than that of ministering to the convenience

of creatures like themselves ; and if they did so suppose, their unquestioning acceptance of such a lot would be little less disgraceful to us than deplorable for them. If they neither asked for nor aspired to anything better than to be treated like well-tended beasts of burden—content to be oxen for the sake of oxen's provender—the greater would be our sin and shame for permitting them so to ignore the privileges of their birthright. And the shame and sin would be increased tenfold if aggravated by hypocrisy ; if, without attempting to lighten the load that bowed our brother to the earth, we mockingly bade him stand upright, and raise his eyes to heaven ; if, allowing him no respite from our work, we solemnly adjured him to work out his salvation in addition.

The consequences of the sin, moreover, could not fail to rebound upon ourselves. It is not possible to acquiesce in debasement which we have the means of checking without becoming ourselves debased. When a living poet declared that 'the meanest life is sacred whence the highest may arise,' he did not mean that two out of every three of our countrymen are greatly sanctified by being used merely as stepping stones, whereby a third may rise higher in the intellectual or moral scale. Neither would that progress be likely to be in an upward direction, which anyone would make who could without repugnance avail himself of such means of rising.

And now be it recollected that the endowment of labour which we have been weighing in the balance, and have found wanting, is not only not the actual one, but is an imaginary amplification of it so great that if it were real, it would be very generally regarded as supplying all that is deficient in labour's estate. Hitherto we have spoken as if a competent livelihood were within reach of every one willing and able to work for it, whereas the notorious fact is that continuous toil often earns barely enough for the maintenance of its own continuity. It is proper, however, here to remark, that there is a good deal of exaggeration

afloat as to the difficulties with which English labour has
to struggle. Misapprehension of our poor-law statistics
often leads foreigners, in spite of their own eyesight, enormously to overstate the amount of pauperism in England,
and to declare that nowhere else is there so much, whereas
it would be, at least, equally near the truth to affirm that in
few countries of the Old World is there so little. The dis-
tinguishing peculiarities of English poverty are not so much
either its amount or its intensity, as the glaring contrast it
presents to the amazing wealth with which it is inter-
mingled, and the magnitude of the relief afforded to it at
the public expense. Absolutely, however, whether relatively or not, there is abundance of poverty to deplore and
to be ashamed of. Although with us, little more than
three per cent.* of the population are in receipt of parish
relief, whereas in France,† corresponding or equivalent

---

* In 1866-7 the number of paupers in England and Wales was
931,546, or four and a half per cent. upon the estimated population of
21,320,000. Of these 137,310 were in-door and 794,236 out-door
paupers, exclusive of 24,379 asylum lunatics. The amount of relief
afforded to out-door paupers, exclusive of asylum lunatics, was
3,358,351*l.*, or, on an average, say 1*s.* 8*d.* per head weekly, or 4*l.* 4*s.* 6*d.*
yearly. But for the entire maintenance of an out-door pauper an
average of at least 2*s.* 6*d.* weekly, or 6*l.* 10*s.* yearly, would be required.
At this rate 3,358,351*l.* would not suffice for a year's maintenance of
more than 516,669 out-door paupers, which number added to 137,310
in-door paupers, would make a total of not more than 653,979, or not
more than three per cent. of the population ; and this, strictly speaking,
is the real percentage of English pauperism.

† 'Il résulte d'un rapport officiel,' says Louis Blanc, 'publié en 1837
par M. Gasparin, que le nombre des indigents secourus dans les 1,329
hôpitaux et hospices du royaume ne s'élevait pas, en 1833, à moins de
425,049. En ajoutant à ce nombre accusateur celui des indigents
secourus à domicile par les bureaux de bienfaisance, l'auteur du beau
livre sur la misère des classes laborieuses, M. Buret, constate, comme
résultat certain des dernières investigations administratives, qu'en
France il y a plus d'un million d'hommes qui souffrent, littéralement, de
la faim, et ne vivent que des miettes tombées de la table des riches.
Encore ne parlons-nous ici que des indigents *qui sont officiels* ; que
serait-ce donc si nous pouvions faire le compte exact de ceux qui ne le
sont pas? En supposant qu'un indigent *officiel* en représente au moins
trois (supposition admise par M. Buret, et qui n'a sûrement rien
d'exagéré), on est conduit à reconnaître que la masse de la population
souffrante est à la population totale à peu près dans le rapport de 1 à 9.'

relief is given to more than ten per cent., still the patent fact that three out of every hundred Englishmen and women cannot or could not, if they were fit for it, find work enough to live upon, speaks very plainly for itself, and suggests an equally plain inference as to the far larger percentage that earn no more than the barest livelihood.

On this latter point we may pick up some useful information, in one or other of the workhouses of which, at the present stage of our discussion, we cannot help being reminded. Let us enter, and have a talk with one of the worn-out agricultural labourers, whom, if our visit be made in a rural union, we shall be sure to find moping by the fire or in the sun. On questioning him about his personal experiences, we shall probably hear some such tale as the following.

As soon as he could earn fourpence or sixpence a day he was taken from the national school to which his mother used to send him to keep him out of the way, and was turned into the fields to look after sheep or to scare away crows from the corn. He was then about ten years old. As he grew bigger, he grew worth more money, and at fifteen he got a place as waggoner's mate, at four or five shillings a week. Subsequent steps of promotion gradually raised him to full bachelor's wages, but within a few months of his coming of age, he found himself one morning coming out of church, with a damsel of seventeen on his arm, whom he had just wedded, tempted partly by her charms, and partly by the premium on early marriage offered by farmers in the shape of extra wages to married men. The first quarters of the young couple were two hired rooms, furnished with articles hired from the broker; and here for a

—'Organisation du Travail. Edition of 1843, pp. 43, 44. It will be observed that in the comparison in the text I take only what Louis Blanc calls the 'official' destitution of England, but both the official and non-official destitution of France. This, however, I consider I am warranted in doing, because, as in England every destitute person is legally entitled to public relief, there may be presumed to be little absolute destitution that is not 'official.'

while they got on pretty well, for though theirs was a dear neighbourhood, yet wages were proportionably high, the husband getting 14s., to which the wife's earnings added on an average 2s. a week. They did pretty well, therefore, as long as they remained childless, and indeed as long as they had only one child; but the family cares of young married people are apt to increase rapidly, and not unseldom, as unfortunately happened in this case, in a ratio of nearly annual arithmetical progression. So in the third year of their married life, they were obliged, for the sake of additional space, to remove to a cottage of their own, where in a few years more they found themselves with half a dozen children on their hands to be maintained on a weekly aggregate income, raised by the earnings of the two elder boys, from 16s. to 24s., or sufficient for a weekly expenditure of 3s. per head. In course of time the elder sons grew up, and left the paternal roof as their father had done before them, but younger boys took their places, while the daughters went out to service, so that the total revenue of the family continued for a good while to bear about the same proportion to numbers. But out of a weekly allowance of 3s. per head, to pay rent, buy food, fuel, and clothes, provide for the repair and renewal of furniture, and meet miscellaneous incidental expenses which the poorest and most economical cannot wholly avoid, involved a hard struggle, and hard was the life which the parents led in consequence.

Wages in their neighbourhood were, as has been said, exceptionally high,* and the man did no doubt allow himself an occasional pint of ale, especially on Saturday nights, but a red herring or a bit of bacon was the nearest approach to

---

* According to Mr. Purdy's calculations, the latest and most elaborate that have appeared on the subject, the average of agricultural wages in England and Wales, in 1860, was 11s. 6d. a week. This was an average of rates ranging from 8s., the lowest known in any of the southwestern counties, to 18s., the highest in the northwest and north. Purdy on ' Earnings of Agricultural Labourers in England and Wales,' in Journal of Statistical Society for Sept. 1861.

flesh meat ever seen within his dwelling, except on very great festivals, and bread and cheese and an onion, washed down with cold tea, constituted as often as not his midday and principal meal. Scant fuel this to keep up the animal heat, and quite as scanty was the fuel on his hearth, and not much more abundant the clothes either on his back or bed. No wonder then that such hard fare, coupled too with hard work, made both him and his wife prematurely old. Before he was fifty years of age, he was sixty in constitution, was pronounced to be no longer worth his 2s. 6d. a day, and was reduced first to 2s. and then to 1s. 6d. This compelled him to lower still further a diet already quite low enough, and low diet, at his age, was little likely to conduce to the conservation of force. By the end of another ten years he was unable to earn enough to live upon ; and as the Benefit Club to which he had formerly subscribed had lately voted him out as a useless incumbrance, his only resource was to apply for out-door relief, to be shortly afterwards changed for in-door relief, on his falling ill and appearing to require nursing and medical attendance which could be most conveniently afforded to him within the sick ward of the 'Union.' Once within the walls of that dreary asylum, the poor old couple—for the wife had to accompany her husband—are in for life. They have sold their cottage furniture, or distributed it among their children, and may now make up their minds to wait as patiently as they can in their separate wards, until death shall come to set them free.*

If our visit had been to a town instead of a village Union, we should have had no difficulty in discovering among the inmates some sufficiently exact counterparts of

---

* For most of the particulars of this poor old fellow's biography I am indebted to an article entitled ' Life of a Farm Labourer,' in the 'Cornhill Magazine' for February 1864. An equally interesting paper, evidently by the same writer, headed 'The Scottish Farm Labourer,' appeared in the same Magazine for November 1864. The 'Fortnightly Review' for October 1868 contains a paper, by Mr. W. A. Abram, on

the rural pauper to whose story we have been listening. We should have found several who, having married without more means than were required to support them singly in tolerable comfort, had thenceforward to strain under their self-imposed burdens, until they finally broke down beneath them.   Wages are, however, in general, much higher in towns than in the country, and a large portion of urban pauperism no doubt consists of persons who, with moderate forethought, might have remained independent, but who having never looked beyond the day, were without provision for the morrow, so that when disease or old age came upon them, it brought hopeless destitution in its train.

No doubt it may be said that the hardships encountered in all these cases were caused or aggravated by the misconduct of the sufferers ; that people who marry with inadequate means, or who consume at one meal all their provision, instead of hoarding it with due precision, have chiefly themselves to blame.   Whether agreeing or not in this, I care not to contest it, seeing that there would be little use in investigating disorders, and as little hope of remedying them, if they proceeded from causes beyond control, and unless personal responsibility for them could be affixed somewhere.   How labour's besetting epidemic may be cured or palliated will be considered hereafter. My immediate object is to demonstrate its existence, and to illustrate its extent; and for that purpose what has already been said may probably be accepted as sufficient.

Assuming, then, that we have arrived at a not inaccurate appreciation of what is, and always has been the normal condition of labour, can we reconcile ourselves to the prospect of that condition remaining for ever unchanged ? Shall we—such of us as are reckoned among the classes to which fortune confines the distribution of her favours— shall we complacently accept, as an overruling necessity,

the ' Social Condition of Lancashire Workmen,' in which the average life of a factory operative is graphically sketched.

the permanence of a monopoly which, however indulgent
to ourselves, excludes the great majority of our brethren
from participation in our most valued blessings? Universal philanthropy is now the order of the day. We
all speak its language; we all profess to share its views,
and not a few of us do no doubt sincerely mean much of
what we profess. But is our ideal of the best possible
human commonwealth—of the highest perfection to which
society can attain—compatible with the perpetual serfdom
of two thirds of society? There are not wanting those
who, by implication if not directly, will not scruple here to
answer 'Yes.' Poverty, they will tell us, is of divine appointment, a destiny with which it is not simply useless,
but rebellious to contend. Is it not written that 'the poor
shall be always with us—shall never cease out of the land'?
So, at the devil's prompting, is Scripture quoted to his
purpose; while cynical scepticism, uniting for the nonce
with religious resignation, sneers, as a powerful organ of
public opinion lately did, at the 'impotence of science,
social or other, to crush those mighty agencies against
which Christianity, with all its divine influences, often contends in vain.' Shall we then screen our stolid selfishness
behind these pious excuses? Shall we, comfortably re-
signing ourselves to the belief that it is God's ordinance
that makes men to differ, content ourselves with being
humbly grateful that some of the differences are so much
to our personal advantage, and abandoning all thought of
raising our brethren to our own level, thank God that we are
not as other men are, even as these helots? Let us not,
at any rate, pretend to be without Scriptural encouragement to a more generous course, for is it not written also that
'the needy shall not always be forgotten: the expectation
of the poor shall not perish for ever'? Endeavours on
behalf of the necessitous are labour in the Lord—labour
which is never thrown away. Yet better that it were
thrown away utterly than that it should not be exerted.
Better, far better, go on to the end of time, expending our

ingenuity on chimerical schemes, on attempts to discover
the undiscoverable, to remedy the irremediable—better
thus waste our energies, thereby at least keeping up
within us some glow of ennobling sympathy—than that
despair of doing aught further for others should render
us thoughtful only for ourselves, should so deaden our
sensibilities as to permit of our making the most for ourselves of such happiness as lies within our reach, blind to
the sight and deaf to the cry of misery on all sides sur-
rounding us.

Blindness and deafness of the kind referred to will not,
indeed, be much longer possible. The upper myriads may
cry Peace, Peace, but there will be no more peace for them,
on the old terms, with the lower millions. Among these
already widely exists, and is rapidly spreading, a profound
dissatisfaction with labour's social position, and a firm determination to readjust it. Among the malcontents are
already many of vigorous and practised intellect, sure to
be succeeded in each successive generation by an ever-
increasing number, with as great or greater powers, who,
whether the movement in which they engage be ultimately
victorious or not, will never permit it to cease until it is.

In saying this I have not the smallest intention of assisting in an apotheosis, which a good many newly-converted
zealots seem bent on celebrating. As a rule mankind
must certainly have the bump of veneration large. Somebody or something they are continually falling down and
worshipping, though fickle enough as to the objects of their
adoration, and often forsaking true gods for some golden
calf, without enquiring very particularly into the purity of
the metal, They are for ever too in extremes. If not
looking down, they must be looking up—gazing with admiring eyes on the very negro, as soon as they have ceased
to trample him under foot. Among ourselves, the latest
object of idolatry is the British workman, in whom devout
imaginations are continually discovering inherent yet pre-
viously-unexpected excellences ; his special merit, forsooth,

consisting in his freedom from enervating and sophis-
ticating culture. No moral growth, we are bidden to
believe, like that which springs spontaneous from un-
broken clods. This is the prime article of a creed now
getting visibly into vogue, and against which those who
dislike it, and are not prepared to bow the knee to the new
Baal, had better speak out in time. I, for my part, am
a firm believer in culture. Be the soil what it may, a
field cannot fail to be improved by being ploughed, and
manured, and planted. Even though a few old weeds
grow ranker in consequence, or a few new ones be introduced, the ground is sure on the whole to be much cleaner,
and the crops much better for the process. And as of the
earth's soil, so of the mind's. The more culture a man
has, the better he is, and the less culture he has, the worse
he is, and by necessary consequence, the cultured classes
(other things being equal) must excel the uncultured in
precisely that degree in which they surpass them in culture.
This is with me a tenet which I cannot afford to relinquish,
for in losing it I should lose all hope for human progress.
If culture be not improving, nothing is ; and if culture de-
teriorate more than it improves, we had better at once
burn our books—those specially by which working men in
their delusion fancy themselves benefited—and betake
ourselves again naked to the woods, as our sole chance of
recovering that excellence of primeval savagery from which
we have degenerated.

Enough, however, of this strange, ungrateful rant which
even those who talk it—one argument, by the way, in its
favour—would not but for the culture they decry be qualified
to talk. Working men themselves do not talk it. They have,
indeed, like the rest of us, their share of vanity, and finding
the smell of incense agreeable, they sniff up what is offered
them with apparent relish, though at the same time with
puzzled looks, as if not understanding why it should be
thought their due, and not perhaps without some secret
contempt of the offerers. For they do not really fancy

themselves able by mere force of genius to leap at once to
truths which other enquirers, however gifted and instructed,
can attain to only by a series of painful efforts.   They
readily acknowledge their inferiority to better taught men,
and are well aware that the difference is due to difference
of teaching.   They acknowledge no oracles of their own
grade.   The authorities whom they do consult, and to
whom they do defer as oracles, belong to those very cultured classes whom now, to their amazement, they find
rendering them such novel homage.   Undoubtedly amongst
themselves are many really extraordinary men, men whose
natural intelligence is perhaps nowhere to be found sur-
passed, and who, having by virtue of that intelligence perceived the value of culture, have made the most of all
facilities for self-education within their reach.   But with all
their natural gifts and artificial acquirements, it is not to
be supposed that even these can have thoroughly divested
themselves of the prejudices in which they were born and
bred.   It is impossible that on many class questions their
views should not be somewhat narrow and one-sided, and
their theories proportionably cramped and crude.   Even
of a class movement, therefore, which has originated with
themselves, they can be, I hesitate not to say, but half-fitted
to be the conductors and directors.   And this they will, I
trust, hear from me without offence when I proceed to add
that satisfactory solution of social problems affecting distinct classes is scarcely to be expected from thinkers of
any single class.   For very different opinions of the same
thing are likely to be formed by those who view it from
opposite points, and those who look down upon it from
above, and those who look up to it from below, are
sure, without very carefully comparing notes, to come to
diametrically opposite conclusions concerning it.   Partly
on this account it may be, though certainly far from
entirely, that attempts made on the part of employers to
indoctrinate the employed on disputed points of economic
science have usually gone so little way towards enforcing

conviction.   Too often in such instances precisely that ground which the employed most vehemently claim as their own and are least disposed to surrender has been quietly taken for granted by their opponents, and then used as premises whereupon to base authoritative arguments.   But preconceived and deeply rooted notions are clearly not to be dislodged in this manner.   Those who would combat them effectively must occasionally condescend to discuss instead of always insisting on lecturing, and on most industrial questions no discussion can be complete in which spokesmen for the working classes do not take an equal share. On several of such questions the majority of working men appear to me to be very seriously in error, confounding almost systematically their wishes with their rights, and their needs with their dues ; but it is idle to expect to convince them of error by appealing to doctrines which, however clear to our own minds, are not recognised by them.   If we would set them right where we believe them to be wrong, we must begin by establishing a common basis of negotiation, and for this purpose we must endeavour to ascertain what they really think.   We must meet them in fair and equal conference, and, without presupposing admissions on their part, or dictatorially obtruding our own sentiments, must listen patiently and respectfully to what they have to say.   We must mutually define our terms, and explain our principles, and agree upon our premises before proceeding to deductions which otherwise can only serve to aggravate mutual misunderstanding.   This, the only suitable mode of conducting a controversy between rational beings, is also the only one which in the present case would be tolerated.   It is accordingly that which is proposed to be adopted throughout this work.

Book II.

LABOUR AND CAPITAL IN DEBATE.

Book II.

LABOUR AND CAPITAL IN DEBATE.

CHAPTER I.

OF SUPPLY AND DEMAND, AND OF THEIR INFLUENCE ON PRICE AND WAGES.

BEFORE entering on our main subject it is indispensable to disentangle ourselves from certain misconceptions which beset us at the threshold, and which unless got rid of now, will continue to cling to and hamper us throughout our subsequent progress.

The actual condition of labour being what it notoriously is, enhancement of the price of labour must be an indispensable element in any very material improvement of that condition. But hitherto everybody has taken for granted that the price of all things, labour included, depends upon the proportion between supply and demand; and if it does really so depend, we are clearly engaging in an almost hopeless enquiry. If the price of labour does so depend, there is plainly but one means by which it can be enhanced: the proportion of demand to supply must be increased. But in order to produce such relative increase no absolute augmentation of demand will of itself suffice. In the case of labour the normal tendency of supply is to keep at least pace with demand. If demand is to continue in advance, the progress of supply must be retarded. In plain language, labourers must place their power of self-multiplication under more rigorous restraint. Unfortunately, restraint of the sort referred to is commonly most wanting where most wanted. Prudence in matters matrimonial is too often in inverse ratio to poverty. As Johnson said to Boswell, neatly compressing into two lines the quintessence of practical Malthusianism, 'A man is poor: he thinks he cannot be worse: so I'll e'en take Peggy.' Labourers can be rendered connubially discreet only by having their standard of living raised. But their standard of living cannot be raised without a permanent rise in the price of their labour, and the price of labour cannot be permanently raised, unless the multiplication of labourers be checked, and that multiplication cannot be checked except at the bidding of connubial discretion. So that, the problem before us being how permanently to raise the price of labour, the dilemma in which the supply and demand theory places us is this: the price cannot be permanently raised unless the supply be first checked, and the supply cannot be checked unless the price be first permanently raised.

For those who do not choose to be confined within this millhorse circle there is no alternative but to cut the supply and demand theory adrift, as I hope to persuade the reader to join with me in doing. Of such of my critics as have been conscientious enough to examine my former pleadings on this matter before pronouncing upon them, one and all admit that I have pointed out real defects in the popular theory. The only difference between these critics and myself is as to the gravity of the admitted defects. With the additional light with which they have themselves favoured me, I hope now to be able to convince them that the defects pointed out are fatal ones—that the theory is not simply imperfect, but radically and intrinsically unsound. I assert positively that the price, whether of labour or of anything else, in no case whatsoever depends on the proportion between supply and demand, and that no definitions ever have or can be given of supply and demand consistently with which price can so depend. To make good these assertions will be the first object of the present chapter; a second will be to ascertain what does determine price if supply and demand do not; and a third to discover whether there is any, and if so, what, difference between the mode in which the really determining cause regulates the price of labour or rate of wages and that in which it operates on prices generally.

From some of the comments which have been made upon my previous statements, I find it to my extreme surprise necessary to explain, that, when speaking as above, I mean by 'price' only *selling* price—the sum, that is, at which a commodity is either actually being or will eventually be sold. This must not be confounded with *market* price, or the sum for which a commodity is merely offered for sale, but which may perhaps never be obtained for it,— the difference between the two being all the difference between asking and getting. Still less must it be confounded with that pure abstraction of the mind, to which its authors have given the name of *normal* or *natural* price, denoting thereby not any sum for which commodities are either sold or even offered for sale, but only one at which they would be sold if certain disturbing influences did not cause them to be sold for a different sum. It is to this abstraction, or at any rate not to *selling* price, to which those refer who, like Ricardo, although admitting that the price of commodities is *temporarily* regulated by supply and demand, say nevertheless that it is cost of production which *ultimately* regulates price. For here as elsewhere the word 'ultimately' means, it may be presumed, 'at last,' but with respect to an individual sale, there can be no separable first and last. A sale as soon as it has taken place, has become an accomplished fact, and at whatever price the sale was effected that price cannot subsequently change. Upon whatsoever conditions it depended at first, it cannot subsequently depend upon any others. It cannot depend upon supply and demand at one time, and upon cost of production subsequently. When price, then, is said to depend *ultimately* upon cost of production, it cannot be selling price that is referred to. With regard to that, the greatest masters have always been at one with their humblest disciples. By both equally selling price has always been understood to be dependent solely and absolutely on supply and demand.*

* It may, I think, be perceived by anyone who reads Ricardo's 30th Chapter with due care, that in speaking of cost of production as ultimately determining price, he meant little more than this, viz., that the price of unmonopolised commodities cannot *for a length of time* remain either above or below the cost of production, because in the one case production would increase, and in the other diminish, proportionately. He only amplifies this idea when he says that ' supply and demand may indeed for a time affect the market value of a commodity until it is supplied in greater or less abundance, according as the demand may have increased or diminished ; but this effect will be only of temporary duration.' He represents, in short, cost of production as the natural price with which market price would always exactly correspond if the continual variations of supply and demand did not cause market price also to vary. This was apparently Ricardo's opinion, and it is identical with that of every intelligent upholder of the popular supply and demand doctrine, and notably with that of Mr. Mill, until lately its most strenuous upholder.

It must be owned, however, that there are considerable inconsistencies in Ricardo's language on the subject. Some of his propositions, indeed, considering whom they come from, are nothing short of astounding. Take, for instance, this : ' Diminish the cost of subsistence of men by diminishing the natural price of the food and clothing by which life is sustained, and wages will ultimately fall, notwithstanding that the demand for labourers may very greatly increase ;' which is almost equivalent to saying that wages must have fallen in England since the repeal of the Corn Laws, instead of rising as they notoriously have done, and which is quite equivalent to saying that in the long run money wages must always and everywhere represent the same quantity of the necessaries of life. Or take this : ' The demand for a commodity cannot be said to increase if no additional quantity of it be purchased or consumed ; and yet under such circumstances its money value may rise.' According to which, the quantity on hand of some particular commodity being supposed to be limited, only sufficient, say, for the want of twenty customers, the demand for it will be the same whether the number of persons desirous of purchasing be twenty or forty.·

With respect to the limit set by cost of production to possible fall of price, Ricardo copies from J. B. Say, who, while stating that ' cost of production determines the lowest price to which things can fall,' is

This is the doctrine we have to examine, and we shall find it more than ordinarily useful to commence the operation by defining our terms.

careful to explain that by 'lowest price' he means 'the price below which they cannot remain for any length of time.' Succeeding writers have not been equally precise in their phraseology. Even Mr. Mill in one place says, without any qualification—probably because he expected every reader to make the necessary qualification for himself—that 'there is a minimum value (or price) determined by the cost of production :' and my reviewer in the 'Times,' surely because he happened to be holding his pen very loosely at the moment, has let slip the following sentences : 'Find out the cost of producing wheat on the worst wheat soil in England devoted to wheat; ascertain the cost of bringing to market wheat from the wheat-growing country most difficult of access or otherwise inconvenient for commerce, and the price of wheat will be found in strict relation to them.' Of course the writer of this cannot mean, though he does distinctly intimate, that the market price of wheat bears some immutable relation to the lowest cost at which any of the wheat in the market was brought thither. For if so the market price of the same wheat could never vary—at least not within the same season. For in any given season the lowest cost being a fixed quantity, the market price would likewise be a fixed quantity, instead of varying, as the official returns show that it does, from week to week, and varying too in opposite directions, now rising and anon falling.

Upon the same writer's clever paradox, to the effect that although cost of production measures price, it is price that measures cost of production, I will merely remark, that clever as the paradox is it has nothing to do with the matter under discussion. There is, however, another point on which—extended as this note has already become—I must still say a few words. I have admitted that by all intelligent believers in the supply and demand theory, its operation is restricted to what Mr. Mill terms 'the perturbations of value during a period which cannot exceed the length of time necessary for altering the supply,' or as the writer in the 'Times' phrases it, to 'those fluctuations of price happening in an open market during the interval necessary for the production of further supplies.' I must take leave, however, to observe that these perturbations and fluctuations are unceasing and everlasting, and that the length of time necessary to accommodate (more than momentarily) supply to demand is an endless period. If in consequence of demand just now exceeding supply, prices rise, supply will no doubt be increased, but by the time that it has been increased to the point aimed at, much of the present demand will have been satisfied, and the augmented supply may very likely be in excess of the diminished demand. In that case production, which

First, then, what is the proper meaning of 'supply'?
What is to be understood by the supply of a commodity?
One thing which may at once be affirmed with regard to it
is, that it is neither more nor less than the quantity offered
for sale. Supply does not comprise any portion of a
dealer's stock which its owner does not propose to part
with. It would not, for instance, comprise the sacks of
wheat which cornfactors, in expectation of a season of
dearth, might reserve for the consumption of their own
families. Neither would it include the contents of corn-
ships, merely conjectured to be on their way to the market,
and which might perhaps exist only in imagination; though
it might include cargoes of corn known positively to be on
their way, and which, though not yet arrived, might at once
be sold. It comprehends everything actually offered for
sale; and everything, wherever situated, may be so offered
provided its ownership can be immediately transferred.
What is meant, then, by the supply of a commodity is
precisely the quantity, and neither more nor less than the
quantity, that is offered for sale, whether the whole of that
quantity be or be not actually present in the market. This
definition will be presently perceived to be defective; something must be supplied to render it a complete description

had just before been stimulated, will now be checked, and, as likely as
not, checked sufficiently to let demand get once again in excess of
supply, whereupon it will receive a fresh stimulus to be followed subsequently by a fresh check. In this manner action and reaction are
continually succeeding each other, and supply and demand are continually reversing their relations. No doubt they are continually
gravitating towards equilibrium, but equilibrium is no sooner reached
than overpassed. The 'point of exact equilibrium,' as Mr. Mill ac-
knowledges, if 'as real as the level of the sea,' is likewise as 'momentary.'
There is never any such 'stable equilibrium' as that of which teachers of
political economy dream, and as a consequence of which things go on
for a considerable time together, exchanging for each other in proportion
to their respective costs of production. Do I therefore say that prices
do not often remain unchanged for a considerable time together? By
no means : but then I am not one of those who believe that stability
or variations of price depend on stability or variations of supply and
demand.

of supply; but so far as it goes it is correct, and for the moment may be permitted to suffice us.

Next what is 'demand'? Evidently not merely desire to possess. There is no demand in the longing with which a penniless schoolboy eyes the raspberry tarts in a pastry-cook's window. His mere eagerness to get at them cannot in the least affect their price. Ability to purchase must also be present. The boy must have some halfpence in his pocket. So much is clear, and demand accordingly is not uncommonly described as consisting of desire to possess combined with power to purchase. But irrespectively of other objections to this definition, there would, if it were correct, as Mr. Mill has pointed out, be no possibility of comparing demand with supply. For supply is a quantity—the quantity offered for sale—and obviously there can be no ratio between a quantity and a desire; still more obviously can there be none between a quantity and a desire combined with a power. The phrase is intelligible only, if by the desire and the power be meant the quantity desired and the quantity over which the power extends. And this is what is really meant. When we speak of ratio between supply and demand, we are thinking of a ratio between the quantity supplied and the quantity demanded : and accordingly these last two words constitute the definition of demand adopted by Mr. Mill.

So far so good, but this definition also is imperfect. If demand admitted of no more precise limitation, the ratio between it and supply would be, not indeed invariable, but one capable of varying in only one direction. Demand might easily exceed supply, but it would be scarcely possible for supply to be in excess of demand. Of any merchantable commodity, of anything at once useful and difficult of attainment, the supply can scarcely be so great, but that some customer will be willing to give something in exchange for it, even if not more than a half a farthing. Only let the price be low enough, and some one or other will be pretty sure to consent to take the whole stock at that price. If goods be offered for sale unreservedly, if the salesman be content to let them go for what they will fetch, the quantity demanded will be pretty sure to be at least equal to the quantity supplied. This consideration may suggest to us a needful emendation of our late definition of supply, which is not simply the quantity offered for sale, but the quantity offered at some specified price; some price or other being in practice always named either by dealer or customer for goods exposed for sale. To correspond with this amended definition of supply, the definition of demand must be similarly amended. The demand for a commodity is not simply the quantity of that commodity which customers are ready to buy at some price or other, but the quantity they are ready to buy at some specified price. As supply is the quantity of a commodity offered for immediate sale at a particular price, so demand is the quantity demanded at the price at which the commodity is offered for sale. The necessity for one of these emendations has been pointed out by Mr. Mill, or at least recognised by him, where he says that the 'quantity demanded is not a fixed quantity, but varies according to the value.' The other is believed to have never before been made in print, possibly because no previous writer thought it worth making. If so, some service will here have been done in pointing out its importance. Any definitions less distinctive than those just drawn would fail to mark the exact outlines of actual or present supply and demand, and of course when we talk in a general way of comparing supply and demand, we can mean only actual supply and demand, for these alone are definite quantities. Future or prospective supply and demand, spoken of with reference to an undefined future or prospect, are obviously indefinite quantities, and between indefinites there can be no definite ratio or proportion.*

* The reader may perhaps like to compare my Edinburgh Reviewer's definitions of supply and demand with those given in the text, and likewise to observe how lucidly the Reviewer discriminates between

The nature and limits of actual supply and demand being thus settled, what is next to be considered is the manner in which they affect price. The prevailing doctrine is variously expressed. Sometimes the statement is simply that supply and demand determine price; sometimes a little less loosely, that price depends on the proportion or relation between supply and demand. Always it is assumed that price rises when demand exceeds supply, and falls when supply exceeds demand. These are the popular ways of putting the case, and in none of them is there anything inconsistent with the more scientific language of Mr. Mill, who, however, besides systematising previous notions on the subject, has made some material additions to the stock. He maintains that price depends on the equation of supply and demand, propounding as the law of value or price that the price resulting from competition will be one at which supply and demand—the quantity supplied and the quantity demanded – will be equalised. These several propositions are quite consistent with each other: they are one and all versions, more or less complete, of a doctrine preached by the first teachers of political economy, and unanimously accepted as axiomatic by their successors. Nevertheless, in opposition to pre-eminent authority and universal credence, the present writer is heretic enough to assert that not one of these propositions will hold good in ordinary circumstances, nor more than one of them in my conceivable circumstances. Such audacity can, I am aware, be justified only by my completely making out my case—only by my completely proving my assertions. This, however, I shall do to the satisfaction of every competent judge, if, in the first place, I show that the theory I am impugning requires and assumes as its

supply and demand and competition. 'Demand and supply,' he says, ' are facts : a large or a short supply of corn at market, the commencement of a war, or the opening of a new outlet for commodities. Competition is the *expression* of these facts. Supply and demand determine price : competition, where it exists unrestricted, prevents either sellers or buyers from rising above or sinking below that standard.'

basis a condition which in practice is almost always absent; and if in the second, assuming, for the sake of argument, the fundamental hypothesis to be realised, I cite examples which .even then would be at variance with all but one particular of the theory. Both these things I undertake to do.

In the first place, it is to be remarked that the theory is never put forward unconditionally. It is not even by its teachers represented to be true, except on two suppositions, of which the first is a perfectly free and open market, with plurality both of competing dealers and competing customers, the former anxious to get the utmost for their goods, and the latter to get the utmost for their money ; and the second, and that which here especially concerns us, that the goods supplied or offered for sale are so offered unreservedly, the owner or owners being content to let them go for what they will fetch. Obviously, this condition is an absolute *sine quâ non.* Obviously, without it, supply and demand must be impotent for the duty ascribed to them. Obviously, as long as a price is reserved at which a dealer is prepared to sell, but below which he will not consent to sell, excess of supply or deficiency of demand will not bring down price. Then, for the time being, price is settled arbitrarily by the dealer. It is only when the latter is content to let such of his goods as he offers for sale go for the highest amount immediately obtainable for them, that it is even conceivable for price to depend upon the proportion between supply and demand, and to vary with variations in that proportion. Now, this absolute *sine quâ non*—this absolutely indispensable condition, without which there is obviously no room for the popular theory, far from being always or generally, is almost never present. With one notable exception—that of labour—commodities are almost never offered unreservedly for sale. Scarcely ever will a dealer sell at a price no higher than that at which the whole of his goods could immediately be sold. Imagine the situation of a merchant who could not afford to wait for customers, but was obliged to accept for a newly-arrived cargo the best offer he could get from the customers who first presented themselves; or imagine a tradesman obliged to clear out his shop within twenty-four hours. The corn-importer who, in the course of a season, sells thousands of quarters of wheat at 60*s.* a quarter, might not get 20*s.* a quarter if, as soon as his corn ships came in, he were obliged to turn the cargoes into money. The glover who, by waiting for customers, would be sure to get 3*s.* or 4*s.* a pair for all the gloves in his shop, might not get sixpence a pair if he were under the necessity of trying to force them on his customers. But it rarely, if ever, happens that a trader finds himself in such a predicament. The nearest approach to it almost ever made is that of a bankrupt's creditors, and even they are, comparatively speaking, able to take their time. But the behaviour of a trader under ordinary pressure is quite different from that of a bank-rupt's assignees. He does not suffer his whole stock-in-trade to be carried off for whatever his customers are immediately prepared to give. He names his own prices, and parts with only so much of his stock as customers are ready to take at those prices. It rarely happens that they are prepared to take more than a very small portion of the entire stock. Ninety-nine times out of a hundred his supply of goods is immensely greater than the quantity immediately demanded at the price at which he offers them. But does he therefore lower his terms? Not at all. He has reserved his price. To such customers as are willing to buy at that price he sells. When they have departed satisfied, he waits for fresh customers to make their appearance. In this way he eventually disposes of his stock for many times the amount which he would have been offered for it at first. But how is it that he has con-trive to secure the higher prices that have produced this increased amount? Plainly, by not selling unreservedly. Plainly, by refusing to sell at prices at which supply and

demand would have been equalised, and insisting on prices
at which supply was greatly in excess of demand.

I must take leave to insist somewhat earnestly on the
importance of what has just been urged. The question we
are discussing is whether it be true that price is determined
by supply and demand;— that price necessarily rises when
demand exceeds supply, and necessarily falls when supply
exceeds demand;—that the prices at which sales take
place are those at which supply and demand are equalised.
Now, no one imagines that prices can be thus determined if
prices are reserved, and we have seen that in ordinary
commerce prices are almost invariably reserved. Goods
are scarcely ever offered for sale in large quantity except
at a price far above that at which the entire quantity could
immediately be sold—far above that, therefore, at which
demand would be equal to supply. Yet price does not,
usually, fall in consequence. On the contrary, far oftener
than not, the goods are gradually sold at the price originally asked, and almost always at prices at which supply is
greatly in excess of demand. It is only when the very
last remnant of the stock in hand is being purchased, that
supply and demand can possibly be equal, for until then
supply consists of the whole quantity remaining on hand,
while demand is only part, and generally but a small part,
of that quantity. This is notoriously what takes place in
the ordinary course of trade. But if so, the controversy is
already all but ended. The question proposed has already
all but received the predicted negative answer. That supply
and demand do not, in existing circumstances, govern
price—so much has been placed beyond dispute. What in
certain hypothetical circumstances they might, could, would,
or should do, is comparatively of little consequence. Examination of that part of the subject may serve to gratify a
laudable curiosity, but can scarcely lead to any more practically useful results.*

* To what was formerly urged by me on this head Mr. Mill has
made a reply, which an unquestionably impartial Westminster Reviewer

Let, however, for the sake of argument, the hypothetical circumstances referred to be assumed to be the real ones.

pronounces conclusive, remarking, with regard to it, that I have been decidedly 'caught tripping.' I protest, however, that in all my life I never felt more sure of my footing.   Mr. Mill considers that in such cases as those supposed by me, supply and demand would be equalised by subtraction from the supply, for that ' reserving a price is, to all intents and purposes, withdrawing supply.'   In explanation he says, ' that when no more than 40s. a head can be obtained for sheep, all sheep whose owners are determined not to sell for less than 50s. are out of the market, and form no part at all of the supply which is now determining price.'   Nothing can be more true ; but I never said anything contrary to this, nor is it in the smallest degree inconsistent with anything I ever did say.   My corn-merchant and glover were not supposed to be asking 50s. a quarter or 4s. a pair at a time when nobody would give more than 40s. or 3s.   What was supposed is, that a certain number of customers were actually buying at 50s. or 4s. ; but that the quantities of corn or gloves which the dealers were offering for sale at those prices, yet would not sell for less, were many times greater than the quantities which customers were actually prepared, or would for a considerable time to come, be prepared to buy.   Now this is what is continually occurring.   A merchant has a warehouse full of wheat. Ask him at what price he will sell, and he will name one at which he will be equally prepared to let you have, either the entire stock or only a single waggon load, or, at any rate, one at which, if he will let you have a single load, he will let you have likewise the entire stock. You take a few loads at 50s. a quarter, but neither you nor any one else will immediately take any more on the same terms, though you may at once have another hundred loads if you like.   These other hundred, then, remain for a while unsold.   But are they therefore withdrawn from sale ?   Why, there they are, offered for sale at the very price at which a few precisely similar loads have just been sold, and at which, quite possibly, these same hundred may all be sold before many days are over.   But, if thus offered for sale, how can they possibly be also withdrawn from sale ?   How can they be both offered for sale and withdrawn from sale at one and the same moment ?

Besides, if, 'to all intents and purposes,' reserving a price be withdrawing supply, then, for any practical purpose, there is scarcely ever any supply at all ; for, as I have shown, and as no one in the habit of entering a shop or counting-house as a customer can help knowing, in ordinary commercial transactions, price is almost invariably reserved. To my 'British Quarterly' Reviewer, so widely may the shrewdest differ, this compatibility of supply with reservation of price, which Mr. Mill refuses to admit, appears too clear to require to be affirmed.   'Is it really possible,' he asks, ' that political economists should have utterly

Let all the conditions most favourable to the theory under examination be assumed to be present, and especially let goods be assumed to be offered for sale unreservedly. I maintain that even on that supposition the theory will not hold good except in one solitary particular. Goods being offered unreservedly for sale, it will be true that if supply exceed demand, price must fall, but it will not be true that if demand exceed supply, price must rise. Neither will it be true that in either case the resulting price must be one at which supply and demand will be equalised. These assertions I proceed to elucidate by examples.

When a herring or mackerel boat has discharged on the beach at Hastings or Dover last night's take of fish, the boatmen, in order to dispose of their cargo, commonly resort to a process called 'Dutch auction.' The fish are divided into lots, each of which is set up at the highest price which the salesman thinks himself at all likely to get for it, and which, if necessary, he gradually lowers until he comes to a price which some by-stander is willing to pay rather than not have the lot, and to which he accordingly agrees. Suppose on one occasion the price agreed to for a hundred herrings to have been 8s. If on the same occasion, instead of the Dutch form of auction, the ordinary English form had been adopted, the result might have been different. The operation would then have been commenced by some by-stander making the lowest bid he thought at all likely to be accepted, and this bid others might have successively exceeded, until a sum was arrived at beyond which no one

overlooked one of the most obvious facts of trade? Could so much as one of them be found who believes that the whole supply of commodities is offered for sale unreservedly?' Incredible as such belief may seem, most certain it is that political economists, almost without exception, have been used to express themselves as if they so believed. Of course they must all have known, or would have perceived at once if they had thought about it, that every dealer does habitually reserve a price; but though they must have known this, they cannot have borne it in mind, or they would never, while admitting that supply and demand cannot operate on prices when prices are reserved, have nevertheless asserted that price is habitually determined by supply and demand.

but the actual bidder could afford or was disposed to go. That sum would not necessarily be 8*s.* ; very possibly it might be only 6*s.* The person too who was prepared to pay the former price might very possibly be the only person present prepared to pay even so much as the latter price : and if so, he might get by English auction for 6*s.* the fish for which at Dutch auction he would have paid 8*s.* In the same market, with the same quantity of fish for sale, and with customers in number and every other respect the same, the same lot of fish might fetch two very different prices.

This is a sufficiently noteworthy case, but its significance is perhaps somewhat liable to be misapprehended. It must not be mistaken for an instance of price varying while supply and demand remain unaltered ; for if we remember and adhere to our definitions of supply and demand, we shall perceive that in the case put these varied quite as much as price. When the price was 8*s.* the supply was not the same as when the price was 6*s.* In both cases it was indeed a hundred herrings; but in one case it was a hundred offered for sale at 8*s.*, and in the other a hundred virtually offered for sale at only 6*s.* ; while the quantity demanded, instead of being simply a hundred for which somebody or other was prepared to pay something or other, was a hundred for which some one was prepared to pay in the one case 8*s.*, in the other 6*s.** But the chief

---

* Notwithstanding my express disclaimer of any such intention, some of my critics have understood me here to mean that at neither of the prices specified would supply and demand be equalised, and Mr. Mill, in reply, contends that what I have really shown is, not that no price would equalise supply and demand, but that two or more prices might equalise them. It seems to me, however, that in this particular case it would not be possible for supply and demand to be equal at two different prices. For the case is one in which demand would increase with cheapness. A hawker who was ready to pay 8*s.* for a hundred herrings, would want more than a hundred if he could get a hundred for 6*s.* There being then but a given quantity in the market, if that quantity were just sufficient to satisfy all the customers ready to buy at 8*s.*, it follows that it would not have sufficed to satisfy

reason why the varying effects of Dutch and English auction have been shown in contrast as above is, that when prices are not reserved, a sale can scarcely take place of which one or other of these forms of auction is not the type. A trader in such desperate straits as to have no alternative but to sell, and sell at once, might probably begin by asking the highest price at which it seemed likely that any considerable portion of his goods would be immediately purchased. If one or more of his customers were prepared to take his whole stock at that price, and if no one, from desire to obtain a larger share of the goods than would otherwise have fallen to him, offered more, the whole business would be settled forthwith. The transaction would be no sooner opened than closed. But if there either seemed to be a probability of part of the seller's goods being left on his hands, or if the eagerness of his customers should suggest to him that he had been needlessly moderate in his demands, he would in the one case be compelled, like a Dutch auctioneer, to lower his price ; in the other, he would be enabled, like an English auctioneer, to raise them. Now, what is here first to be remarked is, that if in the circumstances supposed the quantity offered for sale at a certain price were greater than the quantity which customers were prepared to buy at that price, the said price could not be maintained. No price being reserved, price must fall if supply exceed demand. So much is true ; and it is also true that (no price being reserved) there can be no variation of price while supply and demand remain the same. These, however, are the sole particles of truth to be found in a theory which, as shall forthwith be shown, is otherwise compounded entirely of fallacies. Every one of their fellow propositions shall be proved to be incorrect. Even though no price be reserved, it shall be proved not to be the fact that whenever supply or demand varies, price must vary likewise ; not to be the fact that if demand exceeds supply, price must rise ; not to be the fact that the

them if the price had been 6*s.* If supply and demand were equal at the former price, they would be unequal at the latter.

prices at which sales are effected are those at which supply
and demand are equal.

Suppose at different times or in different places, two
great horse fairs to take place, and as many competing
dealers and competing customers as you please to be present
at both. If you have ever yourself been at a horse fair,
you must have noticed that, however crowded it might be,
there were plenty of animals without a single bidder. You
will have no difficulty then in supposing that there might be
still greater plenty for each of which there were only two
or three bidders. Well then suppose there to be at each
of these fairs a horse to be sold valued by its owner at 50*l*.,
and suppose there to be in the one case two, and in the
other three persons, of whom each is ready to pay 50*l*. for
the horse, though no one of them can afford to pay more.
In both cases supply is the same, viz. one horse at 50*l*.,
but demand is different, being in the one case two, and in
the other three horses at 50*l*. Yet the price at which the
horses will be sold will be the same in both cases, viz. 50*l*.*
Or again reverting to our former hypothesis, suppose that
when a hundred fish were sold by auction for 8*s*., there
were no more fish of the same description in the market,
but that no one except the actual purchaser was willing to
buy any at that price, and that even he did not want to

---

* The Edinburgh Reviewer's note upon this displays all his usual
acumen. 'The two parties,' he says, 'in the first, and the three
parties in the second case, who have predetermined to pay a certain
uniform price, are virtually as one, and there is not, as supposed, any
difference whatever in effective demand between the two examples.'
The reviewer clearly perceives the difference between 'virtual' and
'actual.' He is far from denying that two parties or three parties are
not actually one party : that demand for two horses or for three horses
at 50*l*. is greater than demand for only one horse at the same price.
These are facts quite within the grasp of his vigorous understanding.
Only, he contends, that although the increase of demand is actually
existent, it is quite inoperative. For any effect it has in raising price,
it might as well not be there. In which conclusion I the more readily
concur, because it happens to be the very same as that which I have
in the text announced as my own, and which, while formally assenting
to it, the reviewer fancies he is disproving.

buy more than a hundred. The whole demand then was a hundred fish at 8*s*. But now suppose that, though there were only a hundred of that sort of fish to be had, the actual purchaser would willingly have bought three hundred at the same price if he could have got them; or suppose that two other customers as well as himself, though neither of them willing to pay more than 8*s*. a hundred, would each of them have been glad to take three hundred at that price if he had not forestalled them. The total demand would then have been three hundred at 8*s*., yet the resulting price would still have been only 8*s*., the same as it was when the demand was only one hundred, the supply all the time remaining the same.* Here are palpable examples of the relation between supply and demand varying without any variation of price, even though price be not reserved;

---

* My ' British Quarterly' Reviewer here fairly makes a point which requires to be as fairly met. ' Could,' he asks, ' such a case happen ? If 300 fish were wanted at all, they would be wanted for resale at a profit. But if 300 at 6*s*. could be sold at a profit—and otherwise they would not be wanted at all—it is quite incredible that the only hundred to be got should not be worth more than 6*s*.' Now, I must at least admit it to be, for the reasons given by the reviewer, incredible that one and the same person would be ready to buy 300 at 6*s*., and would yet not consent to give more than 6*s*. for the only hundred to be had. But then I have not supposed this. On the contrary, where I have supposed only one bidder at 6*s*. for 100 fish, I have supposed that rather than not get that 100, he would go as high as 8*s*., because he believed that even buying at 8*s*., he would be able to sell 100 at a profit ; and thinking this he might very well think also that buying at 6*s*., he might be able to sell as many as 300 at an equal profit. Still, quite possibly, no one else in the market might take so sanguine a view of affairs. All his competitors might quite possibly regard 6*s*. as the highest price at which it would be prudent to buy, with the view of selling again. If so, although two or three others beside himself might each be ready to buy 100 at 6*s*., and though he might himself be willing to buy 300 at that price, the only 100 in the market might nevertheless be knocked down to him at that price.

The reviewer will observe that though I have been obliged to alter his figures in order to make them correspond with my own altered figures, I have taken care to preserve the same proportion between them.

and the only thing that prevents such examples from being multiplied at pleasure is the paucity of commercial trans-actions effected without reservation of price. If that con-dition be present, every one *must* see that price cannot vary from the cause in question; and even though that condition be not present, every one *may* see the same thing. Every one may see that at an auction, although no one were disposed to bid more than had already been bidden for some particular article, many besides the last bidder might be equally ready to give as much for it. They might or they might not; but whether they were or not, the price in the circumstances supposed would remain un-altered; that is to say, the price would not vary, whether, while supply remained the same, demand did or did not increase. Clearly it does not follow that because the price of some commodity has reached the utmost height at which any customer will purchase at all, therefore the quantity actually on sale is the utmost which he or any other customer would consent to purchase at that price. But if not, then equally plain is it that the supply of that commodity might be increased without causing price to fall, or the demand increased without causing price to rise.

In the cases just put the demand for horses at 50*l.* each, or of herrings at 8*s.* the hundred, might, we see, have been three times as great as the supply, without causing any increase in the price of horses or herrings. These cases, then, might of themselves suffice to refute the second of the fallacies which are here challenged. But another shall be added. Let us take a solitary draper in a small country town, and, for the sake of the requirements of the argu-ment, suppose him to be impatiently selling off in order to retire from business, but to be, nevertheless, as long as he continues to sell, as desirous as tradesmen in general of getting the highest possible price. Such an one, finding on the morning of an assize ball that he had but a dozen pairs of white gloves left, and knowing that there were no others to be had for love or money within twenty-four

hours, might possibly be able to get as much as 10*s.* a pair
for each of his twelve pairs of gloves. He would be able
to get this, if twelve customers were willing to pay that
price rather than not go to the ball or than go ungloved.
But he could not get more than this if it were the utmost
the first batch of customers could afford or were willing to
pay, even though, while still haggling with them, a second
batch, equally numerous and neither more nor less eager,
should enter the shop and offer the same but not a higher
price. The demand for gloves, which just before had been
iust equal to the supply, would then be exactly doubled,
yet the price would not rise above 10*s.* a pair. Not more
in this than in the analogous cases of horses and fish would
price rise because demand exceeded supply.

Next we come to the supposed dependence of price on
the equation of supply and demand. Here I find myself
immediately in collision with Mr. Mill, feeling, in consequence, a little as Saul of Tarsus might have felt if, while
sitting at the feet of Gamaliel, he had suddenly found himself compelled by a sense of duty to contradict his master.
Truth, however, before Plato ; and truth compels me to
repeat that my objections to Mr. Mill's views have been
rendered all the stronger by his recent explanations. His
opinion is that price is always tending to a point at which
supply and demand will be equal : that price will keep
falling towards this point as long as supply exceeds
demand, and rising towards it as long as demand exceeds
supply. I continue to assert that no part of this theory is
correct. One half of it, I submit, was completely disproved
when examples were given of demand greatly exceeding
supply without occasioning the smallest increase of price ;
and with regard to the other half, also, there is no difficulty
in showing that it is much too inaccurate to satisfy the
rigid requirements of science.

No doubt when, of goods offered unreservedly for sale,
the supply exceeds the demand, the whole stock cannot be
sold unless the price be lowered to a point at which supply

and demand will be equalised ; but it does not follow that the fall of price will then cease. The only thing certain, is that the point at which the fall will cease will be one at which supply will not be in excess of demand, but it may quite possibly proceed to some still lower point at which demand will be in excess of supply. When a hundred herrings, put up for sale at Dutch auction, were knocked down for 8*s.*, it did not follow that a single hundred were all that the actual purchaser was willing to buy at the price, or that other customers would not have been glad to buy at the same price, though it did not suit them to pay a higher. Because a horse, offered for sale at 60*l.*, finds no purchaser, and cannot be sold until its price be reduced to 50*l.*, it does not follow that only one person would give 50*l.* for the horse, or that one would not willingly give 50*l.* a piece for two or three such horses.*

---

* According to the 'Times,' ' the stability of price of a commodity sold under the action of free commerce, where there is more than one potential seller and more than one potential buyer, denotes an equilibrium of active supply and of active demand ; that is to say an equality between the quantities of the commodities sellers *push* upon the market at that price ; and that an effort to *push* more upon the market, or an abatement of the quantities withdrawn by purchasers must diminish the price, while an increase of the price would follow contrary hypotheses. Price is thus a function of supply and demand, and the proposition that supply and demand determine price, means that the price of a commodity in a free market has not reached its normal level until there is such an equality as we have indicated.'

By simply italicising the word ' push,' I have indicated what appears to me to be the proper reply to these observations. Pushing goods on the market necessarily implies that no price is reserved, that they will be allowed to go at once for what they will fetch, or at any rate for some lower price than that for which they are at first offered. Now, if goods pushed in this sense are cleared away by purchasers as fast as they are pushed, and cleared at the price set on them by the seller, there may be fairly presumed to be perfect equality between supply and demand ; the one solitary case of such perfect equality, to which I shall hereafter advert as the only one possible, may be presumed to have been realised. Moreover, if more goods are pushed than customers are prepared to take off at the price first named, price must fall, while if less be offered, whether pushed or not, the seller will probably (though not quite certainly) be able to raise his price.

These propositions are quite undeniable— not only true, but truisms.

It thus appears that of the equation theory one half is
not true, while the other half is diametrically opposed to
the truth; but what is equally worth remarking, and notwithstanding all that has lately been urged to the contrary,
still seems to me as clear as ever, is that if the whole of it
were literally true it would be a truth of small significance.
Let us imagine ourselves in one of those few situations in
which goods are sold without reserve; in the shop, for
instance, of a bankrupt tradesman, whose remaining stock
consisting, say, of a thousand pairs of gloves, must be
cleared away before night. The gloves, we will suppose,
are of a sort commonly priced at 4s., but to expedite the
sale they are on this occasion marked first at 2s. 6d., at
which price three hundred pairs are bought before noon.
Then, still more to accelerate progress, the price is reduced
to 1s. 6d.; and, at four o'clock, it is again reduced to 1s.,
at which two rates four hundred and two hundred pairs,
respectively, are sold, so that when the shop is about to be
closed, there are still a hundred pairs left; and these, since
there is no better means of getting rid of them, some one
of the shopmen is perhaps allowed to take at 6d. a pair,
exhausting both his cash and credit to the last penny in
the operation. Now if unreserved sales always took either
a course exactly like this, or one exactly converse to it, the
equation theory would be very completely realised. Prices

What they have to do with the matter in hand is not quite so clear.
Whether, upsetting all the reasoning in the text, with detached frag-
ments of which they are in perfect unison, they prove that 'price is a
function of supply and demand,' the reader is in a position to judge
for himself. Whether they prove that the 'price of a commodity in a
free market has not reached its normal level, until there is such an
equality as that indicated,' I cannot pretend to say, for I really do not
know what is meant by that 'normal level.' All I do know about it is,
that it cannot mean merely a level at which price may remain stationary for a lengthened period; for, as the examples given in the text
place beyond dispute, such stability of price is in many branches of
trade the normal condition of things, notwithstanding that in those
branches supply habitually exceeds demand.

would be always tending towards a point at which demand
and supply would be equal, until they at length rested at
that point.   They would be always falling towards that
point as long as supply exceeded demand, and always
rising towards it as long as demand exceeded supply.   But
what then ?   Even then it would be but a mere fraction of
the whole stock of goods that would be sold at equation
price, by far the greater part being sold at prices at which
supply and demand were unequal.   Suppose it were true,
which, however, the reader will be pleased to recollect it is
not, that when no price is reserved, the price at which the
last lot of any commodity is sold must be one at which
supply and demand are equal—one at which, there being
of course but one customer desirous of purchasing left,
that last customer could get as much of the commodity
as he desired—the truth might be rather worth knowing
than not; still, seeing that every lot of the commodity
except the very last would have been sold at prices at
which supply and demand were not equal, it is not easy to
conceive a piece of knowledge more barren of practical
utility.*

* My 'British Quarterly' reviewer, whom here, as elsewhere, I have
found it no easy matter to answer, and to agree with whom I would
willingly, if possible, stretch a point, suggests a new reading of the
equation theory.   His notion of it is in substance as follows :—If it
were known beforehand what—at a price equal to cost of production,
plus the ordinary rate of profit thereon, or at what is usually termed
normal or natural price—would be the demand for any commodity,
supply would be sure to accommodate itself to that demand.   Producers would not send more to market, because, if they did, they
would not be able to sell the whole quantity at a remunerative price.
They would not send less, because, if they did, they would not be
availing themselves to the full of an opportunity of making the ordinary rate of profit.   Selling price would always exactly coincide with
natural price.   But such foreknowledge of demand is seldom obtainable, and the best indications of the relations existing at any particular
time between supply and demand are those afforded by selling price.
When this is higher than natural price, producers are apprised that
they may safely increase their supplies ; when lower, they get warning
to diminish them.   But when, after repeated experiments, they have

Here it will probably be objected that all the cases cited above are exceedingly exceptional. To which allega-

at last discovered how much customers are willing to buy at the natural price, they take care to keep the market supplied with exactly so much, and natural price becomes thenceforward permanent selling price. All previous variations of price had been merely oscillations by means of which price settled down thus at last. For instance, if sixpence a yard were the natural price of calico, and 1,000 yards the quantity that could be sold daily at that price (the word 'daily' is an interpolation of my own, which is, however, indispensable for the realisation of the reviewer's idea), producers might begin by supplying 800 or 1,200 yards, but as soon as they discovered that 1,000 yards was the only quantity they could supply without causing price either to rise above or to fall below natural price, 1,000 yards would be the quantity which they would regularly send.

Now if this were authoritatively declared to be a correct rendering of the equation theory, I confess that it would be no longer obnoxious to the objections taken to it in the text. On the assumption implied in the new version, not only would it be literally correct to say, as Mr. Mill says, that price always tends to a point at which supply and demand will be equal, falling towards that point as long as supply exceeds demand, and rising towards it as long as demand exceeds supply ; it would, further, be almost literally true that no sale could take place except at a price at which supply and demand would be equal. The real objections to the new reading are of a different kind. The course of procedure it assumes is quite incompatible with any phenomena of commerce, either actual or possible. By no repetition of experiments could it be ascertained beforehand what in retail, and still less in wholesale transactions, would be the daily or otherwise periodical demand for any commodity. Even if the aggregate amount for some time to come could be approximately estimated, the variations of demand from week to week, and from day to day, would defy all calculation. Neither, even if the daily demand could be foreseen, would it be possible for a number of independent producers to adapt supply to it with any approach to exactitude. It would be impossible for each of the producers to be aware of what the others were doing ; each would have to guess for himself how much he might send to market towards supply of the ascertained demand, and if anyone guessed wrong, supply would inevitably either outrun or fall short of demand, price likewise rising or falling simultaneously. That stable equality to which supply and demand are imagined to be always tending never is and never can be attained. As already intimated, it is but a figment of the economic brain.

Of course the reviewer may here rejoin that the *daily* equation of supply and demand is a gratuitous suggestion on my part ; that he

might occur without being attended by the supposed results, to that same extent the law is shown to be not simply
defective but false, and, what it worse, deceiving. Pur-
porting to apply to all, it applies only to part, without
affording any hint that another part, or any clue as to
what part, is excepted from its operation. Of what use is
a scientific law unless to serve as an immovable fulcrum
whereon our argumentative lever may be rested with im-
plicit confidence ? as an ascertained principle, needing no
further investigation, and not simply a proved truth, but a
standard of truth, convicting of error whatever is opposed
to itself? But if there be one single situation in which the
fulcrum will give way, is there not perpetual danger of the
lever's moving askew ? If the principle contain one single
particle of error, is there not a certainty of its causing both
other falsehoods to be confounded with truths, and truths,
on the other hand, to be mistaken for falsehoods ? If the
best possible answer to these momentous questions be not
furnished by experience of the 'law' of supply and demand,
it is only because that ' law,' instead of containing merely
one stray element of error, is almost entirely made up of
error ; because, instead of there being but one situation in
which it must break down, there is but one solitary situation in which it can hold good.

Secondly, the cases cited are in no greater degree exceptional than it was unavoidable that they should be, seeing
that the sole motive for citing them was to expose the falla-
ciousness of a law, which even by its upholders is itself
confessed not to be true, except in circumstances so exceptional as scarcely ever to occur. The sole purpose they
are designed to serve is that of proving that even when
goods are offered for sale without reserve, price does not
depend on supply and demand. But some exercise of the
imagination is requisite to conceive cases in which goods
are so offered. Of course, then, at least equal use of the
inventive faculty must be needed to discover cases in
which, even though goods were so offered, price would

still not be determined by supply and demand. But the
cases of the latter class cited above, instead of being exceptions to those of the former class, are really typical of them.
For, as has been already said, when prices are not reserved,
it is scarcely possible for a sale to take place, of which either
the English or the Dutch form of auction is not the type, and
every one of my cases will be found on examination to be a
specimen of one or other of these forms of auction. Each one,
too, will be seen to be neither rare nor far-fetched, but only an
ordinary specimen. I have been bantered for my supposed
extravagance in imagining that two or more persons could
anywhere be found each prepared to give 50*l.* for a horse,
yet each resolved not to give one farthing more. ' Don't
you see,' asks a valued correspondent, who dates from the
other side of the globe—from Dacca—'that the seller
would turn to A., and say, "B. has offered me 50*l.*, and I am
thinking of letting him have the horse," and that A. would
at once cry " guineas " then ? ' But if my friend think it
impossible that one bidder should not cry ' guineas,' must
he not suppose it next to impossible that two should not ;
and if so, how is my position affected ? Is it not self-
evident that there must always be some extreme price or
other that will not be exceeded ? that when the most eager
bidder has added the very last farthing he can afford to
his original offer, a price has been reached to which neither
he nor anyone else will add one farthing ? And is there
much more difficulty in supposing that there might be two
persons prepared to pay that extreme price, than that there
was only one ? Mr. Mill says that though such a case ' may
be conceived, in practice it is scarcely ever realised,'—that
it is 'just possible in a very small market, practically impossible in the great market of the community.' But I
submit that it is repeatedly realised ; and if not often in extensive markets, then simply because in extensive markets
unreserved sales do not often take place. It repeatedly
happens in an auction room that the very highest bid
which anyone present is prepared to make is made by two

persons simultaneously; or, though made only by one, would have been made by another if the first had not preceded him.   And as in an auction room, so at a sea-beach auction.   A thrifty housewife who had bought the last lot of a hundred herrings for four shillings, intending to salt them for winter use, might not at all improbably have been willing to buy three hundred at the same rate, and one or two of her neighbours might have been quite as willing as herself to pay four shillings for the hundred she did get, and yet be unwilling to pay more than four shillings.   So, too, in a tradesman's shop.   I confess it to be exceedingly unlikely, that of so many as twenty-four ball-goers, each one should be prepared to give 10*s*. a pair for gloves, while not one was prepared to give more ; but if, after all the rest of the gloves had been disposed of, and when only one solitary pair remained on hand, there were still two customers to be served, there is surely no difficulty in supposing that each would rather pay 10*s*. for his gloves than not go to the ball, and yet that each would rather give up the ball than pay more than 10*s*.   If so, whichever of the twain were preferred as a customer would get the gloves at a price at which his competitor's demand was left unsatisfied.

Thirdly, if in spite of all that I can urge, the cases cited by me as inconsistent with the equation theory are still deemed not less improbable than far-fetched, at least let them be contrasted with any that can be adduced on the other side.   Of such cases there is, as has been intimated, but one.   In order that the price at which goods are sold should be one at which supply and demand are exactly equalised, two things are indispensable : first, the quantity on sale must be as great as the quantity which customers would like to take on the terms offered ; secondly, it must not be greater.   Now, how often are these conditions fulfilled ?   How often does it happen, when horses or fish or gloves are sold, both that not a single horse, or fish, or pair of gloves of the same description remains unsold, and

that no single customer would desire to buy another
horse, or fish, or pair of gloves at the same price, if another
were to be had ?   What combination of analogous circumstances can there be of rarer occurrence ?   Yet it is only
when this combination occurs that equation can possibly
take place.   This is the one solitary case in which it is
possible for supply and demand to be exactly equalised.
How shall the comparatively numerous cases in which the
theory fails be objected to as exceptional when there is but
one solitary case in which it can hold good?

Though asking this question, I dare not pause for a reply,
lest the overwrought reader seize the opportunity to protest
against what, not quite inexcusably, he may be disposed to
mistake for solemn trifling.   'What,' I fancy I hear him
exclaiming, 'can it matter whether amongst a set of cases,
all of which are admitted to be so exceptional as scarcely
ever to occur, those on one side be more or less exceptional
than those on the other?'   Certainly, on a point so minute,
misapprehension might not matter much if it stood alone,
and were not part of a far larger and more serious error.
But it does matter greatly that, when of a practically mischievous doctrine the refutation is attempted, that refutation
should be thorough and complete ; and it will not have
been for nothing that the doctrine I am impugning has
been pursued into its last retreat, if I have succeeded
in showing that even there it has not a leg to stand upon.

This, I venture to think, has now been shown.   I submit
that the negative position taken up has been completely
established, and I shall be greatly disappointed if it has
not been established to the satisfaction of all who may condescend to bestow on this restatement of the argument the
candid examination which it is sure to receive from Mr.
Mill.   For consider what has been done.   The object, be it
recollected, having been to demonstrate that supply and
demand do not regulate price, it was, in the first place, shown
that of the conditions under which alone it is conceivable
that they should regulate price, one, and that the most

indispensable of all, is, in practice, scarcely ever present. Unless goods be offered for sale unreservedly, the staunchest believer in the law of supply and demand will not pretend that it can possibly apply. But goods are scarcely ever offered unreservedly for sale, except at an auction, and not always even there. Whether, therefore, or not, supply and demand might, could, would, or should determine price, it is at all events clear that in practice they scarcely ever do. Secondly, it was shown that even if all the required conditions were present, even then the law would not apply— that even then the relations between supply and demand might vary without being accompanied or followed by variations in price, while, on the other hand, price might vary without any concomitant or antecedent variation of supply and demand. To prove all this, was to disprove at the same time the notion that price depends upon the equation of supply and demand, yet it was further shown that so far from its being true that at the finally resulting price, supply and demand are invariably equal, there is but one conceivable combination of circumstances in which even at the finally resulting price they can avoid being unequal. What more in the way of refutation can be needed? What loophole of escape is there from lines of circumvallation so complete and uninterrupted? For those at least who have accepted, according to its plain and obvious signification, the law we have been examining, what alternative is there but henceforward to abjure it altogether? Some there are indeed who may say again as they have said already that they never intended the law to be construed so strictly as I have construed it: that they never supposed the variations of price and of supply and demand to be precisely and invariably accordant. But this is, in other words, to say that while asserting that price is always dependent on supply and demand, they meant that it is usually independent of them—that while declaring that when supply increases or demand decreases price must fall, and that when supply decreases or demand increases price

must rise, they yet meant that whether supply or demand
increase or decrease, price may remain stationary, and that,
on the other hand, it may move though neither supply nor
demand move. With those who consciously meant this it
would be superfluous to argue, for they are already convinced. They stand self-accused of having been accustomed to say the very reverse of what they believed, and
remorse for such delinquency in the past will, it may be
hoped, induce them to adopt greater accuracy of expression
in future. Yet this is what all those dissidents must have
meant who did not mean what they said, and yet meant
something. Others again, however, probably did really
mean nothing, or, at any rate, would have been sorely puzzled
to explain what they did mean. Probably they have been
accustomed to talk glibly of supply and demand, just as
they let fifty óther formulæ and phrases roll trippingly
along their tongues, not thereby desiring so much to express any thought as to disguise from themselves and others
their want of thought. To these I will take the liberty of
offering a gentle admonition. They may rest assured
that there are few mental habits more dangerous than the
one they have been indulging in. What we say parrotlike
at first, without thinking what we are saying, and merely
because we hear others saying it, we are very apt to believe
firmly at last, merely because we have said it so often.
Our loose thoughtless words by dint of frequent repetition
become converted into rigid articles of faith, shackling most
heavily our subsequent powers of thinking. With regard
to the formula of supply and demand, for instance, whether
those who repeated it understood anything by it or not, or
whether they accepted it in a natural or only a non-natural
sense, nothing is more certain than that one and all have
habitually employed it as if they believed it to be literal gos-
pel truth, summarily rejecting whatever of fact or inference
was found to clash with it. If then the foregoing exposure
of the fallacy of the formula answer no better purpose than
that of causing a correcter phraseology to be substituted,

no small service will thereby have been done. Not that I claim any special credit for such share as I may have had in the exposure, any more than I should deem it matter for boasting that having together with a number of fellow-travellers fallen into a ditch, I happened to be the first to discover it to be a ditch we were all floundering about in. Still the knowledge that we were in a ditch might be an indispensable preliminary to any attempt to scramble out, and those who will not be persuaded that supply and demand do not determine price, are not very likely to find out what really does determine it.

For those, however, who have satisfied themselves on the former point the ground is now cleared for examination of the latter, to which we have next to address ourselves. First, however, in order to prevent recurrence of one marvellous misapprehension to which I have been subjected, let me explain that when saying that supply and demand do not determine price I did not say that they have nothing to do with its determination. I really never asserted, whatever my egregious Edinburgh Reviewer may think, that, other things being equal, goods are not likely to be comparatively cheap when very abundant, and comparatively dear when greatly in request. I should as soon think of saying that a voyage is not likely to be shorter with a favourable than with a contrary wind. Still, just as it remains true that the length of a voyage does not *depend* on the wind, inasmuch as, with the most favourable wind, a ship may be retarded on her way by fifty different causes or may go to the bottom without ever reaching her destination, so it is equally true that price does not *depend* upon supply and demand ; does not, that is, bear any uniform relation to them, need not vary when they vary, nor when it does vary need vary in accordance with their variations; is, moreover, in certain circumstances susceptible of numerous variations, at any one of which supply and demand might be equalised. It is the reverse of all this that other economists affirm, and that I deny, and my denial of which may, I submit, be readily distinguished by any one of ordinary intelligence from the sweeping repudiation of the most patent facts with which one of my reviewers has confounded it.

If, however, supply and demand do not determine price, what does? Or, since it is past dispute that somehow or other they do influence price, how is it that price is affected by them? These questions are more easily asked than answered. To throw down is much easier than to build up, and to point out inaccuracies in one theory than to devise another more accurate in its stead. Unlearning what is wrong is, however, the best preparation for learning what is right; and though getting rid of prejudice is not the same thing as getting at truth, it at least permits truth to be looked for in the right direction. Divesting ourselves, then, of preconceived notions, and commencing the enquiry anew, we have in the first place to observe that there are two opposite extremes—one above which the price of a commodity cannot rise, the other below which it cannot fall. The upper of these limits is marked by the utility, real or supposed, of the commodity to the customer ; the lower by its utility to the dealer. No one will give for a commodity a quantity of money or money's worth, which, in his opinion, would be of more use to him than the commodity itself. No one will take for a commodity a quantity of money or of anything else which he thinks would be of less use to himself than the commodity. The price eventually given and taken may be either at one of the opposite extremes, or may be anywhere intermediate between them, but, with so much latitude for variation, what is it that decides what price shall exactly be? Our best chance of finding this out is by considering carefully all that happens when a sale takes place. Practically, it is almost always the dealer who begins by naming some set-up price. His object is to get in exchange for his whole stock the largest aggregate price which he can get within the period during which it will suit him to keep part of his stock unsold. To

sell the whole stock at a moderate price may be better for
him than to sell part only at an exorbitant price, and have
the left rest on his hands ; and it may also be better for
him to realise moderate prices soon, and so be able soon to
re-invest his capital, than to obtain double the prices after
treble the time, during which his money would lie idle.
He begins, therefore, by naming the highest price at which
he thinks the whole of his stock is likely to be readily
purchased.   We have seen that there is an extreme point,
dependent on the value of his goods in the eyes of his
customers, above which their price cannot possibly rise, but
he scarcely ever, or rather almost never, asks that extreme
price.   Why does he not? Why, seeing that he is eager to
get the utmost for his goods, does he not ask the highest
price which he thinks his customers would consent to pay
rather than not have his goods?   Evidently the one thing
that prevents him is the fear of competition—the fear, that
is, of being undersold by some rival dealer.   It is competition alone that deters him from asking a higher price than
he actually does ask—that may perhaps compel him to
lower his price, or may, if he has over-estimated its force,
permit him to raise his price.   It is competition, wherever
competition exists, that determines price.   Competition
remaining the same, price cannot possibly vary.   For, it is
competition that determines the lowest price at which
goods are offered for sale, and whatever that lowest price
be, goods of the same description cannot be selling in the
same market at a higher price—except, indeed, to persons
of the class described by Mr. Mill, who, ' either from indolence or carelessness, or because they think it fine, are
content to pay and ask no questions,' and with whom
political economy has nothing to do.   In a free and open
market, and among dealers and customers actuated by the
self-interest which political economy always takes for
granted, competition is the only thing which determines
price ; the only thing indeed that directly influences it.

All this may perhaps be rendered more apparent by

being somewhat differently stated. The object of every
dealer is to get for the whole of his goods the largest sum
obtainable within a certain time. If there were but one
single dealer, he would probably ask the highest price at
which he thought all his goods would readily be purchased;
but if he have competitors, he must content himself with
the highest price at which he will not be undersold. All,
dealers, while considering at what price they shall offer
their goods, consider each for himself the actual state and
future prospects of the market. Each takes stock as well
as he can of the quantities already in hand of the commodity he deals in, estimates as well as he can the
additional quantities likely to be brought in within the
period during which he can manage to wait, and also the
quantities which, within the same period, customers will be
likely to take off at different prices, and conjectures as well
as he can to how low a price rival dealers will be obliged
to descend, in order to get rid within that period of the
portions of their respective stocks which they will respectively be impatient to sell. He then considers whether at
that price he will be likely within the time to get rid of
the whole of his own present stock. If so, he adopts that
price. If not, he adopts one still lower. In this manner,
each frames his own calculation, and judges for himself
what would be the best price to ask ; but different dealers
in the same market may calculate differently, or may draw
different inferences from the same calculations. Some may
estimate lower than others both the quantities that will be
brought into market, and the quantities that would be
demanded at different prices, or may think that the same
estimate requires a lower price ; or some may not be able
to wait so long as others, and may be compelled to adopt
a price which will enable them to dispose of their goods
more rapidly than others would care to do. But whatever
be, for whatever reason, the lowest price at which any
resolve to sell, that price becomes, for the time being, the
current price, and what causes it to be so is competition.

What caused certain dealers to adopt that price in the first instance was the fear that, otherwise, competition would prevent their selling as fast as they desired. What prevents other dealers from asking higher prices is the knowledge that they will be undersold by their competitors if they do. Plainly, then, it is competition, and competition alone, that regulates price ; but what regulates competition? According to the account given above, what all competing dealers do is in effect to estimate each for himself prospective supply and demand, the least favourable estimate thereof which any one of them forms being that upon which all the others are compelled to act. But may it not then be said that competition depends on prospective supply and demand?   If by prospective supply and demand be here meant the ratio or proportion between them—and unless this be meant nothing is—there need be no hesitation in giving a direct negative to the question, and that not solely for the reason given in an early part of this chapter. Prospective supply and demand, when spoken of generally, or with reference to an unlimited future, are indeed, as was there shown, indefinite quantities between which no ratio is possible. But if the future over which the prospect extends be confined within specified bounds of time, they no doubt become at once definite quantities admitting of exact comparison.   Every individual's estimate, for instance, of what supply will be and demand will be in the next six months may evidently be expressed in precise figures between which there will necessarily be an equally precise proportion. But though this proportion clearly exist, competing dealers as clearly take no sort of account of it.   No dealer when considering what price he had better charge in order to get rid of his present stock of goods within, say, the next six months, ever troubles himself to enquire at what price not only the present stocks of all his rival dealers as well as his own, but also all the additions likely to be made to those stocks within six months, could be sold within the same time. He

knows very well that the generality of his fellow-traders
have as little idea as himself of completely clearing out
their storehouses within the six months, and he has no fear,
therefore, of any such insane competition as would cause
them to adopt the ruinously low price indispensable for
such clearance. The competition which he apprehends is
that of a variety of men anxious to sell, or believing themselves under the necessity of selling, very different proportions of their actual stocks, and that within very different
periods of time—a competition of men of every gradation
of experience, shrewdness, and neediness ; who, in the first
place, estimate the future probabilities of the market for
very different periods ; in the second, would form very different estimates, even for the same period ; and, in the third,
would be influenced very differently by the same estimate.
Surely such competition can in no intelligible sense be
said to *depend* upon prospective supply and demand. I
do not, of course, deny that there is more briskness of
competition among dealers when supply is expected to be
comparatively abundant, and among customers when it is
expected to be comparatively scanty. What I deny is that
the same expectations will be formed by different persons
in the same circumstances, and that increased briskness on
either side will depend upon the comparative abundance or
scantiness—will bear, that is, any uniform relation to it, or
be in any manner regulated by it. But if not, upon what
does competition depend ? What does regulate it ? To
the latter half of this question, if by 'regulating' be meant
the laying down of rules or prescribing a course which
competition in any given circumstances must follow, the
simple answer is Nothing. There is no regularity about
competition—competition is not regulated at all. . If it can
properly be said to depend upon anything, it depends
partly upon individual necessity, partly on individual discretion ; and as for the first of these there is proverbially,
and for the other manifestly, no law, so likewise is there no
law of competition. Neither, if there be no law of com-

petition, and if competition be, as it has been shown to be, the determining cause of price, can there be any law of price.*

To such conclusions have we come at last: 'conclusions inconclusive—that I own ; yet would I say not vain, not nothing worth.' Vague, loose, they must be confessed to be, ascertaining little, prescribing less, yet not perhaps on that account the less valuable. If little can be learnt from them, much may be unlearned. It is no small gain to have perceived that on the subject of which they treat, little can be known beyond what they teach. Nine-tenths of the confusion and obscurity in which the doctrine of price has

---

* It may not be amiss to enter here, in a note, a somewhat different summary of the same opinions which, in the former edition, appeared as part of the text. 'Actual or present supply and demand do not affect price at all, except in so far as they form part of prospective supply and demand, or except when their limits and those of the latter coincide, as they do when there is no apparent chance of any increase of present supply and demand. Nor do even prospective supply and demand affect price, except indirectly, and by their influence on competition, which, and which alone, is the immediate arbiter of price. Neither is competition affected by them in any uniform or regular manner. Competition does indeed always depend upon the estimate of probable supply and demand formed by those dealers who rate lowest the probable proportion of demand to supply, or who from any other cause are most disposed to sell cheaply ; but the estimate of these dealers need not be always the same in the same circumstances, for the same probabilities of supply and demand may be very differently estimated at different times or by different people, and the same estimates may affect different dealers differently. Thus it is, and in no more definite manner, that wherever or whenever competition exists, prospective supply and demand affect the competition which determines price. Where competition does not exist, where a monopoly of trade is exercised by a single dealer or by a combination of dealers, the case is no doubt materially altered. Prospective supply and demand then become of almost paramount authority, and may be not improperly said directly to influence and even to determine price ; for the price at which a monopolist sells may always be presumed to be the highest at which, judging from his estimate of the probabilities of supply and demand, he expects to be able to sell either the whole of his goods, or as much as he has resolved to sell. Provided, then, that different monopolists at different times estimate these probabilities alike, they will no doubt charge the same prices.'

hitherto been involved have arisen from searching after the
unsearchable, from seeking for some invariable rule for
inevitable variations, from straining after precision where to
be precise is necessarily to be wrong. Supply and demand
are commonly spoken of as if they together formed some
nicely-fitting, well-balanced, self-adjusting piece of machinery, whose component parts could not alter their mutual
relations without evolving, as the product of every change,
a price exactly corresponding with that particular change.
Price is scarcely ever mentioned without provoking a
reference to the ' inexorable,' the ' immutable,' the ' eternal'
laws by which it is governed; to laws which, according to
my friend Professor Fawcett, are ' as certain in their operation as those which control physical nature.' It is no small
gain to have discovered that no such despotic laws do or
can exist ; that, inasmuch as the sole function of scientific
law is to predict the invariable recurrence of the same
effects from the same causes, and as there can be no in-
variability where—as in the case of price—one of the most
efficient causes is that ever-changing chameleon, human
character or disposition, price cannot possibly be subjected
to law. The progress of enquiry, and particularly of the
one in which we are here engaged, need no longer be barred
by this legal bugbear. Price in general comprehends the
price of labour or rate of wages. Whether, therefore, that
rate can by artificial expedients be enhanced, is a problem
which, how much soever its intricacy may discourage us,·
we need no longer be deterred from approaching by the
belief of its being also an unlawful mystery.

We proceed therefore to the third question proposed for
consideration in this chapter: Is there anything special,
and if so, what, in the mode in which the price of labour or
rate of wages is settled ?

Now, the so-called law of supply and demand has been
held to be not simply applicable to the price of labour,
but to apply to it with more than ordinary stringency.
By most teachers of political economy the existence has

been assumed of a certain fund, on the proportion between which and the quantity of labour in a country, the price of labour or rate of wages has been supposed to depend.   On this subject Professor Fawcett speaks as follows :—'The circulating capital of a country is its wage fund.   Hence, if we desire to calculate the average money wages received by each labourer, we have simply to divide the amount of capital by the number of the labouring population.   It is therefore evident that the average money wages cannot be increased, unless either the circulating capital is augmented or the number of the labouring population is diminished' ('Economic Position of the British Labourer,' p. 120).   And Mr. Mill thus describes the popular belief as to the same matter : 'There is supposed to be at any given instant, a sum of wealth which is unconditionally devoted to the payment of wages.   This sum is not regarded as unalterable, for it is augmented by savings and increases with the progress of wealth ; but it is reckoned upon as at any given moment a predetermined amount.   More than that amount it is assumed that the wages-receiving class cannot possibly divide among them ; that amount, and no less, they cannot but obtain.   So that, the sum to be divided being fixed, the wages of each depend solely on the divisor—the number of participants' ('Fortnightly Review,' for May 1869, p. 515). In other words, the whole number of labourers at any time existing in a country constitutes the supply of labour ; a certain sum set apart for the payment of wages consti- tutes the demand.   Divide the demand by the supply, the amount of the wages fund by the number of wage-seekers, and the quotient will be the price at which supply and demand will be equalised and which will be labour's average price.

The reality, however, of any such fund as is here assumed I utterly deny, and Mr. Mill, with characteristic generosity, here goes with me the whole way, not only con- curring unreservedly in my views, but supporting them by fresh suggestions of his own, of which I shall gladly avail

myself in the following exposition of what has now become
our common cause.

If there really were a national fund the whole of which
must necessarily be applied to the payment of wages, that
fund could be no other than an aggregate of smaller similar
funds possessed by the several individuals who composed
the employing part of the nation. Does, then, any individual employer possess any such fund ? Is there any specific
portion of any individual's capital which the owner must
necessarily expend upon labour? Of course every employer possesses a certain amount of money, whether his
own or borrowed, out of which all his expenses must be
met, if met at all. With so much of this amount as remains
after deduction of what he takes for family and personal
expenses, he carries on his business,—with one portion of
that balance providing or keeping in repair buildings and
machinery, with a second portion procuring materials, with
a third hiring labour. But is there any law fixing the
amount of his domestic expenditure, and thereby fixing
likewise the balance available for his industrial operations ?
May he not spend more or less on his family and himself
according to his fancy—in the one case having more, in the
other less, left for the conduct of his business ? And of
what is left, does he or can he determine beforehand how
much shall be laid out on buildings, how much on materials,
how much on labour ? May not his outlay on repairs be
unexpectedly increased by fire or other accident ? will not
his outlay on materials vary with their dearness or cheapness, or with the varying demand for the finished article ?
and must not the amount available for wages vary accordingly ? And even though the latter amount were exactly
ascertained beforehand, even though he did know to a
farthing how much he would be able to spend on labour,
would he be bound so to spend the utmost he could afford
to spend ? If he could get as much labour as he wanted
at a cheap rate, would he voluntarily pay as much for it as
he would be compelled to pay if it were dearer ? It sounds

like mockery or childishness to ask these questions, so obvious are the only answers that can possibly be given to them ; yet it is only on the assumption that directly opposite answers must be given that the wages fund can for one moment stand.   For if in the case of individual employers there be no wages funds—no definite or definable portions of their capitals which, and neither more nor less than which, they must severally apply to the hiring of labour—clearly there can be no aggregate of such funds, clearly there can be no national wages fund.   And be it observed, fixity or definiteness is the very essence of the supposed wages fund. No one denies that some amount or other must within any given period be disbursed in the form of wages.   The only question is, whether that amount be determinate or indeterminate.   If indeterminate, it cannot of course be divided, and might as well not exist for any power it possesses of performing the sole function of a wages fund, that, viz., of yielding a quotient that would indicate the average rate of wages.

It really can only be requisite to bring out plainly that this is the question—that determinateness or indeterminateness is the one point of difference between those who affirm and us who deny the wages fund—to show as plainly which of the two parties are in the right.   The former assume that of the whole circulating capital, which, of course, must at any given time be of•determinate amount, the portions required for business purposes, other than the payment of wages, are likewise of determinate amount, and that consequently the remainder available for wages cannot be otherwise than of determinate amount.   Further, they assume that the whole of this remainder must, and that less than this remainder cannot be disbursed as wages.   Now, in this, we so far agree as to admit that there is at any given time a certain amount, the whole of which may possibly, and more than which cannot possibly be expended on labour.   What we deny is, that because this amount *may* be, therefore it *must* be so expended.   We fully admit that employers may spend upon labour all they have got to spend, and cannot spend upon it more than they have got; but we deny that they are under any obligation to spend upon it all they have got. We admit that if an employer were to confine his domestic expenditure within the very narrowest bounds, were to spend on his plant only just so much as was necessary to keep it in working order, and were to purchase only just so much raw material as it was necessary for him to work up in order to go on working remuneratively, the remainder of his capital would represent both the utmost amount at his disposal for the payment of wages, and also an amount which he both could afford to spend, and would actually spend on wages, rather than not get the quantity of labour he required. What we deny is simply that, though an employer would spend this utmost amount on wages if he could not help himself, he would not if he could. We venture to think that, though he would pay the very highest price he could afford for labour if he could not get it cheaper, he would get it cheaper if he could. The believers in the wages fund, on the other hand, insist that whether labour be cheap or dear the whole body of employers always spend upon labour the utmost amount they can afford to spend. Very possibly they may be unconscious of insisting on this, but, consciously or unconsciously, this is demonstrably what they do insist upon. For they declare that the amount destined at any given time to the payment of wages, is a fixed amount—an amount so rigidly fixed that by applying to it the proper divisor you arrive infallibly at the average rate of wages. And they cannot but admit that this fixed amount *may* be the utmost that employers can afford ; for, clearly, employers would pay the utmost they could afford for labour, rather than not get the quantity of labour they required. But if the fixed amount in question *may* be, it necessarily *must* be that utmost, for otherwise it would be not a fixed but a variable amount.

In this strange doctrine it is, as Mr. Mill has pointed out, 'by implication affirmed that the demand for labour not only increases with the cheapness, but increases in exact proportion to it, the same aggregate sum being paid for labour whatever its price may be.' But though as a rule it be true that demand increases with cheapness, it is certainly very seldom, if ever, that demand increases in the same ratio as cheapness. Few of us, if bread or beer became ten times cheaper, would buy ten times as much bread or beer as before. Even in the limited sense, too, in which the rule is true, it is open to very many exceptions, and labour is almost always one of the exceptions. The quantity of labour which an employer needs, depends upon the work he wants to have done. If there are certain jobs which it is essential to him to get finished within a certain time, he will, if labour be dear, consent to pay pretty high for the quantity needed to complete the jobs within the time. But he will not, merely because labour happens to be cheap instead of dear, hire more than that quantity. If, on Saturday morning, he wants his hay cut or carried before night, and if fewer than ten men would not suffice, he will, perhaps, consent to give ten men 5*s*. a-piece, but he would not engage twenty men for the same service, even if he could get them for 1*s*. a-head. Still less, if he found he could get the ten men for 1*s*. each, would he think of paying them 5*s*. each. Whenever, as in the case of labour, demand does not increase with cheapness, demand, as Mr. Mill has further pointed out, may be perfectly equalised with supply at many different prices. If all the employers get all the labour they require, and if all the seekers for employment succeed in getting hired, there is as complete equation of supply and demand, whether the rate of hire be 6*d*. or 6*s*. But when an employer's demand for labour is fully supplied, he can have no demand left requiring to be supplied. If, at a given rate, he can obtain all the labour he is in a position to employ, he will not, merely because that rate happens to be a low one, either hire additional labour for which he has no

employment, or voluntarily raise the rate, instead of retaining
the difference for himself, and either spending it upon himself or laying it by. But if no one employer will do this,
how can the whole body of employers do it? and if they
do not, how can the same amount be spent upon labour,
whether labour be cheap or dear? and how, again, unless
this be done, can there be a sum unconditionally devoted
to the payment of wages?

I am half ashamed to lay so much stress on points so
glaringly obvious. My excuse is, the pertinacity with which
the opposite points are maintained. A reader new to the
subject can scarcely fail to suspect me of exaggeration in
my statement of the case of my opponents. He will have
a difficulty in believing that notions so inconsistent with
common sense and with every-day experience can be recognised dogmas of political economy. But, indeed, there
are no notions too wild to become recognised, if, because promulgated by authority, they are accepted without
examination. Whether I have been guilty of misrepresentation in my account of the wages fund theory, any one
may judge for himself who will compare what I have said
of it with the quotations given above from Mr. Fawcett and
Mr. Mill, or who will stop to consider whether the theory
is susceptible of any construction beside the one that I
have placed upon it that will not render it meaningless.
The idea of a wages fund, the whole of which needs must,
and more or less than which cannot be expended upon
labour, may be a manifest absurdity. Without presuming
myself so to style it, I readily acquiesce in the designation. But absurd as the idea may be, still no other idea
of a wages fund is conceivable consistently with which
division of the fund by the number of wage-seekers can
determine the average rate of wages which the latter are
about to obtain. No other idea of it can be formed consistently with which it can perform the one sole function
for which it has been devised.*

* To my 'Edinburgh' Reviewer, much meditating over this matter, a

did not raise it higher, simply because, according to the hypothesis, 2*s.* was the highest point it could possibly reach —the utmost which the farmers thought it would be worth their while or that they could afford to give.

Next, still keeping in view three farmers and twelve labourers, similarly circumstanced in most respects as before, let us suppose the farmers to have each just work enough for four labourers, and to be able each to spend just 12*s.* a day on labour ; and further, let us suppose the labourers, though of course anxious to get as much as they can, to be willing to work for as little as 6*d.* a-day rather than not get employment. The highest rate at which all twelve men could then be employed would be 3*s.* a-day ; but it would by no means follow that they would get that rate. What precise rate they would get, would depend— not on supply and demand, whether actual or prospective— not upon the stock of labour either actually in, or expected to come into the market, as compared with the several quantities of labour which customers would be ready to purchase at different prices ; nor upon the number, eager- ness, and purchasing power of the customers ; for without any variation in any one of these respects, the rate might become either 6*d.* or 3*s.*, or anything between them. Which of the extreme rates, or what intermediate rate would result, would depend simply and solely on compe- tition ; perhaps on the competition of the farmers—perhaps on that of the labourers, but always and certainly on competition. If the farmers were more urgently in need of labour than the labourers of work, the latter would be able to name their own terms, and if the dread of each other's competition did not prevent their asking the extreme price of 3*s.*, they might get that extreme price for the asking. But perhaps, and much more probably, the labourers would be more urgently in want of work than the farmers of labour, and some of them, in order to make sure of employ- ment, might offer to take 2*s.*, or 1*s.* 6*d.*, or 1*s.*, or even 6*d.* The competition of the farmers would then relax : they would perceive that they might safely refuse to give more than some one of the lower rates, and whichever might be the rate they offered, that rate the labourers would by their necessities be compelled to accept. Or again : it might be that the farmers, though unable to engage more than four labourers at 3*s.* a-head, had work for more than four, and were each willing to hire as many as six, if they could be got at 2*s.* a-head; or as many as eight at 1*s.* 6*d.* Then, even though some of the labourers should be willing to take as little as 1*s.* 6*d.* or 2*s.*, the competition of the farmers would be pretty sure to raise the rate. Their competition would apprise the labourers that a higher rate was to be had by them all; and the competition of the labourers, relaxing in consequence and correspondingly, would permit them all to ask and obtain a higher rate. The rate would certainly rise above 2*s.*, and might not improbably rise as high as 3*s.* Here, again, without any change in the state of the labour market, the price of labour might vary exceedingly—competition alone deciding whether it should be 2*s.* or 3*s.*, or something intermediate between the two. All these are fairly representative cases, which may easily be so modified as to be made to comprehend the essential conditions of most situations in which competition would have free play. For instance, the farmers, instead of their all having exactly the same demand for labour, might be supposed to want very different quantities, and to have very unequal means of paying for it; or, instead of all the labourers being supposed to be equally in need of employment, some of them might be supposed to be much more eager for it than others, and to be willing to accept it on much worse terms than others would agree to. But, set what examples you please, and vary them as you will, whoever will be at the trouble of working them out, will, I am pretty confident, find one general principle applying equally to all. Wherever competition is permitted to act without restriction, he will find that the price may vary exceedingly without the smallest variation in the relations of supply and demand; and he will also find that there cannot be the smallest variation in the price without a previous and corresponding variation in competition, which, therefore, he will, in the cases examined, be constrained to recognise as the price's determining cause.

So far, little difference may perhaps have been noticed between labour and any other commodity; yet one very material difference has been adverted to. Whereas what determines the price of tangible commodities is almost always the competition of dealers,* we have seen that the price of labour may be determined by the competition of customers, and in practice the latter competition would be infinitely more likely to determine it than the former. This is owing to the fact that labour is almost always offered for sale without reservation of price, which other commodities never or scarcely ever are; and this again is owing to two peculiarities, one necessarily inherent in, and the other habitually united with labour, which distinguish it from all other commodities, and affect its price in a remarkable and generally very unfavourable manner.

In the first place, labour, differing in this from every other commodity, will not *keep.* All other commodities may be stored up for a longer or shorter time, without loss either in quantity or quality. But labour will not keep; it cannot be left unused for one moment without partially wasting away. Unless it be sold immediately, some portion of it can never be sold at all. To-day's labour cannot be sold after to-day, for to-morrow it will have ceased to exist. A labourer cannot, for however short a time, postpone the sale of his labour, without losing the

---

* This, in speaking of tangible commodities, seems to me a more accurate as well as a simpler way of stating the case than to say that the competition of dealers makes price fall, and that competition of customers makes it rise. What the latter competition seems to me really to do is, to show the dealers that a higher price than they previously supposed is attainable, and to induce them consequently to relax their own competition so as to obtain it.

whole price of the labour which he might have exercised during the period of the postponement.

Labourers, or sellers of labour, are consequently liable to a loss to which no other sellers are exposed : for all other sellers—grocers, or drapers, for example, and even those who deal in the most perishable commodities—such as bakers, or butchers, or fishmongers—may hold back their goods for more or less time, and at the end of the time find them still existent, and little or nothing the worse for wear.   The loss, too, is one which, owing to another peculiarity connected with labour, labourers are of all men the least able to bear.   Not only can they in general ill afford to sacrifice any part of their labour by postponing its sale, they could ill afford to postpone its sale even though the postponement involved no ultimate loss.   For in the second place, labour—hireable manual labour alone, of course, being here understood—is seldom found except in such intimate union with poverty as to be scarcely distinguished from it, insomuch that, in common parlance, 'labouring classes' and 'labouring poor' are treated as perfectly synonymous terms.   Labourers who live by the sale of their labour have, for the most part, nothing but their labour to live upon.   Such labourers have never been a saving race.   Their habit has always been to live from hand to mouth, depending on the price of present labour for the supply of present wants, without any other means of even temporary self-support.   But, as Solomon says, and the wisest of men never said a truer thing, 'the destruction of the poor is their poverty ;' and the saying is especially true of poor labourers for hire.   For the well-being of these depends mainly on the bargain they can make for their labour, and extreme poverty virtually disables them from bargaining.   It forbids their standing out, as all other sellers are accustomed to do, for their price. The meanest huckster, if he cannot get what he asks in the morning, can wait till the evening, or till to-morrow, or next week, for with a packful of wares he will surely be able to get food enough upon credit to keep him alive till then. But very poor labourers are almost compelled to deal with the first customers who present themselves. They cannot wait for the chance of better customers, for they are in urgent need of immediate earnings for immediate subsistence. They must, therefore, let their labour go for what it will immediately fetch, provided that be not less than the lowest pittance they can manage to live upon. They must do this for two reasons—firstly, they cannot defer the sale of their labour without certainly having less to sell in consequence whenever they do sell ; and, secondly, even if by waiting they were sure of a better price for the lesser quantity than they could get immediately for the larger, they could ill afford to wait, for fear of half starving during the interval.

And while labourers are thus disabled from bargaining, their customers, on the contrary, have extraordinary facilities for that operation. Customers for anything else, for necessary food or clothing, or even for unnecessary dainties or ornaments, are generally more impatient for the article they are seeking than the dealers in it are for their customers' money. The former are much more likely to be inconvenienced by having to go for a while without the one, than the latter by having to wait an equal time for the other. Customers in general, therefore, are so far at the mercy of the dealers to whom they have access, that, if they are bent on having the dealers' goods, they must pay the dealers' prices, the competition of the dealers alone determining what those prices shall be. Labourers, on the contrary, are as much and more at the mercy of their customers. Customers for labour—who as employers of labour must necessarily have more or less of capital at their disposal, on which, in the absence of accruing income, to subsist for a while—cannot possibly be so urgently in need of labour as destitute labourers must be of work. They seldom, therefore, trouble themselves to enquire how much such labourers expect, well knowing that, whatever be their expectations, they must e'en content themselves with what they can get. What employers have really to regard is simply their own mutual competition ; and whatever be the lowest price which their competition permits them to offer, that price, if they insist upon it, labourers in a state of chronic destitution will have no alternative but to accept. Now in a tolerably well-stocked market the competition of customers is never very keen. If the prices of tangible commodities were settled by the competition of customers, instead of by that of dealers, the prices of such commodities would assuredly, except in times of scarcity, be always very low; and as, except when labour is scarce, its price, if settled by competition at all, is settled by the competition of customers, its price when so settled is sure to be lower than the competition of dealers would cause the price of anything else to be in a similar state of the market.

To make this clearer, I will risk another trial of the reader's patience by recurring once more to an example already given. In one of the cases in which a dozen farm-labourers figured, we perceived it to be quite possible for the men to agree to hire themselves out for 1*s.* 6*d.* or 2*s.* a-head, at a time when the farmers were prepared, if necessary, to hire them at 3*s.* a-head, but had not the means of hiring more than twelve men altogether at that rate. This last rate was, however, in the circumstances supposed, the very highest the men could possibly get. None of them could have obtained employment at more than 3*s.* a-head, even if the farmers had been so much in want of labour that, rather than not get any, they would have paid 6*s.* a-head for two men. For at any higher rate than 3*s.* only part of the whole number could have got employment, and the competition of the others would have been sure to bring down the rate. But if what the men had to sell had, instead of labour, been corn or cloth, the result might, and probably would, have been very different. The utmost that could possibly be got for the whole of the labour was

36*s.*, but corn dealers, or clothiers, in corresponding circumstances, might, by beginning with asking sufficiently high
prices and waiting till they got them, have obtained 36*s.*
for only one-half of their stock of corn or cloth, and still
have had the other half to sell at similar prices as demand
gradually sprang up. But if the labourers had waited until
the middle of the day, in hopes thereby of doubling the
price of their labour, the only certain consequence would
have been their losing half a day's labour. Corn dealers or
clothiers, even if they had failed to obtain the rise of price
for which they stood out, would, when at last compelled to
give in, have had the same quantity of goods to sell as at
first. But labourers who stood out till noon would, at noon,
have only half a day's labour instead of a whole day's
labour to sell. Labourers cannot postpone the sale of their
labour without incurring a loss corresponding exactly with
the length of the postponement. So far as the morning's
labour is concerned, it is of no use to them to know that
the demand for labour will be twice as great in the afternoon as it is now, or that it is twice as great twenty miles
off as it is here ; for the morning's labour cannot be sold
at all if they wait till the afternoon, or if they occupy
the whole morning in walking to another place of sale.
Suppose even that by waiting till the afternoon, or by
walking twenty miles, they succeeded in getting then or
there twice the rate of wages obtainable now or here, or
that, by sacrificing the labour of the first half of the day,
they obtained for the second half the usual wages of the
whole day. Suppose, for instance, a dozen farm servants,
by waiting till the afternoon, to succeed in getting thirty-
six shillings for the afternoon instead of for an entire day.
Even so, they would be much worse off than ordinary
traders similarly circumstanced, for ordinary dealers would
incur no such sacrifice by waiting till the afternoon; and if
by so waiting, they succeeded in getting double price, they
would have an undiminished stock to sell at that price.

But labourers are not merely worse off than ordinary traders by being liable to this peculiar sacrifice. They are further worse off by being in general too poor to be able to make the sacrifice. They generally want the price of this morning's or of to-day's labour for this morning's or to-day's use. They must needs sell to-day, and, in consequence of selling to-day, must content themselves to-morrow with the same low price as to-day. Thus, owing to two causes — one, labour's inability to keep,* the other, the

* My friend Professor Cairnes, who has done me the favour to read this paper in manuscript, and who, I am happy to be permitted to say, concurs generally in the views expressed in it, demurs, however, a little in this place. He considers that the habitual poverty of labourers, which commonly leaves them little choice but to accept the first offer of employment made them, sufficiently accounts for and sums up all the special disadvantages attaching to them in the capacity of dealers in a commodity. He does not think that those disadvantages are increased by the inability of their commodity to keep. In this respect he recognises no difference between labour and any other commodity—corn for, instance. If corn, which might be sold to-day, be not sold till to-morrow, the extra profit which the corn dealer might have realised if he had obtained the price of the corn to-day instead of to-morrow, is foregone, and Mr. Cairnes regards this extra profit as the proper analogue to what a labourer loses by postponing the sale of his labour. For, as he justly argues, a labourer's wages are not all clear profit. His net gain is no more than the difference between the quantity of comfort or enjoyment which he sacrifices by working, and the quantity of enjoyment which his wages will procure for him. It is the difference between these quantities which constitutes his profit, if, selling his labour at once, he set to work at once, and which con-stitutes his loss, if he defer the sale of his labour ; and the loss in the latter case Mr. Cairnes regards as analogous—so far as the two cases admit of being compared—to that incurred by a corn dealer who defers the sale of his corn, and obtains for it eventually no higher price than he might have had at first.

Now I quite agree that the labourer's apparent loss by not working to-day, and therefore not selling the labour of to-day, is not all real loss. Though he loses a day's wages he saves himself a day's exer-tion, and his net loss is no more than the difference between the two, which same difference would have constituted his entire net gain if he had worked. This net gain, this difference between his outlay in the shape of exertion and his gross receipts in the shape of wages, would be in fact his profit, just as the farmer's profit would be the difference habitual poverty of labourers—the labour of uncombined labourers is almost always sold without reservation of price. It is only very exceptionally that isolated labour is not so sold, whereas it is only very exceptionally, or rather almost never, that anything except labour is so sold. Now, when no price is reserved, what determines price is the competition of customers, and of those customers, too, who happen to be actually at hand, for when dealers do not insist on any particular price, it naturally devolves on the customers to decide what the price shall be. Such competition, except in a very scantily supplied market, is sure not to be very keen—is sure to be less keen

between his outlay on the several items of production, and his returns in the shape of the price obtained for his corn.

So far, corn and labour, farmer and labourer, seem exactly alike. But now a very important distinction presents itself. The profit which the farmer fails to realise to-day, may be realised hereafter ; for the corn may be as available for sale to-morrow, or six months hence, as now. But, if the profit which might be made by the sale of to-day's labour be not made to-day, it can never be made at all, for to-morrow there will be none of to-day's labour left to sell. The utmost which a farmer can lose by postponing the sale of corn which he eventually sells at the same price as he might have got immediately, is the second profit which the first profit might have enabled him to make if realised earlier. But, in the case of the labourer, even if any such second profit would not in general be quite out of the question, the first profit itself is irrecoverably lost. The position of a labourer postponing the sale of his labour seems to me analogous, not to that of a farmer simply postponing the sale of his corn, but rather to that of a farmer who, refusing to sell to-day in hopes of a higher price to-morrow, finds to-morrow that his ricks have been burnt down during the night, and so loses the whole value of the corn, and not merely that proportion of the value which would, if realised, have constituted his profit.

The disagreement between Mr. Cairnes and myself is but small, and is besides purely theoretical, and without even the smallest practical importance. We both agree that the chronic poverty of labourers commonly induces them to sell their labour without reserve ; only I think, while he does not, that labour's incapacity for keeping furnishes them with an additional, though perhaps supererogatory, motive for so selling. But the smaller our disagreement, the greater the temptation to me to note it, in order thereby to show to how large an extent I have the concurrence of a writer who, for acuteness in finding his way through the tortuous entanglements of high economics, is perhaps without a superior.

than it would have been if, some price having been reserved, the sale had been delayed and more customers had had time to arrive. The price resulting from such competition is of course correspondingly low. Wherefore, as isolated labour is almost always sold without reserve, whereas tangible commodities are scarcely ever so sold, it follows that the price of such labour must almost always be lower than the price of any tangible commodity would have been in a similar state of the market.

This is a serious disadvantage, but it is neither the only, nor the worst special disadvantage to which labour is subject in respect of price. It would be bad enough for labour that its price, unlike that of every other commodity, should be dependent on the competition, not of dealers interested in selling dearly, but of customers interested in buying cheaply. It would be bad enough that the competition of the customers should ordinarily be too feeble to have much elevating influence on price; but what is still worse is, that even such influence as the competition of customers might occasionally exert is scarcely ever suffered to be exercised, for in practice it is not the mutual competition, but the mutual combination of customers, which, in general, really determines the price of isolated labour. Here again, customers for labour possess certain facilities peculiar to themselves. For most other * objects of trade the customers greatly outnumber the dealers. Wholesale traders are but few in proportion to retailers, and for one retail butcher, baker, grocer, or draper, there are fifty or a hundred consumers of bread, meat, groceries, or draperies. But in

---

* 'Every other,' instead of 'most other' was originally the expression used here, but, as the 'Spectator' very aptly, though with very needless acrimony, reminds me, 'there are other commodities besides labour the sellers of which are overwhelmingly more numerous than the purchasers'—rag merchants, for instance, than paper manufacturers, and rag gatherers than rag merchants. But though these are undoubtedly exceptions to the rule, they are likewise exceptions helping to point the moral intended to be drawn from the rule. It must be much easier for two or three rag merchants than for several scores of rag gatherers to combine, and in transactions between the two, the former, we may be sure, have much the best of the bargain.

the labour market, on the contrary, the dealers usually greatly outnumber the customers. For every employer there are dozens or scores or hundreds of employed. This of itself would make it comparatively difficult for sellers of labour, and comparatively easy for sellers of anything else, to combine; and would also make combination comparatively easy for buyers of labour, and comparatively difficult for buyers of anything else. Combination, too, of buyers of labour would be much more likely to succeed. If the mass of miscellaneous customers in any neighbourhood were to agree together not to deal with some of the shopkeepers without a reduction of prices, they would most likely inconvenience themselves ten times more by foregoing comforts to which they were accustomed, than they would inconvenience the purveyors of those comforts by withholding their custom. Besides, rather than take less than their usual prices, grocers and drapers, and such like, would probably send off their goods to some other market, perhaps removing themselves thither also; and even bakers and butchers, though they might have no alternative at last but to take whatever was offered for their existing stocks, would certainly shut up shop rather than go on killing meat and baking bread at a loss, or at less than the current rate of profit. A combination of ordinary customers would thus have little chance against ordinary tradesmen, because such customers are even more immediately dependent on their tradesmen than the tradesmen are upon them. But between dealers in and customers for labour the relations of dependence are reversed. The customers are seldom so urgently in need of labour as labourers are of their usual wages. If the job which an employer wants done cannot be done to-day, it may generally be done to-morrow; and how much soever he may want it done, his immediate livelihood can very rarely depend upon its being done immediately. But if to-day's wages are not earned to-day, they cannot be earned at all; and not only can the day labourer seldom afford to lose to-day's earnings, he generally requires to have them to-day.

With every labourer it is always, in one sense, Hobson's choice. He cannot have what is offered unless he accept it at once, whereas an employer has generally a chance of getting to-morrow, on as good or better terms, what he refuses to-day. With a very poor labourer it is always Hobson's choice in the fullest sense. He must take the most he can immediately get, for he cannot wait for more; he cannot carry his labour to a better market, for he cannot spare the time to go there; he cannot retire from the profession of labourer, unless, when ceasing to work, he is content also to cease to live. Even if among many destitute workmen there were some few who had saved a little money, their savings would avail them little. To a large employer it would be a small inconvenience to dispense with individual workmen, but the individual workmen, as soon as their savings were exhausted, would be compelled to take fresh employment on such terms as they could obtain. Labourers with savings could do nothing without others to combine with, and labourers without savings could not combine with them. Yet, uncombined, they could have little chance against even single masters, who, on the contrary, would have merely to use their special facilities for combining, in order to have their improvident men completely at their mercy.

Employers have never been slow to perceive, nor backward to avail themselves of the advantages they thus possess. 'Masters,' says Adam Smith, in words not the less strikingly apt and to the purpose because, being so strikingly true, they have been quoted and re-quoted until they have become commonplace, 'Masters are, always and everywhere, in a sort of tacit but uniform combination not to raise wages above their actual rate. Masters, too, sometimes enter into particular combinations to sink wages even below this rate.' Masters scarcely ever allow their mutual competition to raise wages. It is only in very exceptional circumstances that they bid against each other for labour; scarcely ever, indeed, unless they are very urgently in need of a greater quantity than can be immediately procured at any price. This happens in new colonies, in which the extent of land to be tilled, and the number of sheep or oxen to be tended, and of meals to be cooked, and floors to be scrubbed, is generally out of all proportion to the number of available hinds and herds, cooks and housemaids, more especially if a promising gold discovery happens to have enticed away half the able-bodied population to ' the diggings.' Something of the kind happens occasionally, too, among ourselves ; if, for example, a few fine days towards the end of a wet June offer to farmers any last chance of saving their hay, provided they can manage to get hands to make it while the sun shines ; or if, some main sea embankment giving way, the preservation of south-eastern Lincolnshire from a second deluge becomes dependent on the number of navvies who can be got together to ward it off before the next high spring tides. On such occasions the price of labour may be forced up by competition to an extravagant height, but in ordinary times employers see clearly that it is better for them to go without part of the labour they desire, than, for the sake of obtaining that part, to incur the obligation of paying a greatly increased price for all the labour they employ. Accordingly employers in the same neighbourhood, whether they have formally combined or not, commonly act as if they had combined to keep down wages. Much more commonly than not, every employer can get as much labour as he is disposed to pay for at the current rate. Much more commonly than not, the labour market is sufficiently supplied for that. But even though that should not be the case, every employer would probably make shift as well as he could with the labour which he could procure at the current rate, and anyone who should endeavour to tempt away another's servants by offers of increased pay, would be treated by his fellow-masters as a traitor to the common cause. Such is the habitual policy of customers for labour. Instead of suffering the rate of wages to be

settled naturally by competition, they endeavour by combination to settle it arbitrarily. Their policy is for the
most part successful. In the absence of combination among
the labourers, the rate of wages is settled arbitrarily by
combination of employers. It does not follow that the
rate so settled should be lower than that which might have
resulted from competition. The lowest rate which any set
of masters ever arranged among themselves to offer was
probably not quite so low as the very lowest rate which
they might have offered without any danger of being out-
bidden by each other. It is probable that when, in the
years before the famine, Irish farmers were accustomed to
pay their men 6*d.* or 4*d.* a-day, every individual amongst
them might, if he had tried, have screwed his men down to
4*d.* or 3*d.* Labour is sometimes to be had at so very low
a rate that masters will be found of their own accord giving
for it a trifle more than they need give. But on the other
hand, when labour is at all scarce, the very highest rate
dictated by combination is sure not to be so high as that
which would have resulted from competition; for the only
object of the masters in combining is to prevent the price
from being raised by competition. When English iron-
masters arrange among themselves that the wages of rail-
millrollers shall be seven or ten guineas a week, they
do so simply because they fear that, if they did not so
arrange, their mutual competition would raise the rate still
higher.

Here is a second special grievance under which unfortunate labour labours. As if it were not enough that the
competition of customers can never be keen enough to
raise the price of labour to the point which the price of any
other commodity might reach in similar circumstances,
even when there does seem to be a probability that the
competition of customers may raise the price of labour,
that competition is commonly withdrawn, and combination
takes its place. The only cause which could naturally
occasion a rise in the price of labour is the competition of

the masters, and to prevent competition from having that effect, masters commonly combine instead of competing.

And even this is not the worst. Employers, as a class, are not without the average admixture of bowels of mercy among their other viscera. For the most part, they so far accept the principle of ' live and let live' as to be willing that their labourers should have any wages that will not sensibly encroach on their own profit. In fact, it is of little consequence to them how high the wages of labour may be, provided the price of the produce of labour be proportionably high. But if among many liberal employers there be one single niggard, the niggardliness of that single one may suffice to neutralise the liberality of all the rest. If one single employer succeed in screwing down wages below the rate previously current, his fellow-employers may have no alternative but to follow suit, or to see themselves undersold in the produce market. Now, nothing of the kind could occur with regard to the price of any commodity except labour. If, in humble imitation of Shakspeare's Jack Cade, you or I were to ask a baker to let us have seven half-penny loaves for a penny, or to propose to a publican that the three-hooped pot should have ten hoops, the baker or beerseller might perhaps be benevolent enough to tell us he wished we might get it ; but assuredly without suiting the action to the word, and serving us with the quantity or measure asked for, on the suggested terms. Neither, assuredly, would let us have threepence-halfpenny worth for a penny while knowing that, by waiting a little, he would be able to get threepence-halfpenny for it, either from ourselves or others. But it would be quite possible for the customary wages of labour to be two shillings a-day, or some higher rate, and for the majority of employers in the neighbourhood to be readily paying it, and yet for some one employer to get a customary two shillings' worth of labour for only eighteenpence or a shilling. For labour is so rapidly and so easily producible that, except on extra-ordinary occasions, the market is sure to be supplied with

it at least abundantly enough to enable all employers to
get at the current price as much labour as they have employment for. The men with whom our supposed niggard
was higgling might, therefore, have no chance of being
hired by any other employer, all the rest being already
sufficiently provided. They would then be completely at
the niggard's mercy, and would have to submit to whatever
reduction he chose to insist upon ; which reduction would
then, for the reason above stated, probably become general
throughout the trade. Numerous instances of general
reductions of wages brought about in this manner will
readily occur to any one at all conversant with industrial,
and especially with manufacturing, history.

It is to be noted that this exposition has been throughout put forward as applicable only to a normal state of
things, by which is intended to be understood a state in
which working men, seeking for employment, act independently of each other and without any mutual concert.*
True, there probably never was a time when working men
altogether abstained from combination. Men with common
interests and feelings, and speaking a common language,
can scarcely be brought much into contact without occasionally talking together over their common plans. But,
until comparatively recent times, labourers' combinations
were very rare and for the most part very desultory efforts ;
and even now that they have become both numerous and
efficacious, they are still, everywhere but in Great Britain,
only exceptional. Among our own working-classes, indeed,
an artificial organisation has within the last half-century
been matured, some imperfect copies of which have latterly
appeared in a few continental towns : but not the less are
we justified in regarding the normal condition of labour as
one of unorganisation ; and it is to such a condition only

---

* This proviso ought, I think, to have saved me from being charged
with 'over and over again saying that wages are kept low by combination among employers,' as if I imagined that such continued to be in
this country and in these days the ordinary practice.

that the foregoing observations have been intended to apply. Bearing this in mind, let us now sum up the conclusions to which our past reasoning appears to lead; let us enumerate the causes which, when there is no union among labourers to obstruct the natural course of things, have appeared to us to determine the price of labour.

Briefly they may be stated as follows:—In the absence of combination on the side of the employers as well as on that of the employed, the price of labour is determined by competition, which competition, again, depends upon the estimates formed by the several competitors of prospective supply and demand. But, unlike the price of any other commodity, that of labour is generally determined not by the competition of the dealers, but by that of the customers. The reason of the difference is, that labour, in the circumstances supposed, is always, or almost always, offered for sale without reservation of price, which other commodities never, or scarcely ever, are. The consequence of the difference is, that the price of labour, when settled by competition, is almost always much lower than that of any other commodity would be, if similarly settled in a similar state of the market. In this manner, and with this result, is the price of labour determined in the absence of combination on the side either of employers or employed. But it is only very rarely, and when labour is at once very scarce and in very great request, that masters are tempted to compete with each other. At all other times they are in the habit of combining instead of competing, and it is their combination which, in the absence of counter-combination among the labourers, then determines the price of labour, and determines it arbitrarily—not indeed absolutely without regard to the relations between supply and demand, but without any uniformity of correspondence with those relations. When labour is very abundant, masters sometimes, of their own accord, pay more for it than they need do. When it is very scarce, they generally agree among themselves not to pay so much for it as competition would have compelled them to do. Masters seldom or never probably avail themselves to the utmost of the power which they might derive from combination ; but combined masters really possess, whether they choose to exert it or not, almost absolute power of control over the wages of uncombined workmen. They cannot of course force the men to take less than they can live upon, but they both can and do force them to take as little more than the bare means of subsistence as it pleases them to offer. Thus, in a normal state of things—in a state, that is, in which labourers are too poor to combine (and throughout the world's history poverty has hitherto been, at most times, and in most places, the normal condition of labour)—the price of labour is determined not by supply and demand, which never determined the price of anything, nor yet generally by competition, which generally determines the price of everything else ; but by combination among the masters. Competition in a small minority of cases, combination in a great majority, have appeared to be normally the determining causes of the rate of wages or price of labour.

The whole of this chapter is confessedly interstitial ; but no reader, I trust, will consider that it has been needlessly introduced. Its importance in relation to general political economy is just this, that if its reasonings be to any considerable extent sound, no small portion of the science, as hitherto taught, will have to be rewritten. The importance of its bearing on our special subject will become more and more apparent at every step, as we proceed.*

* Some few more last words I must ask leave to add in a note, directed, Parthian-like, against a very able writer who has, by anticipation, taken up a position which, if retained, would enable him completely to demolish mine, not leaving me an inch of ground to return to. I have been endeavouring to ascertain how the price of labour is ordinarily regulated, but Mr. Frederic Harrison (' Fortnightly Review,' No. 13, ' Good and Evil of Trade Unionism ') contends that labour cannot have a price, for that it is not a thing capable of being sold. ' Here,' he says, ' we come to the root of the matter. The labourer,' and he prints the aphorism in capital letters, ' THE LABOURER HAS NOT GOT A THING TO SELL.' To suppose that he has ' is the funda-

mental fallacy which distorts the reasoning of many capitalists, and of most economists.'

Mr. Harrison's reasons for this opinion are three :—1. That a saleable commodity must needs be some 'portable, visible thing,' which, moreover, the owner must not be urged by any immediate necessity to sell. ' If,' he says, ' he was in need of immediate support, he would not be a seller or trader at all.' Whence it would follow that if a citizen of a blockaded city, or a pilgrim in the desert, were willing, in order to save his life, to sell all he had, even all his sub-stance, for a crust of mouldy bread or a cup of dirty water, he could not become a seller, and his substance would cease to consist of saleable commodities, for the very singular reason that his life would depend on his being able to sell.

2. The seller of a visible commodity can in general 'send it, or carry it, about from place to place, and from market to market,' whereas a labourer cannot send away his labour, but must carry it himself, or, at any rate, must go with it wherever it goes. Yet fields and houses, rights of shooting or fishing, mining or water privileges, which can neither be sent nor carried, are not on that account the less subjects of continual sale. How, then, can the fact that a la-bourer 'cannot correspond with his employer, cannot send him a sample of his strength,' 'but must himself be present in the market ' in which he seeks to sell his labour, be any proof that his labour cannot be sold ?

3. A labourer seeking employment, 'seeks not to exchange products but to combine to produce.' When he obtains employment, he con-tracts, not ' to sell something,' but ' to do something,' and on the terms and conditions of his contract depend 'his whole comfort, peace, and success : very often his dwelling ; usually his health, the arrange-ments of his household, his wife's duties and occupations, his home in every detail.' No sale of a visible commodity similarly 'affects the complex network of human relations.'

Now all this may be perfectly true ; but it is certainly rather beside the question. To show that it is of paramount importance to a labourer to make a good bargain in disposing of his labour, is scarcely equivalent to showing that his labour is a thing which cannot be dis-posed of by sale.

The above is the substance of Mr. Harrison's arguments, which will scarcely be considered sufficient to sustain his case. There is, however, a fourth and nicer point, which, though Mr. Harrison has not distinctly adverted to it, may perhaps be thought to afford for his opinion some firm, though narrow, footing.

When a visible commodity is sold, it is transferred bodily from one person to another ; there is a complete change of ownership. What the seller parts with, the buyer acquires. The corn or cloth which did belong to the one, does belong to the other. The former, instead of the latter, has become corn-owner or cloth-owner. But no such transfer, no such change, occurs when what is sometimes termed a sale of labour takes place. An employer, by purchasing labour, does not himself become a labourer. He does not gain any strength or skill, nor does the labourer lose any. It must even be admitted that what he acquires is not labour itself, but the results of labour ; which results, moreover, were never the property of the labourer through whose instrumentality he acquires them. The additional productiveness which land derives from being ploughed, the additional value which wool derives from being woven, never belonged to the ploughman or the weaver, neither of whom, therefore, could transfer what he never possessed. It must, further, be admitted, then, that neither labour nor the impalpable results of labour are capable of being sold in precisely the same manner as tangible commodities, the results of labour and capital combined. Evidently there is some anomaly, at least, if not some defect, in their so-called sale. Either the terms ' sale of labour,' and ' price of labour,' are not strictly accurate expressions, or the transactions to which they both have reference must be of a somewhat special character. Even so ; and accordingly, the speciality of the transaction is distinctly recognised in our habitual forms of speech. In ordinary discourse, we talk not of ' selling,' but of ' hiring' labour—not of the ' price,' but of the ' wages ' of labour. Perhaps these colloquial terms are also the only perfectly correct ones; perhaps, even in scientific discussion respecting labour, we ought to speak always of hire and wages, never of sale and price. So much, at any rate, may be safely conceded to Mr. Harrison, provided he also admit, as with equal courtesy he no doubt will, that the rate of wages is determined by exactly the same causes, in exactly the same way, and with exactly the same result, as the price of labour would be, *if* the transaction which we are accustomed to call ' hiring' labour, could with equal propriety be termed ' selling.'

[The accomplished contributor to the ' Times,' already more than once referred to, observes upon the foregoing note, that 'in all purchases, what is paid for is not the material thing which may be transferred, but the services or labour which the transferrer and his predecessors, if any, have rendered with relation to the article transferred. We speak compendiously of buying fish, but the fish itself is a gratuitous gift of nature ; what we pay for is the service of those who furnished the boat, of the fishermen who manned it, of the fishmonger who brought the fish to our doors.'

This though specious seems to me sophistical, and the fallacy that underlies it is not, I think, far below the surface. If purchasing the results of certain services were nothing more than purchasing the services themselves, then to purchase the services would be to purchase their results also. But whoever, instead of waiting till fish were caught before paying for them, should pay beforehand for the labour involved in catching, taking the chance of any being caught, might discover a material difference between the two operations.]

CHAPTER II.

THE CLAIMS OF LABOUR, AND ITS RIGHTS.

WHEN Proudhon electrified all well-to-do people by the astounding declaration that property is robbery—*la propriété c'est le vol*—the indignation which so outrageous a proposition was calculated to excite was considerably abated by amusement at its extravagance. People in general, well-to-do people, that is, were disposed to take for granted that the speaker was jesting, and that he neither himself believed what he said, nor expected others to believe it. Comparatively few suspected, what was nevertheless the fact, that Proudhon had merely given shape, distinctness, and epigrammatic point to certain confused notions, which, engendered and nourished by discomfort and discontent, had been gradually quickening in the minds of multitudes. Fewer still were aware how fair a show of reasoning might be marshalled in defence of notions apparently so irrational, and how capable these are of being built up into a theory of sufficient regularity and strength to require to be at least attacked in form, in order to be decisively refuted.

The basis on which the theory rests is the assumption that every man who has not by crime forfeited the right, and who has no other means of living, has a right to live by labour. From this modest premiss, a complete series of very exorbitant pretensions may, in manner following, and in something like logical sequence, be deduced.

The right to live by labour is an empty name when the

means of so living are absent. For society, therefore, to
concede the right while withholding the means, is a mere
mockery of justice. The means of living by labour consist
of tools and materials for work; but often these cannot be
obtained, because, together with all other elements of
wealth, society has permitted them to be appropriated by
a portion of its members to the exclusion of the rest. In
thus sanctioning the institution of property, society sanctioned spoliation; it permitted that to be monopolised by
a few which had previously belonged to all in common.
All previously were equally free to live by labour. But
now the poor cannot sow or plant, or gather roots or
berries, or hunt or fish, or build themselves dwellings, or
make themselves clothes, without permission from earlier
occupants of the land or waters, or from earlier collectors
of their produce; and these are authorised by society to
refuse permission. It is thus the action of society which
disables the poor from living by labour, and society, being
therein guilty of injustice, is bound to repair its own
wrong—bound so to regulate the right of living by labour
as to make it a reality—nay, bound so to re-organise
itself as, that from the very essence of its reformed constitution, the certainty of being able to live by labour shall
result to all. But society entirely neglects this, its bounden
duty. Its maxim is to let alone, to leave things to take
their course, heedless that, according to that course, the
less need a man has of growing richer than he actually is,
the easier it is for him further to enrich himself; the poorer
he is, the more impossible to extricate himself from poverty,
inasmuch as in the former case he can better afford to
undersell his rivals, and in the latter can less afford to
refuse to work for whatever pittance may be offered. The
total amount of employment obtainable is unequal to the
demand; but society does nothing either to increase the
amount or to improve the distribution. Applicants for
employment are, therefore, compelled to bid against each
other, reducing the price of labour by their internecine

competition. Thus it happens that, having been placed on earth to live by labour, man is often, in spite of all he can do, in danger of dying by starvation in the midst of abundance which he may himself perhaps have contributed to create. He is eager to comply with all the conditions assigned for his existence. He has strength, skill, intelligence, and industry, and all these he offers in exchange for bread, but he offers them in vain. He can get no work, because those who have taken possession of the field of employment refuse to employ him. Why do they refuse? Not for any fault of his, for he is both able and willing to work. The fault, then, must be theirs, and society, which tolerates the fault, becomes responsible for its consequences. The destitute labourer, having a right to live by labour, and being unable so to live without being hired, is entitled to be hired, and is entitled, too, to the hire of which he is worthy. He is entitled to adequate subsistence for corresponding work, and he is entitled to it from the authority which alone can secure it to him—that is, from society, which, failing to furnish it, withholds from him his indefeasible right, and treats him with manifest and palpable injustice.

To the misery, the hatred, the mutual suspicion and fear—to the countless disorders hence arising—an end must be put. Their more immediate cause is unlimited competition. That, therefore, must be controlled and restricted, if not entirely abolished. Labourers must be freed from the necessity of bidding against each other for employment, and employers must be prevented from bidding against each other for custom. The latter must not be permitted to indulge their propensity to sell cheaply. They must not be let alone in the disposal of their wares. True, to interfere with them in that respect would be a manifest invasion of their freedom of action; but freedom, true freedom, the freedom of all, demands, as indispensable for its own preservation, the violation of the freedom of some. For should not all be free; and how can those be called free who are the slaves of hunger, of cold, of ignorance, of chance? Have not all the right to lead an easy, rational life—to improve their position, to exercise and develop all their faculties? But what avails the right without the power? What avails the right to be cured to the sick man whom no physician will attend? Freedom obviously implies the possession not merely of rights, but also of the means of exercising those rights; and since under a system of competition the poor are often debarred from the exercise of their rights, competition cannot be permitted to continue. Equity requires that steps be taken for its suppression.*

Such is the case of the poor against the rich, as drawn up by one of the ablest and most eloquent among those of their advocates who adopt their extreme views and endorse their extreme pretensions; and if some, starting from the same point, refuse to go the same lengths as M. Louis Blanc, and perhaps even denounce part of his doctrines as exaggerated and mischievous, this is really because they are less consistent in their opinions than he, not having so steadily followed out the necessary deductions from their own principles. Their narrower tenets are, however, completely comprehended within the limits of his more extensive system, and a sufficing answer to him will serve at least equally as an answer to them also. One thing in which they all agree is in demanding adequate occupation as the right of all who need it; and the demand is so seemingly moderate, and the satisfaction of it is so manifestly indispensable for the well-being of those on whose account it is made, that to question its validity cannot but be a somewhat distasteful operation. Nevertheless, and although these pages have little other object than that of determining how the labouring classes may most easily and effectually obtain fully as much as they ever dreamt of asking, the writer is constrained, even in the interest of

* See M. Louis Blanc's 'Organisation du Travail,' *passim*. It will be found that most of the expressions in the text, and all the stronger ones, are translated literally.

those classes, to protest against the theory set up in their behalf. No cause can be permanently maintained that is suffered to rest on fallacies ; and one pervading fallacy, beginning at the very first link, runs through the whole chain of reasoning of which the theory consists.

The right of the poor to live by labour, affirmed as un-hesitatingly as if it were a self-evident proposition beyond the possibility of dispute, is explained to mean not merely the right so to live if they can themselves find the means, but to have the means supplied by others if they cannot themselves obtain them, and to have them supplied, nomi-nally by society at large, but really by the richer portion of it, the rich alone being in a position to furnish what is required. But right on the one side necessarily implies cor-responding obligation on the other ; and how can society, or how can the rich, have incurred the obligation of main-taining in the world those whom they were in no degree instrumental in bringing into it ? Only, if at all, in one or other of two ways. Either mankind were placed in posses-sion of the earth which they inhabit on condition, expressed or implied, that the wants of all the earth's human inhabi-tants should be provided for from its produce; or part of those inhabitants have, by some communal act or institution of the whole body, been dispossessed of the means of pro-viding for themselves. But on the first of these hypotheses, in order that the supposed condition should be equitable, it would be necessary that the earth should be capable of producing enough for the wants of whatever number of inhabitants might obtain footing upon it; whereas it is demonstrable that population would infallibly everywhere speedily outrun subsistence, if the earth's produce were freely accessible to all who had need. Of the other supposition it is to be remarked, that the only institution that has ever been accused of producing the alleged effect is the insti-tution of property ; and very slight advocacy will suffice to absolve an institution from the charge of depriving people of that which, but for itself, could not have existed. Let it be admitted that the earth was bestowed by the Creator, not on any privileged class or classes, but on all mankind, and on all successive generations of men, so that no one generation can have more than a life interest in the soil or be entitled to alienate the birthright of succeeding generations. Let this be admitted, and the admission is surely large enough to satisfy the most uncompromising champion of the natural rights of man. Still it is certain that those rights, if fully exercised, must inevitably have proved themselves to be so far worse than worthless, as to have prevented any but a very minute fraction of the existing number of claimants from being born to claim them. The earth, if unappropriated, must also have remained untilled, and consequently comparatively unproductive. Anything like the world's actual population could not possibly have been in existence, nor, if it had been, would a whole year's growth of the earth's natural produce have sufficed for the subsistence of the earth's inhabitants during a single day. The utmost of which the poor have been dispossessed by the institution of property is their fair proportion of what the earth could have produced if it had remained unappropriated. Compensation for this is the utmost which is due to them from society, and the debt is obviously so infinitesimally small, that the crumbs which habitually fall from the tables of the rich are amply sufficient to pay it.

If these things be so, a strict debtor and creditor account between rich and poor would show no balance against the former. Society cannot properly be said to owe anything to the poor beyond what it is constantly and regularly paying. It is not bound in equity, whatever it may be in charity, to find food for the hungry because they are in need, nor to find occupation for the unemployed because they are out of work. By withholding aid, it is not guilty of the smallest injustice. For injustice implies violation of a right; and not only can there be no breach of right without disregard of a corresponding obligation, but that only can be a right the breach or denial of which constitutes a wrong. But wrong is committed only when some good which is due is withheld, or when some evil which is not due is inflicted. Applying this test we shall find that the poor, as such, have no unliquidated claim against the rich. The latter are doing them no wrong, are guilty of no injustice towards them in merely abstaining from paying a debt which, whether due to the poor or not, is, at any rate, not due to them from the rich. It was not the rich who placed the poor on earth, and it is not the rich who owe them the means of living here. How far the poor may be forgiven for complaining, as of a grievance, of having been placed here without adequate means of living, may possibly be a question for the theologian. But the political economist may fairly content himself with showing that the grievance is at any rate not one with which they can reproach any of their fellow-creatures, except their own parents. No other portion of society was a party to the transaction, and no other portion can justly be held responsible for its consequences.

These remarks may very possibly be misunderstood, and are pretty sure to be misrepresented. It may be prudent, therefore, to explain that nothing can be further from their purpose than to exculpate the existing social system, or to suggest an excuse for continued acquiescence in its enormities. No one can be readier than the present writer to exclaim, in the words of Mr. Taylor's 'Philip Van Artevelde,'—

> Where is there on God's earth that polity,
> Which it is not by consequence converse
> A treason against nature to uphold?

But to affirm that those evils of the existing social polity which constitute the peculiar grievance of the poor are not the result of human injustice, is perfectly consistent with the most vehement denunciation both of the evils themselves and of the heartless indifference that would perpetuate them. It is perfectly consistent even with the admission that the rich are bound to do what they can to alleviate those evils—with this proviso, however, that they are so bound, not by their duty to others, but by their duty to themselves. The obligation is imposed upon them not by injunctions of justice, but by the force of sympathy and the exhortations of humanity and charity. The sacrifices which it may thus become incumbent on the rich to make, the poor are not in consequence entitled to demand. If the sacrifices are withheld, the rich stand convicted indeed of brute selfishness, but they do not thereby lay themselves open to the additional charge of injustice. This distinction is not drawn for the sake of pedantic precision. It is one of immense practical importance. To all right reasoning it is essential that things should be called by their right names, and that nothing, however bad, should receive a worse name than it deserves. The more glaring a sin, the less reason is there for exaggerating it, and in the case before us the use of an erroneous epithet has been a fruitful source of further error. Unless the present constitution of society had been arbitrarily assumed to be unjust, it would never have been proposed to correct its injustice by resorting to means which would otherwise have been at once perceived to be themselves utterly unjustifiable. On no other account could it ever have been supposed that liberty demanded for its own vindication the violation of liberty, and that the freedom of competition ought to be fettered or abolished. For freedom of competition means no more than that every one should be at liberty to do his best for himself, leaving all others equally at liberty to do their best for themselves. Of all the natural rights of man, there is not one more incontestable than this, nor with which interference would be more manifestly unrighteous. Yet this it is proposed to set aside as incompatible with the rights of labour, as if those could possibly be rights which cannot be maintained except by unrighteous means.*

---

* Notwithstanding the keen and searching criticism which, as readers of the 'Fortnightly Review' are aware, these passages have

The defence of competition need not, however, be rested upon abstract considerations. Impartial examination of its effects will show that, though certainly not immaculate, it is infinitely more deserving of praise than censure. The most obvious objection to it is the harm it does to some of the competitors—to some of those who themselves engage in it. These it is very apt to render too eager in the pursuit of wealth, and proportionably unscrupulous in the choice of stratagems for acquiring it ; heedless also of the ruin likely to result from their being outstripped or anticipated in the chase. It is apt to make them careless of others and careful only for themselves, and even for themselves careful chiefly to accumulate that which they do not allow themselves leisure to enjoy. For that excessive strain on the faculties, however, to which almost every one is in these days subjected, competition is perhaps less to blame than the largeness of the scale on which business is carried on. A professional or commercial man is no longer permitted to say, ' thus far and no farther will I go in my avocation.' A physician who refused to see more than a certain number of patients, or a tailor who resolved to make only a certain number of coats, would soon find himself, the one without practice, and the other without custom, for people would not needlessly consent to take merely their chance of being served, and would prefer to go where they would be sure of being attended to. In no species of traffic can success any

had the distinguished honour of receiving at the hands of Mr. Mill, they are here reprinted just as they originally appeared, and without any attempt to answer Mr. Mill's objections. This is not because I have nothing, but because I have a great deal to say in reply, and because any lengthened investigation of the subject might perhaps be deemed out of place in an economic treatise. I hope shortly, however, to have an opportunity of going thoroughly into the matter in a separate essay. In the meantime I will only observe that the doctrine put forward in the text is not justly chargeable with being 'à priori' or ' intuitional.' However defective in other respects, it at least does not pretend to be self-evident, or ' claim to command assent by its own light.' Reasons have been offered as its basis, which, whether good or bad, are at any rate reasons.

longer be reckoned upon except on condition of as much
of the business which is offered being accepted as can in
any way be got through.

Moreover, the same magnitude of modern commercial
transactions gives to large capitals an immense advantage
in competing with small ones, by reason of the many economising contrivances which cannot be adopted except upon
a large scale, and competition thus exhibits a daily increasing and very unedifying tendency to give to those who
have much at the expense of those who have little. These
are great and undeniable evils, but they are evils which
affect only the comparatively small and comparatively
wealthy class of employers, and which, except in so far as
they may promote the practice of adulteration or other
tricks of trade, leave untouched the great mass of the community, to whom meanwhile competition does an amount
of good compared with which its ill effects are but as dust
in the balance. Competition may be truly styled the nurse,
if not the parent, of all the useful arts, and the suggestor of
almost every improvement that has taken place in them.
Without it there could have been no civilisation. Wild
through the woods man would still be running, a noble but
unrobed savage, and we, who are now peaceably philoso-
phising over the nature and extent of his social privileges,
would have met, if we had met at all, only to fight like
hungry dogs for the possession of some wild animal's car-
cass. And even so we should have been still competing,
albeit in hatefullest fashion, for in some shape or other
competition will always continue to exist. If extinguished
in one shape it is sure to reappear in another, and that
other not at all likely to be the better for having been artificially moulded. Left to itself, however, and suffered to
assume its natural form, competition will not fail to exercise
an influence well suited to existing circumstances, whatever
those circumstances may be. Hitherto it has proved the
chief mainspring of every kind of progress. Of all incen-
tives to exertion, those which it supplies are by far the most

powerful, the only ones indeed sufficiently strong for the propulsion of human affairs. Its motives truly partake largely of selfishness, but if they did not, they would be unsuited to the present condition of human nature. The time may come when those motives will be exchanged for others of a higher and nobler character, and those enthusiasts, of whom the present writer confesses himself to be one, who can discern no necessary limit to human perfectibility, may fondly cherish a confident hope that that time will at length come. But the besetting sin of enthusiasts, and notably of enthusiastic philanthropists, is a proneness to anticipate events, a desire to legislate as if mankind were already what it is barely conceivable that they may one day become, and to force upon them institutions for which they can only be fitted by long ages of training, instead of beginning by endeavouring to educate them into fitness for the institutions. Centuries hence, if many happy combinations of circumstances concur to bring about so blessed a result, human beings may be found generally willing to labour for the common good as zealously as for their own, and content to work each in proportion to his ability, yet to receive not more than in proportion to his wants, keeping those wants meanwhile under due restraint. Many individuals have lived, and many are now living, who have attained to this pitch of moral elevation, and there is no monstrous extravagance in concluding that all men may one day become what some are already. The finest specimens of human excellence are very far indeed from being such as to defy imitation. If such a day ever comes, competition will not cease, but will only change its object and abate its excess of energy. Under the generous guise of emulation it will continue to exist, but will prompt men to vie with each other only in doing each other good. Even to dream of such a time is pleasant, and may help besides to hasten its arrival, provided we do not mistake our visions for realities; but it would be a fatal sort of sleep-walking to proceed to act as if the dream were already fulfilled, and to rush into aggression against the competition of self-interest before the competition of self-devotion is prepared to take its place.

It would be strange indeed if even the former species of competition, possessing the recommendations assigned to it, were yet opposed to the interests of labour.   The worst harm it does is done, as has been said, almost exclusively to the comparatively rich.   If its influence on the poor be not exclusively beneficial, at any rate the benefits which it confers upon them are lasting and widely spread, while the hardships it inflicts are transitory and partial.   Those who think otherwise maintain that its inevitable consequence is to reduce the remuneration of labour to a minimum. ' Who so blind,' they exclaim, ' as not to see that, under its domination, the continuous fall of wages, far from being exceptional, is necessarily universal.' *   In so speaking they argue as if the rate of wages depended on the employer's will.   They seem to suppose that a manufacturer, for example, who in order to undersell his rivals, seeks to reduce his workmen's wages, has merely to insist on their being reduced, and that they must fall accordingly.   They further assume that the mechanical or administrative improvements, or other expedients for economising labour which are introduced in rapid succession when competition is keen, must needs displace much of the labour previously employed, which labour, in order to obtain re-employment, is forced to bid against the labour that had remained employed.   And in these assumptions there must be admitted to be some truth, although mixed up with very much more exaggeration, in endeavouring to separate the one of which from the other, it behoves us to be specially on our guard against a very prevalent cant, and carefully to eschew the use of two plausible fallacies very commonly adduced on one side of the question.   We must not, in the first place, flatter ourselves that we are refuting our opponents by

* Louis Blanc, *ut supra*, chap. 2.

simply pointing to supply and demand as the exclusive regulators of wages in accordance with fixed immutable laws which operate quite independently of the will of either employers or employed. As was shown in the last chapter, supply and demand have no such character. What really does, within certain impassable limits, really regulate wages, is commonly, when the employed are content to remain passive, the combination of the employers ; and when these have (as they in practice do far more and far oftener than they get credit for) fixed upon a higher rate than they need have done, they can of course lower it if they please. In such circumstances the *sic volo* of every individual master is to a certain extent equivalent to *sic jubeo.* If he wishes to reduce his servants' wages, he has merely to say the word, and—always supposing they do not counter-combine—they have no choice but to submit. Moreover, if then the master in question avail himself of his saving in wages to undersell his commercial rivals, the latter in self-defence must either lower wages in imitation of him, or contract or perhaps abandon their business. If they take the one course, the fall of wages becomes general; if the other, many, perhaps all, of their workmen are thrown out of employment, which they can only regain by taking service at the reduced wages offered by the underselling employer. Now, among keenly competing employers there are never wanting some who are willing to reduce wages as much as possible. So far as tendency is concerned, therefore, there is no denying that competition has, as asserted, a tendency to minimise wages.

In the second place, we must not allow ourselves to be deluded by the pleasing notion that improved machinery, instead of throwing labour out of employment, creates an increased demand for it as a consequence of the increased cheapness of the commodity which the machinery assists in producing. Such might be the effect of machinery applied to agriculture, if it caused land to produce a sufficiently augmented quantity of the raw material of industry to afford occupation to as much labour in one department as the machinery set free in another.   If, for example, the use of a steam-plough which had permitted the services of one ploughman to be dispensed with, should make a cotton-field produce so much more than before as to furnish occupation for one additional weaver, the direct gain and loss of labour in the transaction would, in the long run, be equally balanced, while the indirect results would be of unalloyed advantage to all concerned.   But, except in such case as this, it is at best but a pious fraud to attempt to blink the fact that the immediate effect of the introduction of labour-saving machinery must be to displace more or less of labour.*   Here, again, those who contend that competition is calculated, directly and indirectly, to minimise wages, appear to be in the right.   It clearly has the tendency they ascribe to it.   Their mistake consists in confounding tendencies with consequences.   The stock answers to their arguments will not suffice, but complete answers may be obtained by reference, first, to the countervailing influence of trades' unionism, and, secondly, to the continually and rapidly increasing amount of employment consequent on the similarly continuous accumulation of capital which commercial competition, with all its various agencies, promotes.   On both these topics we shall have to speak at some length hereafter, but no one who has eyes to see or ears to hear can in these days doubt that trades' unionism does impose a very powerful check on the arbitrariness of employers, and that the adoption of expedients for more and more economising labour does incalculably augment eventually the capital which creates a demand for labour.   No one who looks fairly into the subject can fail to see how amply sufficient the two causes combined are to prevent competition from having that effect upon wages to produce which it does undeniably tend.   True, the operation of the second of the causes

* This point will be found discussed in detail farther on, in the chapter headed 'Good and Evil of Trades' Unionism.'

alluded to may be sensibly checked by the propensity of population to indefinite multiplication. However fast capital and employment may increase, it is quite possible for the number of persons in need of employment to increase still faster. True this, most true, and pity 'tis 'tis true; for it is a truth which lies at the root of almost every social evil. To twist it into an argument against the competition of employers is, however, a little too much. Employers, like all other people, have sins enough of their own to answer for without being made responsible for the superfecundity of the employed. It is a little too much to denounce competition not only for such evil as it does, but also for the good which it leaves undone. ' Is competition,' it has been triumphantly demanded, ' a means of ensuring employment to the poor? Does it contain within itself any means of preventing that homicidal disproportion between work and workmen which dooms so many of the latter to destitution?'* Assuredly not. But is there any principle of action whatever, any motive power, institution, or device of any sort or kind, which is not equally chargeable with the same imperfection? Is remunerative occupation for all who need it ensured by religion, or by education, or by liberty, civil or political? More or less of all and each of these the world has in all ages enjoyed, but was there ever a period in its history without multitudes of hopelessly unemployed poor? Yet religion, and education, and liberty, are not denounced and threatened with penal extinction on account of their deficiency in so vital a particular. Their existence is not the less tolerated for the sake of their good deeds, and similar toleration ought in fairness to be extended to competition, notwithstanding its precisely similar shortcoming. Besides, though competition can, no more than anything else, pretend to secure employment, and still less, if possible, any definite rate of wages to the poor, it does palpably increase the value of whatever

* Louis Blanc, *ut supra.*

wages are actually earned. For by stimulating production it renders commodities more abundant and cheap than they would otherwise be, thereby enabling the labourer, in common with every other consumer, to buy more with the same money, and it enables him, too, to buy many commodities which, but for it, could not have been had at any price. Deplorable as many a poor man's condition is, how infinitely worse would it be if he were shut off from the advantages resulting from modern improvements in all industrial processes! Would not the very worst off be far worse off than he is if those improvements were given up, or if commerce were brought back within limits which would render them inadmissible—if all costly and complicated machines were laid aside, and if the large assemblages of operatives indispensable for the due division of labour were prohibited, and no manufactures permitted but what could be carried on within the walls of a cottage? So put the question answers itself, and the reader will no doubt readily dispense with any allusion to the invariable intermixture of evil with all sublunary good, and to the consequent need in all human affairs of compromises between the two principles. Unless we believe that the steam-engine, the spinning jenny, the power-loom, and the printing-machine do more harm than good to the working man—unless we judge that it would, on the whole, be for him a change for the better to lead the life of a savage, and to be lodged, boarded, clothed, and taught accordingly—we must not stigmatise as detrimental to him the industrial improvements to which he owes such of the blessings of civilisation as he enjoys, nor consequently condemn the competition without which those improvements would never have been made.* What common sense would dictate with respect

* If rivalry of employers were the chief cause of pauperism, the latter could scarcely have been so rife during the middle ages, when hundreds of monastic soup kitchens availed as little for its relief as the whipping-post, the branding-iron, and the gallows did for its suppression. In those days there was very little of commercial speculation

to an agency to which mankind is under such incalculable obligations, is that it should continue to be utilised to the utmost as long as it retains any beneficent capacity, but that anxious search should in the meantime be made for whatever may be wanting to correct its defects and supplement its deficiencies.

While thus engaged in endeavouring to strike a balance between the good and evil of commercial competition, I have been led into a digression, not, I trust, unprofitable, but not perhaps absolutely necessary for my immediate object. To show how infinitely the advantages outweigh the disadvantages of perfect freedom of competition was not, perhaps, indispensable in order to demonstrate that to extinguish or to shackle competition is not one of the rights of labour. For this it might have sufficed to plead that, inasmuch as the property of the rich belongs to them and not to the poor—to those who have it, not to those who have it not—the latter can have no possible right to interfere with the disposal of it, not even so far as to demand that it shall be applied in such a manner as to

or emulation. Almost all traders were members of monopolist guilds, and seem to have come to a mutual understanding that their wisest course was not to over-exert themselves by striving with each other, but to content themselves with the very liberal price which a long-suffering public were content to pay for small work. The last relics of a similar order of things have scarcely yet entirely past away. According to Mr. Charles Knight's description of the Windsor of his boyhood, both its commercial torpor and its pauperism must, in the early years of the present century, have been quite mediæval. 'It is not,' he says, 'within my recollection that anybody worked hard. Absence of extreme competition gave the old settlers a vested interest in their occupations. Some were not behind the counter till eleven. Some closed their hatch when they went to their noonday meal, and no importunities could induce them to open it. The baker, after drawing his afternoon batch, put on his flaxen wig, and went to spend the evening in his accustomed chair at the ale-house. This was a general custom.' But simultaneously there was 'a vast deal of wretchedness around, indiscriminate almsgiving to vagrants, lavish out-door relief, destitution everywhere.'—Knight's 'Passages of a Working Life,' vol. i. Compare pp. 49 and 74.

furnish them with the employment without which they cannot live. If there be any force in the remarks made above on this head, if they prove anything whatever, they prove nothing less than this—that the special claims set up on behalf of the poor, which we have been examining, have no foundation in equity; that society is guilty of no injustice in neglecting to provide employment and subsistence for those whose services it does not need; that, in short, the right of the poor to live by labour, in the sense in which the phrase is commonly used, and in the only sense in which it has any practical meaning—in the sense, that is, of a right against the rich—is an utterly baseless pretension. A shocking paradox this, perhaps; but if a genuine paradox, then not more shocking than true; and for the radical cure of social, as of all other disease, the first essential is to lay bare the whole truth concerning it. But, it may well be asked, if of labour's claims the one which is most loudly and most universally proclaimed, and indeed almost universally taken for granted, be thus flatly denied, what claim is there that will be conceded? What is there that the poor, as such, or that labourers, as such, are warranted in demanding as their due? If labour be not entitled to the employment without which it cannot subsist, what title can it possibly have to anything?

In proceeding to reply to these questions, I must be permitted to continue to use great plainness of speech. Verily, so far as I can discover, labour has no rights special or peculiar to itself. The rights of labour, as I apprehend them, are all such, and none other than such, as belong equally to every other interest with which society is concerned. In common with and to precisely the same extent as every other interest, labour is entitled to inviolability of person and property, and to the punctual fulfilment of contracts entered into with it, and to nothing else whatever. These three particulars appear to me to make up the sum total of what labour can rightfully exact from society. To uphold and enforce these rights, to secure person, property, and the performance of contracts, though by no means the sole purposes for which society exists, appear to me to be the sole duties absolutely incumbent on it—the sole functions which it, or the government which represents it, cannot omit without wronging its individual members by withholding from them what is their due. The relative duties of society at large, and of its individual members, are necessarily reciprocal. What the individuals are bound to do for each other, is precisely so much as they have mutually agreed to do. But individuals do not commonly, when aggregating themselves into society, pledge themselves, either formally or tacitly, to do all they can for each other's general well-being ; and society cannot, therefore, be justly held responsible for the general well-being of individuals. Individuals are not by mutual agreement entitled to demand from society either the means of subsistence, or even such educational training as may fit them to earn subsistence; and society is not, therefore, bound either to feed or to educate its individual members, however desirable it may for its own sake be that it should do at least the latter. But on the other hand, although individuals are not entitled to be fed, clothed, or taught at the public expense, they are entitled to the absolute possession and disposal of whatever belongs exclusively to themselves —of their own persons to wit, and of their honestly-acquired property, and also to the fulfilment of engagements entered into with them : and as they are required to assist in securing thus much to the rest of society, so are they equitably entitled to the like assistance from the rest of society in securing thus much to themselves. Thus the rights of labour, or in simpler phrase, of labourers, are essentially the same, and neither greater nor less than those of every other class of the community, and may be described in the same general terms. Nevertheless, those terms, when applied to labour, although still susceptible of all their more extensive interpretation, may also, without impropriety, be used in a special and more restricted sense,

so as to indicate particularly the following things—viz.,
Exemption of the labourer from compulsory work ; Freedom to engage in any harmless pursuit for which he may
possess the requisite means and materials ; Appropriation
to the labourer of the entire proceeds of his own unaided
industry ; Similar appropriation, when the labourer has
been assisted in his work, of whatever may remain of the
produce of his labour after deduction of the portion which
he may have agreed to pay for the assistance rendered to
him ; and Punctuality of payment to a hired labourer of
his stipulated hire. Of these five heads, under one or
other of which every tenable pretension of labour may, as
it seems to me, be ranged, the first four may be passed by
with comparatively little comment. It has indeed been
said that if a man will not work, neither shall he eat ; and
it may thence with perfect justice be inferred that he who
can work, and will not work, may be made to work, if
otherwise he would become chargeable to other people ;
but it is not the less demonstrable that if the consequences
of his idleness would affect only himself, and if he be
willing to take those consequences on himself—if, in short,
he be content to starve rather than work—he cannot, without violation of natural liberty, be prevented from indulging
his preference of indolence to food. No doubt the case
will be altogether altered if he have a wife or children or
other dependents whom it is his duty to maintain, for he
will then have placed himself in a different category, and
by his own act have forfeited part of his original freedom
of inaction. He will then have contracted obligations to
others which society is bound by its duty to those others
to compel him to fulfil ; and society, therefore, not only
may, but must, compel him to work, to save his dependents
from want.

Again, there was a time when it was generally considered
that none could rightfully engage in certain trades without
first serving an apprenticeship to them, but that, so far as
our own country is concerned, was in the palmy days of

monopoly, and none of us any longer deny the abstract right of all to engage in any businesses whatever, with the exception of those professions the practice of which, whether wisely or unwisely, yet, at least by common consent, and with a view to the common good, has been reserved for those who have undergone a certain amount of special preparatory training.

Further, in support of the labourer's claim to the whole produce of his unassisted labour, it may suffice to remark that the only counter-claim which can by possibility be opposed to it, is one which we shall hereafter have occasion to examine, and which we shall then discover to be too trivial for more than passing notice. And if this be admitted, it will follow that of assisted labour also, the whole produce, less the stipulated price of the assistance rendered, must similarly belong to the labourer.

Of the five several propositions, then, involved in our arrangement of the rights of labour, the first four may, with the qualifications just stated, be probably taken for granted. At first sight, the fifth also might appear to be even more completely beyond cavil, but on closer inspection, so far from commanding universal assent, it will be found to contain within it the subject-matter of almost every controversy to which the claims of labour have ever given rise. The condition of the independent labourer, who possesses or can borrow the means of setting himself to work, affords comparatively little room for discussion. There can be little dispute as to the limitations of his right to work or not to work as he pleases, or to choose his own occupation, or to appropriate either the whole produce of his industry, or the whole produce less what he may have agreed to pay for aid afforded to him in his business. It is around the hired labourer, around him who is dependent on an employer for employment that the real contest rages; and the real question at issue in the hot debate is, how is the amount of hire due to a labourer to be determined ? Not that the simple statement given above of the labourer's right to his stipulated hire is one that can be gainsayed, but to represent this, as I am doing, as the sole right appertaining in any peculiar sense to the hired labourer, is in effect to assert that the wages for which a labourer voluntarily undertakes to work, however low they may be, however inadequate to his requirements, are yet all that he is in justice entitled to receive or that his employer is bound in justice to pay. Now the whole, or nearly the whole, of what is commonly understood by the 'labour question' proceeds upon an assumption the very reverse of this. It arises out of a belief, latent perhaps for the most part, but not therefore the less widely spread, that a labourer's dues, instead of being simply coincident with his earnings, bear a certain undefined relation both to his wants and to the value of his services. This opinion is so universally prevalent that among recent writers on social subjects I cannot point to one who is not more or less imbued with it. One main object of them all appears to be to discover some principle which may help to define the as yet undefined relation, and to ascertain how a remuneration conformable to that relation may be best secured to the labourer. In undertaking then to prove that an opinion so authoritatively upheld is nevertheless unfounded—that the principle sought for does not and cannot exist—that the dues of labour have nothing to do with either its needs or its value, and that the only true criterion of wages is the agreement between the employer and the employed—in undertaking to prove all this, I know well to what I am exposing myself. I know what tremendous opposition I am challenging, and what virtuous indignation I shall provoke—that anything like sympathy with my sentiments is out of the question, and that no more toleration for them must be expected than success in defending them may extort. Of course when Ishmael's hand is against every man's, Ishmael must be prepared to have every man's hand against his.

Not asking, then, nor hoping for quarter, I shall not

hesitate in self-defence to speak my mind freely, and to affirm that in the instance before us we have a remarkable example of an originally self-evident proposition thoroughly mystified by the introduction into it of irrelevant considerations. It is a case in which the misapplication of notions of justice has operated like sunlight on the mists of the Brocken, concealing or distorting the shapes of things and diverting attention from solid realities to unsubstantial illusions. Justice is very gratuitously supposed to require that a labourer's remuneration should correspond with his wants and his merits. Now if this be stated in general terms, I will not venture to contradict it. I will not take upon myself to say that manna from heaven ought not to fall around the labourer in sufficient abundance for his subsistence and reward. But the proposition with which we are here concerned is not really of such extensive reach ; its actual meaning lies within much narrower compass. What we are called upon to consider is, not how much the labourer is entitled to receive from every source, but how much is due to him from his employer. Now it is self-evident that from his employer he cannot be entitled to receive more than his employer is bound to give. But, except under the terms of some mutual agreement, the employer is not bound to give anything. Before joining in the agreement he was under no obligation to furnish the labourer with occupation. Either he might not have required his or any one else's services, or he might have preferred to employ some one else. But if he was not bound to furnish employment at all, *à fortiori* he was not bound to furnish it on any particular terms. If, therefore, he did consent to furnish it, he had a right to dictate his own terms ; and whatever else those terms might be, however harsh, illiberal, exorbitant, or what you will, they could not, at any rate or by any possibility, be unjust. For they could only be unjust in so far as they deviated from some particular terms which justice might have exacted. But, as we have seen, there were no such terms, and it is

manifestly absurd to condemn a thing merely because its
limits do not coincide with those of an abstraction incapable of being realised or defined, incapable, that is to say,
of having any limits at all.

Not improbably, however, before I am suffered to get
thus far, a demurrer may be entered. Not improbably it
may be urged that a person having the means of giving
employment is *not* at liberty to withhold it, and that his
duty does require him to furnish it to the necessitous. His
duty, then, to whom? To God, or to man? to society at
large, or to particular individuals? If the answer be 'to
God,' the rejoinder need only be that duty to God does
not necessarily involve duty to man—that for reasons explained in a former part of this chapter, duty to God can
in this place mean merely gratitude to God, and that in-
gratitude to God, though it may justly provoke divine
displeasure, does not necessarily involve a human grievance.
To do this latter, the neglect of duty constituting the in-
gratitude must be neglect of a duty which man is entitled
to exact ; but how can society or individuals have acquired
the right to insist that whoever has the means of employing
the necessitous shall employ them accordingly? By duty
to any person is simply meant the obligation to do or to
abstain from doing what in the one case cannot be left
undone, or in the other case cannot be done, without breach
of that person's rights ; and so far as active duties are
concerned, the obligation can have been incurred only in
one or two, or at most of three, modes. Either there
must be a special agreement, expressed or implied—a case
requiring no illustration—or there must have been commission of some act imposing responsibility on the actor
or actors, as when parents bringing children into the world
become bound to support them, or when a homicide
causing the death of an innocent person may become bound
to provide for the dependents of the deceased ; or there
must have been receipt of some unearned or unpurchased
benefit, as when a man who is saved from drowning at

another's imminent risk, might perhaps be bound to risk his life in turn for his preserver's rescue. Only in one or other of these ways can duty originate. For duty (*debitum, dovere, devoir*) signifies something due, a debt, indebtedness, and a debt cannot have been incurred for nothing, and without some antecedent step on the part either of debtor or creditor. Either payment must have been promised, whether gratuitously or in return for some real or supposed equivalent ; or it must be necessary to satisfy some claim created by the debtor's conduct ; or it must be claimable in return for some benefit voluntarily conferred by the creditor. But no one of these conditions is present in the case under consideration. Men do not, when becoming members of society, undertake to do more for society than society undertakes to do for them. They engage to assist in the general protection of life and property, and in the general enforcement of contracts, on the understanding that their lives and properties will be similarly protected, and that contracts to which they are parties will be similarly enforced ; but society does not undertake to provide them with employment or subsistence, nor are they bound to provide employment or subsistence for their associates indiscriminately. Neither, unless they have by some proceeding of their own caused or aggravated the distress of certain of their associates, are they, simply in their character of members of society, bound to relieve that distress, except in so far as the laws or customs of their community may enjoin. Nor, finally, can the receipt of benefits from particular individuals affect their obligations, except in reference to those same individuals. It follows, then, that employment cannot be demanded by the necessitous as a right on any terms whatever, and if not on any terms, then of course not on any particular terms ; that to refuse it to them altogether, however cruel the refusal may be, and however inconsistent with common humanity, would yet be doing them no wrong, inasmuch as it would be withholding from them nothing to which they had a right ; that when employment is supplied, no terms to which the employed knowingly agree can possibly, to whatever other epithets they may be liable, deserve to be stigmatised as unjust; that, in short, a hired labourer has absolutely no rights in respect of his employment, and notably in respect of the amount of his hire, except those vested in him by the agreement or contract under which he is employed; and that justice has absolutely nothing further to do in the matter than to see that the terms of the agreement, whatever they may be, are punctually fulfilled.

In order further to test the correctness of these conclusions, let us approach the subject from a different quarter. Hitherto we have regarded the labourer as one offering himself for employment to which he has no inherent right, and consequently as destitute of all pretext for complaining of any conditions on which employment may be conceded to him. But he may also be regarded as one who, having labour of his own to dispose of, offers it for sale—offers to exchange it for an equivalent. Now, whenever a sale, either of labour or of any other commodity, takes place, the price which the seller can equitably take is just as much as he can, without using force or fraud, persuade a customer to give for it. This price, whatever it may be, is the true commercial equivalent of what he sells—its value in exchange—price and value in exchange being, in fact, universally convertible terms. Now, what is it that determines price? Assuredly neither inherent utility nor cost of production has the smallest direct effect upon it. Among material things, by far the most useful of all is the air we breathe, and without which we cannot live five minutes; yet it is only in situations more or less analogous to that of the Black Hole at Calcutta that air has the smallest exchangeable value. Nowhere else will any one pay anything for that which is provided in unlimited abundance without his asking. Only second in utility is the bread we eat, and for which, or for some sufficient substitute for which, any one having the wherewithal would, rather than not obtain it, consent to pay its weight in silver. Fortunately, however, there are generally plenty of bakers ready to sell it for much less than its weight in copper, so that pence, not pounds, are commonly paid for the quartern loaf. Yet if this same bread, which may have cost only a few pence to produce, were introduced into a besieged city as hard pressed as Samaria once was by Benhadad the Syrian, it might not impossibly command a higher price than would then and there be given for the costliest article of jewellery or goldsmith's ware that sparkles unsunned in the Royal Treasure House at Dresden, and on which some Dinglinger or Peter Vischer may have expended almost a lifetime of labour. So little direct bearing has either utility or cost on price. Neither one nor the other can influence it in the least, except indirectly, and by increasing or diminishing supply or demand, and thereby influencing that competition between dealers, which I have elsewhere endeavoured to show to be the real arbiter of price. In the absence of monopoly the price of a tangible commodity depends solely and exclusively on the competition of the sellers. True, unless the commodity were of use to satisfy some human desire, it would not have been produced. True, also, that unless its price be sufficient to cover the cost of production it will not continue to be produced; but having once been produced and brought to market, at whatever cost, neither its cost nor its utility, in comparison with those of other products, will be in the smallest degree considered. The price fixed upon it by the dealers will be simply the highest at which they believe that they will be able to sell as much of it as they have to sell. The price so fixed may be immensely above or immensely below the cost of production, and it may be equally disproportionate to the prices of other articles of equal or greater utility or cost; still, when neither compulsion nor deceit is used, prices cannot be more or less equitable in any one case than in any other. Provided only that plain dealing be observed and freedom of action permitted, all prices must be equally fair; there can be no such thing as an unfair or unjust price, or one by which either buyer or seller can be wronged. For as the seller is under no obligation to sell at any price whatever, no price demanded by him, however exorbitant, can be such as to warrant the buyer in showing more resentment than may consist in refusing to buy. Similarly, as buyers are under no obligation to buy, the seller never can have any right to complain of their refusing to buy except on such terms as they may choose. Surely every dealer in a commodity is perfectly justified in taking in exchange for it its full value in exchange. Surely no customer can be bound to give in exchange for a commodity more than its full value in exchange. Surely these are among the most palpable of truisms. But if so, no price, however exorbitant ('price' being merely another name for 'value in exchange'), can merely, by reason of its exorbitance, be unjust. Neither, however low, can it be so merely on account of its inadequacy as remuneration for the toil, trouble, and expense incurred by the seller, nor on account of its incommensurateness with the utility of the article offered for sale.

What, as much as anything, has served to complicate and obscure the ethics of price is the general belief in the existence of a certain entity denominated 'natural price,' whose very name seems to imply an engaging unsophisticated simplicity, every deviation from which on the part of actual price, would seem to be a corresponding divergence at once from nature and from natural justice. According to Adam Smith, who originally introduced the expression, by the natural price of a commodity is to be understood a price just equivalent to the quantity of labour required to produce the commodity, and consequently just sufficient to ensure its continued production. But it stands to reason that there cannot possibly be any such price. The quantity of labour required for a certain amount of production is not fixed but variable. It varies with the skill of the labourer —itself a thing continually varying even in the same individual—with the efficacy of the tools he works with, and with the time or place at which he works. To select one example from a thousand, the quantity of corn resulting from equal quantities of labour will differ exceedingly, according as the labour is exercised by an East Lothian or a Connaught farmer, according as a steam plough or a plough of Virgilian type is used, according as the seed is sown on Salisbury Plain or the Carse of Gowrie, and according as the seasons in which the grain is grown and garnered are wet or dry. But even suppose that skill, tools, soil, climate, and all other conditions were everywhere and always the same, and that labour consequently was always and everywhere equally productive, would that be a reason why a man should pay for a thing, about the acquisition of which he was comparatively indifferent, the equivalent of the labour requisite to produce a thing, not perhaps more difficult of production, but the possession of which was indispensable to him ? or why, if having of a commodity for which there were a dozen eager applicants, not more than enough to satisfy the wants of one, he should be bound to part with it for cost price, instead of taking whatever price might result from the competition of all his customers ? True, if he took the latter course, he might be said to be taking advantage of other people's necessities, to be profiting by their inability to supply their wants without his aid ; and such a proceeding is no doubt the reverse of generous, and one not to be commended on any score save that of prudence. But it is also a proceeding which is adopted, whenever an opportunity offers, by every one who engages in any species of trade, by every one who buys cheap and sells dear, and by every one who buys at a price less than the expense incurred by the seller. Taking advantage of other people's necessities is indeed the very essence of commercial enterprise, and is and always has been practised by all traders great and small—by the patriarch Joseph, when, having bought up for Pharaoh all the corn in Egypt, he afterwards resold it, getting the fee-simple of the whole

land of Egypt in exchange—and by merchant princes like
the Barings, when, foreseeing a dearth of silk or tallow, they
send orders betimes to all corners of the earth to have it
bought up for them, and do thereby a magnificent stroke of
business.   Nor is it more unequivocally practised by such
gigantic speculators than it is by thrifty housewives—when,
hearing that their mercer is selling off at a 'tremendous
sacrifice,' they hasten to see whether the tradesman's loss
may not prove their gain in the shape of half-price dresses
—or than by the poor widow who late on a Saturday night
higgles with a costermonger for his last lot of sprats or
onions, which she finally obtains for next to nothing because he cannot afford to have them left upon his hands.
Of course this sort of thing could not happen unless selfishness were one of the mainsprings of human conduct.   Certainly it could not occur if all men loved each other as
brethren, and lived together accordingly.   In such a state
of society the parties to an act of exchange might probably
be willing to divide its advantages as equally as possible
between them.   Each might be content to accept what in
the other's position he would have been ready to give.   In
such a state of society, a person who in a season of dearth
should have a full granary, would scorn to enrich himself
by issuing corn at famine prices; he would rather calculate
how far his stock would go towards meeting the wants of
his neighbours, and then distribute it amongst them proportionately, charging no more for each man's share than
he had been accustomed to do in ordinary years.   And on
the other hand, if an unusually abundant harvest should
lower the relative value of what remained to the corn-dealer
from his previously acquired stock, his customers would in
turn be equally considerate.   They could not indeed, without perversely foregoing all participation in the extraordinary bounty of Providence, continue to purchase their corn
at the old rates ; but though they would no doubt buy much
larger quantities and at much lower rates than before,
every one would readily consent to pay for the whole of his

augmented purchase the same sum as he had previously
been accustomed to give for the smaller quantity, and in
this way the dealer's losses would be reduced to a minimum
A blessed state would that be in which men should so deal
with each other, and that to such a state or a better, mankind may, by long process of development, one day come,
I am myself sanguine (or silly) enough to deem not absolutely impossible. God hasten the advent! But how
in the mean time are the best-intentioned men to comport
themselves? Desirable as it may be for the common weal
that this reign of universal fraternity, with or without coextensive equality, should be established on earth, mankind
are under no apparent obligation to inaugurate that beneficial régime, and individuals under, if possible, still less to
anticipate its inauguration. What though my Lord cannot
as yet bring himself to invite Jeames to take his seat at
table, and to propose that each should take it in turn to
wait; or what though you and I do not greatly trouble
ourselves to enquire how our butcher, baker, and clothier
manage to exist on the profits of their respective trades,
and content ourselves with ascertaining that we should not,
by changing our tradesmen, get better or cheaper food or
clothes, is there any dereliction of duty on his Lordship's
part or on ours? or would there be any on the part of
Jeames or the butcher, if the one should threaten to leave
his master's service unless his wages were made double
those of the inferior clergy, or if the other should make, as
in fact he has done, the cattle plague a pretext for charging
half as much again for his meat as the prices he is paying
for his beasts would allow him to sell it for? In all these
cases every party concerned is trying to drive a hard
bargain at his neighbour's expense, is taking advantage of
his neighbour's position; but, however unamiable or worse
his conduct may be, you cannot deny that he has a perfect
right to adopt it, since in so doing he is simply doing as he
will with his own, he is simply refusing to .buy or sell, to
part, as the case may be, with his goods or his' money,

except on such terms as suit him. Surely if there be one right more incontestable and more indefeasible than another, it is this; and if this right be conceded at all, it must be conceded in all its integrity, in all circumstances, and despite of all its consequences. Unless it be utterly devoid of validity, it will suffice for the justification of the most griping monopolist and the most niggardly chafferer. If it will warrant a baker's charging one halfpenny a loaf more than he could afford to sell for, it would equally warrant his charging fifty pence or fifty shillings a loaf, should he so think fit. If it permits you without reproach to cheapen some articles of the stock of an embarrassed shopkeeper, it will serve equally to excuse a pawnbroker for confiscating the table or chairs which their distressed owner has been obliged to pledge for the tithe of their value, and has been unable to redeem. The comparative morality of transactions is not affected by the scale on which they take place. In those referred to, each one of the actors is doing the very self-same thing ; he is simply refusing to buy or sell on terms which do not satisfy him, and is therein exercising a privilege which either does not belong to him at all, or belongs to him unrestrictedly and unconditionally. For it would be a simple self-contradiction to talk of a man's having a right to settle for himself on what terms he will consent to deal, and in the same breath to say that any terms on which he may settle can possibly be unrighteous.

The application of these principles to labour is obvious and easy, and the reader has doubtless already perceived that when so applied they are calculated to operate much more for than against the interests of labour. A labourer offering his services for hire is simply offering labour for sale. No one is bound to accept the offer. No one is under any obligation to buy, nor *à fortiori* to buy at any particular price. There is therefore no particular price to which the labourer has a right, or by not obtaining which he can be wronged. No price can be proposed

either to him or by him which can be one whit more fair
or just than any other price. Any price is just which he
agrees to take and another to give, and this, and not one
tittle more than this, constitutes his due. What will be the
amount of the price so agreed upon depends not at all,
at least not at all directly, upon labour's cost of production.
To that cost it bears no uniform or definite proportion.
The price of labour in general cannot, indeed, long continue below what will enable labourers to nourish and
bring up children, but it need not at all exceed, or it may
very greatly exceed, what would suffice for that purpose.
Neither is there any definite proportion between the price
and the intrinsic worth of labour. The price agreed upon
may be the product of a quantity of labour perhaps very
much greater, perhaps very much smaller, than the labour
for which it is exchanged. The price in any particular
instance, at any particular time and place, will be greater
or less, according as it is the seller or the buyer who is best
in a position to take advantage of the other's necessities.
Sometimes it is the buyer or employer who, although
greatly in need of labour, yet, needing it less than the
labourer needs the employment, can better afford to wait,
and can thereby artificially (or artfully, if you prefer it)
diminish, or, more properly speaking, conceal demand.
Sometimes it is the labourer who can best afford to wait,
and who, in like manner, has artifices at his command by
which he can lessen supply. In the one case, competition
for labour is decreased, and its price falls; in the other,
competition for labour is likely to increase, and its price
is likely to rise. Sometimes employers, by withholding or
delaying their demand, get the labour market so completely under their control, that the price of labour falls to
a pittance barely sufficient for the subsistence of the
labourer, as was notably the case with agricultural wages
in Ireland before famine and emigration had so vastly
thinned the numbers of the peasantry. Sometimes, again,
labourers possess equal powers of control, and use them

quite as unscrupulously; as, for instance, when an India-
bound voyager, arriving at the appointed place of embar-
cation, sees his vessel already loosed from her moorings
and dropping down the river, while the solitary boatman at
hand refuses to put him on board unless paid 5*l.* for a job
for which he would generally be glad to get 5*s.*: or when
the sailors of a wreck-boat, meeting with a stranded vessel,
demand half the value of the cargo as salvage before
consenting to take off it or the shipwrecked crew. This last
is about as glaring an example of brutal selfishness as can
well be cited ; but the condemnation of it need not be the
less severe for being withal a little discriminating. Odious
as the conduct of such salvors would be, their right to act
in the manner described is not to be impugned. There is
no intelligible sense of the substantive 'right' in which it
can be said that they had not a right to put their own price
on services which they were equally at liberty to render or
to withhold, and which, at any rate, no one had a right to
exact from them. However exorbitant, however extortionate their demand, it was in no degree unfair; for to be
unfair it must have been in excess of some price which
they would in fairness have been bound to accept ; and it is
clear that there was no such price, nor, consequently, any
standard of fairness from which their demand could diverge.
But if this be so, and if labourers can, without injustice,
obtain the utmost wages which employers can, without
fraud or force, be induced to give, then, by parity of reasoning, employers can equally, without injustice, accept the
services of labourers on the very lowest terms to which the
latter can voluntarily, and with their eyes open, be brought
to submit. Neither party possesses any relative rights in
the business except those which arise out of their mutual
agreement or contract. Whatever else that contract may
be, it cannot be iniquitous; neither of the contracting
parties can possibly be wronged by it; it can do no
injustice to either. Unless it be legitimate to use words
without any definite meaning, so much as this must needs,

I think, be conceded; but let not any reader who may
be disposed to grant thus much imagine that he will
thereby be making only a verbal concession. Let him
clearly understand that he will be in effect denying the
abstract right of labour, not simply to any specific remuneration, but absolutely to any remuneration whatever;
for that clearly cannot be a right which it is not a wrong to
set aside. He will be admitting that the right of hired
labourers in regard to the conditions of their hire,—
the only one of the rights of labour about which there can
be much dispute—is altogether and entirely matter of
agreement, and has no other basis or extent than those
which the agreement furnishes. He will agree with me
that the just price of labour is precisely that which employers have agreed to give and labourers to take, and
that 'a fair day's wage for a fair day's work' is a phrase
admitting of no other defensible interpretation.

CHAPTER III.

THE RIGHTS OF CAPITAL.

THE last chapter was occupied with an enquiry into the
distinctions between the untenable pretensions and the
genuine rights of labour, and its main purpose was to show
that the equitable remuneration of *hired* labour is simply
whatever may have been mutually agreed upon between
the employer and the owner of that labour—simply whatever the one may have consented to give and the other to
accept. No one rate of wages, it was argued, is intrinsically
more or less fair than any other ; the rate which has
actually been mutually agreed upon, however low it may
be, however inadequate to the labourer's necessities, being
all that he is entitled in justice to demand, or that justice
requires the employer to give.

Members of the working classes, nine-tenths of whom
probably are hired labourers, will not be particularly well
pleased with this definition of their dues. But let them be
of good heart. Theirs is one of the best of causes, and no
good cause ever was or ever will be weakened by plain
speaking. The doctrine summarised above will on further
examination be discovered to be anything but prejudicial
to their interests ; but to enquire in what precise manner it
is calculated to affect those interests would as yet be premature. Before attempting to trace the consequences of a
theory, we should be satisfied of its correctness ; and this
quality we cannot in the present instance subject to a more
crucial test than by comparing with the limits already

assigned to the rights of labour, the boundaries which, after due investigation, shall appear to be those of the conterminous rights of capital.

This comparison will be greatly facilitated if, for the sake of convenience, though at some sacrifice of scientific exactness, we are here permitted to comprehend land under the denomination of ' capital,' thereby excluding from a discussion, of itself sufficiently complicated, the additionally perplexing element of rent. Understood in this enlarged sense, the rights of capital will be found to reach completely up to the boundary which has been represented as circumscribing and confining the rights of labour, and which therefore the latter rights cannot overstep without violating the former. But the rights of capital are of course just as inviolable as those of labour, nor are they so merely on the general ground that all genuine rights whatsoever are by their very essence equally sacred, and that it must always be equally wrong to violate right. There is also an additional and special reason. On looking carefully into the matter we shall find that the rights of capital and of labour rest on precisely the same basis, the former indeed rising out of the latter, so that the validity of the one cannot be called in question without equally impugning the reality of the other. Hence it will be seen to follow that the rights of capital, whatever, when accurately determined, they may prove to be, present an impassable barrier beyond which the rights of labour cannot possibly advance.

To allow of all this being demonstrated, the only concession required is one which few will be disposed to deny, and which those will be foremost to make who are least prepared to approve of the use to which it is about to be turned. It is simply that the whole produce of unassisted labour belongs of right to the person to whom the labour belongs, and by whom it is exerted. The proposition is not indeed absolutely unassailable. The right which it asserts, although one of the least questionable of the claims of human industry, is still not one to which some small

exception may not be taken ; for it is a right which no
individual can exercise without more or less impairing the
corresponding rights of all other individuals.   For human
industry is not a creative process : it cannot make anything out of nothing.   It is ineffective unless it have
materials to work upon ; and these materials, although now
for the most part private property, must in the first instance
have been derived from what at the time was common
property, which no one individual could be entitled to
appropriate without the consent of all the rest.

As soon as Adam's firstborn came of age, so that there
were two men in the world instead of one, neither of them
could pluck an apple, or catch a trout, or snare a rabbit or
partridge, without thereby disabling the other from doing
precisely the same thing, which yet that other had an equal
right to do.   For nothing which the earth contained belonged exclusively either to Adam or to Cain ; everything
belonged to both jointly, and neither, therefore, could seize
for his own sole use on anything, without being bound in
equity to give up part of it to the other on demand.   No
amount of labour expended in acquiring it could give to
either a complete proprietary title to it.   If a horse belonging jointly to A and B break loose and run away, A
cannot by running after it and catching it, after however
long and fatiguing a chase, make it exclusively his own.
Neither could Cain do the like with respect to a primogenial
zebra which his father fancied as much as himself, and
might have captured and broken-in if he had not been
anticipated by his son,

As long as the human family were suffered to revel in
the abundance of the garden of Eden, questions of this sort
could scarcely become very embarrassing, but in the course
of a few generations they began to be sharply contested
between rival hunters and shepherds, whose conflicting
claims to the same hunting or grazing ground could scarcely
be decided except by the sword.   The only law then
in vogue was that modification of the venerable maxim,

'Capiat qui capere possit,' 'Catch who can,' which is embodied in Wordsworth's well-known version of—

> ' The good old rule, the simple plan,
> That they should take who have the power,
> And they should keep who can.'

But it was gradually discovered that without some certainty of being able to keep, few would be at the trouble of taking, and that all activity must come to a stand-still unless individual ownership of whatever individual exertion had acquired were recognised. Thus arose and was established the claim of unassisted labour to the exclusive possession of its own produce, which, however, we see was not so much a right springing naturally from any principles of natural justice, as an artificial privilege built up for the convenience of society out of the ruins of that common right which had previously been the only existing proprietary right.

So microscopic a flaw in the title will scarcely induce any one to dispute the right, which, however, if admitted in the interests of labour, will be found to furnish complete warrant for the most extensive pretensions of capital likewise. If a man be entitled to the whole produce of his unassisted industry, he is of course entitled to all the benefit he can in any way extract from that produce, which therefore he may if he pleases, instead of consuming it unproductively, apply to the purposes of further production, appropriating similarly to his own sole use the whole results of the further production. Now nothing succeeds like success; there is nothing like money for making money; nothing so greatly facilitates and promotes production as the application to it of the results of previous production. A naked savage running after a stag without having made any commissariat arrangements beforehand, will most likely have to give in through hunger and faintness before coming up with his quarry, whereas if he has been prudent enough to take food with him, he may be able to continue the chase until it proves successful. In this latter case, having learned from experience the advantage of fore-thought, he may probably resolve to live no more from hand to mouth, and instead of gorging himself with raw venison, may dry the greater part of it in the sun and so lay up provision enough for several days' hunting. If now he make good use of his time and meat, every separate joint may perhaps serve him as the means of obtaining an entire carcase, and by the time his first supply of food is exhausted, he may find himself in possession of ten times the original quantity. He may then, if he pleases, repeat the same process *ad infinitum*; but it is also very possible that some companion who has witnessed his mode of proceed-ing, may propose to borrow his hunting weapons and appliances, together with a haunch of his venison, on con-dition of repaying the loan with two haunches of the stag which he hopes with its aid and support to be able to run down ; and the owner of the venison may either close with the bargain, or may offer instead to let his applicant have a haunch on condition of receiving the whole produce of the other's chase. The provident savage has, you per-ceive, become a capitalist, his hunting implements and his venison being his capital, which, in one of the cases sup-posed, he lends nearly at cent. per cent. interest, and in the other invests in a speculation from which he expects per-haps three or four hundred per cent. profit.

'What an unconscionable usurer!' you exclaim, and cer-tainly not without reason ; yet in taking the whole of this enormous interest or profit he is taking nothing but what is, in straitest strictness of speech, his own. His hunting tackle he made entirely himself. He might, therefore, if he had pleased, have played the part of the dog in the manger with it, neither using it himself nor letting others use it. His venison, the other item of his capital, was equally the fruit of his own unaided exertions. His own bow and his own spear had gotten him the victory over it. In like manner as the bow and spear, therefore, it was absolutely and entirely at his own disposal. He was quite at liberty to employ it in whatever way he pleased, whether productively or unproductively. He might have eaten the whole of it himself, alternately stuffing and sleeping, as long as it lasted, or have kept it till it rotted, or burnt it on his idol's altar without by such beastly excess or wanton waste, injuring any one but himself, or sinning against anything human but his own conscience. Or he might have used it to sustain and invigorate his own labour, and have increased his store with the increased produce of the labour so increased in efficiency. For in his venison he possessed what in Johnsonian phrase might be called the potentiality of acquiring wealth, of which he might, if he had chosen, have availed himself for his own exclusive advantage. He consented, however, to transfer the use of this potentiality to another on condition of receiving a portion of the resultant wealth ; he suffered his capital to be employed in rendering another's labour instead of his own more efficient. He was under no obligation to make any such transfer. He might, if he had preferred it, have kept his capital entirely to himself, and have used it, or left it unused, as he thought proper, without thereby giving the smallest pretext for complaint to any one. If then he did consent to part with it for a consideration, it was clearly competent to him to determine without appeal what that consideration should be. It could not possibly be greater than he was justified in asking. It could not possibly be so great as to trench on the rights of him who agreed to it ; for the latter had no rights in the matter until the agreement gave them to him, nor any but what the agreement gave. Whatever share, then, however large, of the produce of the combined capital and labour, was assigned to the capitalist by the agreement, belonged to him by the clearest title, while nothing more could belong to the labourer than the share, however small, which might remain for him after the capitalist had taken his stipulated portion.

Further, in taking all this profit or interest he was not

only taking no more than his undoubted due : it is quite
possible also that he may have been taking no more than,
perhaps not so much as, might fairly be regarded as the
creation of his capital.   The hunting tackle and venison
of which that capital consisted, were, as we have seen, the
products of his own unassisted labour.   Nobody had helped
him either to make the one or to use it in getting possession
of the other.   Both were, too, instruments of production
which he might, if he had chosen, have himself used to
increase his store.   He might himself have gone out hunting with them, and if he had, whatever he had bagged in
consequence would clearly have been the exclusive product
of his own industry.   He consented, however, to make over
the use of them to another hunter, thereby enabling that
other to procure a further batch of venison which, according to the hypothesis, he could not have procured without
such aid.   In the circumstances supposed the unassisted
labour of the second hunter would have been fruitless.   It
was the borrowed capital which he was permitted to combine with it that rendered it productive.   But for the loan
of the first hunter's provision bag, and spear, and bow and
arrows, he could neither have come up with the stag, nor
have killed him if he had.   Of course it is not pretended
that the capture of the stag was therefore due exclusively
to the loan.   Of course whoever should put forward so preposterous a claim on behalf of capital, would speedily be
taught that his argument was one cutting equally both
ways by finding it turned decisively against his client.
Certainly labour without capital can do nothing except in
an unappropriated wilderness, and very little even there, but
as certainly capital without labour can nowhere do anything
at all.   Most likely, in the case before us, the second hunter
would have bagged no game without the first hunter's
food and tackle to help him, but most certainly the food
and tackle would have bagged no game without a hunter to
use them.   Still, though the capture certainly was not
owing solely, it was owing chiefly, to the first hunter's

capital. At first sight, when labour and capital are associated, to determine which of the two deserves most of the
credit of their joint productiveness, or how much of the
credit is due to either, might seem as hopeless a task as to
decide which blade of a pair of scissors is most influential in
cutting, or whether the fire or the sirloin has most to do with
the generation of roast beef. But the problem will cease
to appear insoluble if we bear in mind that all capital is the
creation of labour, and likewise the plenary representative
of just as much labour as created it, and if we also consider
how much more of labour is commonly needed to create
capital than to utilise it. In the example before us, perhaps
it took the second hunter the best part of a day to run
down his stag; but perhaps, also, it may have taken the
first hunter the best part of a week to fashion the implements and to provide the food which furnished the second
hunter's equipment. If so, the former contributed four or
five times as much labour as the latter to the common
stock, and was the author of four or five times as much of
the joint result. Consequently, even though in the final
division of the spoil, he gave only one haunch to his companion, and kept the other haunch, both forequarters, and
breast and neck for himself, he would still have been
making a strictly equitable apportionment of the proceeds
of labour, and would have taken as his own labour's share
no more than his own labour had produced. His four or
five hundred per cent., every usurious jot of it, was his
undoubted due by a double title,—by the very selfsame
titles, and by both of them, by which alone hired and unhired
labour are respectively warranted in appropriating their
respective earnings. It was his, first, by special agreement
—on the same ground, that is, on which alone a hired
labourer becomes entitled to wages; it was his, secondly,
as being entirely the result of his own labour—for the
same reason, that is, for which alone a man working on his
own account, and without aid from others, is entitled to the
whole proceeds of his own toil.

The case here selected for the purpose of illustration is
at once very simple and very extreme—quite elementary
in its simplicity, and almost extravagant in the length to
which its governing principle is carried. But elementary
truths continue equally to be truths amidst the most involved of complications, and principles that can be pushed
to extremes without terminating in absurdity, may be
implicitly trusted for guidance in ordinary cases. In the
rudimentary example before us, the rights of capital have
been seen to rest on the very self-same foundation as those
of labour, so that to question their validity would, on the
part of labour, be an obviously suicidal act. But what is
true of capital in its chrysalis form applies to it equally
in its most full-fledged development. It applies not more
to a few ounces of pemmican manufactured by the owner
out of the flesh of game of his own killing, than to
millions of pounds sterling in the possession of one who
has acquired them by gift, bequest, or barter. The prerogatives of capital—its rights over whatever has either
been pledged to it by formal contract, or which it has itself
generated, are always equally extensive, and belong to it
not more in its earlier and minutest embryo stage than
after it as attained to its most complex combinations and
most colossal dimensions. If the earlier of our two hunters
was at liberty to dispose of his venison as he pleased, to
use it or to leave it unused, or to waste it according to his
humour or caprice—if he might do anything with it, in
short, except harm to his neighbour, *à fortiori* he might do
with it anything that did to a neighbour not harm but
good. If he was free to gorge himself with meat, or to let
it rot, or to burn it to ashes, *à fortiori* he must have been
free to give it away, or to sell or bequeath it. The meat
could not be exclusively his own, which, as the fruit of his
unaided toil it incontestably was, unless he could make
over the ownership in all its integrity to another ; and in
so transferring the ownership, he of course transferred with
it all the rights which ownership gave him, while he **to**

whom those rights were transferred, receiving them in all
their entirety, became, of course, entitled to transmit them
in turn in similar entirety to an infinite series of successors.
Some members of the series might probably augment the
capital transmitted to them, by adding to it produce arising
out of the combination with it of labour, either originally
their own, or which they had made their own by purchase,
and by paying for it certainly more than it could have
produced if it had remained unpurchased, and almost
certainly more also than the share which it contributed to
the joint produce of capital and of itself. If so their
rights over each fresh increment became precisely the same
as those which they possessed over the original stock, and
their rights over both became equally capable of transfer
or transmission. In one or other of the modes thus indicated all honestly acquired property must have been accumulated and acquired. Either it must have been the
product of the first owner's unassisted industry ; or it must
have been the product of that product in combination with
industry which, if not originally their own, he or his successors must have made their own by purchase; or, finally, it
must have been the product of one or more subsequent
combinations of the same character as the one just described.
All honestly acquired capital may, therefore, be fairly regarded as the produce of the labour either of the actual owner, or
of a former owner or owners, or of both jointly, but always of
labour, all rights arising out of which are concentred in the
actual owner. Whoever then comes honestly into possession of honestly accumulated capital acquires the same
unbounded ownership over it as would have belonged to
him if he himself alone and unaided had created the whole
of it. He necessarily succeeds to all the rights in connection with it which appertained to any of his predecessors ; and as among those rights was included the right
to all the profit to be got out of property accumulated by
their industry, that right, together with the rest, devolves
upon him and belongs to him, although he be but the

tenth or ten thousandth in descent, as completely as it did
to the earliest of the series.

Neither can differences in the quantity of capital affect
the nature of its rights. It will scarcely be seriously maintained that a man's property is the less completely his own,
or less absolutely at his own disposal, because it happens
to be large. It will scarcely be asserted that the owner is on
that account under any greater obligation to purchase labour
unless he chooses to do so, or consequently to purchase it
at a higher price, or, in other words, to hire labourers at
higher wages than it suits him to pay. Nor, after he has
paid his labourers their stipulated wages, is any advantage
he may derive from their services the less entirely his due
because he happens to be rich. A Manchester millionaire
is entitled just as much, and on just the same grounds, to
take as profit the whole difference between the cost and
selling prices of the finished material which his hundreds
of hired operatives have spun or woven for him, as the
poor Indian who, with wages paid in advance in venison,
had hired another to hunt for him, would be entitled to all
the produce of that other's chase. Nor, again, when capital
and labour act in conjunction, need the magnitude of
the capital diminish capital's share in their joint productiveness. Rather, on the contrary, is capital's proportionate productiveness apt to increase with its bulk. Here
I am compelled to confess that an illustration used a page
or two back is, in one respect, peculiarly favourable to the
pretensions of capital. In it a certain hunter was supposed,
at the expense of four or five days' labour of his own, to
equip another hunter, thereby enabling the latter, at the
expense of one day's additional labour, to run down a
deer. In this instance, one of the hunters, contributing
four or five times as much as the other to the whole stock
of labour, contributed also in the same proportion to the
attainment of the ultimate product. But it must be acknowledged that this hypothesis needs only to be a very
little altered in order to show a very different result. A

very slight addition to the second hunter's equipment might have qualified him to continue the chase for four or five days instead of one, and to bring back four or five instead of a single head of game. Both hunters would then have contributed equal quantities of labour, and both would have contributed in equal measure likewise to the success of the chase. So much must in fairness be admitted; but, on the other hand, it is to be observed that there is also a respect in which the illustration in question is not less unfavourable to capital than it is favourable in another. Being taken from the chase, it is taken from a very exceptional branch of industry, one in which, while the capital employed is almost a fixed quantity, the labour employed is continually increasing, whereas in most other employments the consumption of capital proceeds quite as rapidly as that of labour. Isaak Walton's Venator, Piscator, and Auceps, the three varieties of the *genus* huntsman, differ from all other productive labourers, as being the only ones who, to be enabled to work, require only to be provided with subsistence and implements. To all other labourers whatsoever, materials to be worked up are equally indispensable, and in most occupations, in order that production may go on, fresh materials must be supplied as regularly as fresh labour. Whereas, therefore, in the chase, the proportion of the capital to the labour employed is continually decreasing, in most other occupations the original proportion between the two is in the long-run pretty steadily preserved. And in most occupations, as has been said, the proportion of capital to labour is apt to increase as the amount of capital increases. It is generally greatest in those undertakings in which the capital and labour employed are both greatest. It is far greater, for instance, in a factory in which hundreds of operatives are employed in turning into cloth thousands of bales of wool, than it would be if equal quantities of wool were left to be worked up by a sufficient number of scattered hand-loom weavers. It may not be out of place here to remark that the whole

quantity of labour employed in such a factory throughout
the whole period of its duration, immense as the quantity
would no doubt be, would yet probably be small in comparison with the labour which at various times and places
must have been employed directly or indirectly in the
production of the wool, the construction of the building,
the fabrication of the engines and machinery, and the
provision of the coal, oil, and sundries, without which the
subsequent labour of the factory-hands would have availed
nothing towards the manufacture of cloth. If the thing
were one admitting of calculation, the latter labour would
almost certainly be found to bear a smaller proportion to
the former than the latter's share, in the shape of wages,
of the wholesale proceeds of manufacture would bear to
the share which, after replacing the capital which represented the former labour, would remain as profit on that
capital. How infinitely in all employments whatsoever the
wages of hired labour are likely to exceed what the same
labour would have earned if left unhired, is a point which
has already been once or twice alluded to, and which will
be more fully noticed presently.

An important corollary from what has gone before is,
that a bargain, or other dispute of any sort, between labour
and capital is not a contest between two adverse principles,
but an affair between two things of the same nature and
constitution. The contracting or contending parties are
not labour and something differing in essence from labour,
but merely two different kinds of labour, labour of two
different periods, earlier and later, past and present. Consequently labour, as a whole, cannot be benefited by the
success of either side. Whichever gains, it must always
be labour that loses, and labour's loss must always be at
least equal to what is gained on either side. To whatever
extent labour trespasses on the domain of capital, to that
same extent is the labour which created the capital dispossessed of its rights. Present labour cannot take more
than its due without taking what belongs to past labour.

Moreover, the present labour which has so trespassed will presently become past labour, when, if part of its produce be converted into and employed as capital, it will in turn be liable to loss through repetition of that same denial of the rights of capital by which it had itself previously profited. The rights of capital are therefore not simply conterminous with those of labour, nor do they merely rest on the same foundation. The two may almost be said to be identical. For the rights of capital are really a portion of those of labour, which does not obtain the whole of her dues if capital be deprived of any part of hers. Capital may be likened to a tree which labour has planted and tended for the sake of the fruit which it may bring forth in the shape of profit; if, then, the tree be prevented from yielding its expected fruit, the labour which reared it will be disappointed of its legitimate reward. Labour cannot commit any depredation on capital without plundering herself as well as her victim. She is at best only taking from one pocket to put it into another, and robbing Peter to pay Paul.

Another thing worth mentioning here, though it has but little direct bearing on the question immediately before us, is that, in every bargain between present labour and past labour as represented by capital, whether the latter gain or not, the former is almost sure to gain; indeed, cannot fail to do so except from some miscalculation of its own. However hard be the capitalist's terms, he does not compel acceptance of them; he only offers them for consideration, and he to whom they are offered is free to accept or to refuse. If he accept, it is to be presumed that he sees his account in so doing, and fears that otherwise he will not be able to earn even the little which the terms offer him. The reader, I fear, must by this time be heartily sick of the two hunters of whom such frequent mention has been made, but if he will consent to revert to them once again, he may recollect that one of them could not have hunted at all without the other's help. Left to himself, the best he could do

might have been to look for shell-fish or berries, or to grub
for roots.   In spite, then, of the desperately hard bargain
to which he was fain to submit, he was yet a gainer ; his
gain perhaps being nothing less than the whole difference
between the hind quarter of a fat buck and a handful of
cockles or pignuts.   Nor, except through miscalculation,
does any labourer ever make so bad a bargain with his
employer, that, in spite of its badness, he is not better off
with it than he would be without it.   Clearly, then, no injustice can be done to him, nor can he be injured by terms
which not only were conceded to him by an employer on
whom he had no previous claim, and which no one forced
him to accept, but which he moreover accepted for no other
reason than because he foresaw, or thought he foresaw, that
they would benefit him.

Some of these latter observations are, however, merely
parenthetical.   The chief thing sought to be established in
this chapter is, that of the joint produce of combined capital
and labour the portion rightfully belonging to the former
is whatever share may remain after deduction of the share,
whatever it may be, and however large or however small it
may be, which the latter has beforehand agreed to accept.
That this is so has been argued on two separate pleas—1st
That capital being under no previous obligation to enter
into any arrangement with labour at all is at liberty to reject any arrangement to which she objects, and is entitled
to whatever profit may accrue to her from any arrangement
to which labour and herself mutually agree.   2dly. That
the profit which thus accrues to capital may be fairly
regarded as the produce of the labour by which the capital
was created and which it represents, and would thus, in the
absence of any agreement, belong entirely to capital, for the
self-same reason for which unassisted labour is entitled to
take as its reward the whole of its own produce.   If these
points have been made out, and if capital has thus been
shown to be justly entitled to whatever portion of their
joint produce may be awarded to her by her agreement

with labour, it necessarily follows that the just dues, the rightful wages of labour, cannot exceed whatever under the same agreement may remain for her after capital has taken her share; and this is likewise the conclusion at which we formerly arrived when investigating the claims of labour independently, and with reference only to their own intrinsic merits.

CHAPTER IV.

THE ORIGIN OF TRADES' UNIONS.

STARTING from the principle that a man may do as he will with what has become his own, as being the produce either of his own unassisted labour, or of the labour of others whose rights in respect of that labour have been transferred to him, and following more than one of the paths which branch off from this commencement, we have found them all terminating in one self-same conclusion, viz., that the just remuneration of hired labour is precisely that—and not one tittle more or less than that—which the employer has agreed to give, and the labourer to receive. We have seen that in the matter of wages the adage, that 'whatever is is right,' requires only one obvious qualification in order to make it perfectly applicable. Provided only that a labourer has neither been pressed nor inveigled into service, his actual wages, whatever their amount, are all that he can equitably claim as his due.

Scant measure this, but literal truth withal, and exact justice; so that honest men have no alternative but to accept it, together with whatever attendant circumstances may be available to supplement its scantiness. Fortunately not more in the case of labour than in others must legitimate incomings be necessarily coincident with dues. If all men got their desert, who would escape whipping, and how many would get much else? The smaller the desert the less cause for resting therewith content, and as the world has hitherto wagged, working men have had peculiarly little reason for remaining satisfied with what was owing to them. Hard it must seem to them, on looking round, that the hardest work and hardest fare generally go together ; that those who toil most often earn least; and that in the distribution of fortune's gifts and charges, unceasing labour is imposed upon some, while others are indulged with life-long luxury and ease. Hard it must seem that though it is they who delve and plough, and sow and reap, it is not into their barns that the harvest is gathered ; hard that the yarn which they have spun and the web which they have woven belong not to them, but to a master who, watching them at work from the window of his pleasant villa hard by, seems to have nothing to do but to look on and grow rich. Hard, very hard, all this not only seems, but is. Little would any of us like it were the lot ours. And you, working men, whose lot it is, no wonder that you are dissatisfied with it. The wonder rather is that, in spite of occasional murmurs, you take it on the whole so quietly. Yet, though the hardship of your condition be undeniable, bear with me while I venture to hint that you yourselves perhaps but dimly perceive in what its hardship really consists. It is not, as your flatterers are so constantly telling you, and as you are naturally so apt to believe, that you alone are the bees of this mundane hive, and that your employers and the rest of your fellow-men are the drones ; that it is you alone who gather the honey, while the rest only help to eat it. Your employers are not a whit less helpful to you than you are to them ; nay, little as you may think it, they are really the more helpful of the two. They could more easily do without you than you without them. They take, it is true, an ample share of the honey; but without the flower-beds which they or their forerunners have formed and filled, there would be little or no honey for you to collect. Capital is not the greedy parasite you are so ready to fancy it, fastening like a sloth or glutton on the tree of labour, and growing fat by gnawing its shoots and draining it of its sap. Capital and labour are mutually beneficial, and lay each other under reciprocal obligations. If labour be the parent of capital, capital becomes in turn the foster-mother of labour, its indispensable patroness and purveyor. In every artificial state of society it is capital that imparts to labour all its fertility, becoming itself simultaneously fertilised, and generally contributing in much the larger measure to the combined productiveness. In the share which your employer takes of the joint produce of his capital and your labour, he takes nothing of yours. The share assigned to you is not only far greater than anything which your own unaided labour could have produced; it is also a share which almost always bears a much larger proportion to your labour than your employer's share bears to the labour which his capital represents. Obtaining thus as much or more than can in any way be regarded as the fruit of your labour, what shadow of right, not founded on concession by the owner, can you possibly have to the fruit of labour which is not yours? Is it not clear that by pretending to such a right you are impugning your own otherwise indisputable rights? Do you not see that by claiming, as naturally and necessarily due to labour, anything more than the same labour's own produce, you are denying labour's primordial right to the whole of its own produce, and thereby shaking the foundation of every right which it possesses?

Your grievance, then, does not consist in your having to work for others instead of for yourselves: it is for yourselves, and yourselves only, that you work, since you thereby gain for yourselves at least the full equivalent of what your labour produces. Your employer's profits are not the product of your labour in any sense in which your wages are not at least equally the product of his capital. It is preposterous, then, to stigmatise him as oppressive and tyrannical for simply withholding from you, and keeping for himself, that which does not belong to any but himself. Not but what there is here a real and grievous tyranny by which many of you are sorely oppressed. But the tyranny is not the tyranny of your employers. It is what M. Louis Blanc not inappropriately terms 'the tyranny of circumstances,' though he goes on to speak of it as if 'circumstances' and 'society' were synonymous expressions, and as if society, moreover, were wholly composed of employers and wealthy people. Your connection with capitalists can scarcely be otherwise than beneficial to you, provided it rest on mutual agreement ; your sole grievance consists in your not being yourselves capitalists; in your being so circumstanced as to be unable to get on without capital, yet to have seldom any capital of your own, and to be generally unable to obtain its aid except on conditions which leave you too small a share of the advantage derivable from its use. So has the despotism of circumstances ordained, and against such ordinances it would be meanness not to mutiny.

Born of a race whose heritage is labour, and placed in a sphere in which, if you are to live at all, you must live by labour, you find yourselves, through the fault or misfortune either of your forefathers or yourselves, destitute of those appliances without which labour must be sterile. You have neither land nor materials to work upon, nor tools to work with, nor food to sustain you while working; and the use of these indispensable accessories you can obtain only, and that on their own terms, from such of your fellow-creatures as possess them. But it is not by taking from you that these have become better provided than yourselves ; and it is for you not an evil, but a great good, that there are others better provided, and able, consequently, to supply your deficiencies. The help afforded by them, on whatever terms you obtain it, cannot but be worth to you more than you are charged for it; for otherwise you would not accept it. In obtaining it,. therefore, you are not injured, but benefited, and the mere receipt of benefits can surely afford no pretext for quarrel with benefactors. Your suit, then, against your employers will not lie. The wrong against which you may reasonably remonstrate is your inexorable need of their

assistance, but your need is not their fault.   What wrongs
you is neither their wealth nor their selfishness, but your
own poverty; this being only a comprehensive name for
the combination of 'circumstances' alluded to by M. Louis
Blanc, the despotism of which overwhelms and oppresses
you, prevents your own unaided labour from sufficing for
your maintenance, and sentences many of you to perpetual
penal servitude as the only condition of your obtaining the
aid indispensable to render your labour efficient.   Against
such despotism by all means rise in revolt.   By all means
muster against it all your energies, and God speed your
efforts at self-enfranchisement.   But before you rise, examine
well, ascertain exactly, what it is that is wanting to your
well-being, and to what cause its absence is attributable.
So shall you more easily discover how best its presence can
be secured.

Those 'circumstances'—to continue the use of a metaphor growing now somewhat unmanageable—which press
most hardly on the labourer, are the two negative ones of
want of any capital of his own, and inability to obtain, on
satisfactory terms, the aid of other people's capital.   The
great practical evil hence arising is the inadequacy of the
share which, in the partition between labour and capital of
their joint produce, falls in the shape of wages to the former.
For this there are but two possible remedies, the difference
between which is more real than apparent.   There may be
an augmentation of the wages themselves, or there may be
an addition to them of some further portion of produce as
something over and above and supplemental to wages.   But
as of the whole divisible produce whatever does not, by
virtue of the agreement made beforehand by the parties,
belong to labour, belongs of right to capital, there can be
no augmentation of wages except at the expense of the
capitalist, nor can the labourer become entitled to any extraneous addition to wages, except either in virtue of concession by the capitalist, or in consequence of his becoming
himself a capitalist.   In either of the two latter cases the

interests of capitalist and labourer may be coincident ; but when an increase of, as distinguished from an addition to, wages is in question, those interests must necessarily be antagonistic ; and in endeavouring to gain his point, the labourer must be prepared for opposition on the part of his employer, which by force of one sort or other, moral or physical, or with whatsoever other adjective prefix, he must be prepared to overcome. *Cæteris paribus*, peace is always very preferable to war, and co-operation to conflict ; and this treatise will have been written to very little purpose if, in the proper place, it fail to show that labour can, by alliance with capital, secure at least as much advantage as by antagonism. But in order that labourers may be in a position to judge between the two, they ought to see clearly what each can do for them, and an additional reason for enquiring how much they may expect to gain by aggression is, that their alliance is likely to be courted in proportion to their apparent capability of becoming dangerous adversaries. In their case as in others, evident readiness for hostilities will be the best guarantee for the establishment of satisfactory peaceful relations, and nothing is better calculated to pave the way towards an amicable settlement of disputes between labour and capital than the showing how formidable the former may become if driven to extremities.

On a cursory view, it might, indeed, seem that, even at bay, labour would have little chance against its opponent. In most situations labour not only cannot act, but cannot even subsist without capital, and must perish from inanition if deprived of the sustenance which capital affords ; whereas capital generally, although equally incapable of independent action, can at least feed upon itself, and so prolong a lingering existence until its own substance is entirely consumed. A mere labourer must starve if he cannot get wages, but a capitalist, as long as he has any capital left, need not starve merely because he cannot get profits. The question, then, being simply which can hold out longest, it might seem clear that labour must be the first to give in. And this no doubt is what must almost invariably happen when labour is completely dissociated from capital, and when, at the same time, capitalist employers agree, as they commonly do, to act together.   Commonly employers, instead of competing with each other for labour, and thereby raising its price, combine together to keep down its price, and their combination having hitherto been for the most part directed against improvident, and therefore needy and disunited, labourers, has hitherto been for the most part successful.   Until recent times, in all old or densely-peopled countries, the rate of wages in most, if not all, occupations, has generally depended mainly on the will of the masters, and has consequently, in most occupations been almost always exceedingly low ; so low, indeed, that scarcely ever or anywhere, until recent times, and even then in not more than one or two long-settled countries, has it been more than sufficient to keep labourers in tolerable working condition.   Does this sound like exaggeration ?   One single allusion will suffice to show that it falls short of the truth, and of a truth which is not notorious, only because we can, when we please, be stone blind to things that have stared us in the face all our lives.   In no other old country, either in ancient or modern times, has the average rate of wages been nearly so high as it now is in England.   Yet, even in England, is there one single county the bulk of whose rural labourers, or more than half at most of whose town labourers, can afford themselves food and shelter nearly as good relatively as every carriage-keeping gentleman provides for his coach-horses, or every well-to-do farmer for his cattle ?   The owner values his beasts too well not to lodge and feed them in what he thinks the best way for keeping them in health ; but what proportion of English labourers, think you, is it that are able so to lodge and feed themselves ?   And if the average rate of wages, inadequate as it is even in England, has never here been so low as it was until recently in Ireland—and if even in that unhappy

island it never was, nor can ever, permanently be so low
as it might be, and actually is, in India, what is the explanation of these diversities ? Partly, 'tis true, the greater
relative abundance of labour in Ireland and India ; but
this, besides being only a secondary reason, is calculated to
disguise from us the significance of the primary cause. The
real original explanation is partly that, owing to differences
of climate or of habit, different quantities and qualities of
food, clothing, and cover, either are, or are esteemed to be,
necessaries of life, and partly that absolute necessaries are
naturally more abundant and correspondingly cheaper in
some countries than in others. But scarcely more true is it
of Ireland or of India than of England, that whatever has
at any time been the minimum of subsistence supposed to
be sufficient to enable labourers to go on living as they had
been accustomed to live, that same minimum has been the
measure of the price of labour. Whenever and wherever
masters have had the framing of the scale of wages, this has
been the basis of their calculations. Speaking generally,
and after due allowance for local peculiarities and exceptional employments, there is no exaggeration in saying that
in all long-established and slowly progressive communities,
the wages of ordinary unskilled labour have almost always
been nearly as low as they could be consistently with the
perpetuation of the race of labourers. So low have they
almost always and everywhere been when their rate has
been settled by combination among employers.

Skilled labour, no doubt, has fared a good deal better.
To fit handicraftsmen for their several callings special training is required, which is only submitted to for the sake
of proportionably increased remuneration. Masters have
always been obliged to take this into consideration, and to
offer extra pay to induce certain descriptions of labourers
to take the requisite pains to become skilful. Still, when
settling the wages of skilled as of unskilled labour, they
were until comparatively recent times, but little in the
habit of regarding anything but their own notions of

propriety and expediency. They were not much more accustomed to take manufacturing operatives than agricultural
hinds into their counsels. Until within the last three or
four generations, the former were generally fain to accept
—not perhaps so tamely and submissively, but almost as
helplessly—whatever their employers thought proper to
offer. Three or four generations back, to any one who had
already begun to doubt whether helotism were the fitting
condition of two-thirds of his fellow-creatures, there must,
nevertheless, have appeared to be small probability that
that helotism would ever cease. Rather it might seem
that what had always been would always continue to be,
that the immemorial bondage of labour would likewise be
everlasting—nay, was far more likely to be tightened than
relaxed. For already it might be perceived how marvellously capital was developing its capacities, and preparing to extend and consolidate its sway. What alone
had hitherto mitigated its despotism was the number of
persons among whom it had been distributed : and, now,
behold, its energies were daily becoming concentrated in
fewer and fewer hands. The savings which, when business
is conducted on a large scale, are obtainable from the
command of costly machinery, from the division of labour,
and the comparative cheapness of superintendence, were
already giving to large capitalists an advantage against
which men of inferior means found it difficult to contend,
and before which they were already retiring. That industrial revolution had already commenced, which has
proceeded uninterruptedly ever since. During the last
hundred years, in husbandry, in handicrafts, in trade, large
undertakings have been continually displacing small ones,
and that, too, in a continually accelerated ratio. Hedge-
rows and homesteads have everywhere been thrown down,
to allow of the formation of fields of fifty, and farms of five
hundred acres ; spinning-wheels and handlooms have been
driven out of sight by spinning-jennies and power-looms ;
and for the small adventurer who used to distribute his

wool, or flax, or cotton, or silk among half a dozen cottage families, has been everywhere substituted the enterprising mill-owner, who congregates his factory lads and lasses by hundreds within the same four walls. Retail trade has similarly begun to assume wholesale proportions, and in most of our larger provincial towns, as well as in the metropolis, drapers, mercers, and tailors occupy premises stretching along half a street. If any philanthropist among our great-grandfathers could have pictured to himself these changes—if Great Britain in her present outward aspect, could have been revealed to him in a dream, how melancholy, on the whole, would have been the impression made upon him! It would have been impossible for him not to admire the colossal scale and teeming productiveness of industrial operations, as his eye fell upon stackyards, each large enough and full enough to serve as the granary of a small province; on magazines and warehouses capable singly, after their respective kinds, of supplying all the inhabitants of a populous city; on a forest of shipping, in any one of half a dozen ports, more than sufficient for what was then the import and export trade of the whole kingdom. But as he caught sight also of Scottish hinds shut up at night by scores in bothies, and of hundreds of operatives, English and Scottish, working together far into the night in mills and factories, might not his thoughts have reverted naturally to the *ergastula* of imperial Rome, in which patrician taskmasters used to pen their herds of human cattle? And when informed, with regard to these hinds and operatives, and to the masons and bricklayers and pitmen and navvies whom he might likewise see clustered like bees or swarming like ants on every side, that these several crowds of employed were each in the service of some single employer—some one of the gentlemen agriculturists, or iron-masters, or cotton lords, or railway kings into whom the homely farmers, and petty furnace-owners, and clothiers, and contractors of his own day would be metamorphosed—might it not occur to him that the

progress of civilisation was about to establish among us
a species of serfdom not less stringent than the feudal
bondage which the same civilisation had destroyed? Might
it not seem to him that a time was approaching when, in
the unequal struggle between large and small capitals, the
latter would entirely disappear, and when the industrial
community would in consequence become separated into
two strongly-marked divisions, the one consisting of a few
millionaire employers, the other of many millions of employed without any means of. livelihood except their
periodical earnings, and without the means of earning
anything except by consent of a superior? Might he not
have reasonably apprehended that absolute supremacy on
the one side, absolute submission on the other, were about
to be characteristics of the coming age?

Happily, however, the remedial power of nature—to call
it by no more reverential name—which seldom allows the
germs of evil to attain complete development, has, in this
instance also placed the antidote close beside the bane.
In human affairs extremes are always meeting, action is
constantly followed by reaction, and despotism stirs up
insurrection; and thus it has come to pass that the
seemingly overwhelming preponderance of capital has
aroused against itself an opposition to which it is not unfrequently fain to succumb. Those very multitudinous
assemblages of workpeople, by which capital most im-
posingly displays and most effectually exercises its authority over labour, afford also to labour its most obvious
means of emancipation from the thraldom of capital. Men
are seldom collected together in large masses without
speedily discovering that union is strength, and men whose
daily avocations obliged them to be constantly using, and
by use to be constantly sharpening, their wits, were not
likely to be backward in making the discovery. As long
as agriculture continued to be the main occupation of
nations, and manufactures were carried on chiefly by a
thinly-scattered rural population, while even in the towns

there were no great employers, or none personally superintending extensive operations, workpeople could scarcely
be brought together often enough, or in sufficient numbers,
to allow of their consulting together to much purpose
about their common affairs, or devising mutual arrangements for the promotion of their common interests. In
such circumstances anything like general or continuous
combination among them was scarcely practicable. But
in proportion as trade subsequently succeeded in concen-
trating its operations were the operatives whom it con-
gregated furnished with facilities for association; and it
was, as it were, instinctively that they gradually availed
themselves of these. It was then that with little pre-
meditation or design, and almost unconsciously, they laid
the foundations and put together the framework of those
TRADES' UNIONS which have since become so famous, and
whose rapid growth full surely marks the commencement
of an epoch unparalleled in industrial history.

It is probable that these associations had at first little of
a defensive, and nothing of an aggressive, character about
them. Originally they seem not to have differed from
ordinary benefit societies, whose main purpose is mutual
assurance against the results of accidental calamities. But
though such may have been their primary object, it soon,
if so, became of secondary * importance. When, at stated

---

* Of secondary importance, that is, with reference to the magnitude
of the interests connected with it, for the insurance portion of the
business of trade societies is still in many cases that which occupies
most of their time and attention, and of their money also. Of 49,000*l.*
expended by the Amalgamated Engineers in 1865, little more than
14,000*l.* went to the support of men out of employment in consequence
of their either being on strike or being unable to find work, while
more than 20,000*l.* were distributed among members sick or superannuated, or temporarily disabled by accident. In some societies
there are two rates of subscription, of which members may take their
choice—a higher rate, entitling them to subsistence allowance when
sick, as well as when they have turned out with the sanction or at the
bidding of the society, or when they are unable to find employment;
and a lower rate, which gives no claim to support in sickness. Among

periods, either in select committee or general assembly, the
members met for the despatch of business, after investigating the claims of the sick and disabled, and of widows
and children, counting the cash in hand or due, estimating
future expenditure, and assessing themselves accordingly,
they naturally proceeded to discuss any other topics of
general concernment.   Among these the one pretty sure
to be uppermost in their minds was the chronic unsatisfactoriness of the relations between themselves and their
employers.   Now it is essential to note that this unsatisfactoriness would not consist solely in the lowness of their
wages.   If the price of labour were settled in exactly the
same way as the price of everything else—as, for instance,
of bread—labourers would at once perceive it to be as
absurd for them to reproach employers for not paying
dearer for labour, as it would be for the cheap bakers with
whom they themselves probably deal to reproach them for
not paying dearer for bread.   But labourers see, or if they
do not see, they feel, that there are some material differences between themselves as sellers of labour and the
sellers of any tangible substance like bread.   The nature

the Operative Masons these rates are $7\frac{1}{2}d$. and $4d$. a week respectively,
and the latter would seem to be regarded by trades' unions generally
as about sufficient for what they term their 'trade purposes.'   The
subscriptions of the Amalgamated Engineers and of the Amalgamated
Carpenters are extraordinarily high, one shilling weekly being required
from every member, but the allowances are proportionate.   A superannuated engineer, one too old to earn the ordinary rate of wages, is
allowed from $7s$. to $9s$. a week.   The allowance to a superannuated
carpenter is $8s$. a week after twenty-five years' membership, $7s$. a week
after eighteen years, $5s$. a week after twelve years.   A sick carpenter
get $12s$. a week for twenty-six weeks, and $6s$. a week during the
remainder of his illness.   For the funeral of a member of six months'
standing the carpenters allow $3l$. $10s$. ; for that of an older member $12l$.
A member completely disabled by accident receives a donation of $100l$.
For loss or breakage of tools, compensation to the full extent of their
value is given to the owner if he has been a member for more than six
months ; up to $5l$. if for a shorter period.   Facts like these may assist
us in understanding the hold which trade societies have on the allegiance of their constituents.

of these differences was set forth at some length in a former chapter, which, however, the courteous but cursory reader is so likely to have skipped, that a brief abstract of some of its conclusions may not be superfluous. If bakers cannot get the price they think fitting, they can at the worst leave off baking, but journeymen labourers cannot so easily leave off working. These live generally from hand to mouth : without daily work they must not expect daily bread, and it is only therefore at the risk of being starved that they can refuse to work for whatever hire may be offered. Even bakers—though few tradesmen have so little choice—have yet some choice of customers. Their loaves will be as eatable and saleable at noon as they were before breakfast, and if kept till noon may still be sold without loss. Not so with labour. If the forenoon's labour be not sold before noon, it must remain always unsold, and its whole value will be lost to its owner, who can never, therefore, without some risk of loss, reject the offer of the first customer who presents himself. Moreover, neither bakers nor any other sellers except those who have nothing but their own labour to sell, need be under any apprehension of their customers unanimously insisting on their reducing their prices, for the customers cannot so insist without foregoing the use of commodities they are accustomed to, and customers in general are likely to tire much sooner of going without such commodities than the dealers in them of going without their customers' money. But employers, or customers for labour, on the contrary, can generally wait longer for labour than labourers can wait for wages, so that however low may be the terms on which they may seek to obtain labour, they can generally, if they are un- animous in insisting on those terms, force them upon needy labourers. This is why the price of labour is generally so much depressed ; and that this should be the cause of the depression, rather than the depression itself, is what in the relations between employers and employed really demands readjustment. The employed are placed in circumstances peculiarly unfavourable for the sale of their only staple. In bargaining with employers they stand at a disadvantage, of which the latter do not scruple habitually to avail themselves, generally combining to keep down the price of labour, and even when they do not combine, obtaining it on terms much lower than the labourers would agree to if they and the employers were more equally in need of each other. This is a grievance of which labourers may justly complain, but serious as it is, it is also one which itself indicates a mode of getting itself redressed. If employers are so frequently able to dictate to labourers the terms on which the latter shall be hired, it is because they can generally manage to wait longer without having their work done than their labourers can wait without having work to do, and that they can so wait is simply because they have, in the savings of themselves or others, reserve funds whereupon to subsist while waiting. Obviously, if labourers had similar reserves, they also could similarly wait, and to members of trades' unions an increase of the subscriptions which were already providing for their ordinary insurance business would naturally suggest itself as a ready means of creating such reserves. The adoption of this means would, in fact, be merely an extension of the principle of insurance on which they were already acting. Hitherto the subscriptions had been applied to the support of members disabled for work by physical causes; thenceforward they would be applied also to the support of able-bodied members desisting temporarily from work at the bidding of the association, and in furtherance of its policy. The associated members would then no longer be living from hand to mouth, but would have wherewithal to subsist upon for a while without working. They would be able, consequently, to meet combination with combination, and though as long as they remained idle, standing out for higher wages, they would lose the wages they might otherwise have earned during the interval, they might not unreasonably hope to be subsequently compensated for this first loss. For the disputes between men and masters, no longer depending for settlement on the will of the latter, would resolve themselves into questions of time, which would by no means necessarily be decided in favour of the party possessing the larger reserves, and therefore apparently, and indeed really, the stronger. No doubt, if both parties strained their energies to the uttermost, the men would be the first to give in, but the masters would probably stop far short of such extreme efforts. No doubt they could, if they tried, hold out longest; but most probably they would not try, for to hold out to the last would cost infinitely more to them than to their opponents. To them entire exhaustion of resources would be absolutely fatal, whereas to the others it would be only a temporary collapse. For the capitalist, in losing his capital, loses his all, distinctive class existence included; he ceases to be a capitalist; whereas a labourer, after spending all his savings, may still fall back upon an undiminished stock of personal strength and skill, and still be as much a labourer as before. With very inferior resources, therefore, it might be quite possible for the men to hold out as long or longer than the masters would choose to hold out.

Taking this view of affairs, trades' unions concerted measures accordingly, and that so judiciously, that they have never found it necessary to deviate much from the course which they began by chalking out for themselves. Under great difficulties and against frequent discouragement, through much of evil and very little of good report, they have gone on extending and developing and multiplying themselves till they have become what they are. What that is may be described in two words. Fifty years ago they had scarcely been heard of. Now they are already a distinct power in the State, and are rapidly advancing towards a foremost place among national institutions. Nearly two thousand of them are now spread over the kingdom, ramifying through every county, and ensconced in every town, and almost every trade. In every occupation dependent in any great degree on skilled labour, a large proportion of the labourers are, by their instrumentality, banded together in constant readiness to try conclusions with their masters. Not less than a tenth, perhaps, of all the skilled labourers in Great Britain are thus enrolled, many unions counting their constituents by thousands, and some by tens of thousands; possessing revenues, too, corresponding with their numerical strength. The very names of the societies are a legion in themselves. The list, as Mr. Harrison neatly says, omits no single trade of which one ever heard the name, and includes several of which few have heard the names; the 'Progressive Makers'-up,' for example, and the 'Self-acting Minders.' The reason why these two are so little known to fame is doubtless that, in respect of size, they are very near the bottom of a graduated scale, growing small by degrees and beautifully less as it descends. For trades' unions are of very various dimensions, from the 'Miners' National Association,' which comprises 54,000 members, to some less numerous even than the 'Progressive Carpenters,' among whom Mr. George Potter is registered, and who have not progressed to a higher figure than 130. The one which, though not the largest, and though very far from being the oldest, is on the whole, perhaps entitled to rank above all the rest, is that of the 'Amalgamated Engineers,' established in January, 1851, which now possesses 308 branches or lodges, with altogether 43,000 members, a number increasing at the rate of 2,000 or 3,000 yearly. From two-thirds to three-fourths of all engineering workmen are supposed to belong to this society. Of its lodges, 238, with 27,856 members, are in England and Wales; 33, with 3,218 members, in Scotland; and 11, with 1,371 members, in Ireland. There are also 14 branches, containing 626 members, in the British Colonies; 11, with 498 members, in the United States; and 1, of 30 members, all English, at Croix, in the north of France. Next in order of merit may be placed the 'Amalgamated Carpenters,' though this is only one, and only second in point of magnitude, among several associations in the same trade. It has 190 branches and 8,261 members, 2,500 of whom joined last year. Its rival, the 'Operative House Carpenters,' has 10,000 members, of whom 2,504 joined last year, distributed amongst 1,506 lodges. The 'Friendly Society of Operative Masons' consists of 278 lodges, and 17,702 members, having gained 4,760 of the latter in 1866. The 'Iron Founders' Union,' which has been fifty-eight years in existence, numbers 11,150. These are specimens of what may be termed national unions. Among provincial or otherwise local associations may be mentioned the Boiler Makers, 9,000 strong ; the London Bricklayers, numbering 6,000 ; the Sheffield Bricklayers, 5,242 ; and the Manchester House Painters, 3,960, divided into 58 lodges, of which 14, containing 1,209 members, were formed in 1866. Of all the Plasterers in the United Kingdom fifty per cent. are believed to be unionists.

Then, regarded financially, some of the associations will be found to have resources sufficient, on occasions of great emergency, to admit of a single union's devoting 50,000*l.* or 60,000*l.* to the requirements of a single season. The Amalgamated Engineers, indeed, do nearly as much as this habitually. In 1865, a normal year, their income was 86,885*l.*, and their expenditure 49,000*l.* They have, at present, an accumulated fund of about 140,000*l.* The receipts of the Operative Masons last year were 18,640*l.* ; their reserve fund amounts to 10,000*l.* The average annual income of the Operative Carpenters is stated at 15,000*l.* Of their 'Amalgamated' brethren the receipts and expenditure in 1865 were 10,487*l.* and 6,733*l.* respectively. Their balance in hand at the end of the same year was 8,320*l.*

Nor are trades' unions more remarkable for their numbers and wealth than for the spirit that animates and the discipline that regulates them. Class aggrandisement with them takes precedence of every other consideration. All other interests, individual or social, patriotic or cosmo-

politan, count for little in comparison. And in prosecuting
their object, the celerity and concert of their movements,
their fortitude and constancy, are such as would do credit
to veteran soldiers. They turn out at a moment's notice,
and remain out until they get the word to turn in again,
merely satisfying themselves that the signal has been given
by competent authority, and asking no further questions.
These particulars, be it understood, are mentioned in proof
of their resolution, not of their wisdom : and, in truth, it
would be well if shortcomings in respect of wisdom were
the worst defects with which they are chargeable. The
moral character of trades' unions is just now under a heavy
cloud. During the last few years the exemplary demeanour
and rapid growth of some of the leading societies had been
gradually dissipating the opprobrium which unionism at
its outset had justly incurred. The contemptuous mixture
of pity and disgust with which its early struggles, fraught
with terrible suffering to the unionists themselves, and
often disgraced by ferocious excesses, had been viewed by
impartial lookers-on, had gradually given way, and had
been replaced by mingled admiration and apprehension.
The revelations of the present year have, however, brought
back much of the original feeling with aggravated force,
heightening disgust into abhorrence, and anxiety into serious
alarm. In giving evidence before the Metropolitan Royal
Commission, the representatives of unionism disclaimed for
its theory any of the elevated sentimentalism sometimes
ascribed to it by outside admirers, honestly avowing self-
seeking, pure and simple, to be its ruling passion ; while at
Sheffield and Manchester unionist practices were disclosed
which could not be too violently execrated, provided only
that indignation's shafts were confined to their proper mark,
instead of being suffered to fly about at random. If it
were fair to judge of the whole body from the state of an
out-lying member, the horrors dragged into light at Sheffield would undeniably afford sufficient warrant for de-
nouncing unionism as one uniform mass of malignity, and

so it is accordingly denounced by a multitude of hostile
critics, to whom the opportunity of applying to it the
maxim of *ex pede Herculem* was too tempting to be neglected. Among the more sententious guides and expo-
nents of popular opinion—among the high dignitaries of
our periodical literature—very few indeed have now a word
left to say in its favour. Even those who, after inveighing
against it for a whole generation and more, seemed latterly
to have begun to doubt whether the devilry they had been
picturing to themselves was really quite so black as they
had painted it, cannot now satisfy themselves in portraying
it without deepening their former shades, and grinding still
darker colours on their palette. ' Times,' ' Edinburgh,' and
' Quarterly' seem finally to have made up their minds, all
agreeing that unionism is innately bad, radically and desperately wicked, and proceeding accordingly to pass upon
it sentence, which by no lack of will on their part, is
prevented from serving effectually as one of utter excom-
munication. On this, as on every subject, let all men
speak and write according to their own convictions, and
those whose convictions take the turn just indicated may
well be in the dumps. Thinking as they do, the future
must needs offer to them a dismal prospect; if what they
think were true, there would be but a sorry look-out for
any of us. For whatever else unionism may be, we may
rest assured that it is, at any rate, full of vitality. If it be
all evil, it is destined to be a very long-lived evil, and to do
a vast deal more mischief yet than it has hitherto done, or
is doing. So significant a phenomenon did not arise, so
powerful an agency was not called into being, without
adequate cause, and as long as the widely-spread and
deeply-seated disorder, for whose relief it has been devised, remains unhealed, so long will it likewise continue to
exist, acquiring also fresh strength continually. Its past
growth may be but an earnest of its future stature. For
the organisation of trades ions has a visible tendency
to consolidate and to extend itself, and it is apparently

susceptible of indefinite extension. From local association
to national federation is but a single stage, and from thence
to alliance with foreign federations is but another. Already
preparations for both movements are being made, and
every step taken in either direction will plainly be so much
ground gained. With such capacities, present and prospective, trades' unions are only too certain to have an
important part to play in the drama of the immediate
future, and upon their mode of acting must greatly depend
the general character of the performance. Heaven forbid,
then, that they should go through their part as ill as some
alarmists expect. One thing pretty certain, with respect
to the coming age, is, that it will be either very much
better or very much worse than any that has for centuries
preceded it ; and if the first of these alternatives be, on
the whole, the more probable of the two, it is chiefly the
growing good sense and good feeling of the classes which
trades' unions represent and guide, and whose prevailing
sentiment reacts in turn upon trades' unions, that make it
so. For my own part, making a virtue of necessity, I am
content to rely on the progress, moral and intellectual, of
the working classes, inasmuch as, now that they have been
invested with a preponderance of political power, there
will, whenever they may choose to exercise their new
privileges, be little else to rely upon. But those who, as I
am about to do, stand forward in behalf of unionism, need
not rest its defence on its probabilities of future improvement. I am myself disposed to go a good deal farther.
Even in its present unregenerate state, I am prepared to
maintain that its influence is much more beneficent than
pernicious. I assert, confidently, that its principle is sound
and just ; that most, nay, that all, of its objects are perfectly legitimate, and that though, in the pursuit of those
objects, means have often been resorted to which cannot
be too vehemently reprobated, there is at the disposal of
trades' unions a sufficiency of perfectly legitimate means

to allow of their accomplishing as much of their ends as even in the interests of labour it is desirable should be accomplished. So I say boldly, and in the eyes of those readers whose patience holds out through the next book, I hope to be able to justify my boldness.

Book III.

LABOUR AND CAPITAL IN ANTAGONISM.

Book III.

LABOUR AND CAPITAL IN ANTAGONISM.

CHAPTER I.

THE ENDS OF TRADES' UNIONISM.

IN enquiring, as we may now proceed to do, into the means and ends of Unionism, and in considering how far these can respectively be termed legitimate, we shall find it convenient to treat the two separately. Inasmuch, too, as the former can scarcely be deserving of commendation, if the latter be reprehensible, we shall do well to reverse the usual order of things, and to take the last first. Beginning thus with the ends, we have yet another separation to make. We must be careful to distinguish between what actually is and what possibly might be, and must not allow the charms of a beautiful ideal to disguise from us the homeliness and coarseness of a somewhat commonplace reality. By some uncompromising admirers of Unionism, the loftiness and modesty of its aspirations are alternate themes of praise, and are each in turn urged as sufficient recommendations. By one very zealous and very powerful advocate its object is represented to be nothing less than the entire remodelling of existing industrial arrangements, the complete abolition of hiring and service, and the substitution for those invidious relations between man and man, of a generous partnership in which employers should take their places as 'Captains of Industry,' while the employed cheerfully and trustfully subordinated themselves as rank and file ; the former assuming the duties of superintendence, and finding tools, materials, and immediate subsistence, the latter 'finding strength, patience, and manual skill.' A rose-tinted picture this, and a visionary, yet not impossibly prophetic. It is at least one quite capable of realisation, and one, moreover, which trades' unions might, if they chose, materially assist in realising ; thereby paving the way towards still better things beyond, and, even without advancing farther, amply atoning thereby for all previous shortcomings or backslidings. Hitherto, however, they have been so far from making a move in that direction, that they will probably be both surprised and amused to find any such tendency attributed to them. 'Captains of Industry,' quotha. Yes, verily, every unionist private may perhaps be well enough content that there should be officers in the army of labour ; only with this important proviso, that he himself should hold one of the commissions.

Not more ground is there for the same writer's assertions that Unionism 'aims, above all, at making even, regular, and safe, the workman's life,' and that 'one of its chief functions is to resist the tendency to continual fluctuations in wages.' Let it be admitted to be, as it undoubtedly is, an immense aggravation of the evils of the labourer's lot, that his earnings are liable to continual variation ; let it be admitted that to those who, whether from necessity or habit, live from hand to mouth, lowering of wages may mean 'personal degradation, eviction from house and home, sale of goods and belongings, break-up of household, humiliation of wife, ruin of children's bodies and minds.' But let it at the same time be recollected that fluctuation of wages implies progress as well as retrogression, and sudden enhancement not less than sudden reduction 'by ten, twelve, or fifteen per cent. ;' and let it be asked whether, for the sake of exemption from the one, labourers in general would be content to forego their chances of the other. Would they really agree that their rates of pay, like those of secretaries, managers, and clerks, should, for a longer or shorter term of years, remain absolutely stationary and unaffected by the vicissitudes of commerce ? Was such a proposition ever made by any trades' union ? If it should be made, the most obvious reason why employers might hesitate to accede to it would be a well-founded apprehension that the men would not by extra exertion in busy times make up for their inaction while business was slack. The plan might naturally seem to them unlikely to answer for either party. They might naturally fear that if the men had nothing to gain by working hard, they would set about their work as listlessly and lifelessly as clerks in certain public offices on fixed salaries are shrewdly suspected of doing, and without any of the mutual emulation which brings out individual skill and talent. But be this as it may, before the plan can be adopted, there must be a thorough change in the unionist mind, and a relinquishment of the more attractive half of the things on which its affections are at present set. For at present, at any rate, it is only the retrogressive element in fluctuation to which unionists object. They insist that the rate of wages shall never go back, but they are scarcely less eager that it should be frequently going forward. Mr. Harrison, indeed, assures us that the most perfectly-organised and most powerful of all trades' societies; viz., the Amalgamated Engineers, whose strength is so great ' that no contest with them would have a chance of success, and which is so well known that it never has to be exercised in a trade dispute of their own,' have neither raised wages nor attempted to do so during the last ten years. But this statement is not quite accurate,* nor, if it were, would it necessarily have all the significance that Mr. Harrison attaches to it. Until

* According to Mr. Allan, Secretary of the Amalgamated Engineers, although in London and Manchester, engineers' wages fluctuated little until within the last twelve months, in the North of England and in Scotland, they have improved vastly within the last few years—year after year almost. Mr. Allan also states that there have been three or four strikes within the last ten years, expressly for the purpose of raising wages—two at Blackburn, one at Preston, and one at Keighley.

a few months before he wrote, the London builders had, for an equally lengthened period, similarly acquiesced in a stationary scale of wages; but in their case, at any rate, it is clear that such exemplarly forbearance was the result not so much of moderation as of good strategy. For some years they had continued quietly taking the same wages, evincing indeed a firm resolution not to submit to reduction, but asking for no advance ; but it now appears that they were only waiting until an advance worth struggling for should seem to be obtainable by a struggle. When the opportunity came they changed their tactics at once, put forward a new claim, and on its being refused, struck, and obtained an advance of ten per cent. Without any lack of charity the Amalgamated Engineers may be suspected to have been, and to be similarly, biding their time. No doubt, as long as they have little prospect of being able to do more, they will easily content themselves with endeavouring to prevent a fall of wages ; but no doubt, too, and small blame to them for it, their union, and every other trades' union likewise, will avail itself of the first and of every opportunity of securing a palpable rise.

Small blame to them for this perhaps, but surely quite as little praise. In striving to secure for their constituents the highest possible price for the labour they deal in, trades' unions may be merely obeying the natural instinct of trade, but moderation is not precisely the quality of which they are thereby making the most edifying display. So however it is, by some unionists and by most philunionists, assumed to be. By these a complete justification of Unionism is thought to be afforded by the plea that it aims at nothing more than at placing the sellers of labour on a level with the buyers, and so doing away with the present commercial disparity between them. On this point especial stress is laid. Thus, according to Mr. Dunning, the object of Unionism is 'to ensure the freedom of exchange with regard to labour by putting the workman on something like an equal position in bargaining with his employer.'

According to Professor Fawcett, the object is 'that the labourer may have the same chance of selling his labour dearly as the master has of buying it cheaply.' Mr. Harrison follows with much to the same effect. Insisting on the notoriety of the fact that capitalist and individual workman are not on equal terms, he assumes, as an inevitable inference, 'that the all-important question is, how equality is to be established, and represents the placing of labour on the same footing as capital as the great desideratum.' A whole chorus of vigorous voices are here in complete accord, using the same key-note and ringing the changes on an equality between employer and employed, which is taken for granted to be the latter's inalienable birthright. Nor can it be denied that there is some plausibility in these harmonious utterances. To say that in dealings between man and man there ought to be no preponderating superiority on either side, does sound very like a truism, although, on a moment's reflection, the seeming truism will be perceived to be a fallacy. For to maintain that all men—and when universal equality is under discussion, special claims in behalf of working or any other particular men are of course quite out of the question—to maintain that all men have a natural and inherent right to be placed on the same footing as those who have got above them, is equivalent to saying that no man has a right to avail himself for his own benefit of any superiority, natural or artificial, which he may possess. This is one of those propositions which to state is to refute. However applied, its absurdity is manifest, but when applied by labour in vindication of the rights of labour, it becomes suicidal as well. For every genuine right of labour rests partially on a diametrically opposite principle. Unless men were at liberty to take full advantage of their individual superiority, unassisted industry would not be entitled to the exclusive possession of its own produce. A workman of superior strength or skill, how much more soever he might produce than his fellows, would not be justified in taking for his own use more fruit of his own labour than they were getting from theirs. The whole extra product he would be bound to throw into a common fund for common distribution. Nor is this all. Nothing is easier than to show that if labourers were really on the same footing as their employers, the equality between them would after all be but a sham and a cloak for the extremest inequality. To turn an acre or two of wild land into the counterpart of an English cornfield would, in many situations, demand an immensity of labour. If a single person undertook the work he might find in it abundant occupation for half-a-dozen years at least, first in fabricating the necessary tools and implements, then in grubbing up trees, trenching, draining, and fencing, collecting manure and procuring seed. Yet, when all these preparations had been made, a single additional season's toil would more than suffice for the production and garnering of one season's crop. Now suppose that when everything was ready for beginning that season's work, the reclaimer and owner of the soil became disabled, by sickness or otherwise, and that there should be but one other cultivator at hand whom he could hire to take his place on his little farm. Suppose, too, that in bargaining about terms both should be on an equality, that the one should need the other's services just as much as the other needed his employment. Evidently the latter would be in a position to insist that the season's crop should be equally divided between them, and evidently, too, if he did so, his share would be out of all proportion to his desert, inasmuch as he would get one-half of the fruits of an industry of which he had contributed less than a tenth. This is the sort of demand which servants would be enabled to press by being placed on a level with their masters, and no one, I imagine, will say that such demands deserve to be singled out as being eminently fair and reasonable. Quite as little, it is true, do they deserve to be stigmatised as unfair or unreasonable. Any servant who actually possessed the equality we are speaking of, would certainly have a perfect right to make the most of it, this right of his resting firmly on grounds to which allusion has more than once been made already, and to which we shall again have occasion to recur presently. But, on the other hand, argument cannot be needed to prove that if he did not happen to possess an equality which would enable him to enforce such monstrous inequality of conditions, abstract justice would give him no previous claim to it. Assuredly it would not be natural equity that recompensed a tenth of the toil with half the fruit, awarding that proportion of the harvest to one man for his pains in cultivating a field which another with ten times the pains had previously made cultivable. Nor, besides, is it the fact that trade societies look simply to equality—that they seek only to place the employed on a level with employers, and have no ambition to raise them higher. If we listen to what those societies sometimes say of themselves, as well as to what others say of them, we shall hear a very different story. We shall find that they have no notion of contenting themselves with an equal voice in the settlement of labour questions. They tell us plainly that what they aspire to is 'control over the destinies of labour'—that they want not merely to be freed from dictation but to dictate, to be able to arrange the conditions of employment at their own discretion ; and facts are not wanting to indicate how they would use such discretionary power if they had it. Already every now and then an opportunity offers, when they seldom fail to show that they are fully disposed to drive, on behalf of employed, quite as hard bargains with employers as ever were driven by employers with employed. Candidly professing such intentions, and, as far as their ability permits, conscientiously acting up to their professions, it would be passing the bounds of effrontery for them at the same time to pretend to moderation or to high-mindedness, and accordingly it is not so much unionists who take credit for either, as philunionists who give it them. Their own selected spokesmen have in general too much regard for consistency to lay claim to anything of the sort. They give themselves no magnanimous airs, they do not affect to have any but interested designs, and these they are at no pains to trick out with sentimental or rhetorical embellishments. They will tell you plainly, if you ask them, that the business of the employed is to look after their own interests, leaving employers, customers, and the rest of society to look after theirs,* and to shift for themselves as they best may. They will say that as it is the interest of masters to get labour at the lowest possible rate, so it is their interest as servants to get the highest possible rate of wages; † that they look upon masters as wanting to get the utmost profit out of their capital, and that they for their part seek to get the utmost profit out of their labour;‡ that, in short, their rule is to get as much as they can, and to keep as much as they can get.§

In such outspoken selfishness there is certainly nothing but its frankness to admire. Judged out of its own mouth, taken at its own estimate, Unionism certainly presents itself in no very engaging light. It confesses itself to be altogether of the earth earthy, without one whiff of sanctity about it, without the least spice of spirituality to qualify the grossness of its materialism. But though in its aims and aspirations there be little that is laudable, and a good deal that is very much the reverse, still it is only by reference to a far higher standard than that of ordinary human conduct that anything which there may be in them to condemn can be condemned. Tested solely by the rules of justice, and apart from any more generous considerations, Unionism, in so far as its ends are concerned, will pass the severest ordeal. Those at any rate who accept the principles laid

* Mr. Applegarth in evidence before Trades' Union Commission.— *Question* 149.

† Mr. Allan, ibid.—*Q.* 924.

‡ Mr. Connolly, ibid.—*Q.* 1349.

§ Mr. Allan, ibid.—*Q.* 861.

down in preceding chapters, have no alternative but to pronounce it quite unimpeachable in that respect. The same plea which has already been urged in support of the rights of capital will serve equally to justify the extremest views of Unionism. If an employer have a right to do as he will with his own, and to get the utmost for himself out of it, so equally has the labourer. If the former be justified in refusing to hire labour except on his own terms, however harsh those terms may be, the latter is similarly justified in refusing to be hired except on his own terms, however exorbitant those terms may be. In the sense in which the substantive 'right' has uniformly been used throughout these discussions, the labourer has an incontestable right to drive the hardest possible bargain in disposing of his labour. Before the bargain is struck the employer has no right to his services on any terms whatever, and if he would not be wronged by being refused them altogether, clearly he cannot be wronged by any particular terms on which they may be offered. Whatever, therefore, be the terms which labourers can contrive to extort by simply refusing to work for less, those terms they are fully warranted in extorting, not by reason of any relation they may bear to terms which might have been agreed to if the two parties had been upon an equal footing, but simply and solely because they are actually agreed to by both parties, however reluctantly, on one side or the other. And of course if labourers are warranted in insisting on the highest terms they can thus extort, they must be warranted likewise in raising themselves up to the best position for the practice of such extortion which they can by fair means attain. Of course they have no natural right to stand upon a level with employers, but, equally of course, they have a right to raise themselves artificially if they can, either to such a level, or above it. Now, to assist them in climbing as high as possible, to assist them in attaining to the highest possible vantage ground, is the one solitary thing—a tolerably comprehensive one, no doubt—which Unionism proposes to effect.

Many people, however—most people, indeed, who have no personal motive for thinking otherwise—evidently think that there are certain limits of remuneration which it would be unbecoming for manual labour to overstep. This rate of wages they style reasonable and suitable, that, disproportionate and extravagant. Even one so earnest as Lord Shaftesbury in every good and beneficent work, might not long ago have been heard indignantly declaring it to be altogether a mistake to suppose that Dorsetshire farm labourers are not very well off; for that, what with wages proper, perquisites, and allowances, many of them actually make up in money or kind an income of not less than 15*s.* a week. And it is noteworthy that, although Lord Shaftesbury's statistics were much disputed at the time, it was only with his facts that his critics quarrelled. No one denied that if his premises were correct, his inference would follow; no one questioned the abundant sufficiency of the supposed hebdomadal 15*s.* for an average family of the peasant sort. No one seemed to doubt that less than three-fourths of what many of us are in the habit of paying for a single dinner-ticket when we are about to eat to the success of some charity, might yet be ample to provide a whole week's breakfasts, dinners, and suppers for five or six persons, and to pay their rent, and buy coals and clothes for them besides. On the other hand, with what almost angry surprise some of us, during the iron-masters' lock-out of 1865, heard for the first time of the wages which some descriptions of iron-workers get? How we exclaimed on being told of shinglers with nearly 5*l.*, and of plate-rollers and rail-rollers with as much as five, seven, even ten guineas a week! And do we not still think there was a cause for exclaiming? Five, seven, ten guineas a week!—say, from nearly 300*l.* to between 500*l.* and 600*l.* a year! What business have mere mechanics—fellows with grimed faces and grubby hands—with rates of pay so ill-accordant with

the stations in life to which it has pleased God to call them ?
Why, as a Quarterly Reviewer piteously puts it, lieutenant-
colonels in Her Majesty's Footguards have less than the
highest of these rates, and passing rich among parsons are
those whose tithe commutation comes up to the lowest.
This being so, friends and connections of lieutenant-colonels
and parsons may naturally feel considerable disgust ; and
even impartial persons, unprepossessed in favour of either
the military or the clerical profession, may be disposed to
admit that both are somewhat scurvily treated. Under-
payment on one side, however, does not necessarily imply
overpayment on the other ; and if, instead of summarily
taking for granted that rail-rollers, for instance, are overpaid,
we set about attempting to prove them so, we may chance
to find ourselves not a little puzzled. For now we come to
think of it, what solitary reason, based on natural fitness,
can be assigned why there should be any differences in the
pay of manual and intellectual labour—yes, even of the
meanest manual and of the noblest intellectual ? Why
should not the same measure serve equally well for meting
out the material rewards of both ? Why should any
measure be more suitable than another for apportioning
the earnings of manual labour, or why should any measure
whatever be deemed too prodigal for that operation ? Not,
of course, that such labour has any special affinity for fifteen
or any other number of shillings a week, or that pounds in
equal number would not amalgamate with it equally well,
leaving behind no larger uncombined residuum. Not,
surely that a hard day's work costs less of exertion to a
hand-worker than to a head-worker. The lawyer or
accountant who may fancy that it does, had better take a
turn at the plough or the forge, and see whether, by the end
of the day, he will not be quite as much done up as if he
had passed the whole of it in court or in the counting-house.
Is it, then, because head-work demands for its performance
higher faculties than hand-work ? He is but a shallow pre-
tender to those same higher faculties who does not feel that

their very exercise is in itself a privilege carrying with it its own abundant and appropriate reward. And as for those who, knowing this, nevertheless fancy that *because* they get the pick of the work, *therefore* they are entitled to extra pay for it, their nearest likenesses are those Turkish Janissaries who, after eating a peasant out of house and home, used to exact additional piastres for wear and tear of their teeth during the process. But perhaps it is that coarse recipients of abnormally high wages might not know how to make a proper use of them. Well, possibly they might not, at any rate at first, but, if not, they would very soon learn. Possibly at first they might waste their increased substance in riotous living, guttling and guzzling as their betters used to do not so very long since, when 'drunk as a lord' was a proverb describing pretty accurately, as far as it went, the tastes and habits of high society. But this is a sort of malady which very speedily cures itself. To give money its due, though the root of all evil, it is also an excellent civiliser. There is no better solvent for softening manners and not letting them be fierce. Habitual use of those material refinements of life which it commands, helps, as much as anything, to make people refined. This it was, as much as anything, which caused the Sir Tunbelly Clumsys, the Squire Westerns, and Parson Trullibers of the eighteenth century to be succeeded by our decorous grandsires and fathers, and still more decorous selves. The same cause will no doubt make gentlemen of the sons and grandsons of the roughest and vulgarest, among newly enriched Australian gold-diggers ; and in proportion as the same cause may be permitted to operate on the working-classes everywhere, may those classes be expected to graduate in the humanities. Small fear, then, of high wages ever doing anything but good in the long run, or of their not doing good in proportion to their height. As small reason on this as on every other account why working-men should not try for the very highest they can get.

There is, in short, only a single, though at the same

time an all-sufficient reason, why professional or literate labour is generally entitled to larger remuneration than manual or illiterate, and that is, that owing to various circumstances, among which the special education it requires is but one, it can generally command a better price. It is generally entitled to more, because circumstances generally enable it to get more. But if circumstances should be so changed as to admit of manual labour getting as much or more than professional labour, manual labour would clearly become similarly entitled, and I do not hesitate to express my conviction that in such circumstances manual labour would be consulting the general as well as its own separate weal by insisting on having as much as it could, for a continuance, hope to get. Seeing that in every community the majority must always consist of working-class families, I cannot doubt that any lasting enhancement of wages—even though effected at the expense, in corresponding ratio, of profits—must be for the greater happiness of the greater number. I cannot doubt, for instance, that it would be for our national advantage if, for every millionaire employer among us, there were instead some two or three hundred of employed with revenues of two or three hundred a year each. So vast a change in the condition of hired labour is scarcely among the possibilities ; and even if effected, it would still be far from a thoroughly satisfactory settlement of industrial difficulties, very far indeed from that Utopia of labour of which I would fain hope it is no mark of want of sanity to dream. Many, indeed, may perhaps doubt whether for society as a whole it would not be the reverse of an improvement. But be this as it may, no one, I imagine, doubts that for working men, regarded as a class apart, it would be a change immensely for the better, and these therefore are only showing themselves wise in their generation by striving after the nearest possible approximation to it.

For the separate interests of labour there is but one case in which the remuneration of labour can possibly be too high, and that is when it is higher than the business in which the labour is employed can afford to pay continuously. In attempting to pass this limit, labourers run great risk of defeating their own object, but so long as, they stop short of it their aims cannot be unreasonable in any worse sense than that of being unattainable. Unfair they cannot possibly be in any sense whatever. Not more in their case than in any other can there be any moral default in owners insisting on their own terms for that which they are under no obligation to part with on any terms whatever. Now, to raise themselves into a position thus to insist, is, as has been said, the one sole thing after which trades' unionists seek. To enable themselves to get the highest obtainable wages, and to do in return the least possible work, doing that little, too, with the least possible inconvenience to themselves; to enable themselves, in short, to arrange for themselves, according to their own discretion, in what way, at what times, and on what conditions they will work—such, stripped of its various glosses, and represented in its natural colours, is their simple scheme. This is the whole head and front of their intending. Their Bill of Rights is comprehensive enough in all conscience; but it embraces nothing of which they either are, or, with reference merely to average human disinterestedness, have any cause to be, ashamed. There is not the smallest occasion, therefore, to attenuate its aggregate sternness by splitting it into a multiplicity of meek-looking details. It provides for the redress of all imaginable grievances. It would be superfluous, therefore, even if strictly accurate, to lengthen out the list by enumerating among them, ' excessive labour, irregular labour, spasmodic over-work, spasmodic locking-out, over-time, short-time, double-time, night-work, Sunday-work, truck in every form, overlookers' extortion, payment in kind, wages reduced by drawbacks, long pays, or wages held back, fines, confiscations, rent and implements irregularly stopped out of wages, evictions from tenements, black lists of men, short weights, false reckoning, forfeits, children's labour, women's labour, unhealthy labour, deadly factories and processes, unguarded machinery, defective machinery, preventible accidents, recklessness from desire to save.' It would be useless, even if not otherwise objectionable, to speak of these things as constituting 'a waste of human life, health, well-being, and power, not represented in ledgers nor allowed for in bargains.' So, however, speaks one with whom I have too many feelings in common not greatly to regret that I am so often compelled to express dissent from his opinions, and Mr. Harrison must forgive me for adding, that it may be not simply useless but mischievous also to describe the 'dark catalogue' he has been at the pains to draw up, now as 'one universal protest against injustice from the whole field of labour,' and now as 'one long indictment against the recklessness of capital and the torpidity of the legislature.' For some of the items included in it, the men, if not wholly accountable, are at least as much accountable as the masters, while others are unavoidable and inseparable from the occupations in which they occur. So far, however, as they are remediable, a means of remedying them might, doubtless, be expected to result from acquisition by trades' unions of the predominance to which they aspire. If the tables were completely turned between employers and employed, so that the power of prescribing the terms of employment, which hitherto has virtually belonged to the former, should pass over to the latter, little more would probably be heard from the same side as before, of oppression of any kind ; it would no longer be from the men that complaints of extortion, confiscation, false weights and false reckoning, would proceed, nor would it be their names that would be inscribed in black lists. Ample reason then have they for desiring a predominance which in their hands and for their purposes would possess such remedial efficacy; and to prove that they are fully warranted in aspiring to that which they thus desire, would merely be to repeat what

has been already said. The single aim of trades' unions is to
enable themselves to dictate arbitrarily the conditions of
employment. Whatever of good or evil can be urged for or
against their pretensions may be briefly comprehended in
this saying. Now such dictatorial power, how much soever
their acquisition of it is to be deprecated, is nevertheless, provided only it be attainable by legitimate means, a perfectly
legitimate object of pursuit. For by legitimate is merely
meant that which a man has in so far a right to do, to have,
or to exercise, that he does not thereby interfere with the
rights of anyone else, nor consequently wrong anyone else;
and nothing can be clearer than that labourers cannot possibly be wronging others by merely dictating, however imperiously, the terms on which alone they will part with
labour which they are under no obligation to part with at
all, and which none have a right to exact from them on
any terms whatever. This is the principle which serves
Unionism as its moral basis, and no principle can be more
rigorously or punctiliously just. In so styling it I am far
from saying that all the practical applications made of it
for Unionist purposes are the wisest possible. I do not say
that because the views of Unionism are legitimate they
cannot also be shortsighted. Whether they are so or not
is a question which will come before us in its turn, and to
take it here out of its turn would only lead to confusion.
Still further am I from saying that all the views of Unionism
are praiseworthy. On the contrary, if anyone choose to
stigmatise them as grovelling and sordid, I am not concerned to reply. I have no wish to disguise the partial
truthfulness of the charge. Only one might have supposed
that to be grave while making it would exceed all power of
face. For the domestic charity which begins at home and
never stirs out, is cherished with about equal fondness by all
ranks and conditions of men. 'Everyone for himself and
God for us all,' is a maxim not so much more in vogue
with the poor than with the rich, with employed than with
employers, that the latter can prudently evince any disgust

at the former's addiction to it. The dwellers in the most transparent and brittlest of glass houses are not precisely those who should begin throwing stones at their neighbours. Employers reproaching the employed with sordid greed suggest a number of familiar parallels—Peachum aghast at Lockit—the Gracchi complaining of sedition, or Mr. Beales of Mr. Finlen's Hyde Park demonstrations—Spain keeping fast hold of Ceuta yet abusing England for not giving up Gibraltar. In judging others they condemn themselves equally. The self-seeking they protest against is itself a protest against that exactly corresponding self-seeking of their own, which, from the beginning until now, has inexorably pursued its course, leaving their dependents to shift for themselves in a slough of despond by the wayside, and to sink or to struggle through as they best might. It is but the assertion by the employed of a right of Labour, the exact correlative of a right of Capital which has generally been used directly against them, and which has almost always been exercised with remorseless disregard of their welfare. What need of further words to show that this correlative, must necessarily be also a genuine, right ?

CHAPTER II.

WAYS AND MEANS OF TRADES' UNIONS.

WE come now to the means at the disposal of trades' unions for the achievement of their ends. On this part of the subject public opinion has of late made a remarkable advance. Ten or a dozen years ago, an apologist for Unionism might still have found himself under the necessity of formally vindicating the abstract right of combination, and of humbly pleading that if every individual workman be at liberty, as he obviously is, to refuse to work except on his own terms, any number of workmen must be equally at liberty collectively to refuse to work except on terms to which, after consulting together among themselves, they may have collectively agreed. Ten or a dozen years ago this plea would have been far from superfluous; for though combination in support of the pretensions of labour was no longer punishable by law, it was still so generally confounded with conspiracy, that any attempt to distinguish between the two would have been sure to have been looked upon as over-refining or worse. Ours, however, is a proverbially fast age: the revolutionary novelties of yesterday are the conservative commonplaces of to-day; and no one now, in speaking of trades' unions, would venture to show himself so far behindhand as to dispute the right of unionists to unite. Everyone now concedes to labourers, for the promotion of their common interests, the utmost freedom of collective action not inconsistent with individual liberty. Anti-unionists now confine themselves to alleging that when collective action takes the form of Trades' Unionism, it not only actually does, but necessarily must, interfere very objectionably with individual liberty, both with that of unionists themselves and with that of persons outside the pale of their association. The purpose of the present paper is to determine how much truth there is in the first of these allegations, and whether there be any truth in the second ; but, in order that we may be qualified to answer these questions, we must first acquaint ourselves somewhat particularly with the facts and phenomena to which they relate.

In theory a trades' union is the result of a spontaneous concurrence of atoms. The constituent members are supposed to come together entirely of their own accord, and to remain together solely because it suits them. In theory, too, the constitution is unalloyed democracy. All functionaries are appointed and all laws enacted by universal suffrage, and the same breath which has made unmakes both. Regulations adopted by general consent define the ordinary routine of procedure, and all extraordinary measures, all deviations from the prescribed course, require an equally popular vote to legalise them. This is the theory, and there must have been a time when the practice corresponded. The first apostles of Unionism could not have been in a position to use any but persuasive arts, and must have been fain to content themselves with discoursing or haranguing on the blessings of concord and unity, and the combative efficacy of fraternisation. It can only have been to conviction or importunity that their earliest proselytes yielded. Others may next have come in, enlisted by fellow-feeling or the strong contagion of example ; but no other sort of compulsion either was or could be resorted to, nor was any other force available to secure obedience to rules which were not generally approved. For a while, therefore, voluntaryism and equality may have been exhibited in the most perfect

form compatible with the inherent imperfectibility of all
human things. For a while only, however, and that but
a brief one. As members of a press-gang, even though
they themselves may have originally volunteered for the
service, bring without compunction any amount of pressure
to bear bludgeon-wise on the heads of eligible recruits, so
are professors of Unionism, in whatsoever manner they
may themselves have been converted, accustomed to mingle
a good deal of roughness with their zeal to make further
converts. As long as they are greatly outnumbered in the
shop, or mine, or factory, they may be politic enough to
restrict themselves to simple argumentation ; but as they
grow in numbers, their humility is often exchanged for
insolence, and as soon as they find themselves in a sufficient majority, they become very apt to play the bully.
Sometimes they will not tolerate the presence of a non-
conformist minority, refusing positively to let non-unionists
work in their company. In some societies this is enjoined
by express statute. One rule of the Glasgow bricklayers
is that 'no member of the society shall serve any master
who employs bricklayers that are not members of the
society.' At Bradford and many other places the plasterers
have a rule that 'no plasterer be allowed to work in any
shop more than six days without giving satisfaction to the
shop steward either that he is a member or will join the
society.' The brickmakers and the house-painters of Manchester have similar rules, and so, too, have the Liverpool
upholsterers and shipwrights, the Glasgow bakers, the
printers belonging to the Provincial Typographical Association, and the associated collier seamen of the north-
eastern ports. In a trade under the influence of one of
these societies, a master has to choose between unionists
and non-unionists. If he admit any of the latter, the
former leave him in a body ; generally, however, first
letting him know why. 'But,' continues one of the rules
just quoted, 'if after being properly warned of his error,
and having had the advantages of the society most ex-

plicitly made known to him, he refuse to desist, then, in that event, the whole of the members in said master's employment are to withdraw directly and come upon the box.' To large employers the choice thus allowed, may be practically no choice at all; either they may be unable to get as many non-unionist hands as they need, or the hands, if procurable, may not be of the right sort; for it so happens, and the fact is one of which we shall do well to take particular note, that though there are plenty of unionists who are not good workmen, there are comparatively few good workmen who are not unionists. A master in a large way of business can scarcely, therefore, continue in it unless he consent to employ none but unionists, in accordance with their own exclusive law, which is sometimes so rigidly enforced that a master is not permitted to accept the aid of his own nearest relatives in his own handicraft, but, like Mr. Howroyd or Mr. Dixon, masterplasterers of Bradford, is required to discharge his own nephews or his own brothers if they have not joined the union. Employers on a small scale, requiring fewer hands, enjoy more freedom of selection; but this they cannot always exercise without serious risk both to themselves and to any non-unionists whom they may engage. If they happen to be established in or near Sheffield or Manchester, there is no small probability of their having their machinery and stock-in-trade injured or destroyed, and their horses hamstrung, and of their men being robbed of their tools or personally maltreated. There is also at least a possibility that outrage of the latter description may extend to mutilation or murder. It will be recollected that the offence for which poor Fearnehough had the room in which he was sleeping blown up three Octobers ago, was that of having retired from the union of his trade, and then working with an employer from whom unionist workmen had been withdrawn.

In other societies, in which there is no written law against the employment of non-unionists, the members can very sufficiently supply its want by being a law unto themselves. Without absolutely refusing to work with non-unionists, they can easily contrive that any exceptional non-unionists, working in a shop in which they are themselves in a majority, shall have but an indifferent time of it. The inter-lopers are made to understand that they are there only on sufferance, most likely having got in only because there were not a sufficient number of unionist workmen at hand. They know that, if the main body of their mates were to insist on their being discharged, the employer would scarcely dare to refuse. They know that the only chance of their being borne with consists in their themselves bear-ing all things patiently, and it is sometimes a good deal that is given them to bear. Some of them indeed would not, perhaps, be permitted to enter the union if they wished it, for unionists are not desirous of having incompetent work-men as associates. They do not want to have the expense of maintaining in idleness persons incapable of earning that minimum rate of wages below which unionists are by their own laws prohibited from working. As a pledge of efficiency, therefore, candidates are generally required to have served an apprenticeship to the trade, or at any rate to have worked at it for a certain number of years. For the same reason, candidates in bad health, or of bad moral character, are frequently rejected. Such, too, as having once belonged to the union, had been expelled as defaulters, would most likely be refused re-admission ; and the door is likely to be closed also against those whose allegiance to the alehouse is evidently too exhausting to leave them the means of duly supporting any other institution. Such men, not being desirable associates, are readily exempted from joining ; but similar toleration is not extended to any who cannot claim it on the same ground of unworthiness. Eligible members who will not allow themselves to be elected, but stand aloof for con-science' sake, should be prepared to be martyrised accord-ingly. The gentlest comment passed upon their contumacy consists of reproaches of the meanness that shrinks from the expense and responsibility of combination, yet gladly participates in its advantages; and the contempt which their conduct excites usually vents itself in numberless insults and annoyances. Every occasion is taken to snub them; choice nicknames are invented for them; none but recusants like themselves will drink, or smoke, or chat with them; within a society shop there is little peace and less comfort for them. Yet they are loth to leave; for another fact deserving to be specially noted is, that trade is generally brisker, and that wages are generally higher, in society than in non-society shops. They prefer, therefore, to stay where they are, rather than, by going farther, to fare worse pecuniarily. But few who remain continue proof against the unceasing persecution to which they are there subjected, and their own natural disposition to do as all around are doing, and most before long end by joining the union. Their joining sooner or later is indeed so much a matter of course, that dilatoriness in the matter is sometimes treated as an offence to be punished retrospectively. One eminent trades' union has the following among its rules: 'Any persons, when asked to join this association, being obstinate and causing delegates' deputations or any other expenses to be incurred by their obstinacy, shall pay all such expenses, together with the amount of entrance or re-entrance as the case may be.' Nonconformists are thus admonished that they had better come in at once, since the longer they delay the more it will cost them at last.

Thus, although in trades' unions volunteering may be the rule, pressing, or something nearly akin to it, is an exceedingly frequent exception; and of course recruits who have been brought into a society against their will are not allowed to have altogether their own way in it. At best, they would have to submit to the will of the majority. On whatever policy the greater number of members resolved, in that the smaller number would have to acquiesce, the only alternative for dissidents being to secede from the society, which they would probably be prevented from doing both by the same reasons as had induced them to join, and in addition by unwillingness to forfeit the insurance privileges to which their past subscriptions entitled them. Occasionally their submissiveness is sorely tried, particularly during the continuance of what is technically called a 'strike.' This name, notwithstanding its aggressive sound, indicates, as everyone knows, rather passive than active warfare. The men do not, except as a rare variation from ordinary practice, come to actual blows with the masters ; they simply desert them, taking themselves off in a body, and thereby ofttimes imitating, in more respects than one, the Roman commons, when the latter withdrew to the Mons Sacer, and were taught in consequence duly to appreciate the moral of the ' Belly and the Members.' Having thus struck work, and having consequently no longer any current wages to live upon, they are thrown for support on their own previously accumulated reserves, and on subsidies from fellow-unionists and sympathising allies. These together are often considerable enough to admit of families drawing subsistence-allowance at the rate of 10, 12, or 14 shillings a week ; but it is only when the 'turnouts,' as they are styled, form but a small fraction of the whole society, that so exhausting a drain on the exchequer can be long continued. If the strike, instead of being confined to a few establishments, extend over the union's whole territorial range, the weekly doles grow rapidly smaller and smaller, and their recipients more and more select, until the former dwindle down to almost nothing. While this is going on, terrible are the straits to which hundreds, perhaps thousands, of families are reduced. They had found it hard enough at first to descend from aggregate earnings of perhaps 4*l.* or 5*l.* a week to an alimony of barely twice as many shillings, but when even this pittance fails them, they are compelled, in order to keep themselves alive, to part with every article they possess that can be turned into bread. Watches, ear-rings and wedding-rings, tables and chairs, bedding and clothes, all disappear one after another, each item, as it is given up, diminishing the probability that any good will after all result from so many sacrifices. And among those who thus despoil themselves there are always many who are far from satisfied as to the sufficiency of the cause for their so doing. Several, from the beginning, may have thought the object either hopeless or not worth the cost of a struggle; others, after a brief experience of the bitterness of industrial strife, would be heartily glad to return to their former peaceful routine. Ask any of these, if you can get them by themselves, and out of hearing of their fellows, why, wanting work and having work within their reach, they do not seize upon it, instead of standing idle all the day long, and you will find few with sufficient faith in the policy they are pursuing to attempt to vindicate it. Rather they will lay the blame of their tacitly-admitted perverseness on 'their mates, or the society, or the committee.' They will give you to understand that, if they pleased themselves, they would at once resume their wonted labour, and that it is to please their companions that they loiter about doing nothing, starving themselves, and seeing their wives and children starve. Yet, although in such behaviour self-abnegation and abdication of private judgment are carried to an extreme, still, if that were all, there might not be very much to object to; so far there would be at least no proof of undue compulsion. The majority would indeed be having its own way in everything, disposing of all questions with absolute authority; but this would be no more than must needs happen in every society in which a majority in number is conscious of possessing also a superiority of strength. It must needs be that such a majority will govern, and govern absolutely; and if the society be one to which no member has a right to belong without the consent of the rest, it is no more than proper that the majority should govern absolutely, provided only that it govern also equit-

212 LABOUR AND CAPITAL IN ANTAGONISM. [BOOK III.

ably, and conform in all its proceedings to laws of perfectly impartial operation, which bear upon all individuals
equally. To despotism so tempered no one submits, except in so far of his own choice that he believes it to be
more for his interest to submit than to secede. The freest
and best-governed countries are never without malcontent
inhabitants, the most valuable portion of whose freedom
consists in the privilege of freely choosing between staying
where they are and leaving. When the general voice of a
nation is loudest for war, there are always individuals—all
Quakers, to wit—whose cry is for peace. In our last
opium quarrel with China, the folly and wickedness of
which were so vehemently denounced by Mr. Cobden and
Mr. Bright, it cannot have been otherwise than galling to
those conscientious statesmen to reflect that they were
contributing towards the expenses of an unjust war, and
thereby taking part with the oppressor. Yet an obvious
alternative was open to them. No force was used to prevent their expatriating themselves. They, and those who
thought with them, might have effectually evaded the payment of war-taxes by breaking up their establishments,
winding up their affairs, and transporting themselves and
their property to some neutral soil ; and this course, it
may be presumed, they would have adopted, but that
on weighing the advantages against the disadvantages of
British citizenship, they found the former preponderate.
Quite possibly the acquiescence of dissentient unionists in
a strike or other measure to which they were averse might
be the result of similar calculations. Quite possibly in an
union in which a majority governed despotically, the minority who obeyed might yet be an unforced minority,
deliberately casting in their lot with Unionism, because, in
spite of its burdens and restraints, they believed it to do
them, on the whole and in the long run, more good than
harm.

This would be a perfectly intelligible explanation of
unionist loyalty, and it is accordingly very commonly put

forward by unionist advocates, but it is also one about which a non-unionist public has always been justly incredulous. Observers from without the unionist pale have always taken a more commiserating view of what goes on within. The absolutism of one kind or other which evidently presides there has always been suspected to be that, not of a widely-spread and overwhelming many, but of an isolated and overbearing few. On this point there was, until lately, no basis firm enough for more than suspicion ; little was certainly known, and almost everything had to be guessed ; but the fewer the facts the more scope for fancy, and imaginative minds did not fail to make the most of the mystery. The popular notion used to be that the government of a trades' union occupies much the same place in relation to its subjects as Loyola's Holy Office once did in reference to the Romish Church. On the one side was supposed to be an insolent junta sitting apart in gloomy conclave, and from its secret lurking-place issuing imperious edicts and darting fearful vengeance on the disobedient ; on the other, an abject crowd, brought, in the first instance, under the yoke by cajoling or bullying, and then suffering themselves to be goaded hither or thither as their drivers listed, without more thought of swerving from the appointed track than cart-horses have of turning agninst the carter's whip. Such was the notion inculcated by the 'Times' when it was wont to speak of 'bands of workmen tamely and ingloriously surrendering their natural liberty, and becoming mere tools and instruments of an inquisitorial despotism, which makes terrible examples whenever its secret and imperious demands are disobeyed.' Such was the meaning of the 'Edinburgh Review' when, getting into full rhetorical swing, it used to declare that 'as the Continent is honeycombed by secret political, so is Great Britain by secret trades' societies, which, enforcing mysterious laws and arbitrary obligations by the hands of irresponsible agents, exercise a tyranny more oppressive than that of king or kaiser, extinguish the characteristic freedom

of the English labourer, not leaving him even the free disposal of the labour by which he lives.' Similar was the
purport of some of the clever cartoons exhibited, from time
to time, by artists of *Mr. Punch's* school, representing now,
perhaps, a lean and tattered unionist accepting alms from
a non-unionist at the gate of an union workhouse, and now
the bare interior of another unionist's dwelling, where a
wretched mother crouches with her famished children beside
an empty grate, while a pursy delegate is rating the father
with the words, ' Going to work, are yer ? Going to give
in, are yer ? Not if I know it ! '

The exaggeration of such conjectural delineations is
patent on the face of them, and would indeed seem to be
by this time tacitly admitted by the draughtsmen themselves, who seldom now, in treating the same subject,
indulge in quite the same hyperbolical style. Yet over-
charged as the pictures are, there is beneath their over-
drawing and over-colouring a considerable underlayer of
substantial truth. In their most essential particular, that
of representing trades' unions to be under subjection to
close minorities or cliques, they only require to be somewhat reduced and toned down to be made to conform
pretty accurately with the reality. It is not far from what
is actually the truth to say that every trades' union is virtually, and either directly or indirectly, ruled by a minority
small enough to be called a clique—is either ruled by such
a minority plainly and openly, or, if ostensibly ruled by a
majority, then by a majority which is itself ruled by a
minority. That such is the actual condition of affairs has
now been established on evidence, but, previously to being
ascertained as a fact, it might have been confidently inferred, for the polity involved in the state of things assumed
is precisely that which might have been expected to result
from the acknowledged circumstances of the several cases.
It is in vain that constitution-mongers are everlastingly
trimming the balance, straining their ingenuity to discover
some means of maintaining an equipoise of political forces ;

average human intelligence must rise a good deal higher than it has ever yet done before the nicest arrangement of checks and counter-checks will avail aught against the resolute tendency of political power to concentrate itself in a few hands. The only thing much worth trying for, meanwhile, is to direct power into the hands most likely to wield it for the general good. These are assertions borne out by the experience of all communities, small and great; of trades' unions as well as of nations. In the former unalloyed democracy is invariably the theory, and in some unions no expedient that the wit of man can devise to maintain democracy in all its purity would seem to have been omitted. As an example may be mentioned the Amalgamated Carpenters, whom I select for the purpose as being likely to be better known to the general reader than most other trades' societies, through the vivid sketch of them which Professor Beesly, in his own savage Salvator Rosa-like style, dashed off some months ago in the pages of a popular Review.*

The union in question had, in the early part of last year, 190 branches or lodges, comprehending 8,260 members. A branch must consist of not less than seven, nor more than three hundred members. Each branch is itself a completely organised body, choosing its own officers, collecting, holding, and disbursing its own funds, and generally managing its own business. Its president and committee-men, if it be large enough to have a full complement of executive functionaries, are elected quarterly; its steward half-yearly; its secretary, treasurer, referee, and trustees annually; all at general meetings at which it is obligatory on every member to attend, on pain of being fined threepence if absent without written excuse. Once

---

* See 'Fortnightly Review' for March, 1867, Art. V. Professor Beesly will not regard the epithet in the text as other than complimentary, if he will recollect the following line in the 'Castle of Indolence' :—

'Which savage Rosa dashed, or learned Poussin drew.'

a week, for the transaction of ordinary business, the branch holds a general meeting, to which the minutes of any committee meeting held since the last general meeting are submitted for confirmation, and by which appeals are heard from any individuals who, having been aggrieved by branch officers, have already appealed in vain to the branch committee, and who will yet, if they desire it, have one further appeal to an executive council in London. At the same fortnightly meeting the branch decides how much money shall be held by the treasurer for the purposes of the next fortnight, the balance being handed over to the trustees to be banked. The treasurer is required to give security, and is forbidden to disburse money except on written order from the secretary.

The central authority of the society is vested in a general council, consisting of a president and sixteen members, of whom six are elected by the metropolitan branches, and the rest by the country branches. Half the council retire every six months. But as the country councillors could not conveniently attend frequent meetings in London, the ordinary management is intrusted to the six London members, and to a chairman elected by the London branches, who together compose what is termed the executive council. This ministerial cabinet is clothed with large but carefully-defined authority. Its business is to see that the branches conform to rules, to maintain the several branches in financial equilibrium, to decide appeals from them, to authorise the establishment of new branches, to initiate, sanction, and terminate strikes. It can require a rich branch to subsidise a poor one, or can insist on the latter making up a pecuniary deficit by extra levies on its own members. If a branch get its accounts into confusion, or give any other cause for suspicion, the executive council can order a special audit, or send a deputation to investigate. If a branch disobey rules or resist lawful requisitions, the same council may lop it off.

But in the discharge of these functions the executive

council must adhere as nearly as may be to written law. Where the law is silent, it may decide summarily, trusting to a subsequent act of indemnity ; but it cannot alter or suspend a rule, or make a new one. These things can be done only either by a meeting of branch delegates, specially deputed for the purpose, or by the general council, which, in cases of adequate emergency, make a general collection of votes in all the lodges. A delegate meeting, being a slow and costly mode of procedure, has been resorted to only twice during the whole term of the society's existence. Usually the business of legislation has, through the medium of the general council, devolved upon the society at large, to whose decision, likewise, would doubtless be referred any question of practical policy of sufficiently extensive interest to warrant the reference. This would be done, for instance, in the case of a general strike throughout the trade, though industrial warfare has rarely, if ever, as yet, been waged on the scale that would be implied by a rising in mass of one of the larger unions. To the society at large is also, by the Amalgamated Carpenters, reserved supreme appellate jurisdiction. If any branch, by a majority of two-thirds, disputes a decree of the executive council, it has an appeal to the whole community. A statement of each side's case is printed and circulated through all the branches, and a majority finally decides. In short, the proceedings of both branch and central authorities are open to inspection, and liable to be checked at every step. Everything possible is done to keep the executive officers in their places as mere instruments for giving effect to the popular will.

The Amalgamated Carpenters and the Amalgamated Engineers are model societies, whose excellence of organisation none of the others have yet reached. Their pattern is, however, followed more or less closely by all such of the societies as, like themselves, are framed on a scale of national magnitude, so that the outline just drawn of the Carpenters' scheme of internal management may suffice to indicate the leading principle of the political constitutions of most trades' unions of the first class. Those of a somewhat lower grade, which, as being confined to one or two counties or other considerable districts, instead of ramifying over the whole kingdom, may be classed as provincial, have kept the same constitutional principle in view in the fabrication of their governmental machinery. Indeed, the acquisition or exercise by presidential functionaries of irresponsible or discretionary authority would seem to be, if possible, still more difficult in the 'provincial' than in the 'national' societies. In the former, the executive and general councils are still more frequently superseded by general meetings, and large questions of practical politics are referred, not exceptionally, but systematically and habitually, to universal suffrage. Now, practical politics, when the expression is used in connection with trades' unions, is commonly little more than an euphemism for strikes, and a strike in which an union of national dimensions engages is seldom or never extensive enough to involve all the associated branches in active operations. Usually, the actual 'turnout' is confined to one or to a few districts, while the others participate in the strife chiefly by contributing the material aid necessary for its maintenance. Strikes on the part of the larger unions are consequently almost always local, and among the Amalgamated Carpenters, and probably amongst most societies of national rank, it is the executive council that decides whether a local strike shall take place. But the largest of 'provincial' societies is not too large nor too much scattered to allow of the whole body striking together, or otherwise engaging simultaneously in a concerted and combined scheme. In order, however, that the whole body should be thus committed, their laws provide that the whole body should be consulted. According to a graphic account given by Mr. F. Harrison of the mode of procedure, before a general or other important measure is determined on, regular voting papers are sent round to all the members of the society. The step is discussed night after night in every separate lodge, and being one with the character of which every voter is familiar, and which 'touches his comfort, his family, and his future in the most vital manner,' is doubtless discussed with as much individual earnestness as so multitudinous an assemblage is capable of in discussing anything. Occasionally deliberation is facilitated by the deputation of delegates from every lodge, by whom frequent conferences are held, often followed by fresh appeals to the constituencies. The discussions, which are sometimes prolonged for months, are practically public, and the result is at length ascertained by a simple comparison of votes.

According to this programme, a fair share in the conduct of affairs is secured to every individual who is willing to accept it. Each associate possesses a potential voice, not merely in the choice of the society's governors, but in the determination of the society's policy. Selected helmsmen are placed in charge of the rudder, but the whole ship's company shout out collectively how the vessel is to be steered. Every single member is consulted before any law can be passed—before any course of action is resolved upon. He belongs to a commonwealth resembling, in its looseness of texture, the freest of ancient republics. In Athens itself less pains seem to have been taken to insure universal diffusion and equal distribution of political privileges. In Athens itself democracy was not so absolute or so little tempered, even by representative assemblies. If mere forms and institutions could suffice to create and to preserve spirit and substance, what M. Comte terms 'sociocracy' would here be flourishing in full development,—that latest and grandest conception of advanced reformers, 'a government of all by all and for all,' would here be completely realised. Unfortunately, very similar contrivances have signally failed in very nearly analogous cases elsewhere, and it cannot be said that signal success has attended those tried here. Railway boards of direction, not less than the executories of trades' unions, are hedged in on every side by constitutional checks. Their members likewise are elected by universal suffrage, hold their offices during pleasure, are required periodically to give account of their stewardship, and are liable to be summarily dismissed if they fail to give a good one. Yet we all know, and many of us to our cost, how easily and habitually railway directors overleap the barriers set to keep them in, playing ducks and drakes with their constituents' money, and sacrificing their public trust to some silly crotchet or personal pique or private end of their own. The shareholders have only to interpose in order at once to put a stop to these malpractices; yet they generally prefer to let things take their course, looking quietly on, or more probably not looking at all, while land-owners and lawyers, contractors and engineers, in league with the directors, are fattening at their expense. Scarcely ever, except when, Beelzebub dividing against himself, some offended member of the board turns informer against his colleagues, and exposes their and his own iniquities, will the shareholders bestir themselves sufficiently to turn out the old and call in a new dynasty, most likely thereby merely inaugurating a fresh era of misrule.

Now, on no account would I do the office-bearers of a specimen trades' union like the Amalgamated Carpenters the injustice of supposing them to be on the same low level in point of morals as the generality of railway directors; but there can be no offence in suggesting that the former exercise an authority, acquired in much the same manner, and much the same in nature and extent, as that which the latter so shamefully abuse. Both sets of func-tionaries owe their elevation to the same cause—their well or ill deserved reputation. Trades' unionist council or committee-men are, in the first instance, like the first batch of railway directors, appointed because they are believed to be the fittest persons for their situations, and for the same reason they are subsequently continued in office, or from time to time re-elected. Mr. Applegarth, the estimable secretary of the Amalgamated Carpenters, has occupied his post for six years uninterruptedly, and, if his constituents are wise, will be continued in it as long as he may be willing to retain it. Half the councillors with whom he is associated are understood to retire at the end of every six months; but probably, like railway directors, they are immediately re-eligible, and in general are re-elected accordingly. If so, council and secretary may exercise concurrent jurisdiction. If not, then new and inexperienced councillors will, as such, be all the more disposed to follow the guidance of an experienced secretary. But whether the secretary avowedly take the lead with the council backing him, or whether he more modestly concur with the council in the prosecution of measures of his own prompting, there can be no reasonable doubt that even in a trade society as jealously framed as that of the Amalgamated Carpenters, the office-bearers of the society—those appointed to be its servants or ministers—have, like ministers in general, the virtual direction of affairs. On this point it is permissible to theorise somewhat confidently. No special knowledge of the facts, only some general acquaintance with human nature, is required to convince us that one or more master-minds must be the motive spirits of trade societies as of all other associations.

Of course the associated mass need not be moved against its will—of course it may act for itself, if it please; but acting for oneself implies thinking for oneself, and there is scarcely any operation of which most men are so anxious to be saved the trouble. Ninety-nine out of every hundred met together for the express purpose of comparing thoughts will generally let the hundredth do all the real thinking, if he offers. In the noisiest assembly the echoes are always out of all proportion to the voices. When Solomon spoke of there being wisdom in a multitude of counsellors, he was clearly either joking or thinking only of that sort of sagacity which a parliamentary leader sometimes shows in educating his party, even to the following him in a leap down Niagara in the dark. Mankind must become very different from what they either are or ever have been, before they will cease to permit themselves to be led like sheep. In Athens, when Athens was freest, the chief use which the collective citizens made of their freedom was to determine whether Pericles or Cleon, Demosthenes or Æschines, should lead. To follow their own devices was an idea that seldom entered their heads; and as seldom, in all probability, do the Amalgamated Carpenters take much greater liberty than that of similarly choosing between Mr. Applegarth and his colleagues and some knot of rival aspirants seeking to supplant them. In every trades' union, the actual occupants of office, provided only they be tolerably firmly seated, are almost certainly in possession of quasi-dictatorial authority. They must be presumed to have been selected from their fellow-unionists because they were more generally esteemed and trusted than any others, and in due proportion to the confidence reposed in them will be their influence with respect to any question coming under discussion. They can, if they please, have the immense advantage of the initiative ; and whatever proposal or opinion they put forward will, simply as coming from them, be likely to be favourably received by the district branches. The members of each of these are indeed free to form an independent judgment, but the judgment of many of them will at once be that which the central council think best : in the same conclusion many more will agree because they see others agreeing, and more still from modesty and unwillingness either to run counter to the general feeling or to put themselves forward in what is as much everybody else's business as theirs. In this manner is commonly made up the majority which in all the larger trades' unions ostensibly rules, but which, though in a certain sense it may be said to take its own course, quietly permits a select minority to determine what that course shall be.

So it is that things are managed in unions of national or provincial rank. But there is also a third class, consisting of those which do not extend beyond the limits of one or two towns, and which even within those limits are not perhaps the only unions of their respective trades. In unions of this description, which we may distinguish as 'urban,' the members are comparatively both few in number and closely packed. In them, therefore, there are greater facilities than in the others for a government of all by all ; but it is in them, nevertheless, that there is the greatest concentration of the governing power. Universal suffrage might in them easily insist on being appealed to as constant referee in all matters, small and great; yet, instead of doing so, universal suffrage may occasionally in these smaller unions be found evincing its not unfrequent predilection for imperialism, by really leaving everything to be settled by one single individual. We paid some of the 'national' unions the compliment of comparing them to the Athenian commonwealth. If we would find parallels for the 'urban' also in the ancient world, we must turn to those small democracies of early Greece, which, as an apparent consequence of their diminutiveness, degenerated rapidly into aristocracies or autocracies. When those petty republics were being constituted, the most capable, or otherwise most influential, citizens were naturally installed in all places of trust: because of their capacity or influence, they were subsequently left a good deal to themselves in the discharge of their functions, very little watched, and still less interfered with; for the same reason they were continued permanently in office, and were, moreover, allowed to fill up vacancies among themselves by nominations of their own. By degrees the prerogatives thus habitually exercised acquired the sanction of prescription, so that men who had begun as servants and agents of democracy ended by transforming themselves into an irresponsible self-elected oligarchy. If among these oligarchs one should make his appearance of more force of character than his colleagues, he might thereby acquire supremacy over the rest, and assume the same relation to them as they were bearing to the rest of their fellow-citizens. Very possibly, if our knowledge of the subject were sufficiently detailed, we might find that it was by a process like this that Orthagoras became tyrant of Sicyon, and Theagenes of Megara, and Kypselus, and after him Periander, of Corinth; and our knowledge of circumstances does actually warrant our asserting that it was in this way that Mr. William Broadhead became tyrant of the Sheffield Saw-grinders. This last-named celebrity would seem to be a sort of genius in his own evil way, and to have been enabled, by his peculiar talents, to attain to an autocratic sway which no other unionist functionary has succeeded in reaching. Evidently he lorded it over his colleagues as completely as he and they together lorded it over their union. But though the ruling junta to which he and they belonged may have been a phenomenon almost unique in some particulars, still, reasoning from analogy, we may confidently assume that in most 'urban' trades' unions there are corresponding juntas bearing considerable resemblance to it in functional attributes, however dissimilar in the personal characters of the members. We shall, at any rate, not be far wrong in concluding that the concentration of governing power which we have perceived to be tolerably close in 'national' and 'provincial' unions, is in 'urban' unions still closer, and still more incompatible with the existence of any real governing majority.

How the power which, in one or other of the modes thus indicated, an unionist executory is permitted to acquire, may be used for the coercion or persecution of refractory unionists may be easily imagined, and not the less easily because, as is frequently objected, the persons supposed to be coerced are members of the body from which is derived whatever power, coercive or other, the executory possesses. Everyone knows how often it happens that persons who evidently might be masters of the situation, if they chose, as evidently are not, tamely suffering themselves to be browbeaten and led by the nose by their own creatures and dependents. No one can at any rate need to be reminded how often a husband's life is made a burden to him simply because he will not take trouble enough, or pluck up spirit enough, to keep a termagant in order. And in such a case the superiority of brute strength is always on the side of the husband. It is nothing but superiority of mind that gives the wife her victory over matter. So that if the commanding spirits who commonly compose an unionist executory were seen to be, by virtue solely of their mental ascendency, riding roughshod over a reluctantly submissive constituency, there would be nothing unprecedented in the sight. In reality, however, such an executory, in dealing with re-cusants, has generally a majority of loyal adherents at its back—a majority sometimes zealously active, sometimes only passively acquiescent, but in either case affording powerful support, physical or moral, or both, to the con-stituted authorities. Thus backed, the latter need be at no loss how to make their power felt. In the prosecution of any policy of which the bulk of the society have formally approved, the bulk of the society naturally go with them, sanctioning, as a matter of course, when any recognised regulation is broken, infliction of the punish-ment for that case made and provided—pecuniary fine, probably, or expulsion, if persistent contumacy seem to demand so extreme a penalty. But even though no es-tablished law be infringed, and even though lukewarmness in the common cause, or non-unionist proclivities, be the worst delinquencies to be corrected, popular opinion will be apt to wink at the adoption of various irregular modes of making the offenders sensible of the general displeasure. And unionist authorities are in possession of the full average amount of official facilities for annoying opponents and rewarding adherents. It is to them that large em-ployers in want of hands commonly apply. They can therefore assist men in getting work, or prevent their getting it, or they can secure good employment to some, and leave to others only such service as would be sure to be refused if there were any choice. In their gift are delegate-ships, and other paid agencies, appointments greatly coveted by unionists of a peripatetic disposition, or with a taste for diplomacy—just the persons, by the way, most likely to become troublesome rivals to those in power if not con-ciliated. In their keeping, too, is the box which furnishes the subsistence allowances of men out of work, and in the distribution of whose contents favoured idlers may easily be permitted to obtain more than their due shares. A witness before the late Sheffield Commission avowed that he had been 'on the box' for four years continuously, drawing regularly 17s. 6d. a week, and doing nothing all the time but what the box-keepers bade him. 'And it warn't bad wage neither,' added he jocosely. Many of this fellow's mates—no less than eighty, he said—had been permitted to do the like. From the same box secret service money in a variety of other shapes can as easily be drawn by those who have the charge of it. Should, then, these be inclined towards persecution, they need not re-frain for want of suitable instruments to carry out their plans. No association held together by a common creed, social, political, or religious, is ever without its zealots and ruffians, and its mixtures of both; and trades' unions have quite an average proportion of all three descriptions. We have now positive evidence, and if we had not, we might still be almost equally sure, that in every large body of trades' unionists, individuals may be found as ready as Italian Carbonari or Irish Ribandmen to do whatever their leaders require and will pay for.

From what has been said, it is clear that unionist executories have all the requisite capacity for practising the compulsion with which current belief charges them. It is moreover certain that they all do actually practise it to a greater or less extent, the precise extent depending in each instance partly on the collective character of the particular union concerned, partly on the separate characters of the unionist officers, both of which conditions vary immensely in different cases. Trades' unions differ from each other not more in magnitude than in every other attribute. In moral sentiments and in all the outward manifestations thereof, their range embraces every gradation, from the decorous sobriety of the Amalgamated Engineers or Carpenters, to the fiendish excesses of the Sheffield Saw-grinders. And as of the aggregate associations, so likewise, or rather more decidedly, of the individual associates, between whom the shades of difference are more numerous still. No one can have had extensive intercourse with unionist functionaries without having met with many amongst them as honourable and upright, and, in proportion to their opportunities, as intelligent men as any living. No one, on the other hand, with any experience of life, can doubt that among persons at once so much trusted and exposed to so much temptation, there must be plenty, also, of arrant knaves. Many of them are probably, as Mr. Harrison says, ' the best workmen as well as the best men in all respects ' of their several trades; and in addition to this general commendation, they often deserve the special praise bestowed upon them by the same writer as ' honest, sensible men of business, of tried character and ability, going through much of hard clerk's routine and reports ' for very scanty remuneration. But though the good often deserve all the good that has been said of them, the bad quite as often are as bad as bad can be, noisy, greedy demagogues, ' all tongue and stomach,' getting into office by dint of rant and cant, and seeking it only for the sake of its loaves and fishes, its beer and brandy-and-water, its petty state and privileged laziness, and the facilities it affords for embezzle-ment and peculation. Of such lures to low ambition there is generally no lack. The bare official salaries are indeed invariably small. The Engineers, whose society is probably as liberal as any, give only 25*s.* a year to some of their branch secretaries, and less than ten guineas to those best paid. The general secretary of the Amalgamated Carpenters gets 130*l.* a year. To members of their central executive committee the Engineers allow eighteenpence each for an ordinary evening attendance. These moderate rates, however, may be materially supplemented by extraordinary additions. For attendance at a day meeting, an Engineers' committee-man gets the full equivalent of his usual wages, plus 5*s.* or 7*s. 6d.*, according to the distance he may have had to come. A delegate of the same society on deputation gets, over and above both his usual wages and his actual travelling expenses, 7*s.* a day for 'expenses.' The year before last the Sheffield Operative Bricklayers held a meeting of delegates to revise laws. It sat for a fortnight, and cost the society 1,088*l.*, each member receiving 11*s. 6d.* a day, besides money for lodging and railway fares, and 6*d.* a day for refreshments. Some five-and-twenty years ago a working-class friend of mine, then a weaver's boy, was sitting in a bookseller's shop at Stockport waiting for a parcel, when another customer entering, was greeted by the shopman with the words, 'Well, Jack, what art doing now?' 'Oh! I'm delegate for Preston strike,' was Jack's reply. 'And that pays better nor weaving, I'll be bound,' rejoins the first. 'And so the Preston lads be out still, ay?' 'Ay, that they be,' answers the other, 'and, by G—d, I don't mean 'em to go in again as long as they gie me my two guineas a week and my travelling expenses.' Then, though in every union there is plenty of office business to be done, it is in general very unequally distributed among those who are supposed to have the doing of it. 'What are the duties of a committee-man?' was asked by the Sheffield Commissioners of a witness who had been serving for sixteen weeks in that capacity. Witness 'didn't know.' 'What did you do yourself?' 'I sat still and supped ale.' 'What did the others do?' 'Many of them supped ale, too.' At the particular meeting about which the witness was being questioned, he had, he said, signed a paper drawn up by the secretary, but he had not read it, nor heard it read, nor did he know what was in it. 'Had, then, committee-men no duties besides that of supping ale ?' Deponent couldn't say ; during his sixteen weeks of office he had not discovered any. On this last point some additional light might perhaps have been thrown if a Lancashire operative instead of a Sheffield artisan had been under examination, and if it be true, as I have been credibly informed, that during the great Preston strike, the deputies from the central committee denied themselves the public use of ale, and bound themselves under penalty not to drink any liquor less 'respectable' than brandy. As for the probity of gentry of this description, that there can be no breach of charity in presuming to be in about inverse ratio to their self-indulgent propensities. One of our principal courts of so-called justice has latterly pronounced fraud and robbery not to be crimes when committed against trades' unions, thereby, as it were, giving public notice that those associations may henceforward be cheated and pillaged with impunity. How trades' unions will henceforward fare, after having been thus formally outlawed, is a question which may well cause them much anxiety, for even while still supposed to be under ordinary legal protection, they were already sufficiently exposed to depredation. Even the Amalgamated Carpenters have suffered seriously from the dishonesty of their trustees and other officers ; and when all the precautions of the best regulated societies did not save them from loss from this cause, more negligent societies of course did not escape. Against one of these, frauds to the amount of 640*l.* are recorded to have been committed in one year. As may readily be imagined, little security against the faithlessness of unionist functionaries is afforded by the obligation imposed on them of furnishing periodical balance-sheets. Some of the concoctors of those documents are evidently adepts at the peculiar branch of cookery which the business requires, perfectly understanding how to make an account balance by omitting receipts on one side or inserting imaginary disbursements on the other, or by entering items of both sorts on both sides indiscriminately. The results of this method of book-keeping are indeed liable to subsequent audit, but this is an ordeal as to which accountants who nominate their own auditors have no need to be apprehensive. Besides, if falsification of documents should seem likely to be insufficient, other more decisive modes of screening pecuniary misappropriations can be resorted to. Cases have occurred of suspected treasurers being required over night to bank on the following morning the sums which according to their books ought to be in their hands, and of their houses being burnt down or broken into and robbed during the interval. Secretaries have not scrupled at a pinch to tear from their ledgers inconveniently communicative pages, and by one of them the ingenious expedient was adopted of letting his book fall into the fire and leaving it there until consumed, because, as he pleaded afterwards in excuse, as there were no tongs in the room he might have burnt his fingers if he had attempted to remove it. Tricks like these, it need scarcely be said, are played only by fellows at the very bottom of that scale of executive morality, at the top of which stand the specimen functionaries of whom honourable mention was just now made. The space between the two extremes is occupied by an intermediate set more numerous than both the others united, and as much superior in character to those below as inferior to those above. Its members are selected for office, not indeed without reference to their official qualifications, but with considerable reference also to other recommendations, among which, by all accounts, convivial qualities figure conspicuously. It is perhaps indispensable that they should have scholarship enough to be able to draw up a plausible report or a flaming manifesto, but it adds greatly to their credit to be known also as jolly companions, discreetly merry over their cups, and able to sing a good song and tell a good story. Unionist functionaries are, in short, susceptible of the usual tripartite classification of some good, some bad, and many indifferent. The worst of them shrink from no means of accomplishing a desired end. The many middling, though much more scrupulous, not seldom play sufficiently fantastic tricks with the authority in which they are dressed, and even the select few whose habitual sobriety and decorum contrast most favourably with the excesses and vagaries of the others, are not absolutely unimpeachable on the same score. For the best of them are after all but human. That great labouring class from which all unionists, good and bad, are drawn, is composed, not of saints or angels, but as Mr. Gladstone justly insists, of 'our own flesh and blood,' of men of like passions with ourselves, liable to be tempted at all points just as we are, and not less liable to yield to temptation. Even working men's native instincts will not always serve them as infallible guides. Their 'bright powers of sympathy' are not always an adequate drag upon their 'ready powers of action.' Self-interest will now and again warp their judgment, self-importance puff them up, gusts of passion carry them away. In seasons of extraordinary ferment, during the excitement of a strike, or the provocation of a lock-out, even the most exemplary of unionist functionaries, being human, relax somewhat their ordinary exemplariness.

Here it may be useful, parenthetically, to advert to a suspicion somewhat prevalent with respect to unionist functionaries—that, viz., of their instigating or fomenting strikes from personal motives. I believe that for any charge of the kind there is much less foundation than is commonly supposed, and none at all so far as unions of the first rank are concerned. These seldom, if ever, have a general strike, and the management of their local strikes is usually assumed, not by the central, but by the branch authorities. Before a strike can be 'legally' commenced, the former must indeed have given their consent; but when they have consented, their share in the affair may almost be said to cease, the conduct of active operations, and all the honour and glory thence accruing, being monopolised by some little knot of local officers. These it is who hold cabinet councils or public levees in ale-houses, preside over large open-air gatherings, meet their late masters on equal terms at conferences, and see their names and speeches printed next morning in the county newspapers, while the central authorities remain apart in unnoticed obscurity, without other part in what is going on than that of making grants in its aid from the central treasury. This can scarcely be supposed to be an occupation much to their taste. They take a natural pride in the wealth of their society, and do not like to see it wasted, and experience has taught them that, even when there is an object worth striking for, a strike is a very wasteful mode of attaining it. The consequence is, that the executory of any one of the larger trades' unions, instead of being the most bellicose, is commonly the most pacific section of the whole community. Instead of originating strikes, it sanctions them only as a last resource, and systematically discountenances them when either the pretext seems inadequate or the time unseasonable. Continually it will be found remonstrating with a branch eager to fight, telling the latter, either that its demand is unreasonable or that its grievance is one that the society cannot recognise, or that other branches are more aggrieved and must have their turns first, or that though its case is a good one, the society have a heavy strike already in hand or impending. 'At least twenty times in as many months,' says Mr. Allan, of the Amalgamated Engineers, 'we have recommended that a strike should not take place.' 'About one third,' says Mr. Applegarth of the Amalgamated Carpenters, 'of the applications made to us to strike during the last few years have been refused.' 'Our parent society,' says Mr. Macdonald, of the House Painters' Alliance, 'never originated a strike, but it has stopped many.'

The same pacifying considerations exert a similar though less powerful influence on the presiding functionaries of unions of the second or provincial class. The largest of these is not so large as to prevent all its branches from engaging simultaneously in one general strike, of which the central authority would naturally take the direction, or to prevent the same authority from exercising immediate supervision over every local strike. That authority, therefore, is affected in only a lesser degree by the personal motives which the chief authority of a national union has for discouraging strikes, and the recent case of the Staffordshire Puddlers may be cited as one in which action on the part of the central executory was undoubtedly the exciting cause of the strike of a large portion of the men. One remarkable feature of this case was that when the Puddlers of the northern division of the county, having first turned out in compliance with a notice from headquarters, presently afterwards got an order to turn in again, they refused to obey. The leaders had in this instance forgotten something of their usual tact, and the men took huff at being so plainly given to understand that they were supposed to have no more will of their own than so many sheep.

It is, however, to the heads of unions of the third or urban class that the charge of fostering industrial strife is least likely to be altogether inapplicable. These naturally undertake the management of every strike that takes place within their narrow jurisdiction. They like its bustle and excitement; taking the lead in it tickles their vanity. All the money spent upon it passes through their hands. They have no reason, therefore, for being averse to a strike on their own account, and it is quite conceivable that they may now and then be tempted to get one up, perhaps to gratify a grudge against an obnoxious employer, perhaps for the sake of the additional emoluments and importance which they will obtain in consequence, perhaps out of the mere wantonness of conscious strength. Yet even in these smaller societies it is certainly only exceptionally that strikes are initiated by the constituted authorities. More commonly they originate with the men themselves, springing out of some grievance, real or supposed; and, more commonly still, their authors are the professional agitators, of whom, wherever unionism flourishes, a certain sprinkling is sure to be found hanging loosely about its skirts. In the clothing districts of Lancashire and Yorkshire, there is a regular gang of these vagabonds who have been at their dirty work for years, and of whom very edifying tales are told—not unfrequently by themselves, for among their intimates they are ready enough to boast of their skill in duping and selling their dupes. They will relate exultingly how at Stockport, after persuading a set of operatives to turn out, they arranged with the masters, for a consideration, to get them to turn in again; how at Bolton they got 50*s.* a head for persuading some factory hands on strike to go back to work on the same terms as before; how this or that master has connived at their proceedings; and how when a certain master, fearful lest his connection with a certain agitator should be betrayed, offered the latter 100*l.* to leave the country, the latter took the money and stayed at home all the same. There are few kinds of mischief-making for which fellows of this stamp are not ready, provided only they are paid for it. Some of the gang I am speaking of did actually once try to get up a Tory manifestation at Manchester against the repeal of the paper duties, as they would, any of them, be equally prepared to-morrow to get up a demonstration for or against anything whatsoever, the ballot or universal suffrage, or trades' unionism itself. But their special vocation is to kindle or fan dissension between employers and employed, and wherever they fancy they see a chance of setting these together by the ears, there are they presently in the midst of them, whispering some, haranguing others, spitting poison or spouting nonsense. These, from what I have been able to gather, I am inclined to believe to be the real authors of nine out of ten of such strikes as are not justly provoked by unreasonable pretensions or obstinacy on the part of masters. Nine times out of ten I believe such strikes are not instigated, but are simply sanctioned by the recognised unionist leaders, although sanctioned with very different degrees of facility by the leaders of different unions.

The temper and spirit with which strikes are carried on depend less than might have been expected on the mode in which they originate. Those who have the immediate direction of proceedings, although most probably they may not have instigated, but only assented to the outbreak, soon catch the contagious enthusiasm of strife, and enter into the contest with all their energies, showing themselves quite as eager for its success as if they had been its authors. Now, the success of a strike depends mainly on two things,—on the strikers obtaining sufficient funds for their maintenance, and on their preventing others from occupying the employments they have themselves vacated. To the securing of these two things, therefore, the directors of the strike, whether they be branch or central functionaries, devote their chief attention.

Money, the sinews of all modern warfare, is so in an especial manner of industrial belligerence. The latter's two principal operations, strikes and locks-out, are each of them a species of blockade, whereby one party is striving to starve the other out. Either the men take the initiative by turning out, in hopes that the masters will have to submit for want of labour, or they themselves are shut out by the masters in the hope that they will have to submit for want of food. When the strike is neither a general one, nor has been met by a lock-out, the men's best chance of being able to resist the necessity to which they are expected to be reduced, lies in their being regularly supplied by those of their fellow-unionists, who, when they took the field, remained, in accordance with usual strike tactics, quietly at work. Upon these, extraordinary levies are then made by the unionist authorities, four or five times as great, perhaps, as their usual subscriptions; but acquiescence in such heavy exactions involves a severe strain upon patience. To prevent, therefore, a virtue so easily fatigued by exercise from flagging, a system of counter-irritation is usually resorted to. One expedient for the purpose is the following. During the continuance of a strike, periodical balance sheets of receipts and expenditure are printed and circulated amongst those interested; but the contents of these documents are not always confined to dry financial details; their figured statements are occasionally diversified by miscellaneous interpolations, on reading which skulkers and defaulters are liable to find their delinquencies exposed in terms like these:—

'John Webster won't pay,—Blackburn's shame on him!'

'If W. Townson would spend less money on drinking, carding, dog and cock-fighting, he might spare something for the Preston Lock-outs.'

'If the single young women of —— Mill will pay their contributions more freely, we will find them sweethearts.'

'Those pretty things, the Jephsons, won't pay, because they are saving their money to buy mushroom hats.'

'If Rogers does not pay, Punch will tell about her robbing the donkey of a breakfast to stuff her bustle with.'

'If that young spark, Ben D——, that works at Banter's Mill, does not pay, Punch will tell about his eating that rhubarb pudding that was boiled in a dirty night-cap.'

'If that nigger in Uncle Tom's Cabin does not pay up, Punch will tell what he saw him do one night.'

'If squinting Jack of Goodair's does not pay up, Punch will stand on his corns.'

'If those three or four spinners do not pay their subscriptions, Punch will bring his iron clogs.'

'If Croft does not pay this week, we will give him another dip.'

At Sheffield, when a man is behindhand with his subscriptions, one of the mildest modes of remonstrance is to place an unsigned scrawl on his trough, intimating that if he does not clear off his arrears, Natty will come to make him. If he neglect this warning, he is likely, before long, on coming to work, to find his tools broken or gone, and the bands cut that connected his trough with steam or water power.

These are punishments for mere luke-warmness; for graver offences there are heavier applications, and these are designed even more for non-unionists than for recreant unionists. For a strike is emphatically a case in which not to be with, is to be against. Neutrality on the part of any who come in contact with it, is scarcely distinguishable from open opposition. Merely not joining in it tends to prevent its succeeding. Everything depends on the ability of the men who have relinquished employment to dispense with it longer than the employers whom they have left will be disposed to dispense with their services. In this view it is all important that all the old hands should leave those particular employers, and that no new hands should take their places. Any, consequently, who either remain, or subsequently come into a proscribed shop, are looked upon by those who have left as enemies, and, if unionists, as traitors into the bargain, and no opportunity is neglected of making them feel how they are regarded.

Previously to 1824, while the combination laws were still unrepealed, and when, consequently, trades' unionists on becoming such, became also *ipso facto* outlaws, there seemed to be no ruffianism to which unionists would scruple to resort, in their dealings with opponents. Consciousness of being singled out as victims by a partial and iniquitous law directed exclusively against themselves, naturally excited in them both general prejudice against all law, and special rancour against those in whose behalf the specially obnoxious law had been enacted: while consciousness of their being already amenable to punishment as criminals, as naturally made them reckless about committing crime. Those were the days of vitriol-throwing, incendiarism, and assassination, when neither any one who worked for a proscribed master, nor the master himself, could stir out after dusk, without risk of being pistolled, or of having his eyes burnt in his head, or could lie down at night with any confidence of not being blown up before morning.

Those days may now be said to have passed, recent experience of Sheffield and Manchester notwithstanding. Even at Sheffield, according to the Commissioners of Enquiry, not more than twelve trades' unions out of a total number of sixty were implicated in the atrocities which have made that town so infamous, and only the grossest ignorance or the perversest prejudice will venture to assert that in more than one or two other places has unionism afforded the smallest pretext for being suspected of similar implication. It has indeed been charitably insinuated that Sheffield practice is but the necessary result of unionist principles, so that, though as yet but the exception, it must eventually become the rule; but to this it may suffice to reply that the exception in question has already really been the rule, of which it is now one of the last lingering remains. It is not very long since assassination and cognate crimes were such frequent concomitants of unionism that there might have been decent excuse for reckoning them among its invariable characteristics; yet, instead of having since become commoner and commoner in connection with it, they have, on the contrary, been growing rarer and rarer, until not more than two or three places can be named in which unionism is still disgraced by the connection. Clearly the inevitable inference is that the real tendency of unionist principles is to purification of practice—just the opposite of the tendency imputed to it.

Without, however, going the length of murder, maiming, or gunpowder plots, there are many questionable modes of persecution which unionists both may and do employ. There is ' rattening,' or the destruction or abstraction of an obnoxious workman's tools, and this, though more prevalent at Sheffield than elsewhere, undoubtedly prevails in many places besides. There is wanton destruction of an employer's property, as when newly-made bricks are rendered unsaleable by having a quantity of pitch thrown over them, or when clay about to be moulded into bricks is rendered unuseable by having a quantity of needle-ends mixed with it. Then there is 'picketing,' with which Londoners were made familiar during the tailors' strike of the summer before last,* when the number of sentinels clustered in front of every noted tailor's shop made walking rather difficult in parts of Sackville Street, Clifford Street, and Savile Row. The office of pickets is to intercept those who seem to be approaching interdicted shops in search of work, to turn them back if possible, or, if they persist and succeed in getting work, to follow them or send after them on their way back, and endeavour to induce them to give it up. The records of the London Police courts show that the tailors were not at all particular what arts they employed for these purposes, and by all accounts, pickets engaged in the service of provincial strikes are less scrupulous still. At Preston, Stockport, Blackburn, Glasgow, or Hull, to say nothing of Sheffield or Manchester—in the coal districts of Durham or Northumberland, in the coal or iron districts of Staffordshire, or in any other part of the 'Black Country,' whoever should presume on dubious errand to come near workshop, or factory, or mine, or foundry, which in unionist phrase had been declared 'illegal,' would most likely have to run the gauntlet through a lane of scowlers, scoffers, hissers, and hooters, pelting him with the names of 'black,' 'black sheep,' 'colt,' 'knobstick,' 'sniveller,' and others too coarse to be found anywhere in print except in the pages of the most old-fashioned of slang dictionaries. And he would be lucky if he were assailed with words only, and if these were not accompanied by actions to match, beginning, perhaps, with shoves and pushes, but passing rapidly into blows and kicks, the slightest resistance to which would be gleefully hailed as an excuse for their tenfold multiplication and aggravation. Lists of persons deemed suitable subjects for this sort of discipline are regularly printed and circulated

---

* *i.e.* of the summer of 1867.

for the benefit of all interested, and these documents—
'black lists' as they are significantly called—are so much
in demand that, though their price is only a halfpenny or
so a-piece, yet in one society—that of the Operative Masons
—between nine and ten pounds' worth of them have been
bought by the members in a single season. On the owners
of the names thus catalogued intimidation is also brought
to bear. Distinct notice is generally given them by some
kind friend or other that, over and above present ill-usage,
there is something worse looming in the future. They are
warned that though they are now in clover, while their
brethren on strike are starving, their own lean years will
come on in due course ; that when existing differences
with the masters are adjusted, and the men who are now
out have gone in, the latter will insist on those who are now
in being turned out; that, since these have hitherto not
chosen to enter the union, no choice shall then be left
them but to enter a union of a very different sort.

Here let it once for all be explained that neither the
foregoing statements nor any like them are designed to
apply to all trades' unions indiscriminately. Those associations differ not more widely in disposition and character than in habits and customs, so that it is quite impossible
for any generic description, unless consisting only of extremest outlines, to be so drawn as to embrace them all.
Of the secondary practices, however, enumerated above,
there is not one which is not adopted by some society,
while many societies are perfectly familiar with them all.
In so far, too, as any of the practices prevail in any society,
in so far are the authorities of that society responsible for
their adoption, and it is mere hypocrisy on their part to
pretend otherwise. No one can doubt that whatever of
rattening, or of assault and battery, or intimidation takes
place in any union, takes place, if not with the express
sanction, yet with the full concurrence of the governing
powers. If these do not know who are the perpetrators, it
is simply because they do not wish to know. They have
always, at any rate, a very shrewd guess, which, if they

were willing to be enlightened, would at once be converted into certainty. Most assuredly neither rattening nor anything of the kind would go on if the authorities were as anxious to put a stop to it as they are to put down anything of which they really disapprove—piecework, for example, or overtime.

Unionist means of attaining unionist ends being, then — exclusively of some clearly unexceptionable—such as above noted, the question which next presents itself is, whether any of those means are legitimate, and if so, which. Some heads of the enquiry need not detain us long. Murder and its kindred sins are viewed with as much horror by the great majority of unionists as by all other respectable people. It is unhappily only too true that in the course of five or six years, five or six unionist murders or attempts at murder have taken place at Sheffield; but it is equally true that within about much the same time much the same number of members of the medical profession have been known to put an end to their too confiding patients with over-doses of strychnine or arsenic. Unless the second of these facts afford sufficient reason for stigmatising the College of Physicians as a corporation of poisoners, the first can furnish no excuse for speaking of a class to which Mr. Allan, Mr. Applegarth, Mr. Conolly, and Mr. Dunning are proud to belong, as if it were made up of miscreants like Broadhead, Crookes, and Hallam. With regard to this last-mentioned trio, the reader will perhaps allow half a dozen lines to be employed in pointing out some moral distinctions between its individual members. About Crookes and Hallam there is nothing at all remarkable. They are mere commonplace, professional murderers, who thought as little of killing a man as a butcher of felling an ox, and who, if they had been offered the indispensable fifteen pounds for the job, would doubtless as lief have shot Broadhead at Linley's bidding, as one of them did actually shoot Linley at Broadhead's. But Broadhead himself may not impossibly be a monster of a somewhat different species. It is not inconceivable that his temper may originally have been as mild as other people's, but perverted and hardened since by mischievous sophisms. My own notion of him is that of a Robespierre,—of coarser grain and with narrower opportunities—of whose wholesale cruelties, unbounded self-conceit was the true mainspring. He had a theory of his own about the amelioration of his trade, as his prototype had about the amelioration of his species, and the same self-sufficiency which prevented him from doubting the justice or the importance of his views made him think any measure allowable that might help to carry them out. This little bit of psychological analysis will not, I trust, be construed into an attempt at apology for Broadhead's enormities. The real purpose of its introduction is that it may serve as a peg whereon to hang a far from superfluous moral, to wit, the following: An extra reason for never doing evil in order that good may come of it, is, that though we are sure of the evil we may be mistaken as to the good; as Broadhead himself, with tears in his eyes, confessed, when the murders which he had instigated for the good of his union were found out, and both he and his union were found to be none the better but immensely the worse for them.

Words would be equally wasted in lengthened inculpation of rattening, of assault and battery, or of any of the minor forms of personal molestation under notice. It cannot be worth while to join issue in earnest with the Sheffield notable who declared it to be 'the duty of a trades' union to thrash into submission all who got their living by a trade and would not obey the laws of that trade without thrashing.' To every individual, by all means, let the utmost liberty of striking work be conceded; but for anyone to suppose himself warranted in striking another because that other does not choose to strike with him, is certainly carrying rather far the converse of the injunction to turn the other cheek to the smiter. If A choose to work for fewer halfpence than B thinks fitting, that is surely no reason why B should insist on making up to him the deficiency in kicks.

Neither can a word be said in excuse of the unionist practice of defamation. This is a point which, for all Englishmen, was settled long ago by Shakspeare, and that filching one's good name is worse than stealing his purse, has ever since been as a proverb amongst us. Those skulking scoundrels who invent wicked stories about one young woman's bustle and another's night-cap, clearly deserve to be well kicked, and it is not very creditable to unionists in general that they so seldom get the kicking they deserve.

All such practices as these, then, may be summarily disposed of. They clearly admit of no excuse, and no decent unionist would dream of excusing them. But when passing from these we come to the remaining ones on our list, we shall find the legitimacy or illegitimacy of the latter to be much more of an open question. To begin with the refusal of unionists to work with non-unionists : the consequence of such refusal may doubtless be as serious to those affected by it, as if they had been subjected to personal restraint. If it be impossible for A to obtain work unless B will consent to work with him, and if B refuse, A is thereby as effectually disabled from earning a livelihood as if B had bound him hand and foot or shut him up in prison. And if A thereupon, in order to induce B to work with him, yield to B's wishes in some disagreeable particular, he is no more a free agent than if B had been a slave-driver standing over him with his whip. Nevertheless, although A may be as much to be pitied as a slave, it does not follow that B is as much to blame as the slave-driver, or is indeed at all to blame. In B's behalf a plea may here again be entered with effect which has already often stood us in good stead. B, be it observed, is doing nothing to A, good or bad. He merely abstains from doing something which A wishes him to do, but which he is under no obligation to do. He is not infringing A's liberty of action, he is only exercising his own liberty of inaction. A has no claim upon his companionship, and cannot therefore be wronged by being refused it. Nay, circumstances can easily be imagined in which the refusal would be not only unobjectionable but meritorious. Suppose A to be a thief, or an obscene talker, or to be in the habit of chastising his wife with the poker, the sternest moralist would not think the worse of B for refusing to work, or otherwise associate with him, so long as he continued his evil courses. Although B's holding aloof would still be equivalent to leaving A to starve, yet if he should at the same time make A aware that he had merely to reform in order to obtain the desired co-operation, B would be generally admitted to be sufficiently blending mercy with justice, and to be marking with no more than proper severity his disgust at A's immorality. But in the estimation of a zealous unionist, disaffection or treachery to unionism is quite as heinous an offence as theft or wife-beating ; and if so, why may he not with equal propriety adopt the same mode of testifying against both ? You may say, perhaps, that he is quite mistaken in his estimate ; but that is no better than saying that you think he ought to see with your eyes, and act according to your notions of right and wrong instead of his own. If we would judge fairly of the proceedings of unionists, we should endeavour to place ourselves in their situations, and look at things from their point of view. If our country were engaged in a life-and-death struggle, should we have any qualms of conscience about denying the substantial advantage of our co-operation to any of our countrymen who should obsti-nately refuse to aid in the national defence ? But what patriotism is to all right-minded Englishmen, unionism is to a large number of English workmen—a cause in which, mistakenly or not, they believe self-sacrifice and self-de-votion to be as virtuous and glorious as everyone considers them to be for the sake of one's country. How then can we blame them for adopting with regard to those whom they look upon as traitors a system of non-intercourse, which in like circumstances we should not hesitate to adopt ourselves?

The matter just noticed is a passive portion of unionist demeanour. Among active modes of annoyance, one of the most prominent is that of 'picketing' shops which unionism has placed under its ban. Upon this, of late, has in due form been passed sentence of judicial condemnation, which has been somewhat prematurely accepted as final by the great majority of those whom it does not affect. For simple picketing, unalloyed by any of those outrageous proceedings which render whatever they are mixed up with as indefensible as themselves, a very tolerable case may nevertheless be made out. Such picketing may easily be shown to be always permissible at least, and sometimes in its general effect beneficial. It cannot, indeed, be otherwise than irksome to a shopkeeper to have sour-visaged sentinels mounting guard constantly at his door, and casting black looks on himself or on any friends of his who come nigh his dwelling; but this intrusion on domestic privacy must be admitted to be, at any rate, a smaller evil than such an interference with liberty of rest or locomotion as would prevent anyone with a fancy for the pastime from spending the day in lolling against some particular lamp-post, or promenading up and down some particular street. It cannot be otherwise than irksome either to non-unionists, to be pursued to their homes with taunts and reproaches for merely taking work where they could get it. Yet it might be difficult to say why less license of remonstrance should be allowed to their pursuers than to the active parish priest whom many would praise for his zeal in similarly dogging the steps of wanderers from his fold, and since they would not come to hear him at church, insisting on preaching to them in the streets. Both may be equally satisfied that their advice and their motives for obtruding it are good, and both in so thinking may be equally right or equally mistaken. Provided the reproaches of pickets and their emissaries comprise no baculine arguments, and do not go beyond hooting or upbraiding, keeping clear also of obscenity and profanity, they may quite possibly be, in spite of their roughness, good for the mental health of those against whom they are launched. 'Oh wad some power the giftie gie us, to see oursels as ithers see us.' There are none of us who might not be the better for such enlargement of vision. Few kinds of knowledge are more useful than the knowledge of what our associates think of us and of our conduct, and hooting, hissing, and calling names are, among working people, favourite and effectual ways of interchanging such knowledge. Ways ill adapted, doubtless, to ears polite; but then, you see, working people have not got polite ears. They are used to plain language, and never think it necessary to call a spade anything but a spade. Besides, they understand each other all the better for being plainly spoken to, and if they are so unfortunate as to be looked upon by their fellows as traitors to the common cause, or opponents of the common interest, it is highly desirable that they should be distinctly apprised accordingly. Though to hear such things must indeed to them be grievous, yet it is also safe. If there be any foundation for the bad opinion entertained of them, their recognition of its partial truth is calculated to shame them into self-amendment. If, on the contrary, they have the approval of a good conscience as to their public conduct, undeserved blame will be calculated to confirm them in it, in which case the edifying spectacle of their patient continuance in well-doing may serve even to convert their maligners. In either case good will result. To the inestimable privilege of unlicensed speaking it can never be advisable to set other limitations than those necessary for the exclusion of filthy, or blasphemous, or libellous language. Short of these there should be no restrictions but those imposed by the taste or discretion of the speakers themselves.

Intimidation is another thing with which unionists are freely charged, and the word has so ugly a sound that to prove the charge seems almost equivalent to proving the guilt implied by it. The intimidation in question, however, consists wholly of threatening, and, whatever be the motive for threatening, the mere act of threatening is not necessarily wrongful. Whether it be so or not depends on the nature of the threat. Threats of injury to person or property belong to the same category as the injury itself, and are equally reprehensible. Putting in bodily fear may be as bad as, or worse than, inflicting bodily pain; and both, when no adequate provocation can be urged in their excuse, may be equally flagrant violations of justice. But for the most frequent of unionist threats, that of refusing to work in company with non-unionists, the same justification will suffice as we have already found to answer perfectly well in nearly analogous cases. Whatever course it is not improper for a man to take, that course it cannot be improper for him to threaten to take. If there be no harm in his not doing a certain thing, how can there be any harm in his giving notice beforehand that he will not do it? If, for instance, he be justified in refusing to work with another, how can it be unjustifiable on his part to warn that other that at some future time he will so refuse? It is admitted that he may refuse, even though the consequences of his refusal be the other's ruin; how then can he be denied the right of apprising the other that he means to take a course which may involve him to ruin?

It is so difficult to see how these questions can be answered, that, instead of getting direct replies to them, I expect rather to be told that certain things which one person may lawfully do, become unlawful when two or more persons join in doing them. Something to this effect I should doubtless be told if I were discussing the matter with my honoured friend Baron Bramwell. That eminent judge would not dispute that any one person may, with the view of deterring others from some particular course, lawfully give them notice that, if they continue in that course, **he** will neither work nor in any other mode associate with

them, or that with the same view he may lawfully cast
upon them the blackest looks he can muster up. But after
admitting this, my honoured friend would certainly add
that if two or more should combine with a similar view to
give similar notice or to cast similar looks, then those two
or more would become guilty of an indictable offence.
Such was, by Baron Bramwell, in his charge to the jury at
the recent trial of certain unionist tailors, declared to be
the law of the land, and that he says so is sufficient assurance that the law is so, for no one is entitled to speak on
the point with more authority. For a dissatisfied suitor
there is therefore no help but to appeal from law to equity,
and to point out how inconsistent in the case before us
the former is, not only with justice, but also with common
sense. That to conspire to attain even a lawful end by
unlawful means, or to attain an unlawful end by any means
whatever, must itself be unlawful, is at once understood ;
but why that which is lawful for one should be unlawful
for two passes a plain man's comprehension. It is not
pretended that combination is in itself unlawful. It is
admitted that men may combine to any extent, provided
they use none but lawful means, and aim at none but
lawful ends. It is not pretended that in the case before
us either means or ends are unlawful. It is admitted
that the one may be used with a view to the other,
either by one single person or by any number of persons acting separately and without intercommunication.
But although to combine is lawful, and although both
the means and the end particularly referred to are lawful,
still to combine to use those particular means for that particular end becomes in some hopelessly enigmatical manner
unlawful. What solution can there possibly be of this
mystery ? What conceivable explanation can there be of
its being unlawful for two to join in doing what either may
do apart? It can avail nothing to urge that the combination
is designed to deter people from following their own inclinations, and thereby to interfere with liberty of mind and

of will, and that this liberty is as much under the protection of the law as the freedom of the body. It is admitted that any number of persons acting singly may interfere with the liberty of mind and will in the manner supposed. It is not then the interference itself which is unlawful. Neither can it avail anything to urge that the combination is in restraint of trade, whatever that may mean. It is admitted that any number of individuals acting separately may lawfully do in restraint of trade those very same things which it is unlawful for them to do collectively. It cannot therefore be its trade-restraining tendency which renders the combination illegal. What it is, is a thing which in Dundreary phraseology ' no fellow can make out.' What would you think of a law which sanctioned a pickpocket's plying his trade by himself, and punished him only in case he had an accomplice? But if you think such a law the height of absurdity, how can you think otherwise of one which permits a man to cast black looks at his neighbours, or to deprive or threaten to deprive them of the advantage of his company; yet if another join with him in doing the very same thing with the very same object, sends them both to prison ?*

* This may to many appear too strongly stated, and I am myself half disposed to fear that it must be so, seeing that among those who think it is, is one so little afraid as Mr. Mill of carrying out principles to their extreme consequences. Very possibly there may, as Mr. Mill says, be cases in which the 'number of agents may materially alter the essential character of the act.' The particular case adduced by him, however, is scarcely a case in point. No doubt in a country in which duelling was legalised, the immunity to single combatants would not be extended to numerous assailants of a single opponent. But the question before us is one not of law but of justice. Duelling is a wicked absurdity in the guise of which the foulest murders may be and frequently have been committed : a practice which cannot be justified and ought never to be legalised. But if we suppose circumstances in which, by reason of the law's defect, a man could not get justice done except by doing it himself, we shall, I think, perceive that whatever he would be warranted in doing for that purpose, others might be equally warranted in joining him to do. If the young Canadian who in broad daylight and before a crowd of spectators, lately pistolled

On the special subject of this chapter I have nothing left to say. Never one tittle either extenuating or setting down maliciously, I have exhibited the ways and means of unionism exactly as by careful research I have discovered them to be. Some of the practices examined speak sufficiently for themselves, and are condemned at once and without appeal, by their own foul-mouthedness. Others, however, despite their questionable shapes, have, when put to the question, borne the test perfectly. Many practices of very ill repute have thus shown themselves to be perfectly legitimate in the only proper sense of that term when it is confined to dealings between man and man. They have been perceived to be right in so far, at least, that they violate no right, and that no one therefore can complain of being wronged by them. And there is no reason to doubt that these, the strictly legitimate means of unionism, have sufficient efficacy of their own to be able to dispense with illegitimate aid. In proof of this it need only be remarked that those trades' unions which are freest from suspicion of employing illegitimate arts, are likewise those whose power and influence are immeasurably the greatest.

The efficacy of trades' unionism is, however, a distinct branch of my enquiry, which, in order to be treated properly, must be treated by itself.

the seducer of his sister, was justified in that act of condign punishment, all his brothers would have been equally justified in assisting in the act, had their assistance been requisite to ensure its performance.

CHAPTER III.

EFFICACY OF TRADES' UNIONISM.

As to the efficacy of Trades' Unionism the question is two-fold. Firstly, in quarrels between employers and employed, how far is unionism calculated to give victory to the latter? Secondly, how far are the fruits of victory so obtained likely to be those which the latter expect? There are such things as barren victories. It is quite possible for labourers to get the better of their masters without becoming themselves at all the better off in consequence. Even when surrendering at discretion, masters cannot surrender more than they have under their own control. They may promise compliance with conditions that cannot permanently be complied with; or it may be that fulfilment of the promise would be not beneficial, but injurious to those by whom it had been extorted. It is not then enough to ask whether unionism is calculated to be instrumental in enabling the employed to prevail against employers; we must also endeavour to ascertain of what use it would be to them to prevail. The two subjects of enquiry are distinct, and will be the more easily understood for being treated separately.

With regard to the first, the story told by past experience may seem a little self-contradictory. A review of the industrial warfare of this country during the last forty or fifty years will show, on the one hand, that when differences between masters and men have led to very severe and pro-tracted struggles, the masters have invariably come off conquerors, yet will show, on the other, that in all the intervals between their victories the masters have been continually giving way. Repeatedly they have been seen successfully maintaining their ground against the most desperate assaults, and then presently afterwards tamely retreating without waiting for a renewed attack. Repeatedly they have put themselves to enormous expense in resisting their men's demands, for little other purpose apparently than that of having a decent excuse for subsequently admitting them. During nearly half a century all signal triumphs have been on one side, all substantial success on the other.

In all those more extensive and prolonged strikes whose duration proves that though strenuously maintained they were likewise firmly resisted, the men have invariably put forth their utmost strength merely to find that strength miserably inadequate ; invariably they have met with what a tender-hearted opponent, regarding their proceedings with eyes not the less commiserating because those of an iron-master, has aptly termed ' the same dismal uniformity, the same miserable monotony of defeat. * The great strike of the Manchester spinners in 1829, when a quarter of a million sterling of wages was forfeited ; the Ashton and Staleybridge strikes of 1829 and 1830, in which 30,000 spinners took part, and in which another quarter of a million was similarly lost ; the strikes of the Tyne and Wear pit-men in 1832, in each of which thousands held out gallantly for months ; the Manchester builders' strike in 1833, when 72,000*l.* of wages were foregone ; the ' terrible ' strikes of the Preston spinners, first in 1836, when thirteen weeks of voluntary idleness cost the men 57,200*l.*, and secondly in 1854, when 17,000 persons underwent all the misery implied in their remaining out for thirty-six weeks and giving up 420,000*l.* of wages ; the engineers' strike in 1853, of fifteen weeks' duration, in which 43,000*l.* of wages were sacrificed ;

* ' An Ironmaster's View of Strikes,' by R. W. Hopper, in ' Fortnightly Review' for August 1, 1865.

the obstinate strike in the metropolitan building trade in 1860; and the still more memorable strikes of the iron workers of Staffordshire and the North in 1865, and of the London tailors in the summer of 1867: these are but a few of the more salient among the very many instances in which terrible suffering and heroic endurance on the part of the men have terminated in their eventually capitulating at discretion, and returning to work on terms little if at all better, and not seldom worse, than those against which they had revolted. Here is evidence in abundance to show that of the war that has been going on between the two parties, the masters have had most of the honour : all the more extraordinary is it therefore, though equally certain, that the men have had all the profit. The bone of contention for which each side has been fighting is the power of dictating to the other the terms of employment, the men seeking to have the price of their service raised and its length abridged—to get more pay for their work, and to give less work for their pay—and also to enforce conditions as to the way in which their work shall be done, and as to the kind and quantity of labour that shall be applied to it ; the masters on the contrary seeking to keep down wages and to keep up working time, and claiming for themselves the exclusive privilege of defining the nature and character of work for which they have to pay. This being what the two parties have been battling about, what has been the practical result of their contention ? On all great occasions the masters have been victors, yet every concession made has been made to the vanquished. Wherever the masters have persevered, they have reduced their men to submission ; but there is no great exaggeration in saying that for every instance of such successful persistence on their part, there have been a hundred in which they have yielded or compromised the matter at issue, perhaps after a short fight, but as often as not after merely waiting to be convinced that the men were in earnest about fighting. In all trades under the influence of unionism, wages, though subject to occasional fluctuation, have, ever since that influence began to make itself felt, been on the whole continually rising. In some they are twenty-five or thirty, and in one fifty per cent. higher than they were forty years ago, and in all the average rate is probably at least fifteen per cent. higher than it was then. In several of the trades, too, the hours of labour have been somewhat, and in some considerably reduced; and in many it is quite as frequently the men who decide for the masters as the masters for the men which and how many of the latter shall be employed at all, and which and how many of those employed shall be set to this or that description of work; how many apprentices shall be in training; whether working by the piece or overtime shall be permitted, and whether newly invented machinery or processes shall or not be tolerated. Where the relations between masters and men are least unsatisfactory, these and cognate matters are provided for by regulations mutually agreed to. Where no such regulations are in force, it is no longer enough for a master to say to his men that he wants a thing done, he must also enquire whether they will be pleased to do it.

The truth of these assertions has latterly become pretty notorious; but if any corroboration or illustration of them be required, the Social Science Association's Report on Trades' Societies, the files of the ' Beehive ' Newspaper— that Royal Gazette of working men—the annual Progress Reports issued by some of the larger societies, and, above all, the Reports of the two Royal Commissions on Trades' Unions, will furnish abundance. Amidst the copiousness of testimony the chief difficulty is that of selection, with regard to which I have myself derived a good deal of assistance from the researches of earlier enquirers. Mr. Harrison, whom I am especially bound to mention as having gone over much of the same ground before me, refers particularly to the West Yorkshire, the Lancashire, and the Edinburgh masons, who within the last few years, by actual or threatened strikes, repeatedly obtained higher wages or

shortened times, or both ; to the Glasgow carpenters, who,
out of seven strikes between 1852 and 1858, failed only in
one, and by means of the others got their wages raised from
22s. to 26s. a week, and their hours of work reduced from
sixty to fifty-seven a week ; to the Glasgow painters, whose
wages, in consequence of two or three strikes between 1845
and 1855, rose from 3½d. to 5d. an hour ; and to the
'Operative Bricklayers,' of whom some rather fuller particulars which I have found elsewhere may be added to those
given in Mr. Harrison's account.   This last-named association ' began to extend itself into the provinces in the autumn
of 1861, after the terrible ordeal it had passed through in
the lock-out of 1859 and 1860, and the no less protracted
struggle against the hour system in 1861.'   In the three
following years it organised strikes in twenty-five towns in
England and Scotland, of which four lasted only a few
hours, eleven only a few days, and only one more than a
few weeks, but of which the aggregate result has been that
not only in the said twenty-five towns, but also in nine
others, in which the mere threatening of strikes sufficed, the
wages of bricklayers have risen on an average 3s. 6d. a week,
while their working time has on an average been reduced
two hours weekly.   Of the Amalgamated Carpenters and
Joiners, their Secretary, Mr. Applegarth, in his Report for
1865, says that the Society, although at that time only five
years old, had, out of the ninety-four towns into which it
had thrown out branches, obtained for the men an advance
of wages in no fewer than fifty-two, and a reduction of
working hours in thirty, the advances of wages ranging
from 8d. to 4s. a week : that in Bradford, since a branch had
been established there, eight and a half had been taken off
the weekly total of carpenters' working hours, and 1s. added
to their weekly wages ; and that in many towns the Society
had got the masters to agree to a code of rules, previously
' approved' by the men, for the regulation of their mutual
relations.   The secretary goes on to describe the mode in
which these changes had been effected:—'In many instances,'

he says, ' the advantages were granted when asked for in the best possible spirit; in others after repeated meetings with the employers, and mutual concessions. Only in some few instances, after vainly trying to avoid it, were we obliged to resort to the *old* way of settling differences.' In his Report for 1866, Mr. Applegarth says that the advantages gained for the members of the Society had been still greater during that than in the preceding year, and he inserts a tabular statement fully bearing out his assertion. The following miscellaneous facts regarding other trades are taken almost at random. When Mr. G. Potter became a ' Progressive '. carpenter sixteen years ago, London wages were 5*s.*; they are now 6*s.* 3*d.* a day. The London masons in the course of 1865 and 1866 got advances of a penny an hour, or ten pence a day, merely by ' respectful representations.' When the Plasterers' Union had been seven years in existence, plasterers' wages, which had previously been 26*s.*, had risen to 30*s.* a week. According to Mr. Trollope, the eminent contractor, the wages of building operatives in London were 33*s.* in 1859, but are now 8*d.* an hour, or 39*s.* per week, though a week at present consists of only fifty-eight and a half working hours. In 1866 the Manchester House Painters' Society obtained for their constituents the following increments of wages: 1*s.* a week in Bradford, Halifax, and Leeds; 1*s.* 9*d.* in Bolton and Eccles; 2*s.* in Leigh, Northwich, Preston, Lincoln, Ulverstone, Blackpool, Nottingham, Shrewsbury, and Chorley; 2*s.* 6*d.* in Manchester, Liverpool, and eight other towns. The ' Operative House Carpenters and Joiners,' a ' national' Society, had twenty-two strikes in the four years ending with 1866: during the same period they obtained augmentations of wages in different places from 20*s.* a week to 24*s.*, 26*s.*, and 32*s.* About twenty years ago I was at some pains to collect accurate particulars of the wages current in different parts of England, for insertion in a work on which I was then engaged, and on referring to which I find among other items the following. At Manchester in 1832 the highest

wages of male weavers were 16s. 10d. a week, and spinners'
wages ranged from 20s. to 25s. At Stockport in 1835, the
average earnings of male adult factory hands were 16s. 6¼d.
a week. In Mr. Bright's mill at Rochdale in 1844, the
average weekly wages of adult males were 16s. 2d. At
Bolton in 1840, carpenters got 25s. a week. Colliery and
other miners were, in or about 1845, earning from 15s. to
18s. in Staffordshire and Warwickshire, and from 20s. to
30s. in Yorkshire, Durham, and Northumberland. At
present, according to Mr. Edwin Chadwick (Address to
Social Science Association in 1864), the average weekly
earnings of a male factory labourer are at least 18s. 6d. in
Lancashire: a weaver in that county may earn from 17s. to
22s., and a spinner in full work 30s. 10d. a week. In most
Lancashire towns carpenters' wages now range from 28s. to
32s. a week. What twenty years ago would seem to have
been the maximum of miners' wages in the midland and
northern counties is now probably nearer the minimum.
And be it recollected that wherever higher pay than
formerly is given, it is probably given also in return for less
work ; for wherever the price of labour has been increasing,
the hours of labour have in general been simultaneously
decreasing. Of course it is open to any one to question
whether the enhancement of labour's remuneration which
has thus been going on at both ends is due to the influence
of Trades' Unions, and whether it would not have taken
place equally if the price of labour had been left to find its
own level without extraneous interference. The questioner
here, however, may very properly be left to answer himself,
as he may satisfactorily do, by proceeding to enquire how
often any portion of the enhancement referred to has been
volunteered by the masters, and how often it has been only
yielded to solicitation with force in the back-ground. He
will find the instances of masters spontaneously raising
wages to be about as numerous as those of workmen
conscientiously believing themselves to be overpaid and

coming forward to insist that their wages should be reduced.

Thus much with respect to the influence of unionism over the remuneration of labour. Its control over the distribution and application of labour is often even more strikingly exemplified, but of this there will be a better opportunity of speaking hereafter, when we come to consider how flagrantly its power in that respect is occasionally abused.

The sort of retrospective review in which we have been engaged is well fitted to fill unionists with exultation. They are fond of indulging in it, and are excusably apt to become jubilant in consequence. If they do these things in a green tree, what shall be done in the dry? and the tree by whose branches they are sheltered is as yet but in the bud. As yet there are very few trades in the United Kingdom in which more than ten per cent. of the men employed are unionists; there is but one, that of the plasterers, in which as many as half are. Even in the same trade, too, the unionists seldom belong all to the same union. They are generally divided amongst many separate unions which have little connexion with each other, and still less or none with unions of other trades. An immensity is thus still practicable in the way both of the consolidation and of the extension of trade societies, and in each way rapid strides are being taken. At the present rate of proselytism, it will take but few years more for all eligible workmen in this country to become converts to unionism, and enrolled members of trade societies; the formation of all these societies into one national league will naturally suggest itself as the next step, and the formation of this and of similar foreign leagues into an international federation may be expected to follow in due course. But by such accretions and alliances the strength of the strongest of existing societies would be centupled, while the weakest would be raised to a level with the strongest; for the cause of any one trade or of any section of a trade, would then be taken up as the cause of all trades, and a strike on the part of any body of workmen would have the support, if required, of all the workmen comprised within the international confederacy. Surely every national league forming a component part of such a confederacy would be supreme within its own sphere. Surely it could dictate arbitrarily the conditions of employment, for the supply of labour would be entirely in its hands. At home there would be no efficient labour outside its pale, nor would there be any abroad that would be suffered to come into competition with the domestic labour under its protection; while at the same time the maintenance of any labour which, in furtherance of its policy, a national league should be compelled to keep unemployed, would be a burden easily borne, since, instead of devolving entirely on the men employed in a single trade, it would be undertaken by the universal mass of employed labour. Reasoning in this manner, sanguine unionists are disposed to accept the past only as an earnest and instalment of the future. For every inch given they intend to take a full ell, evidently thinking nothing done while aught remains to do, and thinking too that their capacity is quite equal to the accomplishment of all that remains. That control over the destinies of labour after which they have been straining seems to them to be drawing fast within their reach, the word 'destinies' in this particular phrase being understood by them as synonymous with 'employers.' These last once stood to them in the relation of inexorable fates, but hereafter their relative situations are, they believe, to be completely reversed, and nothing less will satisfy them than bringing the very fates under subjection.

In thus counting up their future conquests, they are, however, decidedly reckoning without their hosts. Their progress hitherto has been due less to their own strength than to their opponents' weakness of purpose. In all struggles with their men in which the masters have really put forth their powers, the latter have invariably gained the day, but they have rarely been willing to exert themselves sufficiently. Generally, like easy-going husbands, they have preferred to put up with a good deal for a quiet life. Their victories too have always been in a double sense Pyrrhic, teaching the vanquished how to manage better on subsequent occasions, and teaching the victors increased respect for the vanquished. Each hardly won fight has rendered the masters more and more shy of encountering antagonists perceived to be continually growing more and more formidable. Rather than incur the ever-increasing cost of war, they have chosen to give up a good deal for the sake of peace ; and they have given up so often and so much, that, as we have seen, during forty years or so, whatever has been lost has been lost by them, whatever has been gained has been gained by the men. There is a line, however, beyond which the veriest Jerry Sneak will not permit himself to be tamely goaded, and English masters are at last showing by very plain symptoms that they consider themselves to have been driven quite as far as is at all reasonable. They have discovered that their men's acquisitive appetite is not to be appeased by concession, but on the contrary grows by what it feeds on ; and they are also becoming aware that permanently organised aggression cannot be adequately met by mere spasmodic resistance, but requires, in order to be withstood, an organisation as permanent and matured as its own, and as capable of exercising the most approved tactics. Hitherto want of concert between individual masters has placed them at a great disadvantage as compared with the men. The latter have almost from the beginning evinced a judicious appreciation of Napoleonic strategy. Their favourite practice consists of manœuvres to which they have given the appropriate name of ' sectional struggles.' The plan is for the workmen of only some one or of some few firms to turn out, while the bulk of the unionists in the same trade, remaining at work, are able by contributions from undiminished earnings to maintain those on strike. With

such extraneous aid the turnouts are often more than a
match for isolated employers, who are in consequence
obliged to come to terms with them ; other employers are
next assailed in like manner, and others subsequently, until
all are either beaten in detail or submit as soon as sum-
moned, in order to avoid being beaten. But this, though
a very pretty game, is also one which either side can play,
and which the masters have occasionally tried, and never
without evincing their superior capacity for it.

When in 1833 the Manchester Builders, in 1853 the
Amalgamated Engineers, and in 1860 the London
Builders commenced operations with a partial strike, the
masters replied with a general lock-out. The refusal of
certain unionists to work was met by a refusal to employ
any but non-unionists. All the shops in the trade were
closed against society men, and no master permitted his
establishment to be used as a foraging ground for the support of men engaged in blockading his fellow-masters. The
turnouts, in consequence, presently found themselves in the
position of a besieging force, round whom in their turn
lines of circumvallation had been drawn by allies of the
besieged, while the lock-outs, instead of being able to send
supplies to their friends, were themselves cut off from their
own sources of supply. The associated workmen had proposed to bring the whole weight of their association to
bear on scattered detachments of the enemy, but to their
dismay they found themselves instead confronted at every
point by an overwhelming force, which gave to each of
their own scattered bands more than enough to do to help
itself without attempting to help others. Still, although
taken so disagreeably by surprise, they did not immediately lose heart. Shame continued to sustain them after
hope had forsaken them; and as long as they could they
stood out gallantly, but to stand out very long was in such
circumstances impossible. Without Ceres and Bacchus to
assist in keeping up the vital heat, Mars as well as Venus
cools down rapidly. There can be no prolonged fighting

on empty stomachs, and a locked out trades' union is like an army in a desert abandoned by its commissariat. So after a while Associated Builders and Amalgamated Engineers, though still too proud to sue for peace, were fain to accept the good offices of mediators in order to obtain it, and the quarrel between them and their employers ended in a mutual agreement that the exchange of labour for subsistence should be resumed on much the same terms as those on which it had been broken off.

Similar strategy was adopted by the masters at Preston in 1836 and 1854, at Padiham in 1859, at Colne in 1860–1, and more recently and memorably in opposition to the strikes of the Staffordshire and North Country puddlers in 1865, and of the London tailors in 1867. Similar, too, were the results, nor can the results ever be very different when the masters take the same pains and use the same means. As in these cases it did actually fare, so will it in future inevitably fare with labour, whenever labour and capital encounter each other in the same relative force as that in which they are spread over the whole field of industry. And it rests with the masters to prevent labour from ever encountering capital on less disadvantageous terms; it rests with them to prevent its massing itself against more than its rateable proportion of the whole stock of existing capital—to ensure that the largest masses of hostile labour shall always and everywhere be met by preponderating masses of capital. To be able to arrange matters in this way, they must indeed first form themselves into associations corresponding at all points with those of the men, and there is no small amount of prepossession and prejudice, of narrow-minded selfishness and mutual distrust to be got rid of by them, before they will be prepared to combine with the requisite cordiality and compactness : while if they do not choose of their own accord to combine, there are no means of compelling them. An union, for trade purposes, among masters must be completely voluntary with regard to every single individual taking part in

it. A trades' union of masters could practise none of the
coercion habitually adopted by a workmen's union in order
to draw reluctant recruits into its ranks. Employers in
any particular trade, millowners, mineowners, ironmasters,
or what not—do not form a class apart, the members of
which are dependent on each other for companionship and
cooperation. If any set of employers were to send one of
their number to Coventry, he might still have abundant
choice of acquaintances outside of his profession. If they
withdrew from all business transactions with him, he
would as likely as not be pleased therefore, for he does not
need the cooperation of his fellow-masters; he rather fears
their competition, and has no desire to be brought into
commercial contact with them. As for personal maltreat-
ment, defamation, and the like, these are not things in the
usual line of employers, and no employer against whom
they were practised would scruple to take the law of his
persecutors in order to obtain redress. Employers, then,
could scarcely be forced into joining a trades' union by extraneous pressure. They can scarcely become unionists
except of their own free will and consent, and there are
certain special reasons why they may hesitate to consent.
Unionism requires more self-sacrifice from them than from
the men. The temptation to swerve from its principles
after having adopted them is much greater. When workmen strike merely because their companions have struck,
or refuse employment at better pay than their own which
their companions on strike have vacated, the loss which
they sustain, however severe, is still but temporary, the
gain which they forego is but inconsiderable. As long as
the strike lasts their labour may be idle, but it will be as fit
for action as ever as soon as the strike is over, and they
may then find themselves in much the same position, in
respect to daily earnings, as they were before it began.
And if instead of striking they had continued at work, and
had even got better paid work which their companions had
left, still their extra earnings might probably have ceased

as soon as the strike ceased, without lasting long enough
to do them any permanent good. But when employers
join in a lock-out, the loss they risk is much more than
the temporary loss of their ordinary profits. Their capital
is not simply lying idle, it is perhaps also gradually dis-
appearing. If, as usually happens, any part of it be
borrowed, compound interest is sure to eat large holes in
it, while whatever portion of it consists of perishable materials is liable to be deteriorated in quality by being kept,
and to be depreciated in value through fluctuations of the
market. In these ways an employer's means may be sensibly diminished during a lock-out; and while such are his
losses, the gains he foregoes may be still greater. For
among employers, the embarrassment of some is the opportunity of others. If, while these are obliged to suspend
business, those are in a position to go on, the latter may be
able to get all the former's previous custom. If they can once
get it, they may hope to keep it: if they can keep it, even
for a time, they may during that time obtain extra profits
more than sufficient to compensate them for any subsequent reduction of profit. To induce them, with such
chances of making rapid fortunes, not merely to renounce
the extra profits within their reach, but to give up for a
time even their ordinary profits, some very urgent motive
is required. To induce them to do it for the sake of their
fellow-employers, they must be provided with some adequate substitute for the public spirit which actuates the
men, and which they not only do not possess, but are
never likely to acquire, for they cannot even understand it.
To them the subordination of individual to class interest,
which the men so remarkably exhibit, is a standing mar-
vel, and an inexplicable folly to boot. So far from
dreaming of merging themselves in their order, they do not
even regard themselves as belonging to an order. The
great ambition of every employer is to cease to be an employer. He busies himself unceasingly for nothing so
much as to be able the sooner to leave off business. By

what course he grows rich enough to retire, or at least how much that course may interfere with the progress of his fellow-employers, he cares very little. If anything, he rather plumes himself than not on cutting out his rivals. It is an additional feather in his cap, an additional proof of his superior cleverness, if, besides reaching the goal himself, he so jostle and hustle his companions in the race for wealth as to prevent their reaching it too.

With such mutually repellent feelings, employers will scarcely be disposed to combine for the defence of their common interests, except either under the pressure of necessity, or in consequence of their acquiring wider and more enlightened views of their individual interests. Such views, however, they are beginning to take. Much as they might prefer standing alone, they are beginning to understand that they may not be able to stand at all unless together. They are becoming aware that the continually growing force of their men's unionism is not to be resisted by them without a corresponding unionism of their own—without their combining with each other just as the men do, with equal heartiness and steadiness, equally prompt obedience to orders from central authority, and equal readiness to make sacrifices for each other, or for the common cause.

To do all this will go greatly against the grain with employers, for it will involve a complete change in the employing mind : it will require that employers should have learned to trust each other by showing themselves worthy of each other's trust. Things are beginning to look, however, as if they would either have to do this, or to abandon their employing functions ; and the world is not yet—whatever it may hereafter become—prepared to dispense with an employing class. We may reasonably assume, then, that in case of need, employers will undergo the moral transformation indispensable for the maintenance of their independence. The instinct of self-preservation may be fairly expected to invest them with those qualities

without which they cannot adopt the measures necessary
to enable them to retain their class existence. Whether or
not to adopt those measures rests evidently with themselves.
They can, if they think proper, form associations analogous
in all respects to those to whose aggressive tendencies
they are exposed. They can arrange like the men to act
in concert, and to suspend business operations unanimously
on a given signal. In the same proportion in which the
men contribute out of their wages, they can contribute out
of their profits to a common fund for the indemnification
of those who have been called upon to suspend business.
In whatever way the men assist each other during a strike,
in that same way, or in some exactly corresponding way,
the masters can assist each other against a strike, or during
a lock-out. All this they can do if they think proper; and
whenever they may think proper to do it, they will find
themselves far more than a match for the men. It will be
very much easier for them than for the men to combine,
and their combination will be much more efficacious for its
purpose. They are at least ten times less numerous, and at
least ten times as well off: and in about the same proportion it must be easier for them both to unite and to
subsist for any definite period on their united means —
easier both to make mutual arrangements, and to fulfil
mutual obligations. Their whole body can afford to shut
up their establishments better than the whole body of the
men can afford to be shut out. And should any of the
former go on with their business, they can quite as well or
better spare a tithe of their profits for the support of their
fellow-masters, than the men they employ can spare a tithe
of their earnings for the support of their unemployed comrades. In trials of strength between associations, equally
compact and equally resolute, of masters and men, the
latter have not the smallest chance. The question being
simply whether a few can hold out longest on large means,
or many on small means, there can be no doubt as to the
answer. A general strike met by a general lock-out of

corresponding extent cannot possibly succeed if the masters exhibit anything like the same spirit as the men. If when the men of one employer, or of a few employers, strike, all other employers either lock out or share their profits with those against whom the strike is directed, the strike must necessarily fail. The two organisations being equal in scale, and animated with equal ardour, that of the masters must inevitably prevail ; the cause of the men is absolutely desperate.

In illustration of this I will, according to my wont, take the extremest imaginable case, believing that there is no way so satisfactory of proving a principle as that of carrying it as far as it can be made to go, and finding that it does not terminate in absurdity. Let all the workmen in all the trades, not only of our own country, but of all neighbouring countries, or of the whole commercial world, be formed into trade unions, each comprising all the workmen in its trade, yet composed of none but loyal and devoted members; let all the unions in each country constitute a national labour league, and all the leagues one grand international labour federation, and let there be the same adhesiveness throughout the whole structure of the federation, and of each league, as throughout that of one of the latter's component parts. Let, in short, the web of unionism be supposed so strongly spun, and so widely spread, that no industrial quarrel could anywhere take place without the whole community of workmen in the same commercial sphere taking part in it on labour's side, insomuch that any half dozen of journeymen tailors, striking for higher wages at Wick or the Land's End, could depend on having any needful cooperation of all the labourers of every description between Archangel and San Francisco. In supposing this, we are supposing the realisation of the most romantic dream ever dreamt by unionist seer in his most rapturous trance: we are supposing the association of labour to have attained to the utmost extension and perfection of which it can be conceived capable. For fairness of comparison, we must assume the associative capacities of capital to have received equal development. Among employers unionism is as yet in its infancy. There was not until the other day, if indeed there be really even yet, any society of masters of a permanent character, which, either in its composition or its objects, bears more than a faint resemblance to what workmen understand by the term of Trades' Union. There may be one or two with ramifications sufficiently expanded to entitle them to the epithet of national, but there is not one whose individual members are either formally pledged, or deem themselves in honour bound, to share equally in the burdens which resistance to unionist aggression may impose on any of their number. Hitherto masters' associations have been for the most part only local or temporary expedients devised to meet local and temporary emergencies. They have rarely extended beyond one or two counties, and have generally been confined to one or two towns. When the Preston Mills were closed in 1854, those of neighbouring Blackburn remained open, and from them succour was sent to Preston, which enabled a strike to be prolonged for nine months, that without such aid might probably not have lasted half as many weeks. When in 1865 the iron-masters of Staffordshire and the northern counties locked out their men, those of Shropshire and South Wales, remaining neutral, as they called it, allowed their yards to be converted into magazines for the supply of the men with whom the former were contending. While even in the same trade masters have thus been divided, those of different trades could not be expected to coalesce. Hitherto in all great disputes, the associated masters of a single place or district have had to deal with the men of a far wider area, nor yet with the men of their own trade only, but with those of other trades besides. Such has hitherto been the embryonic state of unionism among employers, who, however, need nothing but the will to raise it at once to the maturity which it has attained among the men, or to make it keep pace with any further advances which it may make among the latter. Let us then, for argument and for comparison's sake, suppose employers to have become, equally with the men, convinced of the necessity of helping each other, and to have made equally judicious arrangements for mutual assistance. Let them be supposed to have constituted themselves first into trades' unions, then into national trade leagues, finally into international trade confederacies, all in their several ways as comprehensive, and composed of members as zealous, as those of the men. And having thus assumed associative organisation to be equally good in its way on each side, let us suppose the rival organisations to engage in a trial of strength. Let us imagine, if imagination will stretch so far, the whole labour of any commercial region striking against the same region's whole capital ; or let us, if we please, confine ourselves to imagining a strike, whether general or partial, in any one trade, supported by all the labourers in all the trades within the same sphere, while all the employers combined to support the employers against whom the strike was directed. In either case the result could not be for a moment doubtful. Resolution on both sides being equal, victory would infallibly be with the superiority of wealth ; and however great might be the pecuniary resources of the men, those of the masters would be many times greater, and better able to bear the drain upon them. The smaller treasure-chest would then be exhausted first ; and when it was empty, labour would have no alternative but to surrender at discretion. This would inevitably happen if labour and capital each pitted against the other its utmost strength ; and what would happen in an experiment on the largest scale would happen equally on any smaller scale, provided the same proportions between the contending parties were observed. In all their disputes employers may always have the employed at their mercy by adopting the same tactics, and persisting in them as doggedly.

During perusal of the last few pages, vials of wrath have probably been filling, which are now about to be emptied on my devoted head. No lock-out has ever taken place without being accompanied by a tremendous outcry from the locked out and their partisans against the tyrannous atrocity, cruelty, and injustice of withholding from the poor the work by which alone they live, and of withholding it equally from the unoffending and offending. Yet am not I, with Machiavellian cold-bloodedness, suggesting to the masters constant preparedness for a course, of which even the exceptional adoption is deemed to warrant such outbursts of virtuous indignation? Were this even so, I do not know that I should have much cause for shame. Working men, and Englishmen to boot, ought not to be such babies as to complain because in a fight of their own challenging they have to take as much or more than they give, and to whimper because, having struck the first blows, they get heavier blows in return. If they are not prepared for rubbers, they had better not play at bowls. Locks-out are almost invariably replies to strikes; and even if entirely unprovoked, they would still be the exact correlatives of strikes, and in so far as the latter are justifiable, would be equally justifiable on precisely the same grounds. Even as no one can be wronged by the men's refusal to take work which they are under no obligation to take, so can no one be wronged by the refusal of masters to give work which they are under no obligation to give. If any of my richer and unemploying readers think otherwise, if they think that employers, merely because they have employment to give, are bound to give it to those that need, why do not they themselves set up as employers? Why do not they, since they have the means, establish themselves in business, and so place themselves in a position to provide means of livelihood to the industrious poor? Or if they do not recognise this last as part of their duty, with what consistency can they represent it as the duty of others merely because those others happen to be actually engaged in business? Are not the latter at liberty, if they think fit, to relinquish business altogether, and thereby to cease altogether to afford employment? And must they not, therefore, be at least equally at liberty to suspend their operations, and to cease temporarily to afford employment? If the poor, as such, have a right to be in any manner maintained by the rich, there can be no limit to the applicability of that right short of equal division of all wealth among all human beings. If wealth belong in any measure to its owners, it belongs to them to the full extent of being completely at their own disposal for any purpose not injurious to others. Even though locks-out, then, were initiative proceedings, spontaneous manifestations of wanton caprice, they would still be perfectly justifiable on the ground and in the sense on which strikes are justifiable — on the ground, viz. that capital is as much the capitalist's own as labour is the labourer's own, and in the sense that neither capitalist nor labourer can be wronged by the other's doing as he pleases with that other's own.

But a lock-out is never initiative—it is always retaliatory: never the first step in an industrial quarrel—always the answer to an actual or threatened strike. Proceedings are commonly begun by the men employed by some few masters exercising their incontestable right of turning out. Some few masters are thus first singled out, the men in the employment of the others still remaining at work. So far the actual strikers are apparently the only sinners, the rest of the workmen merely affording them pecuniary aid, while none apparently are sinned against except the masters against whom the strike is directed. Perhaps, then, it behoves the other masters to remain quiescent, and to keep on their men until the latter may find it convenient to strike? This or the like is often seriously urged, but to give it a serious reply would be an insult to the reader's good sense. Hostility does not the less require to be guarded against because veiled with hypocrisy. Wolves are not the less to be driven from the fold because they have entered it in sheep's clothing. No doubt it is peculiarly mortifying to the engineer to be hoist with his own petard ; but how much soever we be vexed at being foiled with our own weapons, we shall only be laughed at instead of pitied for accusing our adversary of unfairness in using the same weapons as ourselves, and those, too, the only weapons that could place him on a par with ourselves. Besides, even if the men locked out were as innocent as they pretend to be, it would ill become unionists to reproach masters therefore. Unionists do not abstain from striking on account of the misery which a strike often entails on hundreds of workmen in no degree interested in its success. The 600 spinners who *turned out* in one of the Preston strikes never gave themselves the smallest concern about the 7,840 innocent piecers, card-room hands, and others whom this act of theirs *threw out* of work, and thereby deprived of bread. Men as well as masters when arrayed against each other should, for decency's sake, refrain from those childish recriminations in which they are on such occasions so prone to indulge. They should remember that the debate they are engaged is, as Mr. Dunning says,* ' simply a bargain in which the employer is the buyer, and the employed the seller,' and in which there is no room for a sense of wrong—no excuse for the seller's being angry because he cannot get the price he asks, for making it a point of honour not to take less than he began by asking, or for abusing the customer who presumes to discontinue his custom. It is a sad pity that the candour and good sense of counsellors like Mr. Dunning should be counteracted by less judicious advisers. It is quite cause enough of irritation to the employed, that their interest and that of their employers are so often of necessity opposed. There is not the smallest need to inflame their passions by telling them that their rights, as well as their interests, are affected by the defensive measures of the

---

* ' Trades' Unions and Strikes : their Philosophy and Intention.' By T. J. Dunning, Secretary to London Bookbinders' Trade's Union, p. 25.

masters, and that they are thereby not simply baffled and disappointed, but outraged and oppressed.

One word in explanation of my own share in the controversy. To blow hot and cold alternately—now to expose and now to excuse the practice of one or the other side —is not precisely the way to gain a favourable hearing from either. Not the less, desiring as I do, not to please, but to convince, shall I continue to speak the truth without respect of persons or consequences. Of all social disorders, and notably of all unsatisfactoriness in the relations between labour and capital, the mainspring is that universal selfishness which is, and has always been, the governing principle of all human institutions. To discredit that principle ought to be the first object of every social reformer, but this, no more than any other worthy object, is to be accomplished by misrepresentation. Even selfishness is entitled to fair treatment, and should be allowed full credit for as much of good as is mingled with its evil. In so far as unionism may be perceived to be capable of furthering the well-being of working men, in so far let its beneficent capacity be admitted. But it is equally essential that unionism should always be presented in its true colours, and should not be fitted with different epithets, according to the company in which it is found. There is no kindness to working men in leading them to suppose that what is allowable for them to do to others can be just matter of reproach when done by others to them, or that they will be permitted to practise with impunity what, if practised towards themselves, they would violently resent. Far better for them to be told plainly that their unionism and that of their masters are both of a piece, one being indeed the legitimate offspring and natural consequence of the other; that as they sow, they must be prepared to reap; that while practising aggression they must not expect forbearance, but if they will go on striking, must lay their account with being every now and then locked out. My own object in telling them this is not—as, after all I have already said, I need scarcely say—to denounce their unionism, but only to let them see with what risks it is attended, and to enable them better to compare with the advantages which labour in antagonism with capital is capable in extorting, those which labour and capital in alliance might obtain for their respective shares.

We return to a point from which we have for a few moments wandered. However perfect the organisation of the employed may be or may become, employers can always, if they think fit, raise up in opposition to it an organisation of overwhelming superiority. It may indeed be suggested that hereafter the workmen of this country may endeavour to bring forward, in aid of their unionist pretensions, their newly acquired political power, and, in imitation of the example set lately in Illinois and Wisconsin, get wages raised and working time reduced by law. There is, however, small danger of English working men being tempted to this last extreme of folly. Those among them to whom the others look for guidance are much too quick-witted not to see clearly that the real effect of any legislation of the sort referred to would be the direct opposite of what its authors desired. To enact that employers should give higher wages than they thought they could afford, would not of course cause such wages to be given: if it did anything, it would only cause employers to cease employing, and would so put an end to wages altogether. But to a truth so patent, men chosen for their shrewdness to be unionist leaders are not likely to be more blind than other people, and it is scarcely therefore to be apprehended that they will desire to have the action of employers shackled by legal chains. But provided masters be left free, and provided they be as extensively united and as much in earnest as the men, their union must always be so much the more powerful of the two as to be able to render vain the other's utmost efforts. Both organisations being equally perfect in their respective ways, and both extending over the same area, that of the masters has only to use adequate exertion in order to secure complete predominance. Nevertheless, although it would thus appear that whatever influence the men's unions have hitherto exercised belongs to them only as it were by sufferance, it by no means follows that the same influence will not be suffered to continue. It does not follow that the masters will avail themselves as they might of their capacity for combination, or will use the exertion requisite to place and keep their workmen in subjection.

Until the masters in any trade shall have so far perfected their union as to render its resistance instantly overwhelming, resistance will always be liable to cost them dear. Although it is always the men who suffer most during the continuance of a strike or lock-out, it is generally the masters who suffer longest from its consequences. For a time, while the 'turn-out' operative or artisan, after spending his last shilling, and pawning his last stick of furniture and last shred of clothing, is staring hopelessly into his empty grate, averting his eyes from the hungry looks and shutting his ears against the piteous cries of his children, his employer may perhaps, as represented by Leech or Tenniel, be sipping his claret beside a blazing fire, rather pleased than not with his respite from his accustomed drudgery, and taking perhaps an extra glass because, having less business to attend to, he has more leisure to sit over his wine. Though his business is at a stand-still, he has money in hand and a balance at his banker's, and interest or dividends may be coming in from investments in stocks or shares. With these resources he can go on for a time without any change in his style of living. But if the strike be much prolonged, his position grows at first gradually less and less easy, and then rapidly more and more uneasy. In one or other or all of the ways formerly alluded to, he sees his capital draining away, and capital is to him as his life-blood; when it leaves him he becomes industrially defunct; whereas the labourer who is trying conclusions with him, provided only that his health be not permanently impaired by the privations he is meanwhile enduring, in preserving his thews and sinews, preserves also his stock in trade and industrial vitality intact. Masters, too, are generally fond of peace and quietness. Their hearts are in their business pursuits ; they are eager to be doing, and dislike proportionably to be checked in mid-career. They are in consequence so averse to industrial strife, and incur so much inconvenience and risk so much loss by engaging in it, that, great as have been their past concessions for tranquillity's sake, they would not improbably concede a good deal yet if they could believe that any concessions would suffice, or could see any end to the exactions continually practised upon them. There are indeed obvious limits within which their utmost concessions must be confined. They cannot, of course, consent to rates of wages incompatible with rates of profit sufficient to compensate them for the toils and cares of business ; but, on the other hand, rather than retire from business, they would, if need were, content themselves with the very lowest compensating rates of profit. It is not inconceivable that continuous and dexterous importunity might so weary them out as to render them thankful to rest at last on a minimum of profit admitting of no further diminution. It is not inconceivable that the men, by striking or threatening to strike, might eventually get the maximum of wages which masters could afford to give and still go on employing. Whether this or any part of this will actually happen, will depend mainly on the men's own management. If, persisting in their past policy, they seize greedily on every favourable opportunity for preferring some new claim, their reckless rapacity will infallibly overreach itself by raising up in opposition to them a combination still stronger than their own. If, on the contrary, they are discreet enough to disguise their ultimate aims, and to bide their time for the accomplishment of their designs, there is no saying how far unionism may not enable them to advance, short of the limits just alluded to as impassable.

Briefly now summed up, the following are the results

thus far obtained on the matter immediately before us. Hitherto Trades' Unionism has proved itself decidedly efficacious, obtaining for many sections of the labouring class many and very considerable advantages. This, however, has been owing entirely to the apathy and negligence of employers, who can at will create unions of their own, in comparison with which those of the men would be absolutely powerless. Such unions employers will doubtless eventually create, if they continue to have as much reason as at present for believing that there is no other way of preserving their independence. But they will do this very reluctantly, if at all; and they will probably never do it if the men's unions learn, before too late, to conduct themselves with prudent moderation. If the latter grow politic enough to abstain from giving intolerable provocation, the masters may continue to postpone any adequate imitation of their organisation, and may continue to prefer propitiating to opposing it. By being wise betimes the men may at least preserve all the influence over their masters which unionism has already given them, and may perhaps materially increase it.

We enter next upon the second of the questions proposed for consideration at the commencement of this chapter. Will the advantages extorted from employers by trades' unionists be lasting? So far as those advantages relate merely to the mode of performing work and do not affect its remuneration, there is no reason why they should not. The relative force of the contracting parties remaining the same, there is no reason why the men should not be as well able to keep any advantages of this kind as they were in the first instance to get them. But the amount of labour's remuneration is very commonly regarded as being determined by Nature herself, and as being incapable of being changed, except very temporarily, by art. Any disturbance of the balance in which Nature weighs wages must, it is believed, speedily readjust itself; generally, too, with a force that will fall heavily on all who have presumed to tamper with the scales. If this opinion be correct, unionism, in the most pretentious of its aspects, is after all but a delusion and a snare. To consider what foundation there is for this opinion must be our next step, which, however, in order to be taken properly, will require for itself all the room of a separate chapter.

CHAPTER IV.

EFFICACY OF TRADES' UNIONISM (*continued*).

To go on asserting that unionism *does* not raise wages, and that to all appearance permanently, would now-a-days be running too completely counter to every-day experience. To assert that it *cannot* raise them, is the utmost extent to which any but the hardiest theorists still venture to go. The majority of objectors no longer deny the fact: they only pronounce the fact to be impossible. According to them, whatever augmentation of wages a union may succeed in extorting, either would have eventually been conceded without the union's intervention, or will not be durable. If it be one which employers can afford to grant, they must, it is contended, have granted it eventually of their own accord. If they cannot afford it, then of necessity they must, after a while, leave off paying it. This statement of the case, we may note in passing, admits in part the very thing it purports to deny. Even though a trades' union never obtain any lasting rise of wages which would not have been conceded without its intervention, still, if the union cause the rise to be conceded sooner than it would otherwise have been, then the intervention has secured a substantial advantage. Whatever is gained in time is gained in money also. This, however, is comparatively a trifle. The important question is whether unions can really extort nothing permanent which would not have been granted without them, and in favour of an affirmative reply arguments are brought forward of various degrees of cogency. Some of them are only new versions of the old story of supply and demand, as to which one of its latest narrators has authoritatively declared that there is no dispute among economists. 'The payment of labour,' says this writer, 'is determined by the proportion between the circulating capital which forms the wages' fund, and the number of labourers seeking employment—in brief, by the law of supply and demand.' But then he continues, with droll misapprehension of the only sense in which the term 'law' can be applied in the sense in which he desires to apply it, 'laws are of no avail unless means are provided for their execution;' and how is the law to be enforced? 'For trades' unions,' he proceeds, 'instead of simply enforcing the law of the market, resort to illegal and extortionate action in order to strain that law to their own advantage, thereby excluding the action of supply and demand by forcibly cutting off supply.'* Of all which the only assignable meaning is that demand and supply would determine the rate of wages if adequate force were at hand to compel the rate to be so determined, but that unfortunately the force of unionism acts quite the other way, opposing instead of aiding the action of supply and demand, and so oftentimes regulating wages according to a fashion of its own.

The subject is not, however, always so artlessly treated. More elaborate reasoning is sometimes used. As recently propounded *ex cathedrâ* by a writer of co-ordinate authority with the one just quoted, the argument, though starting as usual with the stock assertion that 'the price of labour depends on the demand for it,' almost immediately diverges from the beaten track. Presently 'the demand for labour is said to depend on the rate of profit, because if profits are high, fresh capital will be attracted into the trade,' which fresh capital, requiring for its utilisation additional labour, increases in consequence the demand for labour, and raises its price, while from a trade in which

* Edinburgh Review, October 1867, p. 446.

profits are low capital is withdrawn, the demand for labour in consequence decreasing and its price falling. Whence it is inferred that 'the real cause of a high rate of wages is a high rate of profit,' and a further deduction is, that if a trades' union compel employers to pay higher wages than they would have done of their own accord, the rise of wages thus obtained must be followed by a fall of profits which will cause wages to fall again to the point from which they rose.*

According to this, profits and wages are somewhat like two buckets at a well, of which neither can rise without the other's falling. Wages cannot rise without profits falling, and profits cannot fall without wages falling in their turn. So that the conclusion at which we are finally landed is that it is quite impossible for wages ever either to rise or fall permanently, for that every rise must necessarily be succeeded by a corresponding fall, and every fall by a corresponding rise. At all places and at all times, wages must be and have been nearly stationary at or about one and the same point, all variations in their rate being mere oscillations, of which that point is the unvarying centre. Never and nowhere can the rate have been, except temporarily, lower than it is at present. The earnings of metropolitan carpenters or bricklayers, for example, must, whatever Greenwich Hospital tables may say to the contrary, be now, or be about to become, the same as they were at the beginning of the century ; and what they were then, they must have been a hundred years before, or, for that matter indeed, at the time of the Conquest.

These are specimens of the sophistry, thus easily reducible to absurdity, with which, in their mania for bringing commercial phenomena under the jurisdiction of natural laws, economists of repute are doing their best to bring the science they profess into contempt. They talk of natural or scientific laws being interfered with, without considering, very likely without knowing, that a law that can be

* Quarterly Review, October 1867, p. 357.

interfered with, cannot possibly be a natural or scientific law at all. They talk of laws, the very essence of which is invariable recurrence, governing operations in which the ever-varying judgments, appetites, passions and caprices of men are principal agents, necessitating continual variations. Workmen are solemnly adjured by them, in the name of political economy, not to try to get their wages raised, because success in the attempt must be followed by a fall of profits which will bring wages down again. They are entreated not to better themselves, because any temporary bettering must be followed by a reaction which will leave them as ill off as before ; not to try to raise the price of labour, because to raise the price is to lower the demand, and to lower the demand is to lower the price. As if a great demand for labour were of any other use to the labourer than that of raising the price of labour, or as if an end were to be sacrificed to means whose whole merit consists in their leading to that same end. Against such teaching, robust understandings of working men instinctively revolt. If all the political economy opposed to trades' unions were like this, trades' unions would be quite right in opposing political economy.

There is, however, more serious opposition from the same quarter yet to be encountered. In all trades in which capital is allowed unrestricted ingress and egress, the rates of profit current in the same country usually afford much about the same compensation to the capitalist for the trouble he takes, the inconvenience he incurs, and the risk he runs. The rates may differ very considerably in different trades, but the differences between them cannot long continue to be much more than proportionate to differences in the trades themselves. If a butcher's business be more profitable than a baker's, the reason is that it is in an equal degree more disagreeable, or otherwise more objectionable. If the extra profitableness were to become more than proportionate to the extra objectionableness, we should be sure to see bakers turning butchers, in sufficient number to restore the former proportion of profit between the two trades, by increasing the quantity of capital in one, and diminishing it in the other.   In all free and unmonopolised trades the rates of profit are in the same country always either in, or tending towards, equilibrium.   Except when disturbing causes are temporarily operating, they are all equal in the sense of affording equal compensation to the capitalist.   While thus in equilibrium, the rates are such that no material augmentation or diminution of the rate current in any particular trade can take place without bringing capital in or driving capital out of that particular trade. If now, while in trades generally profits were at the usual rate, an improvement in business or other cause should in some particular trade—say the cotton manufacture—raise profits above the usual rate, cotton manufacturers would have to choose between two things: either they might themselves at once raise wages, in compliance or not with unionist demands, or they would see them raised in spite of themselves, for if they declined to take the initiative in the matter, their extraordinary profits would attract into the cotton trade additional capital, the competition of whose owners would increase the demand for labour, and raise its price.   Thus either way a rise of wages would be in the circumstances of the case inevitable.   A trade's union might very probably in such circumstances be able to extort a rise of wages, but with or without the union's interposition, a rise would be sure to occur. If, on the other hand, in any trade, say again the cotton trade, an advance of wages should be conceded to unionist demands, at a time when profits in that trade were at only the usual rate, profits would in consequence be reduced below the usual rate, below the rate requisite to keep the cotton trade on a level, in point of attractiveness, with other trades.   But rather than submit to such a reduction, cotton manufacturers would transfer their capital to some other business, whereupon the demand for labour in the cotton trade would decrease, and wages would fall and go on falling, until, by reason of their fall, profits in the cotton trade rose again to their former level. The advance of wages obtained under these circumstances would thus be only temporary.

Such is the real economic case against unionism, and it is one evidently possessing considerable force. Of the two propositions which it embraces, viz., that whenever the state of any unmonopolised trade is such as to allow of a rise of wages taking place without being succeeded by a fall of profits below the usual rate, that rise will take place whether extorted by a trades' union or not—and that no advance of wages can be lasting which cannot be made without bringing down profits below the usual rate—the former is partially true, and the latter is wholly true in most of the cases to which it is applicable. Neither the one nor the other, however, is both wholly and invariably true, even where applicable, and the cases to which neither of them applies are very much more numerous than those to which either of them does. In order to perceive this, we must follow the two propositions through their respective bearings. To do so properly may require close attention, but it will require nothing more, and whoever is willing to bestow so much on the enquiry, will, I venture to say, find himself amply rewarded for his pains by the additional insight he will have gained into a problem quite as important as it is difficult.

First it is affirmed, that when profits are above the usual rate, wages also must necessarily rise, and so no doubt they must to some extent, if the causes to which the elevation of the rate of profit is due, be not merely temporary ; but it by no means follows that the rise of wages which would take place in the natural course of things, would be as great as that which an union might have obtained artificially. When profits rise in any branch of trade above the usual rate, the masters evidently could, if they chose, afford to make over to the men as additional wages the whole difference between their old and their new profits. They could do this if they pleased without reducing profits below the previously current and usual rate. And being able to do this, it is conceivable that they might by a powerful union be constrained to do it. It is conceivable that the men might, by means of their union, get the entire increment of profit transferred to them as additional wages, and there is nothing in the supposed circumstances to prevent a rise of wages so obtained from being permanent. It is certain, however, that the men could not get this nor any similar rise without demanding it. If they asked nothing, they would be pretty sure to get next to nothing. Left to themselves, the masters would certainly go on pocketing the whole of the enhanced profits as long as they could, and until the fresh capital attracted into the trade had, by its competition, brought down the rate of profit. This competition would no doubt raise wages somewhat, but only to a comparatively inconsiderable extent. For one of the first effects of the influx of capital would be, even while raising wages, to stimulate production, and thereby to lower prices, reducing consequently the very fund out of which alone any increase of wages could be made. But prices being thus, owing to the influx of fresh capital, reduced, the utmost enhancement of wages which the masters could then afford, could not possibly be so great as that which, before prices were so reduced, it would have been possible for a union, strong enough to dictate terms, to have extorted.

Thus much to show what large abatement must be made from the first of the propositions under examination before it can be admitted. According to the second, an advance of wages extorted by unionist action cannot be maintained if it be greater than the masters can afford to pay without reducing their own profits below the usual rate. As a general proposition, this might perhaps pass muster. There are several cases to which it is applicable, and in most, though not all of those cases, it holds good. Wages, it is clear, cannot rise without one of two consequences following. Either prices also must rise, or profits must fall. If circumstances be such that prices

cannot be raised, and raised at least as much as wages have
risen, then profits must needs fall; and unless they had
previously risen above the usual rate, they must needs fall
below the usual rate. Then, unless the fall have been
general in all trades, and not confined to some one trade,
either a portion of capital will be transferred from that one
trade to other trades in which the usual rate of profit is
still to be obtained, or that trade will be, wholly or in part,
transferred to some other place or places. This latter has
in fact been in repeated instances the effect of misdi-
rected unionist force. It was in this manner that Spitalfields and Coventry ceased to be the chief seats of the
English silk manufacture, and it is for this reason that ships
which would otherwise have been repaired in the port of
Dublin, are usually sent to Belfast or Liverpool to be
docked. But though where applicable the rule be generally
a good one, yet, even among the cases to which it would
seem to apply, there are some in which it does not hold
good, while the cases to which it obviously does not apply
at all are so numerous as almost to deprive it of practical
value. Even when prices cannot be raised, and when consequently if wages are raised profits must fall, the rule
does not hold good unless there be other trades at hand by
being transferred to which capital may be employed at an
unreduced rate of profit. It need not apply at all to a trade
which is the subject of monopoly, nor to one in which
simultaneously with an advance of wages there were either
increased productiveness or increased demand for produce.
It does not apply either when masters are in a position to
prevent profits from falling by raising prices, nor when,
owing to the adoption of improved industrial processes or
other causes, there is an increase in the quantity of produce they have to dispose of which answers for them the
same purpose as a rise of prices. A few illustrations may
usefully elucidate the nature of these several exceptions.

A rise of wages need not affect profits, if it be accompanied by a corresponding rise of prices, and there are

cases in which a rise of wages may itself bring about a rise of prices sufficient for its own maintenance. This might happen in any trade protected against distant competition, in any trade in which the employers enjoyed a local monopoly, and such is every trade the produce of which it is much more convenient for customers to obtain from producers on the spot, than to procure from a distance. Such, for example, is the building trade. Building work can everywhere be done most conveniently, and generally too most cheaply, by builders of the same neighbourhood. Whoever wants a house built or repaired, will, on many accounts, prefer employing some builder near at hand. Often he has no alternative. Local builders, therefore, by acting on a common understanding among themselves, can often virtually impose their own terms upon local customers, who have often no choice between paying what the builders choose to ask for the work, or not having it done. If, then, by means of a successful strike, the workmen of any of the many branches of the building trade have extorted an advance of wages, their employers can generally compensate themselves by raising prices, and so, notwithstanding the rise of wages, preventing their own profits from falling. And this is what has actually taken place of late years in a variety of instances. Strikes have been more frequently and more signally successful in the building than in any other trade ; the men in it have gained greater advantages over their masters, having indeed in some towns got completely the upper hand of them, and for this plain and simple reason, that master builders suffer less than any other masters by yielding to strikes, and are consequently less interested in opposing them. Whenever and wherever the wages of journeymen masons or bricklayers, or carpenters or plasterers, or plumbers or painters have been raised, the masters have immediately availed themselves of their special facilities for reimbursing themselves, by charging more to their customers. Whenever they have consented to pay higher wages than with existing prices they could afford to pay, they have at once raised prices. What they have chiefly to consider, is how much their customers can afford to pay, and would rather pay than not have the work they require executed : within the limits of their customers' means and desires, they can generally extort whatever price is needed to cover the increased expenses of their business. The advances of ten, twenty, or thirty per cent. which within the last fifteen or twenty years have taken place in the wages of most descriptions of journeymen fabricators, have taken place entirely at the expense of the customer, who has had to pay the employer at least as much more for the work done as the employer has paid more to the journeyman for doing it.

The advantage thus gained by labourers in the building trade has not indeed been quite unqualified. All men, whatever else they may be, are customers or consumers as well. Journeymen bricklayers must lodge, and if owing to enhancement of their wages the cost of houses has increased, they will have to pay proportionately higher rent for their lodgings. This, it is true, is a comparatively small matter. What the journeyman loses by having to pay additional rent for part of a house which he has helped to build, is but a small deduction from what he gains by getting higher wages whenever he is engaged in building. There is, however, another and more important deduction.

Other circumstances remaining the same, as the cost of builder's work increased, the demand for it would diminish. More or less of repairs and improvements would be postponed, and either fewer houses would be built, or some of those built would be smaller or otherwise inferior. In one way or another, there would be less occupation for building labourers than before ; not enough to keep the same number fully employed, and some would be left without work. One of three courses would then have to be followed. The unemployed men might compete with the others for employment ; or they might tamely submit to be excluded from their former trade, and consent to seek their livelihood in other occupations; or it might be agreed among the whole body of workmen, that none should leave the trade, but that only so many should seek employment in it as could obtain the enhanced rate of hire, the remainder being maintained in idleness out of the increased earnings of those at work. In the first of these cases, the men's combination could scarcely have raised the rate of wages, before their competition would bring it down again, and prices, also, would return to their previous level, so that the only result of the strike, over and above the evils inseparable from all strikes, would be some transient disturbance of wages and prices. In the second case it may be thought, that although the workmen who continued in the trade might gain, and gain permanently, through enhancement of wages, they could gain no more, if so much, than their former mates would lose by being excluded from the trade ; while in the third, it may appear that no portion of the workmen could be any better off than before, if so well, or that, if any were better off, they could only be so at the expense of the rest. Apparently if, out of the aggregate of wages received, the men actually employed got a larger amount than before, it could only be because the unemployed men got less. Thus it may be concluded either that the effects of the strike would be only temporary, or• that if it had any permanent results, those results could be beneficial to one portion of the men only in the same degree in which they were injurious to another, while they might be absolutely and altogether mischievous; in the latter event being no other than these, that building work of all kinds would become dearer, that the master builders, though by enhancement of prices obtaining an undiminished rate of profit, would obtain that rate on a more or less contracted business, and that part of the workmen, instead of maintaining themselves, would be living in idleness maintained by the labour of the others.

These conclusions are, however, only partially true. They are based upon the assumption, that though (or be-

cause) building work had grown dearer, the whole amount
paid by customers for such work would be no greater than
before, if so great. If this premiss were sound, the inference from it would be sound likewise. The total receipts
of the master builders remaining the same, the portion
of those receipts which, without diminishing their own
profits, they could pay away as wages, would also remain
the same. If this portion were divided among the same
number of workmen as before, the average rate of wages
would at once become again what it had been. If it were
divided among a smaller number, or among the same
number in a different manner than before, whatever some
of the men gained would be completely counterbalanced
by the losses of others. The premiss, however, is not
sound. It is not the fact that if unionist action causes the
prices of building work to rise, the demand for such work
must fall off *proportionably*. It is quite possible that even
during a period of commercial stagnation,—even without
any increase in the number or wealth of customers,—the
cost of builder's work may rise a good deal without occasioning any very sensible diminution in the demand for
it ; quite possible, therefore, that building labourers may
gain more by an enhancement of wages which has raised
the cost of their work than they can lose through consequent diminution in the amount of employment for them.
Whatever of comfort or luxury people are accustomed to
in their habitations, they are apt to regard almost as a
necessary of life, and are exceedingly unwilling to give up.
Most people would rather put down their carriages, or leave
off going to public entertainments, or giving private ones,
or would even rather stint themselves in dress or diet, than
not have showy drawing rooms and airy nurseries. They
would economise in a good many other things before
making any change in a particular of so much importance
to their domestic convenience and social appearance. If
building work became very dear, orders for it would no
doubt fall off, but in all probability not nearly so much as

its cost had increased.   In all probability, therefore, customers would pay a good deal more for the smaller quantity of dearer work which they continued to order, than
for the larger quantity of cheaper work which they had
been in the habit of ordering.   The total receipts of the
master builders would thus be increased, and the total sum
divisible as wages among the workmen would also be
proportionately greater.   In whatever manner, then, this
greater sum were divided among the men, the whole body
of them, taken collectively, could not fail to be benefited.
If it were divided among the whole number and the same
number as before, as it might be if all took their turns of
working and idling, the average earnings of all would be
increased.   If it were divided among only part of the
previous number, to the exclusion of the rest, although the
latter might lose all they had been accustomed to earn, the
former would gain more than the latter lost.   If it were
permitted to be entirely appropriated in the first instance
by part of the previous number, on the understanding that
its first recipients should out of their augmented wages
maintain their unemployed companions, the former would
be able to allow the latter as much as these latter had been
in the habit of earning, and yet to keep for themselves
more than they themselves had previously been used to
earn.   Regarded as a section apart and distinct from the
general mass of labourers of all descriptions, the building
labourers who had extorted the enhancement of wages
would in their collective capacity be better off than before.
As a body they would benefit, even though individuals
amongst them might suffer, and quite possibly the advantage to the whole body might be unaccompanied by any
individual suffering.   Such, even in a state of the trade not
specially favourable for strikes, may be the effect of a successful strike in the building trade, or in any other trade, the
tailoring or bootmaking to wit, which is the subject of local
monopoly, and the products of which are in urgent and
universal demand.   In all such trades, though in some more

than in others, triumphant unionism may, even in a period of only ordinary commercial activity, occasion a permanent advance of prices, which will permit wages also to be permanently raised.

In addition to these, there is another set of trades in which the same thing may occur. In those just spoken of, employers have little competition to fear except that of their immediate neighbours. There are others in which, though exposed to the competition of similar employers established in other parts of the same country, they enjoy considerable protection against that of foreigners. Almost every country has an advantage over most others in the production of certain descriptions of goods. Great Britain has this advantage in a very marked degree in several branches of industry. Thanks to her insular position, her excellent means of internal communication, her richness in some of the most useful minerals, the abundance of her capital, and the efficiency of her labour, she is without a rival in some kinds of raw, and many kinds of manufactured produce. Coal and iron, cottons and woollens, machinery, hardware and earthenware are but a few among many things in which she can undersell most other countries in their own markets. She might raise her prices for these and several other exports, without danger of being undersold. Manchester indeed could not raise the price of her chief staple, except in concert with the rest of Lancashire and with Glasgow, nor Sheffield with the fear of Birmingham before her eyes ; but by common consent of all British producers, the prices of many articles of produce might be safely raised all over the kingdom. For in the trades in which the articles in question are produced, British employers enjoy a qualified monopoly ; within certain limits of price they are secure against foreign rivalry ; within those limits they can, under the pressure of necessity, raise prices. In this they resemble the master builders just referred to, and, possessing an advantage similar to theirs, they would, no doubt, in similar circumstances make similar use of it.   If constrained by a trades' union to raise wages, they would, no doubt, raise prices proportionately, thereby acquiring the means of continuing to pay the enhanced rate.   They could not, indeed, adopt this course, unless the same were adopted simultaneously by all other employers of their class throughout the country.   A rise in spinners' wages, obtained by a strike confined to Manchester, could not, in all probability, be maintained, for the Manchester manufacturers could not afford to pay higher wages than before without raising prices, and could not venture to raise prices for fear of being undersold by rival manufacturers in other parts of Great Britain.   But if the strike at Manchester were accompanied or followed by equally successful strikes at all other seats of the British cotton manufacture, there would be no reason why the manufacturers should anywhere hesitate to take the steps necessary to compensate themselves for the concession they had made.   Of such strikes, permanent advances of wages might very possibly be the results, for they would not necessarily involve any diminution of employers' profits.   In any branch of industry in which Great Britain possesses a marked productive superiority, British manufacturers might, by raising prices, compensate themselves for any advance of wages not so great as to require that, in order to compensate for it, British prices should be raised to the level of foreign prices. In any such branch of industry, therefore, it would be quite possible for a rise of wages, brought about by unionist action, to be permanently maintained, for much the same reasons for which a permanent rise might by the same means be brought about in such a trade as the building trade.*

* There is some reason to apprehend that the limits within which unionist exactions ought in prudence to be restrained, have already been in some cases overstepped.   The importation into Hull of doors and window frames from Stockholm, the order from Russia for 40,000 tons of iron obtained in 1866 by a Belgian firm in opposition to English competition, the contract with the Dutch Government for rails wrested in the same year by a Liège house from English ironmasters, the fact of Belgian rails having been laid down on the East

Here again, however, as in the building trade, the advantage to the workmen would be subject to certain drawbacks. If the cotton trade were the one affected, those operatives, the enhancement of whose wages had caused the prices of sheeting and shirting to rise, would, like all other people, have to pay more for their sheets and shirts in consequence. The demand for the particular goods whose price had risen would at the same time fall off both at home and abroad, and with the demand for the goods the demand for the labour employed upon them would likewise fall off, bringing down with it (not, indeed, the rate) but the aggregate amount of wages, and, on the supposition that the demand for goods had fallen off as much as their price had risen, bringing down the aggregate of wages to the sum at which it had stood before the rate was raised. On that supposition any benefit to the men which might at first seem to have resulted from the strike, would at best be neutralised, and most probably the benefit would be more than counterbalanced by subsequent injury. If, however, the goods that had thus become dearer, were in very urgent and general request, the falling off in the demand for them, and consequently for the labour requisite to produce them, might not be proportionate to the increase in their price. If they were cottons or woollens, for example, customers might very probably prefer retrenching in some less important branch of expenditure, in order to be enabled to keep up as nearly as possible their customary stocks of inner or outer clothing. Although purchasing probably somewhat less of these than before, they would probably pay for what they did purchase a larger sum total than before. If so, the total receipts of the masters would, as in the parallel case already

Gloucestershire Railway, and of there being French locomotives running on the Great Eastern line—these, after every abatement of their significance that can be suggested, are still ugly symptoms, which our unionist workers in wood and iron cannot wisely disregard. I have seen it somewhere stated (by Messrs. Creed and Williams, if I recollect rightly) that the order for 40,000 tons of iron, alluded to above, involved wages to the amount of 150,000*l.*

described, be greater than before, and the portion of those receipts divisible as wages would likewise be greater.   In whatever manner the increased aggregate of wages were divided among the men, the latter, regarded collectively, could not fail to be benefited.   If it were divided among all, the average earnings of all would be increased.   If among part, to the exclusion of the remainder, the losses of the remainder would be more than counterbalanced by the gains of part.   If among so many only as could obtain employment at the enhanced rate of wages, and if these should, according to unionist custom, take upon themselves the maintenance of the others, those so maintained might get as much as they were getting before, and yet their maintainers might have left for themselves more than they had before.

Two distinct cases have thus been shown, in which a rise in the rate of wages, although due solely to unionist interposition, might yet be permanent, because it might take place without occasioning a reduction in the rate of profit. In one of these cases, all employers of certain descriptions in the same neighbourhood; in the other, all employers of certain descriptions in the same country, have been perceived to possess local monopolies.   In both cases they have been seen to be up to a certain point protected against distant competition—the former against any but that of their immediate neighbours, the latter against any but that of their own countrymen.   Up to a certain point, therefore, they can in the event of their consenting to raise wages, indemnify themselves by raising prices.   It has been seen too that they can do this, even though there be nothing in the state or prospects of trade to cause or to facilitate an advance of prices or otherwise to augment the resources of employers.   Hitherto both business in general and the community transacting it have been spoken of as unprogressive.   No account has been taken either of the improvements in industrial machinery and processes which are continually being made, or of the accumulation of capital which is continually going on in every civilised country. The subject has been treated as if not only there were no increase of production, but as if production were equalled by consumption, and as if there were therefore no growth of national wealth. Yet even amidst such general stagnation we have seen that in certain trades—those, viz. in which the employers are, to a certain extent, monopolists, and of which the produce is in great and urgent demand, unionism might obtain permanent advances of wages.

In scarcely any country, however, and certainly not in our own, is commercial stagnation the normal condition of things. Most civilised lands are to this extent at least thriving, that a year's production commonly more or less exceeds the same year's consumption, and that there is consequently an annual addition to the public's wealth and purchasing power, and, together with this, a continually increasing demand for all sorts of goods. The opening of new foreign markets and the enlargement of old ones also tend to increase the demand for many kinds of home produce. Now, if in any trade, whether monopolised or not, in which, from these or other causes, the demand of customers were increasing, unionism should succeed in extorting an advance of wages, that advance would not necessarily be followed by any reaction, but might continue for an indefinite period without abatement. For though, in order that employers should be able to raise wages it might be necessary that prices also should be raised, and although the natural effect of the rise of prices would be, by diminishing the demand for goods, to diminish the demand for labour, and consequently to bring down wages again, yet this effect might be completely counteracted by the opposite tendency of the increasing wealth of the country to increase the demand for goods, and consequently for the labour requisite to produce those goods. If, for instance, a rise of wages, occasioning a rise of prices, should be obtained in the building trade at a time and place in which customers were increasing in number and wealth, the increase of de-

mand for builders' work from the latter cause might fully
counteract any tendency to decrease of demand from the
former cause, and, notwithstanding the enhancement of
price, the demand for new houses and repairs, and for the
labour required to construct and execute them, might
continue as great as before.   Or, again, slightly varying the
hypothesis, and taking, moreover, as an example one of
those least favourable to the conclusion sought, let us suppose that at a time when increased demand on the part of
customers was raising the price of silks or glass ware, a rise
of wages should be extorted in the silk or glass trade,
both trades in which British employers, instead of possessing
anything like monopoly, are barely on a level with their
foreign rivals.   That rise of wages would not necessarily
require for its maintenance any further enhancement of
prices, nor would it consequently be necessarily followed
by reaction of any kind—by any diminution of demand
either for goods or labour : there would be nothing in the
circumstances to prevent the rise from being permanent, or
from lasting at least as long as the causes, whatever they
were, that had given extraordinary impulse to trade.   For
as the rise of prices which preceded the rise of wages must
have raised the rate of profit above its usual level, the
employers would not, by conceding an advance of wages
commensurate with the advance of prices, cause their profits
to fall below the usual level.   In fact it would be much
more the interest of the consumer than of the employer
that would be opposed to such an advance of wages.   The
employer would surrender no advantage that he could
permanently retain, even though he consented to pay away
in increased wages the whole difference between former and
present prices.   He would really have no choice between
raising wages eventually in that proportion, and letting
prices fall again just as much as he had forborne to raise
wages.   So long indeed as he could delay raising wages, so
long he might gain by getting more than the usual rate of
profit, the consumer meantime suffering through enhance-

ment of price. But the employer's extra gains would presently attract fresh capital into his trade, and whether in consequence wages rose or not, prices would certainly fall low enough to bring down profits again to their original level. If, on the other hand, employers had begun by raising wages as much as owing to the rise of prices they could have afforded to do, there would have been no extra profits of theirs to attract fresh capital into the trade, nor any reason on that account, therefore, why prices should fall, or why wages should not remain indefinitely at their enhanced rate. Whether wages were or were not increased, it would be impossible for the employer long to continue making extraordinary profit ; but in the one case the labourer would benefit at the expense of the consumer, in the other the consumer would benefit in consequence of the labourer not benefiting.

Now the cases thus put hypothetically are pretty exact representations of what has actually taken place in a variety of instances. The building trade, in particular, has for a considerable time been in an exceedingly thriving condition. London may almost be said to have been for some time past in process of reconstruction. So too may quarters of Liverpool, Manchester, Glasgow, and other provincial capitals. In fact, among either English or Scotch towns, with the exception of the few so unlucky as to have been left by our network of railways quite out in the cold, there is scarce one of any note which is not annually increasing by the addition of houses enough to form one or two new streets. In every part of the country the number of persons requiring and able to pay for house accommodation is continually increasing. In every branch of the building trade the rate of wages has simultaneously increased. Journeymen masons, bricklayers, carpenters, painters, plasterers and plumbers, are in many places earning a fifth or a third more than they did a few years ago, and masters' charges have kept pace with journeymen's wages. But the tendency of continually rising prices to diminish the demand for builders' work, has been more than counteracted by the increase of demand consequent on the simultaneous growth of national wealth.   The demand is doubtless not so great as it would have become if prices had not risen, but it is nevertheless as great and greater than it was before prices rose.   There is as much employment and more at the higher rate of wages than there formerly was at the lower.   There is no more reason, therefore, why the higher rate should now be reduced, than there was why the lower rate should have been then.   There is no reason why the higher rate should not be maintained as long as the advancing prosperity of the country keeps up the demand for builders' work.   And as of the building trade, so of many other branches of industry.   The increasing demand for coal and iron has permitted coal miners and iron workers to obtain both enhanced wages and more employment at those wages.   Journeymen tailors, hatters, printers, bakers, are employed at higher rates, yet in greater numbers than formerly.   These are but a few of the businesses in which unionism has gained higher wages for its clients, by taking advantage of the ability of the public to pay higher prices.

Another state of affairs of which similar advantage may be taken exists when, by the adoption of labour-saving machinery or processes, the efficiency of labour is materially increased.   If, for instance, the quantity of labour previously required to convert 50,000*l.* worth of wool into cloth, could now, with the help of some new invention, convert 100,000*l.* worth, the total value of the cloth which the manufacturer would have to dispose of would bear a greatly increased proportion to the whole cost of production, the difference being so much additional profit.   Not only without raising prices, therefore, but even although he reduced them, he might raise the wages of his labourers, and yet retain for himself his accustomed rate of profit.

In the cases hitherto adduced it has appeared to be possible for advances of wages, though artificially obtained, to be permanent, mainly because circumstances were either such as of themselves to indemnify employers, or such as to enable employers to indemnify themselves by raising prices, and so escaping the reduction of profits which the enhancement of wages must otherwise have occasioned. A case may be conceived, however, in which an advance of wages similarly obtained may be maintained permanently, for a diametrically opposite reason. The reason why in a trade in which employers are exposed to unlimited competition, and for the products of which there is no increasing demand, a rise of wages cannot generally be maintained, is that in such a trade employers are not at liberty to raise prices, and that unless prices are raised when wages rise, profits must fall, their fall naturally causing part of the capital invested in the trade to be transferred to some other trade in which the rate of profit has not been reduced. Circumstances may however be imagined, in which there would be no such other trade. If the unionist dreams adverted to in the last chapter should ever be realised, so that all the trades in the country should be united in a national league, connected by offensive and defensive alliances with similar leagues in all neighbouring countries, it is conceivable that such a league might succeed in extorting equal and simultaneous enhancements of wages in every trade whatsoever. The immediate consequence of such a universal rise of wages would be a correspondingly universal fall of profits, which would prevent employers from being any longer able to improve their position by changing from trade to trade, or from country to country. Abroad and at home, they would find wages everywhere equally raised, and profits equally depressed, in all employments. Their least unpromising course might then seem to be to raise prices as universally as wages had risen; but so to raise prices, and yet to keep their whole capital employed, would be impossible; neither, if it were possible, would it afford them much relief. As long as all kinds of business continued to be prosecuted on the same scale, and with the same vigour, so that there was no falling off in production, and that the quantities of all kinds of goods continued to bear the same proportion to each other and to the quantity of money in circulation, there could be no general rise of prices. Neither, if there were, could the rise be of much service to the employers, who would be little the better off for selling their own products more dearly, if they had to pay proportionately dearer for everything they bought. Prices, however, would not rise, and profits therefore could not escape a depression, to which capitalists would have no choice but to reconcile themselves, unless some of them should prefer retiring from business altogether, or at least withdrawing from it part of their capital. Unless this were done, the universal rise of wages would be entirely at the expense of profits, and there would be nothing in the circumstances to prevent the rise from being permanent. In each particular trade employers would have to go on paying away as additional wages what they might otherwise have appropriated as profit, because in any other trade they would have equally to do the same thing.

A universal labour league strong enough to enforce its demands, and demanding a universal augmentation of wages, might indeed easily overshoot its mark and overreach itself. If the increase of wages obtained trenched very far upon profits, the growth of capital would infallibly be checked, and more or less of the capital already invested might very probably be withdrawn from business. When people save money instead of spending it, or store up commodities instead of consuming them, they are abstaining from immediate for the sake of prospective enjoyment, sacrificing the present for the sake of the future. What they especially look forward to, is a permanent income to be derived from the profit or interest of their accumulated capital, and the inducement to accumulate is in proportion to the expectation of such profit or interest, which must be of sensible amount to serve as any inducement at all. Cent. per cent. would make almost everybody a miser. Half per cent. would prevent nobody from being a spendthrift. An excessive rise of wages might thus encroach so much upon profits, as to leave to employers little to save, and little inducement for saving, and still less for risking savings in trade. If any of them still continued to save, it might be rather with the intention of living on their savings, than of living by them. Instead of adding to their trading capital, they would be more likely to take from it, and so, by not making good its wear and tear, allowing it gradually to dwindle away. Universal unionism might then too late repent of its foolish rapacity, discovering that through blind greed for overpaid employment it had put an end to employers, killing the gold-laying geese—which the latter in the case supposed would have clearly shown themselves to be—for the sake of their eggs.

This is what unionism completely in the ascendant might get by abusing its power. For all parties concerned, however, there may be consolation in reflecting that a good while must elapse before it can have so much power to abuse, and that in the interval it may learn moderation enough not to use a giant's strength barbarously, when it becomes a giant. For all except unionists it may be additionally consoling to reflect that nothing but the apathy of employers either could have permitted unionism to become as strong as it is, or can permit it hereafter to grow stronger. If unionism ever does attain to sufficient predominance to be able to raise wages simultaneously in all employments, it will be entirely the fault of employers, who are more likely, however, to take warning from the past, and not to go on repeating their former errors. Still, though it is not probable that their past negligence will continue, it is possible; and the horoscope of our working classes cannot be duly cast unless the possibilities as well as the actualities of unionism be taken into account, and its latent as well as apparent energies be fairly gauged. We cannot show conclusively, what it is the great object of this treatise to show, that whatever unionism may be able to do for working men, industrial co-operation can do still more, unless in our comparison of their respective capacities we give the former credit for the utmost it could do in any conceivable circumstances.

With this view we have yet another set of circumstances to consider—those, viz. of a trade in which there is so much scope for the employment of capital, that a large capitalist might prefer remaining in it to removing to some other business in which, though the rate of profit were higher, he might not be able to obtain that profit upon so large a capital. Thus a manufacturer with half a million invested in his business, and making twenty per cent., or 100,000*l.* of annual profit, might very possibly prefer paying 10,000*l.* a year more in wages, and getting consequently only 90,000*l.* a year profit, to setting up in some fresh business, in which there would not be room for more than half of his capital, and in which, therefore, though the rate of profit were twenty-five per cent., his total annual profits would be only 62,500*l.*

Adding this to the cases previously cited, we have six in all, in which it is possible for unionism to bring about a permanent increase of wages. It may do so: 1st, in any trade of which, owing to some peculiarity in its nature or character, the employers in the same neighbourhood have virtually a monopoly: 2nd, in any trade for the prosecution of which one country possesses a marked advantage over others: 3rd, in any trade the demand for whose produce happens, owing to the growing wealth or growing number of customers, to be at the time increasing: 4th, to any trade in which, without any increase, and perhaps notwithstanding a considerable reduction in prices, the increased productiveness of industry places an augmented quantity of produce at the disposal of the masters, and increases, consequently, their total sale proceeds: 5th, in all trades whatever, provided the rise take place simultaneously and equally in all trades: and 6th, in any trade in which the scale of business is such, that a greater aggregate

profit can be made in it at a low rate than in others at
a high rate. These several cases are so many exceptions
to one or other of the two so-called general rules, that
wages cannot be artificially raised without depressing profits, and that profits will not consent to be permanently
depressed for the benefit of wages ; and the exceptions will,
on further examination, be found to cover so much more
space than the rules, that the latter, rather than the former,
really deserve to be termed exceptional. The exceptions
include many of the more necessary trades—those in particular which furnish us with shelter, and with the more
essential articles of food or clothing. These last, for the
same reason as the building trade, are very apt to be locally
monopolised. Any one who likes to have his clothes or
his boots made to measure, and is at all particular about
the fit, will rather pay a good deal dearer for them in the
nearest town, than send for them to some place fifty or
a hundred miles off. Most of us would rather let the
baker in the next street charge an extra penny for each of
his loaves, than have to send from Belgravia to the City for
our bread ; and there are few London families who do not
put up more or less quietly with the notorious extortion of
London butchers, notwithstanding the repeated assurances
of newspaper correspondents that they might save half the
price of their meat if three or four of them would only
club together, and order up from Wales or Devonshire a
whole sheep, or half a bullock, at a time. The exceptions
include all those numerous trades in the products of which
this country is able to undersell others in their own or in
third markets. They include, that is, most of the employments which have converted Manchester and Glasgow,
Birmingham and Sheffield, Newcastle, Merthyr Tydvil, and
Middlesborough, into perfect hives of industry. In an
age like the present, when national wealth is everywhere
rapidly increasing, and when customers consequently are
everywhere becoming richer and more numerous, there is
scarcely any trade which the exceptions do not, or may

not, occasionally include. In the possible, however improbable and remote, contingency of unionism becoming universal, they might include all trades. In all these cases it
is possible for unionism to raise wages permanently. The
only cases in which it seems absolutely impossible for
unionism so to do, without first gaining paramount control
over the domain of industry, are the exceedingly exceptional ones of trades which are both completely unmonopolised, completely free and open, and carried on in
periods of complete commercial and industrial stagnation.
Under all other conditions, or, in other words, under all
conditions of ordinary experience, one or other of the aforesaid exceptions becomes the rule. We knew before that
in existing circumstances unionism is continually raising
wages, and to all appearance permanently. We have
now discovered that there is nothing in political economy
to prevent its doing that which it manifestly is doing, and
the discovery cannot fail to be acceptable to those tender
consciences which, though their faith in theory is too firm
to be shaken by facts, nevertheless prefer that facts should,
if possible, be in accordance with theory.

Some very few words I must here be forgiven for saying
in corroboration of the doctrine laid down in one of the
earlier chapters. Unionism has undoubtedly, in repeated
instances, raised wages for a longer or shorter period.
That, at all events, is a palpable piece of statistics, patent
to all observers. But it would be simply impossible for
unionism or any other artificial cause to raise wages for
any period whatever, if their rate were, as is popularly
believed, determined naturally by supply and demand in
any of the ways in which supply and demand either are
supposed, or can be conceived, to act. What notoriously
does continually happen is this. Supply and demand
being in some particular state, standing towards each other
in some particular relation, and possibly exhibiting some
species of equation, and there being also some concomitant
rate of wages, a number of men refuse or threaten to refuse

to work unless that rate be raised. Perhaps it may be thought that this refusal or threat of theirs has disturbed the previous relations of supply and demand, and whether this be thought or not will depend upon which of their many different interpretations be attached to the words supply and demand. But whatever be the opinion on this head, if the men succeed in getting what they ask, and return to their work on increased wages, then, whether supply and demand have been temporarily disturbed or not, there can be no doubt that they are now restored to their previous condition, that they again stand towards each other in precisely the same relation, and are just as much equalised as they were before the men struck or threatened to strike. The number of labourers, and the number, requirements, and pecuniary means of their employers, are precisely the same as before. But if supply and demand determine the rate of wages, and if supply and demand have not changed, how can the rate have been changed? Is not the fact that it has changed, conclusive against the popular idea of the causes which regulate the rate?* If, notwithstanding such proof to the contrary, political economists are, as an Edinburgh Reviewer asserts, 'all agreed that supply and demand do determine the rate,' must they not all be equally agreed in resisting the evidence of their senses?

There is still one collateral question to be considered: At whose expense are unionist gains obtained? The most sanguine admirer of unionism will not venture to credit it with the merit of adding anything to the yearly national income; but if that remain the same, and if one part of the community get more of it, another part must get less. When a body of labourers, by striking or threatening to strike, succeed in getting their wages raised, what they gain

* I would invite the particular attention of the British Quarterly Reviewer to what is here said in reference to his remark that ' the effect of Trades' Unions is to lessen the supply of labour, and therefore to alter to the advantage of labour the *proportion* between labour and capital.'

some other persons must lose. Who then are the losers? The answer will vary according to circumstances, according as the rise of wages takes place in a close or in an open trade, or during a stationary or a progressive period, according as it is confined to some one or some few trades or is universal throughout all. In trades which are locally monopolised in the sense in which the building, tailoring, and certain other trades have been so styled, employers can usually by raising prices fully indemnify themselves for raising wages. The products of almost all such trades are commonly regarded as necessaries of life, the aggregate expenditure of the public upon which is likely rather to be increased than diminished as they grow dearer. Employers therefore, although paying higher wages than before, have proportionably increased receipts out of which to pay them, and are consequently no losers. The chief and most obvious losers are the customers, who, according to the hypothesis, are paying a larger total than before, and getting a smaller total in return. If the period be one of commercial stagnation, however, they are not the only losers. At such a period monopolised trades are the only separate trades in which a rise of wages can be brought about by unionist action; and if at such a period and in such trades a rise of wages be so brought about, whatever is gained by the recipients of the increased wages is lost twice over, first by the consumers, and next by the main body of the labouring class, into whose pockets the extra amount paid by consumers would have gone if the successful unionists had not intercepted it. For at a time when national wealth was not increasing, the quantity of money which the public had to spend upon goods and products of all kinds would be a fixed quantity, so that the more was required to be spent upon one sort of products, the less would be left for all other sorts. The more customers were compelled to pay to master builders, for instance, the less they would have to spare for all other employers. Just as much as, by paying higher prices to the former, they enabled these to pay higher wages, just so much, by diminishing their dealings with the latter, would they disable those from paying even the wages they had been accustomed to pay. Just as much as building labourers gained, just so much would all other labourers lose. The good done to the former would be done at the expense of twice its amount of evil, undergone in equal moieties, first by the mass of the consuming public, and secondly by the mass of the labouring population.

The circumstances, however, in which unionism thus appears to so little advantage, are among those of rarest occurrence. If, all other particulars remaining the same, instead of a stationary, a prosperous and progressive period were supposed, in which the wealth and purchasing power of the public were steadily increasing, the only positive losers might be the customers. These, although obliged to pay more for the products of the trade in which wages and prices had risen, might still be able to spend as much as before on the produce of other trades. They might be paying more than before to master builders, and yet be as good customers to all other master traders, which latter, therefore, might still have the same means of employing, and the same demand for labour—not indeed as much of either as they would have had if the building trade had not forcibly drawn towards itself more than its fair share of the public's increasing custom, but still as much as before. The enhancement of wages in the building trade would not therefore occasion any positive reduction of wages in other trades. There would be no positive losses of labourers in general, to set off against the special gains of building labourers. The former would be deprived of nothing they had been accustomed to : they would merely be excluded from participating in unaccustomed gains of which they would otherwise have had their shares.

Limitation of the number of participants is indeed at all periods, whether of stagnation or progress, indispensable, if exceptionally high wages are to be maintained in any trade. Whether with respect to employers the trade be close or open, the workmen in it must be monopolists of its employment, and must be able to impede the entry of interlopers, if they are to retain any peculiar advantages. Such advantages trades' unionists generally endeavour to keep to themselves, firstly, by placing restrictions on the admission of new members into their society ; secondly, by forbidding unionists to work with non-unionists.

This is not the place to make these matters of fact serve as a pretext for the introduction of moral reflections. There is no doubt that in the pursuit of their own separate and sectional objects, trades' unions are accustomed to proceed always without reference to the interests of labour in general, and often more or less in direct opposition to them. But it would be equally little to our immediate purpose to descant on the narrow selfishness of such proceedings, and to bring forward *tu quoque* arguments in their excuse. What though it be true that unionist carpenters or bricklayers try to get and keep for themselves as much as possible of labour's aggregate remuneration, without thinking or caring how much they take from or how little they leave for labourers in general. Or what though they be thereby doing no more than any other associations or individuals would do if similarly situated. What though exact parallels to their proceedings may be found in those of honourable East India and Russia Companies, and honourable Societies of the Temple and Lincoln's Inn, and Colleges of Physicians and Surgeons, and worshipful guilds and corporations without number, and in those of all patentees, and, in a word, of all persons or parties whatsoever, who, having got possession of part of Mammon's gold field, endeavour by all possible means to shut out interlopers. I shall neither, on the one hand, impute as a special enormity to unionists their doing in the world as the world does, nor, on the other, speak as if I thought that the universality of wrongdoing can make wrong right, or that universal selfishness is the less disgusting because it is but another name for universal human nature.

I shall content myself with placing before unionists, what appears to me to be the truth as to the effect of unionist policy on the general interests of labour, leaving them to form their own judgment as to the propriety of such policy. And among those of its consequences over which it may be well for them to ponder, are included, as we have seen, the following. In a country commercially stationary—in which national wealth is not increasing—when a permanent advance of the rate of wages is obtained artificially by unionist action, there must needs be a corresponding lowering of wages in other trades. Even in a country commercially progressive, it is impossible for unionism to raise wages in any particular trade, without causing the demand for the produce of other trades to be less than it would have been, or without equally checking the demand for labour in those other trades. Whether a country be stationary or progressive, an exceptionally high rate of wages cannot be maintained in any particular trade, unless the workmen of all other trades are prevented from entering that particular trade, and endeavouring to get the same rate. Unionism cannot keep up the rate in one trade, without keeping it down in others. It cannot benefit one portion of the labouring population without, during a period of stagnation, injuring the remainder, nor even in a season of prosperity, without at least shutting out the bulk of the labouring population from the advantages secured for a portion.

Now, whether a policy devoted to such narrow aims be or be not deserving of reprobation, it can at any rate have but little claim to public sympathy, and it would, no doubt, be more seemly on the part of trades' unions if, while pursuing each exclusively its own separate ends, they put forward less pretension to an enlarged public spirit. Nevertheless a motive may be suggested which, if avowedly acted upon, might serve as a complete justification for unionist procedure, even when regarded from the point of view from which we are now observing it. The union or unionism, which by the labourers of isolated trades has been discovered to be strength, would clearly be far greater strength if it embraced all the labourers of the same country, or the same commercial range. In thus becoming national or cosmopolitan, it would improve too as much in special aptitude as in general power; for whatever benefit universal unionism conferred on any labourers, it would confer on all, whereas partial unionism cannot benefit any part of the labouring population, except more or less at the expense of the rest. But though in the interests of universal labour the formation of national and cosmopolitan unionism be thus clearly an end to be aimed at, the best, if not the only means to that end is the previous formation and bringing to maturity of separate trade unions. The thing is scarcely to be done, if done at all, in any other way. National unionism is only to be built up piecemeal. To begin by laying foundations coextensive with the area to be finally covered, would be a sure way of never getting beyond the foundations. The only plan at all feasible, is for separate sections of labourers to organise themselves independently, and for each separate organisation to confine its attention to its own affairs, wherein it would long find abundant occupation, without troubling itself about those of its neighbours, until it and they, having grown strong enough to stand alone, should perceive it to be for their mutual advantage to coalesce and stand together. This is the plan which, unconsciously perhaps for the most part, trades' unions are at present following; each, in obedience to its own selfish instinct, seeking only to do the best for itself, yet each doing thereby the best for the others also. That this or any other plan will ever really eventuate in the formation of a confederacy embracing the entire working population may to most people appear an utterly chimerical notion, and no doubt the chances are great against its realisation. But the thing, however improbable, is not more improbable than some of the actual phenomena of unionism would not long since have appeared. Half a century back, while the marvellous organising aptitudes of working men lay dormant and unsuspected, it would have been quite as difficult for anyone to look forward to the existing 'amalgamation' of little less than 50,000 engineers or 70,000 miners as it is now to imagine that in another century or so—no very long period in a nation's life—a combination of these and of other associations may weld together the whole community of British workmen as one brotherhood. At the present rate of progress less than a hundred years would suffice for the operation. Upon data furnished by the last census, the entire adult male labouring population of England and Wales may be roughly estimated at 4,000,000, of whom, to keep well within bounds, we will suppose that less than eight per cent., or say 300,000, are at present unionists. During the last year or two, however, unionism, if its general progress has been equal to what we know have been its advances in particular quarters, must have been joined by fresh recruits at the rate of 40,000 annually, and a continuance of the same rate for three generations would bring every non-unionist into its ranks. Now if anything like this should ever happen, and if the example set here were followed by our foreign neighbours, that machinery would be matured which has already been alluded to as conceivably capable of effecting an universal enhancement of wages. As to the economic bearings of such a phenomenon, not to try the reader beyond all endurance, I will confine myself to pointing out that the advantage resulting from it to the whole labouring class would be obtained by them without any drawback. According to the hypothesis, there would be no diminution of production and no rise of prices, so that in their quality of consumers they would be in no degree the worse; while, as there would be the same amount of employment for them as before, and as that employment would be better paid, they would in their quality of workmen be better off. Their gain in the form of augmented wages would be pure unalloyed gain, and would be gain in which the whole of them would participate, none getting more than others or getting what they got at the expense of others of their own class. Of the entire community, the only class that would lose would be that of employers, and even to these there would be the consolation of reflecting that they were the few suffering for the good of the many. We may imagine them revelling in retrospect on the sacrifices sustained by them for the advantage of an appreciative public, even as Strasburgh geese have been supposed, amidst their liver-enlarging tortures, to glory in foreknowledge of the added zest which the discriminating epicure would in consequence discover in his *pâté de foie gras.*

Here it occurs to me that the economic case against unionism has not yet been fully stated. An important portion of it still remains untouched. That unionism may and often does raise wages will perhaps be admitted to have been placed beyond dispute, but at what expense does it do this? Is the advantage to the men worth what it costs them? Is not their loss generally greater than their gain? On this point, diametrically different opinions are maintained by different writers. On one side, Mr. Harrison seems to think that even in an unsuccessful strike the men's apparent loss is really no loss at all, but only deferred gain. The notion of the wages then temporarily foregone being permanently forfeited is ridiculed by him as ' puerile,' ' sophistical,' and ' a juggle of words.' ' The wages' fund,' he says, ' or the sum which the capitalist devotes to the payment of wages, is, or most of it, sooner or later paid to the workmen in that capitalist's trade.' For, as long as the strike lasts, the wages' fund must, he supposes, remain intact, its owners being unable to employ it, except temporarily, in any other way than in the payment of wages, so that, as soon as the strike is over, there is the fund ready to be divided among the men who were engaged in the strike, and who then get what, but for the strike, they would have got before. ' Strikes,' he proceeds, ' are usually preceded and followed by extra production and labour which nearly equalise the rate for the whole period.' Consequently the men's gains are much the same in the end. 'In the long run they get the gross sum though somewhat discounted,' the chief difference being that it comes to them 'spasmodically,' instead of 'regularly.'*

I refer to the passages of which the above is the substance, principally for the sake of showing how dangerous it is to follow that economic Will o' the Wisp, the wages' fund, and how far the shrewdest intellect may be led astray in consequence. Mr. Harrison will only need to be reminded of what he has written, in order at once to perceive its fallacy. Merciless as he habitually is on what he is wont to call the 'jargon of political economists,' he will see that he has for once been imitating it. On one moment's consideration, he will of course admit that for wages sacrificed during an unsuccessful strike there cannot possibly be compensation in higher rates of wages immediately preceding or succeeding the strike. He will not require to be told that a strike resulting in a rise of wages would not be unsuccessful; still less that the high rate which sometimes precedes a strike cannot possibly be the result of a strike that follows it, nor make amends for the expense of a strike that puts an end to it. Neither, in all probability, will he contend that if the so-styled wages' fund, instead of lying intact and consequently unproductive throughout the continuance of the strike, had during the same period been distributed among productive labourers, and expended in giving them employment and subsistence, it might before the termination of the period have been reproduced and again distributed as before, so that but for the strike the labourers might have got twice or oftener what in consequence of the strike they got only once. Mr. Harrison has of course only to look again in order to see all this clearly enough, and to admit that labourers do incur real loss during a strike, and that if the strike be unsuccessful the loss is irrecoverable.

* 'Fortnightly Review' for Nov. 15, 1865, *Good and Evil of Trades' Unions*, p. 40.

Dr. Watts of Manchester differs widely from Mr. Harrison, but seems to me to go sometimes as much too far in an opposite direction, as, for example, when he treats of wages forfeited during a strike as so much capital which would otherwise have been saved and have gone on accumulating at compound interest. Many of Dr. Watts's arguments, however, are deserving of all respect. The more important among them may be briefly summarised as follows. In a strike on account of wages, the amount in dispute is sometimes not more than two per cent., often not more than five per cent., seldom more than ten per cent. of the rate actually current. The duration of a strike varies much. It may be only a week or less—it has been as much as fifty weeks. But a single week is very nearly two per cent. of a year, three weeks are more than five per cent., and six weeks than ten per cent.; and, while on strike, men of course get no wages. Wherefore, even though the strike aim at as large an advance as ten per cent., and though it last no longer than six weeks and then be quite successful, the men will have lost more during the six weeks than they will recover in a twelvemonth. If the strike had lasted twelve weeks, it would take them more than two years to recover what they had lost ; if eighteen weeks three years, and so on. During the great Preston strike, 15,000 operatives were out for thirty-eight weeks, during which time they must, at the rate of 15*s.* per head per week, have forfeited 427,000*l.* of wages. Eight hundred during the Padiham strike of twenty-nine weeks lost 17,400*l.*, and 1,500 during the Colne strike of fifty weeks lost 56,250*l.* In 1859, when 10,000 London building labourers were out for twenty-six weeks, they gave up 25*s.* per head per week, and must have lost altogether 325,000*l.* All these strikes were failures, but if they had been complete successes, and if the men had got their wages raised in consequence by one-tenth, it would still have taken the Preston men between seven and eight years, the Padiham men nearly five years, the Colne men more than eight years, and the Londoners more than six years, to repay themselves the expenses of their respective triumphs. Whereas if the Prestoners, for instance, or the Londoners, had gone on working uninterruptedly, they might, without stinting themselves more than they actually did while on strike, have saved, instead of sacrificing, 427,000*l.* and 325,000*l.* respectively, and have thereby at once secured as much as the advance of wages sought for could have given them in between seven and eight and six years respectively. The moral hence sought to be deduced is, that even when a strike succeeds the utmost gain from it can scarcely repay the cost, while equal gain might without a strike have been obtained quite certainly at equal cost.*

All this is strongly put, so strongly indeed, that if it represented the whole instead of only part of the case, I do not see how it could be answered. If the immediate results of a successful strike were its only results, and if the persons interested in or benefited by its success were those only who took actual part in it, a strike likely to be severely contested could never be a judicious measure. As we have seen, even if the 15,000 operatives who gave up 427,000*l.* in thirty-eight weeks had then succeeded in obtaining the ten per cent. advance they had struck for, still if that advance were followed by no subsequent advance, and if the advance were obtained only by the 15,000 who struck for it, these latter must have waited for seven or eight years before the additional wages due to the strike would have equalled the amount of wages lost during the strike. Now, many of them would be sure to be dead in seven or eight years' time. It would plainly then have been more prudent for the 15,000 to have begun by saving and putting by thirty-eight weeks' earnings, and thereby making sure at once of a seven or eight years' ten per cent. advance. It is, however, to be remarked in the first place, that the ulterior results of a strike are generally of much more importance than the immediate results, and in the second that what

* 'Workman's Bane and Antidote,' by John Watts, Ph.D., pp. 8-10.

the actual participants in a strike gain, they gain not only for themselves but for many more besides. A set of men who by a thirty-eight weeks' strike had gained an advance of wages, would very probably have created such an impression by their successful pertinacity as would enable them to obtain many similar subsequent advances before eight years were out. The London builders, 10,000 of whom gave up 325,000*l.* without at first getting anything for their money, have since had their wages raised by successive steps from an average of 25*s.* to one of 30*s.* a week, and that without being again obliged to resort to a general strike, or to any strike on a large scale. All their recent strikes have been what are termed 'sectional,' and in many instances they have not had to strike, but have got what they wanted by simply making it clear that they were prepared to strike unless they got it. Chiefly by this means it is that they have succeeded in getting 5*s.* a week or twenty per cent. added to their wages. Now 5*s.* a week is 13*l.* a year, which multiplied by 10,000 comes to 130,000*l.* or forty per cent. on the original outlay, which now yielding such interest must be admitted to have been really, in spite of first appearances, a very tolerable investment. And this twenty per cent. advance, it must be recollected, is not confined to those who struck for it, but is general throughout the building trade of London, and indeed of the greater part of the kingdom. Nay, the pertinacious strikes which have taken place in the building, the engineering, mining, and some other businesses, have exercised an influence which extends far beyond the limits of those particular businesses, and is felt almost equally in every occupation in which unionism has been established. By teaching employers in general how much resolution unionist workmen in general are capable of exhibiting, they have disposed the former to make considerable pecuniary concessions rather than provoke a spirit among the latter which it might cost them still more to allay. Hence it is, that speaking of a trade 'which has never known a serious strike,' an unionist writer can boast of an addition of one-fifth to wages, and of a deduction of one-tenth from working time, obtained merely by ' respectful representations.' Of several other trades a similar boast might equally well be made. It is indeed notorious that in all trades whatsoever in which unionism prevails the unions have of late years been able materially to raise wages. Now the trades in question number their labourers literally by millions, for there is scarce a branch of manufacturing or mining industry which has not its union or unions ; and if it be recollected that non-unionists as well as unionists participate in the fruits of unionist action, the number of such participants in Great Britain will not perhaps be deemed to be greatly over-stated if set down at the same figure as that of the whole male adult manufacturing and mining population of Great Britain at the date of the last census, or at nearly 2,600,000. Suppose, then, the average earnings of these labourers, before affected by unionism, to have been as low as 15*s.* a week, and to have been raised by unionism no more than five per cent., still five per cent on 15*s.* a week, multiplied by 2,600,000, is equal to 97,500*l.* a week, or to 5,070,000*l.* a year, and there is every reason to suppose that the aggregate gain of the whole labouring population has been quite as much as this. There can be little doubt that the aggregate annual earnings of labour in this country are, thanks to unionism, greater now by full five millions sterling than they would have been without it. From such an aggregate, five per cent. interest on all the expenditure that has ever been incurred by unions,—five per cent. on all their outlay, ordinary and extraordinary, swollen as the latter has been by the many quarter and half millions devoted to strikes,—may be deducted and yet leave a very considerable residuum. Rate that expenditure at the high-est conceivable figure. Suppose it to have been during the last forty years not less than forty millions sterling. Still if this amount be now yielding to the working population an annual interest of five millions, or 12½ per cent., Dr.

Watts himself will not deny that, with reference solely to the welfare of the labouring class, as distinct from that of the general community, the money has been very tolerably invested.

The chief recipients in the advantages resulting immediately or eventually from a strike may not indeed be the actual strikers. Many of these, even when victorious, may die too soon to enjoy much of the fruit of victory, their lives, moreover, having not impossibly been shortened by the privations they underwent during the strife. Still, if voices could come from their graves, they might not improbably be heard parodying Horace's famous *Dulce et decorum*, and proclaiming it to be not less sweet and glorious for a proletarian to perish for the sake of his class than for the patriot for the sake of his country. In one case as in the other the consolation would be the same. In both equally, although what had been fought for was not gained by the combatants for themselves, it was through their prowess acquired for those who came after them.

There is another point of Dr. Watts's raising, to which I only allude in passing, because, though he lays considerable stress upon it, I cannot myself consider that it possesses any real importance. Dr. Watts thinks that to the direct loss incurred by workmen during a strike, through forfeiture of wages and expenditure of previous savings, ought to be added the injury done to them indirectly, by the stop put, during the stoppage of business operations, to the growth of employers' capital. All increase of the future wages' fund, he argues, comes out of the profits of the employer and the invested savings of the workman. Arbitrarily to interrupt, therefore, the production of wealth as certainly lessens the future demand for labour, and the future rate of wages, as if the employer's workshops and plant had been burnt, or his wealth cast into the sea. Here, again, we have the irrepressible 'wages' fund' casting its delusive shadow. But what if there be no such fund? Or what if the term be at best allowable only as representing, not any sum that is devoted or destined, or must inevitably be applied to the maintenance of labour, but only that amount which is the utmost that employers can afford to expend upon labour if they please, and if they cannot get all the labour they require for a smaller sum? An addition to the wages' fund in this its only intelligible sense will not necessarily raise the rate of wages. Dr. Watts himself would not expect it to do so, if while the employer's means were increasing, population were increasing, as it commonly does, with equal speed. But even if population were stationary, it might not, and most probably would not, have this effect, unless an enhancement were formally demanded by the men, and demanded by them too with unionism at their back. Otherwise, ninety-nine times out of a hundred, employers would consider it no sufficient reason for raising wages, that they had grown rich enough to raise them. Far rather, as they almost always do when they are dealing with disunited labourers, they would agree among themselves to let wages remain at the previous rate, and to let their own profits rise instead.

Briefly now to recapitulate, we perceived in the last chapter that labourers may by combining acquire an influence which, if exercised with moderation and discretion, employers will in general be willing rather to propitiate than to oppose. Among the concessions which may in consequence be obtained by unionists, the most material are those which affect the remuneration of labour, and these, it is commonly supposed, cannot when due solely to unionist action be of permanent operation. We have learnt, however, in the course of the present chapter that the fact of an increase in the rate of remuneration having been artificially caused, furnishes no reason why in the great majority of cases that increase should not be lasting—no reason why it should not, first in trades in which employers enjoy more or less of protection against competition, and can therefore by raising prices indemnify themselves for raising wages ; or, secondly, during a period in which prices are rising from causes unconnected with unionist action, and in which consequently no special steps need be taken by employers for their indemnification ; or, thirdly, in the event of wages having been raised equally and simultaneously in all trades. These three classes of cases comprise all those of ordinary occurrence, and we have seen that in all these it is possible for unionism to increase permanently the wages of labour. Such being the efficacy of unionism, there is no difficulty in accounting for its popularity without resorting, in explanation of unionist loyalty, to any of those terrorist theories, the exaggerations of which have already been exposed, and on which no additional words need here be expended.

CHAPTER V.

GOOD AND EVIL OF TRADES' UNIONISM.

ENOUGH, it is hoped, has now been said to justify the further assertion that, in the actual condition of the world, unionism is to the employed in a double sense a necessity. It is indispensable alike for their protection and for their advancement. Without it, they must be completely subject to the dictation of employers; with it, they may themselves become, within certain bounds, dictators. Disunited, they are helpless to prevent the price of labour and the other conditions of employment from being imperiously reduced. United, they frequently succeed in getting them materially raised. And for the purposes to which unionism is adapted, nothing can adequately supply its place. The service which it renders nothing else can render equally well—no Conseils de Prud'hommes, no Courts of Arbitration or Conciliation. All honour to the excellent men who, like Lord St. Leonards, Mr. Kettle, and Mr. Mundella, seek to supplant its aggressiveness by such pacific substitutes. All honour and all possible success, but only moderate success is possible. The proposed courts or councils may be advantageously grafted upon unionism or planted by its side. They may usefully supplement, but they are incompetent to supersede it. In so far, indeed, as their purpose is to arbitrate in trade differences, they can scarcely be of much service, for in the great majority of such differences there is really nothing to arbitrate about. Arbitration, as the name itself implies, is a mode of settlement suitable only

where right or title is called in question, and when a disinterested referee may fairly be supposed to be better able
than either of the interested parties to judge which has
justice on its side. A case in point is that of the 'Alabama'
claims, which England, probably, would never have hesitated
to refer to arbitration, except that, conscious of her own
international unpopularity, she feared that no impartial
umpire could be found, and which America's still lingering
hesitation so to refer is not easy to account for, except on
the supposition of her entertaining serious misgivings as
to the validity of her demands. But what in unionist
language are known as trade differences rarely involve
any question of justice. Men do not often strike or
masters lock out on account of an ambiguity in a subsisting contract. The matter at issue is in general, not
what terms have been agreed to for the past, but what
shall be agreed to for the future; and with respect to
the future both masters and men are clearly entitled
to make the best terms they can. Either side is clearly
at liberty to put forward whatever claims it pleases. The
only question is whether it is strong enough to enforce
its claims; but that, like the one as to the recent Austro-
Prussian claims upon Sleswick-Holstein, is a question not
of right but of might, and of a question of might the
parties chiefly concerned naturally consider themselves the
best judges. Whether Austria and Prussia united were
more than a match for singlehanded Denmark was not a
point on which they could be expected to ask counsel from
their neighbours; nor is it much more likely that masters
or men, persuaded that they are strong enough to extort
important advantages by locking out or striking, will consent to let others decide whether they shall or shall not
take advantage of their superiority of strength.

And even though this preliminary objection to arbitration
were removed, another equally serious would immediately
present itself. Even though employers and employed consented to refer their differences to one of the proposed

courts, pledging themselves to abide by its decision, there would be no means of compelling them to keep their pledges. The point for the court to decide would be on what terms certain employment should be given or certain work should be done. But, even though its decree were invested with the sanction of law, it could not possibly be enforced against employers under no obligation to employ, or against workmen under no obligation to work. The former might be forbidden to pay less than a certain rate of wages, but if that rate were higher than it suited them to pay, instead of paying it they would discharge some or all of their workmen, thereby practically locking out. The latter might be forbidden to demand more than certain wages, but if those wages were lower than it suited them to accept, instead of accepting they would cease working, thereby practically striking. Arbitration, if not compulsory, would be a pretence. If compulsory, instead of preventing collisions of masters and men it would be just as likely to create and multiply them.

Nevertheless, though the proposed courts could not for the purpose of formal arbitration be, at best, otherwise than failures, they might, without much change in their composition, become of very material use. Converted into councils of conciliation, they would be calculated to exert a very salutary influence. So metamorphosed, though they could no more than before do away with the necessity for unionism, they might greatly mollify its character; though they could not render strikes impossible, they might often, perhaps always, prevent their occurrence. Their possible efficacy may be estimated from actual experience of institutions of the kind at Wolverhampton, where the following arrangements, established under the auspices of Mr. Kettle, Judge of the Worcestershire County Courts, have been for some time in operation. In three branches of the building trade—those of carpenters, bricklayers, and plasterers—twelve delegates are selected, half by the masters and half by the men, and, together with an umpire appointed by themselves and unconnected with their business, form a court, to which are referred all disputes occurring between such employers and such employed as are parties to the arrangement. Those who are so have notices to that effect hung up in their places of business, whereby they are held to be pledged, legally as well as morally, to abide by the court's decision, and though for the reason just explained these pledges are not really binding on any who do not choose to be bound by them, in practice they are said to be faithfully observed, insomuch that since the courts have been in existence, no disputes have occurred within the trades which recognise their jurisdiction that have not been amicably adjusted by their means.

A similar system has since 1860 existed, and been productive of similar harmony, in the hosiery trade of Nottingham. A board composed of seven manufacturers and seven workmen, with one of the former for president, takes cognizance of all disputes about wages and the like, and manages so satisfactorily that during the eight years of its existence, although a period of great distress in the trade, not a single strike or lock-out has taken place in a branch of industry which, during the previous eighty years, had been more frequently and more violently convulsed by such disorders than almost any other. Of these Nottingham arrangements, which are in some particulars improvements upon those in force at Wolverhampton, Mr. Mundella, the newly-elected M.P. for Sheffield, was one of the chief originators, as he is still their most zealous and energetic promoter. The object of Lord St. Leonards' Bill of the last session was to cause similar courts to be generally adopted, and it is much to be desired that some such measure as that which he proposed should become law.* His lordship's enactment was not indeed intended to be more than permissive and enabling, but this would have been one of

---

* While these sheets are passing through the press, I learn that Lord St. Leonards' Bill did pass last session as the ' Equitable Councils of Conciliation Act of 1867.'

its merits. To have made its provisions compulsory would have been nugatory, if not mischievous, whereas simply to notify by express declaratory statute that the courts in question might be legally instituted in a certain manner would be tantamount to an authoritative recommendation very likely to be generally attended to. And it would be an immense point gained if in consequence, at all the chief centres of industry, machinery should be established which would be always at hand for the amicable adjustment of industrial quarrels. The mere fact of the machinery being constantly available for use would often suffice as a reason for using it. Merely because the courts were there for no other purpose than that of being resorted to by masters and men, masters and men would often be tempted to resort to them. Moreover, their being so resorted to would be a sort of pledge for their not being resorted to in vain. Many of the bitterest trade contests have their origin quite as often in some sentimental provocation as in any more substantial grievance. The men often care less about the claim they put forward than about the way in which it is received, or rather not received, by the masters. What irritates them beyond endurance is the latter's high and mighty demeanour, their haughty refusal to confer with the men's representatives, or to vouchsafe them any other reply than an intimation of their sovereign will and pleasure. Wherever Lord St. Leonards' recommendations were acted upon, this stumbling-block of offence at any rate would no longer exist. Merely by agreeing to meet by delegated proxies in court, masters and men would be evincing mutual respect, and they would meet there with avowedly amicable motives, instead of, as they must have done if they had met elsewhere, in mutually defiant mood. Meeting, too, for the avowed purpose of reasoning, they would be obliged for consistency's sake, and in order to show themselves reasonable, to avoid mutual recriminations, and to listen patiently to each other's explanations. They would thus have all instead of only half the circumstances of the case set before them, and with ampler materials for judging, would be so much the more likely to form a wise judgment. So too, and for the same reason, would the outside public, which in important cases would not fail to take cognizance of the debates, and when sufficiently interested in them to declare decidedly in favour of one side, would almost certainly induce the other to give way. For to persist obstinately, in opposition to strongly pronounced public opinion, is to be either more or less than human. No one who has ever seen can have forgotten Carlyle's grim picture of De Launay in the cellars of the Bastille. There he sits, the stern old governor, with a lighted torch in his hand and a barrel of gunpowder by his side, waiting for the proper moment to blow up the fortress ; and now that moment has come. He only delayed until the halls and galleries should be full enough of besiegers, and now the whole place swarms with them. He hears them shouting and yelling above, around, on all sides, and their very shouts paralyze him, for every voice he hears is a vote against his purpose, and to be outvoted by thousands to one is too much for his faith in his own principles. Much less extraordinary cases would suffice to make ordinary men show themselves as unstable as so many De Launays. However well satisfied previously of the rectitude and propriety of their procedure towards each other, neither associated masters nor associated men would often be found persevering in it after the public voice had begun to cry shame upon their perverse obstinacy.

No doubt, with this assistance from the public, courts of conciliation might so greatly improve the relations between employers and employed that both would be well content to let many of the habitual functions of unionism fall into desuetude. Yet it must not therefore be supposed that the courts in question can ever completely take the place of trades' unions. On the contrary, without the latter the former could not subsist, nor in all probability would ever have been thought of. Disunited workmen could not depute delegates to represent their united body, nor could the resolutions of delegates be binding upon disunited work-men. Neither would masters condescend to depute delegates of their own, to treat with the men's delegates, if they did not know that these were backed by an union ready to fight if not appeased by diplomacy. The masters consent to negotiate, only to avoid the alternative of fighting, but it is unionism alone which gives them that alternative to apprehend. But for unionism, masters would again be able to dictate as of old. Without it, the men could not have that preparedness for war which, in theirs as in every other case, is the best guarantee for peace. Even though all concerned were desirous to substitute conciliatoryism for unionism, the thing would be impracticable. The former would still require the latter as its basis.

As long, then, as the existing industrial system endures, as long as a broad line of demarcation continues to separate employers from employed, so long unionism may as well be recognised as one of the social necessities of the time. So I am myself constrained to term it; yet if anyone choose to term it, in addition, a necessary evil, I am not disposed to contradict. Some unionist abuses have already been set forth in sufficient detail, but there are many other objection-able circumstances connected with the constitution, or regu-lations, or practice and deportment of trades' unions, which cannot be left unnoticed in any faithful portraiture of unionism. To these I will now briefly advert, in the order in which I have classified them, beginning with a grave con-stitutional defect.

All unions which seek, as most do, to combine the pur-poses of 'benefit' with those of 'trade' societies, rest upon bases financially unsound. The incomings of the richest among them are insufficient even for their ordinary and calculable liabilities, and they are liable in addition to ex-traordinary calls, the amount of which cannot possibly be calculated beforehand. Few, if any, other unionists tax themselves nearly as heavily as the Amalgamated Engineers and Amalgamated Carpenters, who pay a shilling a head weekly, or three or four times the more usual rates of $3d.$ or $4d.$; but according to the principles by which the proceedings of ordinary insurance companies are regulated, the taxation of these engineers and carpenters ought to be three or four times heavier still, in order to provide duly for the allowances which their associations are pledged to make for the support of sick and superannuated, and for the burial of deceased, members, independently of their miscellaneous obligations towards members who are desirous of emigrating, or who have lost or broken their tools. It is true that the proportion of its promises to pay which a trades' union is likely to be actually called upon to keep is smaller than that of an ordinary life insurance company. Almost everyone who has begun to insure his life goes on regularly paying the premium, until, on his death, the company has to pay in turn to his heirs; whereas it is a very common thing for unionists, after paying their weekly groats or shillings for a year or two, to stop their subscriptions on changing their place of residence, and thereby to forfeit all future claims upon their society, leaving to it all their past contributions as so much pure gain. The Amalgamated Engineers, during the first sixteen years of their existence, profited in this manner at the expense of 13,317 of their members. For the profit which a trades' union thus obtains, however, it is indebted mainly to its own immaturity. Not a single union is as yet more than half grown: not one includes more than half the whole number of workmen belonging to its particular trade, and not many, more than a tenth. Of the Carpenters, nineteen-twentieths are still unamalgamated. But every trades' union is sanguinely looking forward to a time when all eligible workmen in its particular trade will be comprised within either its own or some similar incorporation; and when that time comes, no unionist will be able, without going abroad, to go anywhere very far away from some one of his union's lodges, or where he will not be within reach of the union's aid, if he still belong to it, or of its persecution

if he do not.   It may be presumed, therefore, that there
will then be few temporary secessions, and that once
a member always a member will then be the rule.
But in proportion as the permanence of membership increases, so too will increase the proportion of members'
claims which the society will be required to satisfy, until
there will be at length no difference in that respect between
it and an ordinary assurance or benefit society.   Such an
increasing drain upon its resources no trades' union, with
its present financial arrangements, would be able to bear.
Of the Amalgamated Carpenters, for example, it is arith-
metically demonstrable that one of them could not, by
subscribing a shilling a week for twelve years, secure to
himself thereafter an annual pension for life of 18*l.*, and much
less several miscellaneous intermediate payments in addition,
if a benefit society could afford only half the same yearly
amount to a similar subscriber of thirty years' standing.
Nor will the Amalgamated Carpenters be permitted to go
on till their association is full grown without finding this
out.   Hitherto, it is true that both they and the Engineers
have not merely paid their way, but have been steadily and
rapidly making money, but the reason is simply that
neither society is old enough yet to have had its solvency
fairly tested.   There has not been time for many members
of either to become superannuated.   Most of them are
still young or middle-aged men, who have been content to
go on paying without any immediate return, and solely for
the sake of prospective return.   Hitherto, therefore, the
incomings have greatly exceeded the outgoings.   But as
both the society and the individuals composing it get on
in years, the former will be called on to make greater and
greater returns for the advances it has received, and to
which its outgoings will then bear a very different proportion.   Even though the association should not become
numerically stronger, the strain upon its resources must
henceforward be much harder than it has hitherto been.
But if it continue to grow as it has done of late, the strain

will be more than it can possibly bear. Sooner or later it must inevitably become bankrupt, unless it either raise its rates of subscription or reduce its allowances, and the sooner it adopts one or other of these expedients the better. By doing so betimes, with due advertence to the doctrine of chances, it may sufficiently guard against ordinary contingencies. But even then there will be little less danger than before to be apprehended from extraordinary contingencies, against which it will be impossible to be sure of having taken sufficient precaution, because their extent cannot possibly be foreseen. No definite provision can be depended upon for an indefinite drain. No subscriptions, no accumulations, can afford complete security for ordinary claims, if these are liable at any moment to be indefinitely swollen by irregular and extraordinary claims of unforeseeable amount. As long as the cost of a strike or a lockout is held to constitute a first lien on union funds, no unionist can be certain that his application for the superannuation or other allowances to which he may have become entitled will not be addressed to an empty exchequer. The evil thus to be apprehended is real and serious, but both it and the danger of it are very apt to be exaggerated. Workmen, it is to be presumed, do not join an union blindfold. They understand the differences between the primary and the secondary objects of unionism, and are intelligent enough to judge how far the two are compatible with each other. And the primary object occupies, as of right, the first place in their estimation. They may be likened to speculators who invest in a joint-stock undertaking for the sake of a dividend, with the hope of a bonus. If they get the first regularly, they are content, as in these days they have good cause to be. If they get the second in addition, they may deem themselves preternaturally lucky. Now, to unionists, support when, in seasons of industrial discord, they throw themselves or are thrown out of work, is as a dividend ; superannuation allowance as a bonus, the latter being viewed as only a possible gain, and as only subsidiary to the more assured provision which, if they are wise, they will make for old age.

Experience besides has shown that, as an union grows in strength, the chances of collision between it and employers diminish. The stronger unionists are, the more anxious are employers to propitiate them. The richer they are, the less willing are they to risk their money. As long as they have little or nothing to lose, they raise the song of battle recklessly enough—*cantabit vacuus*—but as their coffers are filling, then, as a good old gentlemanly vice, they gradually take up with avarice, and get to look upon strikes as extravagances to be resorted to only in extremity. For several years the Amalgamated Engineers have had only two or three strikes, and the Amalgamated Carpenters very few of any note; and if, as may be fairly expected, they go on advancing in discretion as they advance in age and experience, they will in all probability cease before long to have them at all.

In this their gradually growing peaceableness of disposition, rather than in the high-handed measures occasionally prescribed by hasty advisers, is indicated the best security against the particular danger under consideration. It has been suggested that trades' unions should be required to divest themselves of their composite character, and that, leaving their provident functions to be performed by distinct provident societies, they should confine themselves to purely industrial concerns. Those who recommend this flatter themselves, perhaps, that when deprived of the support for which they are indebted to their provident pretensions, trades' unions would decline into insignificance; but a much more natural result would be that, when subsisting only as purely militant bodies, they would, instead of being rendered harmless, become of a more fierce and warlike temper. The humanizing influence which the performance of friendly offices towards their constituents is calculated to have over them would then in a great measure cease. When the sole end of their being was that of carrying on hostilities, they would naturally be on the look-out for favourable opportunities of acting on the offensive. Such a habit would not of course tend to the establishment of improved relations between the employed and the employing, and a widening of the angry gulf of separation between them would be a heavy price to pay for the additional stability acquired by unions.

A modification of the same suggestion is that unions, without formally dissolving in order to reconstitute themselves as independent societies, should keep the funds destined for different operations completely separate, so that the provision for provident purposes should no longer be liable to be swept away in trade disputes. This plan is pronounced by experienced unionist functionaries to be impracticable : whether really so or not, it would certainly prove ineffectual. The proposed separation, if made, could certainly not be maintained. It is not to be supposed that, when reduced to extremity, unionists would hold any money of their own sacred, or that they would scruple to use to-morrow's provision for to-day's sustenance, when the only apparent alternative was their doing away with to-morrow's need, by perishing intermediately from starvation. To prevent such malversation on their part some writers have indeed gone so far as to insist that trades' unions should be compelled by law, either to relinquish provident functions, or to place their provident funds out of reach of misapplication. Whereupon, suffice it to observe that a reformed parliament certainly will never think of enacting the requisite law ; and that it is perhaps just as well no unreformed parliament ever did. English workmen are no longer children, and are not at all of a temper to permit themselves to be again placed in leading strings.

We come next to certain unionist regulations which are sometimes stigmatized as tyrannical towards unionists themselves, besides being otherwise objectionable in their bearing, both on the general community and on the labouring sections of it. Objectionable in many respects they certainly are, but tyrannous or oppressive, in regard to the unionists who have adopted them, they as certainly neither are nor can be. *Volenti non fit injuria.* No man can be made an unionist except by his own consent, and no member of a society which he need not have entered unless he had chosen, and which he would not have been entitled to enter without permission from the other members, can possibly be aggrieved by any law of the society, which applies to him only in common with the rest, and does not involve a breach of faith with himself. None of the society's laws, provided only that they be of impartial operation, and do not violate the original conditions of admission, can, however preposterous their purport, be correctly designated as unjust to the associates—not even though they require the right hand to be cut off, or the right eye to be plucked out ; or though, like the statutes of the Fat and Lean Clubs commemorated by Addison, they make it a disqualification to grow in the one case thin enough to pass through an ordinary door, or, in the other, stout enough to be distinguished from a living skeleton. If the majority of unionists did not like the rules about minimum wages, piece-work, overtime and the like, they would not, it may be presumed, have permitted the rules to be passed ; while the minority who dislike them may similarly be presumed to find, in certain parts of the unionist code, abundant compensation for its objectionableness in others.

The fact, however, of regulations not being unjust is no proof of their not being injudicious, as all of those just adverted to must be admitted to be, although in very different degrees. To the fixing of a minimum rate of wages, the chief objection appears to be that the thing sought is not attainable. Nothing could be more proper than to insist that no workman should accept a lower wage than would suffice for a man's decent maintenance, if the so sufficing wage could thereby be secured to every one requiring it. But at any given time the whole quantity of work to be done is a fixed quantity, and the utmost which employers can afford to pay for having it done is a fixed amount, and if the latter be too small to admit of all work-men earning the prescribed wages, and if they are for-bidden to take less, some must necessarily remain earning nothing. Something of this kind frequently occurs under the operation of the rule in question. Trade grows slack, so that employers can no longer afford to pay the prescribed rate except to the best workmen ; or the best workmen grow old, and cease to be worth the minimum rate. Many an employer would, nevertheless, prefer keeping on the old hands, but the union leaves him no choice between dis-charging them and paying them more than they are worth, and the union alone is to be blamed if he adopt the former alternative.

Another objection is that a minimum is almost sure to become a maximum rate. When workmen of varying de-grees of strength and skill insist on being all paid at one and the same rate, that rate must be above the deserts of the worst amongst them; for if not, it would be below the deserts of all except the worst. But an employer, com-pelled to pay too much to some of his men, is compelled in self-defence to pay too little to others. Even for his own sake, he would prefer to encourage extra merit by extra reward; but if he be forbidden to make distinctions in one direction, he cannot afford to make them in the other, and so he treats all his men alike. True, the uniform rate at which he pays them all may very probably be higher than the mean of the varying rates which would have been adopted if the men, instead of acting together, had bar-gained separately, each for himself. Quite possibly it may be as high as the highest of those rates would have been. If so, and as long as affairs continue so, none of the men will suffer in pocket, while many may profit considerably. Still the arrangement, besides being detrimental to the general public, will, even to the workmen with whom it has originated, prove the reverse of advantageous in the long run. When good and bad are paid alike, the bad are deprived of the strongest motive for improving themselves ; and the good, of one chief reason for wishing to keep up their superiority. The efficiency, and with it the productiveness, of their aggregate labour may therefore be expected to fall off eventually, when a reduction of their remuneration will naturally follow.

As to overtime, workmen's dislike of it is easily explained. Those engaged in any particular trade may very plausibly argue thus : So many hours of our work a day are as many as a man of average powers can do without impairing his health and constitution, or as any man can do without encroaching on the leisure for self-culture and for recreation which every man must have in order to be anything better than a mere working machine. By working an hour or two longer we might earn more, but ten to one our extra wages would be spent upon the extra gin which we should require to repair our overtasked energies, and at all events the earning of those extra wages would occupy time which might otherwise have been spent very much more to our advantage. Besides, the extra wages so obtainable by any of us could often be obtained only at the expense of our fellows. There is seldom in our trade more than enough employment to keep us all at work for as many hours as we are able to work without doing ourselves harm. If then some, by working overtime, get more than their shares of employment, they will not leave enough for the rest. By making it a rule then not to work overtime, except when the quantity of work is too great to be got through in time without, we are consulting at once both our united common interest, and most of our individual interests, and though to a few possessed of superior strength the rule may be of less use than to others, the restrictions which it imposes are no greater than persons of any public spirit ought readily to submit to for the public good.

The whole of this reasoning applies almost equally to piece-work, which is open to all the same objections as overtime, but to several besides. It similarly tends to make men overtask themselves, and to contract intemperate habits, and it similarly diminishes the quantity of employment left for those workmen by whom it is not practised. The charge too brought against it, of tendency to lower the remuneration of labour, is not without foundation. Men working by the piece, and finding that by extra exertion they can earn half as much again as before, say 30*s.* instead of 20*s.* a week, may by a cunning master be easily wheedled into accepting terms which will not admit of their earning with the same exertion more than 25*s.* a week. And whatever terms piece-workers agree to may plausibly be set up and easily used as a standard for determining the proper remuneration of time-workers, all the more easily because the more work a master gets done by piece the less need he has of the assistance of time-workers. This is a serious drawback from what is frequently put forward as a conclusive recommendation of piece work—viz. that, in the interest equally of employer and employed, it proportions the reward of labour to the labour exercised ; that when a man is paid by the piece he is paid in proportion to what he does, he being secure of money for money's worth, and his master of money's worth for his money, whereas if paid by time he might earn no more than some idle companion who, working with him on the same job, had done only half the same work in the same time. But a man may fairly doubt whether he gets full money value for his labour if, though working half as hard again as before, he earns only a fourth part more. Piece-work, again, is exceedingly liable to become scamped work. Men whose earnings depend on the quantity of work they do, are not likely to give themselves much avoidable trouble about its quality. They will rather hurry as fast as possible over the surface, hastily covering up what builders call 'pockets' or other defects, and not caring to lose time in getting unseasoned timber or cracked bricks or spongy iron exchanged. On the other hand, overtime and piece-

work are no doubt among the readiest expedients to which
a man can have recourse for turning extra strength or skill
to profitable account, or for supplying the wants of an increasing family, or for extricating himself from pecuniary
embarrassment, and to be arbitrarily interdicted from such
obvious means of self-help must often be felt as a cruel
hardship.

With regard to both overtime and piece-work, the great
unionist error consists in interfering paternally with individual liberty in matters which chiefly concern individual
interests, and in insisting on things being done which,
unless done cheerfully, had better not be done at all. The
error is one of a sort to which leading unionists, and working-
class leaders generally, are peculiarly prone. A favourite
notion of theirs is that whatever seems to them right to be
done, people ought to be made to do, and a most pestilent
notion it is to be entertained by the foremost men of a class
who have just been formally invested with the power of
making people do whatever they please. Would that these
could be persuaded to take ‘Mill on Liberty’ as their daily
manual and bosom companion. There are few of us who
have not much to learn from that inestimable little book,
but there are none, unless perhaps parsons, who so much
require its precious counsels as those to whom I am specially recommending it.*

‘That machinery does not diminish, but enlarges the
field of employment, is’—says a recent writer, the same
as he who has already been quoted as asserting the un-
disputed authority of supply and demand over price—‘a
thesis which he would be ashamed at this time of day to

---

* A collateral recommendation of piece-work is its occasional use in
technical education. When, according to a not uncommon practice
in certain trades, a superior workman takes from his employers a sub-
contract for the performance of a certain job, he generally associates
in it with himself a number of inferior hands, apprentices and others,
whom it then becomes his interest to instruct in his and their business,
instead of leaving them, as apprentices are generally left, to pick up
instruction as they can.

argue.' By this ill-timed bashfulness, on the part of one little wont to give way to such an infirmity, the world has been deprived of some unhesitating counsel on a point on which it is desirable to have all possible materials for making up one's mind. In the absence of the light thus denied, I am myself unable to understand how mere labour-saving machinery can possibly, if no counteracting cause intervene, fail to diminish the demand for labour. If, indeed, the machinery increased the productiveness of labour in a greater ratio than that in which it saved labour, its influence on employment would be different. If, by using improved implements, one man were enabled not merely to do the work of two, but to turn out more produce than the two together had formerly done, the demand for labour might remain unabated, or might increase. If with only half the previous expenditure of labour two ears of wheat were made to grow where but one grew before, or twice as much ironstone were brought to the pit's mouth, or twice as many herrings were caught, those men for whom there was no longer place in the cornfield, or in the mine, or on the fishing-ground, might yet find full employment in making the additional wheat into bread, or in smelting the additional ore, or in curing and packing the additional fish. But if there be no more corn, and no more ore, and no more fish than usual, if the new machinery has created no new work, and has only enabled the old work to be done with fewer hands, thereby causing some of the old hands to be discharged, how can it be asserted that the field of employment is enlarged? how denied that it is diminished?

The result would be the same if the labour saved had been accustomed to be employed, not in raising raw produce, but in subsequently manipulating it. It seems to be supposed that, if an improved jenny or power-loom enabled a single spinner or weaver to make as much yarn or cloth as two could previously, yarn or cloth would then become so much cheaper, and the consequently increased demand for it would be accompanied by such an increased demand for the labour required to make it, that the tendency of the labour-saving jenny or loom to diminish the latter demand would be more than counteracted. It seems to be thought, in short, that if only half the previous quantity of labour were required to fabricate a given quantity of goods, those goods would grow so much cheaper, and the demand for them would be so much increased, that as many or more labourers would be required in the trade than before the labour-saving processes were introduced. It is forgotten that, of all manufacturing and of most other production, the labour immediately employed is only one, and only a minor, element, and that consequently no saving in the quantity or cost of that labour can in any commensurate degree cheapen produce, or thereby increase the demand either for produce or for labour. If, for instance, with the appliances at present in vogue, two weavers at 50*l.* each were required to convert 1,000*l.* worth of yarn into 1,300*l.* worth of cloth, and if, thanks to some mechanical improvement, one weaver would thenceforward suffice for the job, the saving in the cost of making cloth would be at most 60*l.* in 1,300*l.*, or less than five per cent.; and there would be no reason why the price of cloth should fall, or why the demand for it should rise in any sensibly greater ratio. For every 1,300 yards previously bought 1,360 or thereabouts might now be asked for; but, in order that all the weavers displaced by the machinery should receive employment, it would be necessary that the demand for cloth should be doubled instead of being increased by one-twentieth; that, for every 1,300 yards formerly bought, 2,600 instead of 1,360 should now be asked for. With an increase of no more than one-twentieth in the demand for cloth, only one weaver out of every twenty thrown out of work could again get into employment. The other nineteen would have to remain out.

It need not, I trust, be explained that these observations are not offered in vindication of the conduct to which they refer. About the senselessness of such conduct there can be no reasonable question. Not to use machinery because it saves labour is about as wise as it would be to resolve to use only the left hand because one can work so much better with the right.   But the more transparently false a notion is, the less excuse is there for rebuking it with pious falla-cies—as palpable too as pious.   To argue that the less labour employers can contrive to do with, the more labour they will require, is like arguing that the larger the pigeon pies, the more of them it will take to make a John Browdie's breakfast, or that the more light lamps give, the more of them will be needed to light up a room.   Since labour-saving machines must needs save labour, and since the more labour can be saved, the less of it will be needed for any given purpose, the direct tendency of labour-saving machines cannot possibly be otherwise than to diminish the demand for labour.   So much is—not indeed incon-testable, for many are perverse enough to contest it—but at least abundantly clear.   What, however, must be con-fessed to be equally clear and notorious is that, although more and more of labour-saving machinery is continually coming into use, the demand for labour, instead of diminish-ing, is continually increasing ; of which phenomenon the obvious explanation is that national wealth likewise is continually increasing, and that its increase increases simul-taneously the demand for all kinds of produce, and there-fore the demand for all kinds of labour also, more than any causes of an opposite character diminish them.   Here is a concomitantly counteracting influence which has hitherto rendered machinery harmless in the only particular in which it is capable of injuring labour ; and the same in-fluence may be expected to continue to operate until the extreme limits set by nature to the progress of material wealth shall be approached. One day or other perhaps, every accessible inch of the earth's surface may have been brought under the best possible cultivation, its mines and fisheries too being simultaneously utilised with equal completeness. When that day arrives there can be little or no further augmentation of the stock of materials that industry will have to work upon. Any further extension of the field of labour will be almost an impossibility, and thenceforward working men will require no excuse for doing their best in self-defence to prevent the adoption of labour-saving innovations. That day, however, is somewhat too distant a morrow to need to have much thought taken for it as yet, and in the meanwhile labour's hostility to machinery is quite as great a mistake as it is called. Over and above the injury it does to those general interests in which labourers share in common with all other classes, it easily may do, and frequently does, a special injury to labour. For wherever labour is not in excess, whatever causes less labour to suffice for certain productive processes sets more labour free for other productive purposes, thereby increasing the productiveness of the whole mass of labour, and facilitating the accumulation of further capital for the employment of further labour. In this manner the very machinery whose immediate tendency is to diminish employment may, and often does, foster the growth of that which subsequently increases employment. Wherever labour is not in excess, whatever harm machinery does to labour directly it undoes indirectly, doing besides a residuum of superabundant good. Of this residuum labour, by opposing itself to machinery, does its best to deprive itself.*

For the conduct of certain unions in opposing the

---

* The observations in the text refer to universal labour. If attention were confined to labour, nationally or otherwise localised, the case in favour of machinery would appear still stronger. It is impossible that mere labour-saving machinery should not tend to diminish the total quantity of employment in the world, and equally impossible that it should increase the total of the world's demand for any kind of produce in a greater ratio than that in which it cheapens the same produce, unless indeed by cheapening goods of one description it causes those goods to be largely substituted for others previously in use for similar purposes ; and even when it does this, although it increases employment of one kind it diminishes equally employment of another kind, occasioning in fact a mere transfer of labour from one occupation to another. It is however quite possible for labour-saving

employment in their respective trades of any who have not been regularly apprenticed thereto, and at the same time endeavouring to limit the number of apprentices, the only excuse I can think of has been suggested in a former chapter. To show how injuriously such conduct may affect not merely labourers in general, but even some of the very unionists by whom it is adopted, very few details are necessary. A journeyman is not permitted to teach his own son his own trade, nor, if the lad managed to learn the trade by stealth, would he be permitted to practise it. A master, desiring out of charity to take as apprentice one of the eight destitute orphans of a widowed mother, has been told by his men that if he did they would strike.

machinery to increase the demand for a particular product of a particular country more than it lowers the price of that product. In the example given in the text, in which it was supposed that machinery reduced the price of cloth five per cent., it was assumed that the demand for cloth would not increase more than five per cent. in consequence, and the assumption would be quite correct if the improved machinery were adopted at the same time in all the countries in which cloth was made. But it might be that the use of the machinery would be, temporarily at least, confined to a single country, which might then be able to make cloth five per cent. cheaper than any other, and, underselling all others in consequence, might, thanks to the machinery, obtain a positive increase of employment for its weavers at the expense of those of the rest of the world. Something of this kind has, no doubt, frequently happened in Great Britain, and the consideration of it is an important one for the workmen of a country, enjoying, like ours, peculiar facilities for the adoption of costly machinery.

Another consideration not to be overlooked is, that the fact of capital being invested in costly machinery may, in seasons of commercial stagnation, cause employment, which would otherwise have been withdrawn, to continue to be afforded to labour, for there is sometimes less loss in manufacturing goods to be sold without profit than in suffering costly machinery to remain long idle. Suppose 100,000*l.* to be invested in an unemployed factory : there is then an annual loss of, say, 5,000*l.*, or five per cent. on the capital so sunk. But if the factory be set at work and employed, in conjunction with 20,000*l.* worth of labour and materials, in making cloth which is subsequently sold for 25,000*l.*, the loss is reduced from 5,000*l.* to 1,000*l.*, or to five per cent. on only 20,000*l.* Even if the cloth were to sell for no more than 20,000*l.*, the loss would be reduced from 5,000*l.* to 3,000*l.*

A bricklayer's assistant who by looking on has learnt how to lay bricks as well as his principal, is generally doomed nevertheless to continue a labourer for life. He will never rise to the rank of bricklayer, if those who have already attained that dignity can help it. About the motive for this exclusiveness there is no attempt at disguise. That it is designed for the advantage of a privileged few at the expense of the many is frankly avowed. The only apology that can be offered to the many is, that without the sacrifices exacted from them, the privileges enjoyed by the few could never be preserved ; and that, moreover, the sacrifices may be only temporary, for that the best chance the whole labouring population have of advancing is by each of its separate sections advancing separately, and that therefore each trades' union is best consulting the general good by attending in the first instance exclusively to its own. In this world of conflicting good and evil, where man so often ' by choice of means must needs offend,' I am not prepared to pronounce trades' unions very blameable for using the best means, however harsh, of accomplishing the great end imagined for them.

There are other unionist proceedings which, only by being enumerated, are almost sufficiently condemned. Some unions divide the country round them into districts, and will not permit the products of the trades controlled by them to be used, except within the district in which they have been fabricated. In most parts of Lancashire the brickmakers and bricklayers' associations are in alliance, offensive and defensive, one consequence of which is that within certain arbitrarily fixed limits, no bricks can be laid that have not been made within the same limits. At Manchester, this combination is particularly effective, preventing any bricks made beyond a radius of four miles from entering the city. To enforce the exclusion, paid agents are employed ; every cart of bricks coming towards Manchester is watched, and if the contents be found to have come from without the prescribed boundary, the bricklayers at once refuse to work. Four miles from Manchester and two from Ashton-under-Lyne, runs a canal which the Manchester brickmakers have thought fit to take as their boundary line. On the Ashton bank of this canal lies, unfortunately for its owners, an extensive brickyard; and there, a few months since, 500,000 bricks, besides 300*l.* worth of plant, were remaining as so much dead capital, because in the Ashton townships no building was going on, and because an embargo was in force against the passage of bricks across the canal. The vagaries of the Lancashire brickmakers are fairly paralleled by the masons of the same county. Stone, when freshly quarried, is softer, and can be more easily cut than later: men habitually employed about any particular quarry better understand the working of its particular stone than men from a distance: there is great economy, too, in transporting stone dressed instead of in rough blocks. The Manchester masons, however, will not allow Yorkshire stone to be brought into their district if worked on more than one side. All the rest of the working, the edging and jointing, they insist on doing themselves, though they thereby add thirty-five per cent. to its price. A Bradford contractor, requiring for a staircase some steps of hard Delphstone, a material which Bradford masons so much dislike that they often refuse employment rather than undertake it, got the steps worked at the quarry. But when they arrived ready for setting, his masons insisted on their being worked over again, at an expense of from 5*s.* to 10*s.* per step. A master mason at Ashton obtained some stone ready polished from a quarry near Macclesfield. His men, however, in obedience to the rules of their club, refused to fix it until the polished part had been defaced, and they had polished it again by hand, though not so well as at first. Two winters ago a builder at Heywood, willing to keep his men employed during the bad weather and short days, when otherwise there would be little for them to do, allowed them to work up a quantity of stone to be ready for use in the spring. When spring came, however, the very men who had worked the stone, struck work on account of its going off to be fixed at other places. A church was being built at Barrow in Furness, for which some moulded limestone bases or plinths were required. At first it was intended to have the stone for these brought from the quarries to Barrow and worked up there, but as the Barrow masons had not got the proper tools for that particular limestone, and as they might reasonably object to having to buy them for only a few days' use, the contractor finally resolved to have the stone sent to his own yard in Liverpool, to be made into bases there by members of the Operative Masons' Society, who are paid at a higher rate than the Barrow members. This was done, and the bases came to Barrow, and were fixed upon the walls; but immediately afterwards the Barrow lodge, discovering that one of their local rules had been infringed by the importation of worked stone into Barrow, demanded first, that the bases should be worked over again; secondly, when this was refused as an impossible interference with the architect's design, that as much time as would have been required to rework them should be occupied by the Barrow masons in standing over them. Finally, the matter was compromised by the contractor's consenting to let the bases be taken from their beds and refixed, and promising not to introduce any dressed stone into Barrow again. Much in the same spirit, though somewhat different in form, is another piece of Lancashire practice. According to a rule laid down by the operative bricklayers, whenever a town master undertakes work away from the town he inhabits, one-half the men employed on the work must belong to that town, and if an uneven number be employed, so must the odd man also. In deference to this rule, an unfortunate Manchester master, who had got an order for the Bury Railway Station at a time when the building trade was brisk at Manchester, did everything in his power to get Manchester men for the job, applying for them, among other quarters, to the union; but everywhere without success. Then fancying that, in such peculiar circumstances, he might venture to treat exclusively with Bury men, he engaged eleven of these, taking good care that they should be society men; but scarcely had he set them to work than two of the society's delegates came down upon him from Manchester, bidding him discharge six of the eleven and replace them with Manchester men, or, if he could get none of the latter, then to stop the work till he could; concluding by asking for their own day's wages, amounting to 7s. each, and 3s. each for first-class railway fare from Manchester, for coming to give him what they called their 'orders.' The upshot of the affair was that the master did as he was bid in every particular, and had to take men from his other jobs in Manchester to work in Bury, although at the time a large number of bricklayers were out of work in Bury and its neighbourhood.

Some unions, from the minuteness and rigour with which they insist on the division of labour, would almost seem to be bent on establishing among English workmen the obsolete slavery of Hindoo or Egyptian caste. The following examples will show how far they sometimes go in that direction.

In one or two of the northern counties, the associated plasterers and associated plasterers' labourers have come to an understanding, according to which the latter are to abstain from all plasterers' work, except simple whitewashing; and plasterers in return are to do nothing, except pure plasterers' work, that the labourers would like to do for them, insomuch that if a plasterer wants laths or plaster to go on with, he must not go and fetch them himself, but must send a labourer for them. In consequence of this agreement, a Mr. Booth, of Bolton, having sent one of his plasterers to bed and point a dozen windows, had to place a labourer with him during the whole of the four days he was engaged on the job, though anybody could have brought him all he required in half a day. It appears to be usual in some places, for the same persons to be brought up as plasterers and bricklayers, learning both trades together. A Scarborough builder, however, who had given his brick-layers some plastering to do, after they had finished their bricklaying, got notice from the Plasterers' Union, that if he let the bricklayers proceed, he would have to finish with them, for that no regular plasterers should in that case be permitted to serve him. One of the adepts at both trades, who, from having been in business on his own account was reduced to go out as a journeyman, got employment as a plasterer, from a master who had known him in better days. The other plasterers, however, would not let him stay: as he professed to be as much a bricklayer as a plasterer, he should not, they said, work as a plasterer: he might go somewhere else, and work as a bricklayer. In vain the poor fellow pleaded the wife and large family dependent upon him for bread. His persecutors were obdurate, and left his and their employer no alternative but to part either with him or with them.

At Bolton, some bricklayers passing by a Mr. Day's place of business, and hearing some hammering of brick-work going on within, looked inside and saw a carpenter who had been sent to fix some joists, enlarging the holes which had been left in the brickwork for the joists. For suffering the carpenter to do this, the bricklayers fined Mr. Day 2*l.* At Ashton-under-Lyne, Mr. George Colbeck sent a joiner and a bricklayer to make some alterations in a house, the door of which was to be re-moved half the width of itself. The bricklayer built up the part requiring it; but because the joiner, instead of standing idly by while this was being done, presumed to pull out some few bricks that had to be removed, the bricklayer struck work and left the job. Colbeck in consequence was fined 2*l.* by the Bricklayers' Union. He naturally asked what for? The reply was, that he had infringed rules by permitting a joiner to pull out bricks, which ought to be done by a bricklayer, and that all the jobs on which he was engaged should be stopped: so he paid. At another place

a builder was fined 5*l.* His offence was that, after waiting
five days for a bit of brickwork—the widening of one
window opening—which he could not get his bricklayers to
do, because they were away on a prolonged drinking bout,
he at last in despair got a mason to do it. These are bricklayers' feats, but there is nothing they do which masons
cannot cap. Some of both were employed together in re-
storing the old church at Kenilworth, of which part of the
old stonework had to be cleaned down, and the joints raked
out and pointed. This is work which, in that part of the
country, bricklayers are specially qualified for, and which
masons do not understand. No sooner, however, were two
of the former set upon it, than all the latter struck, although
on being questioned, they were obliged to admit that there
was not one amongst them who could do the work at all.
In the neighbourhood of Sheffield, two bricklayers had
been sent to 'tuck point' a wall ; but when they had been at
it for a week, their master was compelled to withdraw them
because his masons threatened to strike if he did not. The
masons were then asked whether they could do the work,
and one and all replied that they could not, some adding
that they would not if they could, for that they would be
obliged to get new tools for it, such as they had never used
before. Still they would let no one else do it, and the wall
in consequence remained unfinished for months. If members of the painting craft, less frequently than their masonic
cousins, resent foreign interference, it can only be for want
of opportunity. That the spirit of exclusiveness is as
strong in them as in any other building operatives, will be
made manifest by one single example. The book-keeper
of a house-painting firm at Blackpool wanting to measure
up some work, and finding the marks on his measuring rod
nearly obliterated, took up a little paint, and painted the
feet and inches upon it afresh ; whereupon his employers got
a letter from theirs 'respectfully, the committee, Blackpool
Operative House Painters,' stating, that what the book-
keeper had done had come to their knowledge, and desir-

ing that he should not be allowed to do so again, 'he not being a painter.'

Very many unions, in their anxiety to prevent over-exertion, scarcely tolerate ordinary activity of movement. They often show themselves scarcely less desirous that masters should get as little as possible of their work done, than that the men should get the highest possible pay for the little they do. Making work is generally what they really mean when they talk of doing work,—a new distinction, unknown to the schoolmen, being thus pointed out between *opus operans* and *opus operatum.* 'Sometimes,' says Mr. G. F. Trollope, the eminent London builder, 'I have said to some of my men who were at work in the joiner's shop,' "Now come, do you mean to call that a fair day's work?" And the answer has been, "Well, sir, it is not, but I am not allowed to best my mates."' 'I have been quite surprised,' says Mr. George Smith, 'knowing what my own disposition would be, to see men working down to so low a level, because it is more difficult to work slowly, or to do anything else slowly, than to do it at proper speed.' Mr. Trollope once asked a young man who was walking along the street about two o'clock in the afternoon, where he was going. 'Oh, I am going to Mr. So-and-so's to work.' 'And at what time do you expect to get there? At the pace you are going, not, seemingly, till it will be time to leave off.' 'I am very sorry, sir,' was the man's apology, 'but we are not allowed to sweat ourselves if we are walking in your time.' 'Not besting one's mates' has by several unions been made the subject of special enactment. 'You are strictly cautioned,' says a bye-law of the Bradford Bricklayers' Labourers, 'not to overstep good rules by doing double work, and causing others to do the same in order to gain a smile from the master. Such foolhardy and deceitful actions leave a great portion of good members out of employment. Certain individuals have been guilty, who will be expelled if they do not refrain.' The Manchester Bricklayers' Association have a rule providing that 'any

man found running or working beyond a regular speed
shall be fined 2s. 6d. for the first offence, 5s. for the second,
10s. for the third, and if still persisting, shall be dealt with
as the committee think proper.' As also shall be 'any
man working shorthanded, without man for man.' In
the building trade, working too fast is technically called
'chasing.' The secretary of the Operative Masons being
questioned as to its prohibition by his society, represented
the object to be to prevent a man's destroying himself by
over-exertion. He admitted, however, that a man of
strength and skill so much above the average as to be able
to do more and better work than his fellows without the
slightest extra exertion on his part, would still be required
to observe the same pace as they. He would have equally
to conform to the injunction, ' not to take up less time than
an average mason in the execution of each description of
work.' Some antichasing regulations are, like this one,
rather vaguely expressed. Others are explicit in defining
what is to be understood by a proper or average quantity
of work. At Liverpool, a bricklayer's labourer may legally
carry as many as twelve bricks at a time. Elsewhere, ten
is the greatest number allowed. But at Leeds ' any brother
in the union professing to carry more than the common
number, which is eight bricks, shall be fined 1s.' ; and any
brother 'knowing the same without giving the earliest
information thereof to the committee of management, shall
be fined the same.' At Birmingham, by agreement between
masters and men, the number of bricks that may be
carried varies with the height to which they are carried—so
many to a first floor, so many less to a second floor, and so
on, and generally different ladders are used for different
floors. But one day an Irish labourer was caught by his
master carrying only eight bricks to the first floor, yet
insisted that he was in order. ' Why,' cries the master, ' it
is only the first floor.' ' Ah shure,' retorts Pat, ' but then
'tis a three-storey ladder.' At certain places the labourers
have ordained that bricks shall be carried only in hods,

however preferable it might be to wheel them in barrows. At Birmingham, a master, who was doing some heavy work at the canal side, laid planks across from the boat, and wanted his labourers to wheel the bricks from the boat straight to the place where they were to be used ; but the labourers would have none of such new-fangled notions, and threatened to strike if the bricks were not all unloaded in the ordinary way, and stacked on the canal side, and then carried by hod down to the works. Every reader may not have quite perceived what was meant when, a few sentences back, men were spoken of as not being allowed to sweat themselves if walking in their masters' time. In most country districts, though not in London or its neighbourhood, it is an understood thing that when a man has to walk any distance to his work, half of the walking is to be treated as part of his day's labour, and paid for accordingly, the man usually walking one way in his own time, and the other in the master's time. Where the men are in the ascendant, however, they often put their own interpretation upon this understanding : sometimes they insist that every one employed at a distance from his master's headquarters shall be allowed walking time, even though he himself be living close by ; sometimes that all the men employed on the distant job shall meet at some common starting-point in order to walk from thence to their work, even though, in order to reach the place of rendezvous, they must pass their final destination.

It is when masters are entangled with time contracts which they are bound under heavy penalties to fulfil, yet cannot fulfil without the cooperation of their men, that they are most completely at the mercy of the latter, who too often use the opportunities so afforded them without shame or remorse. But, indeed, the strain which some unions habitually put upon the letter of their most extravagant regulations is, if possible, more preposterous than the regulations themselves. Neither do they shrink, when it suits them, from improvising a regulation for the nonce.

According to the rules of the Glasgow Bricklayers' Association, 7*d.* an hour being the ordinary wage, overtime is to be paid as time-and-a-half, and Sabbath work as double time, and, in the case of a country job, the fare going and returning, and likewise full wages for the time spent in travelling, are to be paid by the employer. Under these rules, a bricklayer sent from Glasgow to Bristol claimed, for not quite nine days spent upon the voyage there and back, 9*l.* 13*s.* 7½*d.*, exclusive of steamboat fare. The total was reached by charging full wages for all the ordinary working-hours spent on board, charging all the nights as overtime, and two Sundays as partly double-time and partly overtime, and charging in addition 1*s.* a day for twenty-eight and a quarter days, on account of having been for nine days, more than three miles distant from Glasgow Cross, and another shilling for each of the nights of the said nine days. The employer, astounded at the exorbitance of the claim, appealed against it to the union, and had the satisfaction of being laconically assured by the secretary in reply that 'the charge was quite reasonable, and would require to be paid.' Messrs. Monteith, calico printers, of Glasgow, engaged with a Mr. Beeton for the plastering of a house they were erecting. Beeton failed in the middle of his contract, leaving one week's pay due to his workmen, who continued to hang about the premises for another week, without, however, doing any work. Messrs. Monteith then got authority from the Sheriff for Caird, another plasterer, to finish the plastering ; but the Plasterers' Union would not let Caird's men begin until Beeton's men were paid by the Monteiths, not only for the week for which Beeton owed them, but also for the week in which they had idled. And this case, monstrous as it may seem, is by no means unique. It is quite common for unionists, after a successful strike, to make it a condition of their resuming work that they shall be paid full wages for the time they have been on strike. During the building of the Manchester Law Courts, the bricklayers' labourers struck because they were desired to wheel bricks instead of carrying them on their shoulders. In consequence of the labourers' strike, time was lost by the bricklayers, who afterwards claimed for the time so lost, and struck because refused. On this occasion the joiners, without pretending to have any grievance of their own, struck to support the bricklayers, on condition of being subsidised out of the latter's funds.

It can scarcely be necessary further to multiply illustrations, nor is there much to be gained by dilating on the characteristics of those already adduced. The contemptuous disregard of anything like fair play, the disgusting mean-ness and outrageous insolence exemplified throughout the proceedings described, cannot need to be more than pointed out to any whose moral vision is not hopelessly obfuscated. No doubt it may be tauntingly asked of me, in what respect the worst of these specimens of unionist conduct differ from others which I have not scrupled to defend; or whether the very selfsame excuse repeatedly urged by me on behalf of some, will not apply equally to all. Even when unionists desert an employer merely because he chooses to have his bricks carried in a wheelbarrow, or does not choose to have no more than eight at a time carried in a hod, or because he declines to pay for work done for another instead of himself, or not done at all; is not even then the worst that can be said of them that they are driving a hard bargain with their employer? and are they not perfectly entitled to drive the hardest bargain they can? Have they not a right to propose any conditions of employment, how-ever preposterous? Even so, I still reply; yes, even to the equiring their employer to dance on his head for their amusement, or to give his daughter to one of them in marriage. Undoubtedly they have full right to ask for what they please: their asking will not cause it to be granted, unless the employer perceive more of advantage for himself in granting than in refusing. But it does not follow that whatever one has a right to demand one is therefore right in demanding. On the contrary, there is often nothing more execrable than to stand on one's extreme rights. Shylock was doing no more when insisting on the pound of flesh which Antonio had pledged to him, but no one detests him the less on that account; and unionist exorbitance, besides being odious, is of suicidal tendency as well. This last point likewise, however, is one regarding which elaborate demonstration would be thrown away upon those who cannot recognise it without. Such unionists as are silly enough to imagine that to make themselves general nuisances can ultimately conduce more to their interest than to their credit, may as well, for any good that can be done by reasoning with them, be left to find out their mistake for themselves. Sooner or later their short-sighted folly will be followed by its inevitable penalty, when the mischief they have wrought, rebounding on their own heads, will teach them convincingly how stupid those heads have been.

Besides, there is the less reason for adding to our catalogue of unionist abuses, because it is not on account of its proneness to abuse that unionism most deserves to be styled a necessary evil. Among the manifold extravagances and enormities of which it is too often guilty, there are none which can be said to be inherent in its nature: they are all excrescences, from which the more respectable unions are already comparatively free, and from which the rest may reasonably be expected to free themselves in proportion as they advance in enlightenment. And it has scarcely, perhaps, been sufficiently observed how well adapted trades' unions in some respects are to serve as instruments for diffusing that combination of sweetness and light, on which Mr. Matthew Arnold has of late been laying such judicious stress. Sufficient note has not perhaps been taken of the educational office which unionism is silently and unconsciously performing, and of the softening and composing influence which it is insensibly exercising over its constituents. Mere union, quite irrespectively of any special object, is of itself beneficial discipline. The mere act of association is of itself a wholesome subordination of the individual to the general. Merely to combine for some common object, causes people to take pride and pleasure in that object, whatever it be, and renders them ready to make sacrifices for its furtherance. And if the object be mutual defence and mutual support, then, for the associates to take an interest in it and in each other, is one and the same thing. Among trades' unionists accustomed to look to each other for assistance in sickness, in distress, and in old age, the sense of mutual dependence begets mutual attachment. In their official intercourse they speak of each other as 'brothers;' and the word is not an empty sound, but indicates the sort of relationship which they at least desire should subsist between them, and which, because they do desire it, is sure to grow up. So far their sympathies have already widened, and it is characteristic of all moral expansion never to cease expanding. Those who, from caring for none but themselves, have got so far as to care for their fellow-workmen, will not stop till they have learned to care for all their fellow-men. Love of their class will prove to have been only an intermediate stage between self-love and love of their kind. Nor is it only indirectly that unionism is qualified to contribute towards this moral development. Certain of its arrangements are calculated to lead straight towards the same result. Hitherto, protection against material evil and acquisition of material good have been its chief care, but higher objects are beginning to claim attention, and intellectual and moral improvement are coming in for a share of solicitude. In the lodges of the London bricklayers, drunkenness and swearing are expressly interdicted. Under the auspices of the Amalgamated Carpenters, industrial schools are being established. These are straws on the surface, showing how the current of unionist opinion is flowing. The day may not be very distant when increasing *esprit de corps* will make Amalgamated Engineers and Carpenters as proud individually of their respective societies, as jealous of their honour, and as unwilling to disgrace them, as the officers of the old Bengal Engineers used to be of their connection with that pre-eminently distinguished corps ; and in proportion as those feelings become general among unionists, in the same proportion may unionism be expected to divest itself of its offensive attributes, exchanging eventually past violence and extravagance for as much moderation as its nature will admit of.

Still, even when so modified and chastened, the necessity for its continuing to exist at all will continue to be an evil. The one constitutional vice, inherent in and inseparable from unionism, is its being a visible and tangible embodiment of that antagonism between labour and capital, which has always been the curse of the one and a thorn in the flesh of the other. The reason why they have always got on so ill together, is, that their mutual relations have always hitherto been settled by bargaining ; and it is an essential part of the business of trades' unions to keep up the practice of bargaining, perpetuating thereby a conflict of adverse interests. With the most amiable dispositions on both sides, it is scarcely possible for one man to desire to sell his labour dearly, and for another to buy it cheaply, without their conceiving for each other sentiments akin to those with which Yorick and his landlord descended into the inn-yard at Calais, to treat about the transfer of a post-chaise. ' I looked at Monsieur Dessein,' says Yorick, ' through and through, eyed him as he walked, in profile—then *en face* ;—thought he looked like a Jew—then a Turk ;—disliked his way,—cursed him by my gods, wished him at the devil.' Truly, as Yorick adds, it must needs be a hostile kind of world, in which a beggarly account of three or four *louis d'or* at most can kindle such malevolence in sentimental bosoms, and a hostile kind of world it must needs remain as long as trades' unionism continues to exhibit itself as a symbol of contentiousness, keeping the two largest portions of society apart.

A system which, when purged as completely as possible

of existing impurities, will still retain so much that is anti-social, cannot be without a large leaven of ineradicable evil. The utmost successes of which it is capable can never be such as well-wishers of their fellow-men, with any catholicity of sympathy, will be much disposed to rejoice over. Its highest achievements must always fall very short indeed of the consummation to which speculative philanthropy loves to look forward, when labour and capital, no longer needing to keep each other's aggressiveness in check, shall cordially combine for mutual cooperation. What ground there is for hoping that such alliance will eventually displace existing antagonism, will be considered in the remaining division of this treatise ; but until the alliance is effected and as long as the antagonism subsists, trades' unionism will continue to be an indispensable auxiliary of labour, and the sooner it is so recognised, both by the Legislature and by capitalists, the better for the public peace. There must be an end of all such tall talk as certain privileged declaimers have lately been indulging in, about putting down unions by act of parliament. The earliest parliamentary action regarding them is pretty certain to take quite an opposite direction, and to consist in extending to their property that protection, now so shamefully withheld, which every government owes to the property of all its subjects indiscriminately, good and bad alike. Another session will surely not be allowed to pass without an enactment for treating those who rob or defraud trades' unions, as all other thieves or swindlers are treated.* And when a provision to this effect has become law, it will soon cease to be believed that the law could ever have been otherwise. If trades' unionists were the vilest of criminals,

---

* [This prediction has been fulfilled. Towards the close of last session (1869), Mr. W. H. Smith having given notice of his intention to move for leave to bring in a Bill for the protection of unionist property during the interval which, it was then seen, must precede matured legislation on unionist affairs, the Government anticipated him by bringing in and getting passed a short bill for the same purpose.]

instead of composing, as they do, the very flower of the
working classes, that, though a very good reason for transporting or hanging, could be no reason for outlawing them.
But the offence for which they are actually outlawed is no
more than certain action, or rather inaction on their part,
deemed by the Legislature to be in restraint of trade.
Whether rightly so deemed or not, matters not a jot. In
either case the next generation will find it equally impossible to understand the confusion of ideas, that could lead
a House of Commons, for the sake of suppressing such
an offence, to make such crimes as theft and swindling
legal.

Employers, too, have something in their deportment to
correct. ' To him that worketh,' says St. Paul, ' reward is
reckoned not of grace but of debt ;' but modern industrial
magnates, looking at the subject from a point the direct
opposite of that of the Cilician tentmaker, are for the most
part slow to take this apostolic view. They behave as if it
were they, instead of their men, who are really creditors.
They cannot readily rid themselves of the notion that they
are doing favours to the latter by using them as hewers of
wood and drawers of water, and that they lay them, in consequence, under a debt of gratitude not to be fully liquidated
without large duty-payments of respectful words and
gestures. But, since unionism has become rampant, not
only, they say, have these supplemental dues ceased to be
regularly paid, but even common civility is often withheld.
There is no doubt truth in this complaint, but where it is
true, the masters have themselves in great measure to
blame. Almost universally, until latterly, they used to
give themselves those very offensive airs, in dealing with
their men, which the latter, when they have a safe chance,
now so greatly disgust them by parodying ; and even now,
they not unfrequently offend in the same manner as of old,
representing as an impertinence the interposition of unionist
committees or delegates. What else but rudeness can they
expect in return for such discourtesy ? They will have no

go-between, they say, 'twixt themselves and their men.
But what if the men insist on having a go-between? On
what pretence are they to be denied the privilege of having
their cause argued for them by attorney? It is high time
for masters to free themselves from an obsolete delusion,
the relics of which are still darkening their perceptions.
Henceforth they should understand, that respect being
really no more due to them from the men, than from them
to the men, is henceforth only to be expected from the
latter on condition of reciprocity.

Book IV.

LABOUR AND CAPITAL IN ALLIANCE.

Book IV.

LABOUR AND CAPITAL IN ALLIANCE.

CHAPTER I.

INDUSTRIAL PARTNERSHIP.

IN THE estimate attempted in the last chapter of the merits and demerits of Trades' Unionism, one of the former was intentionally omitted. No allusion was made to the powerful reason which unionism furnishes to employers for desiring to improve the relations between themselves and the employed. This was designedly kept back then, with a view to its being more effectively brought forward now.

In the same chapter the paradox was started that unionism is, in the natural order of things, destined to mollify hereafter that antagonism between classes, which in its earlier stages it undoubtedly does its utmost to foment. It was treated as having, together with its more obvious and immediate functions, an educational office to perform, and was credited, in consequence, with a portion of that humanizing influence which education, of whatever kind, can scarcely fail to exercise. Whether justly so credited, time must be left to show. As yet, it must be admitted to have done little to deserve the praise bestowed upon it by anticipation. Hitherto, far from mollifying, its general effect has been that of very greatly aggravating that hostility between capital and labour, which is only too apt to grow up spontaneously and without any external fostering.

Wherever it prevails, it has extinguished whatever mutual kindliness a sense of patronage on the one side, and of dependence on the other, had engendered, and for such faithfulness and attachment as previously existed, has generally substituted an embittered discontent, that grudges payment of even its acknowledged dues. In the words of one of the last to be suspected of speaking with undue harshness on such a point, ' the rich are regarded as a mere prey and pasture for the poor—the subject of demands and expectations wholly indefinite, increasing in extent with every concession made to them. The total absence of regard for justice or fairness, in the relations between the two, is as marked on the side of the employed as on that of the employers. We look in vain, among the working classes in general, for the just pride which will choose to give good work for good wages. For the most part, their sole endeavour is to receive as much, and return as little in the shape of service as possible.'*

So speaks Mr. Mill, and so (or similarly) thought and felt M. Leclaire, house-painter in Paris, when, finding it 'insupportable to live in close and hourly contact with persons whose interests and feelings were in hostility ' to him, he set himself seriously to consider how more amicable relations could be established with them.

He had begun business, he says, with the usual mistake of paying the lowest possible wages, and dismissing for the slightest offence; but he soon found that this would not do and that, without some permanent connection with his men, there was no hope of his getting on satisfactorily with them. He tried, therefore, to attach them to his service by raising their wages, and he succeeded so far as to render them loth to leave so liberal a paymaster, but not so far as to induce them to take more pains with their work than they thought necessary to prevent their being discharged. As long as he was personally superintending, there might be a fair show of diligence, but this

---

* Mill's Political Economy, Sixth Edition, vol. ii. p. 342.

lasted only while he himself was looking on. As soon as
his back was turned, the men slackened their pace, and at
the end of the day they would be found to have done
barely two-thirds of what might fairly have been expected
of them. He was not, however, disheartened by the failure
of his first expedient, but went on wrestling manfully with
the necessity of the case, which in due course became
mother of a more promising invention. He considered
that his men, having no obvious interest in common with
him, had no sufficient motive for desiring to promote his
views. Being paid the same whether they did more or
less, they did, he observed, no more than they could help.
The surest way, he inferred, of getting them to do more,
would be to proportion their remuneration to the value of
their exertions, and he resolved, accordingly, to distribute
among such of them as should in his judgment prove
themselves worthy, a portion of any increased profits that
might result from their increased or improved labour. The
outlines of his plan were as follows:—He announced that
when the accounts were made up at the end of the year,
out of the net profits which might then appear, should be
taken, first, interest at five per cent. on the capital invested,
and a salary of 6,000 francs for himself as superintendent
and manager, and that the surplus should be divided
rateably, according to the sums-total of wages or salary
they had severally earned, among those, himself included,
who had been selected as entitled to participate. The
promise thus made was hedged round with sundry precautions. Only certain of the workpeople were admitted
as participants, and the determination of the number and
the selection of the individuals was reserved by M. Leclaire
entirely to himself. No one either had a right to see the
books without his consent. Who should be sharers, and
how much, or whether anything should be shared, depended
entirely on him. It would not have been surprising if a
proffer so qualified and hampered had not appeared particularly tempting, and had not acted as much of a

stimulant on those to whom it was made. M. Leclaire, however, knew his men, and his men knew him too well by experience to have any fear of his deceiving or defrauding them ; and they entered cordially into his arrangement, which came into operation early in 1842. Very soon afterwards the waste of time that had previously so much vexed him almost entirely ceased. His best hands redoubled their exertions, and in presence of their activity, the old idlers became ashamed to be seen lolling about with their arms folded. At the end of the year there was so considerable a surplus to divide that, of the privileged participants, there was not one who had worked as many as three hundred days, whose quota was less than 450 francs, or 14*l.*; while the utmost amount of bare wages which—at M. Leclaire's highest rates, of four francs a day in summer and three francs in winter — anyone could have earned within the same number of days, was only about 1,050 francs, or 42*l.* That the surplus which thus permitted their incomes to be augmented by little less than two-fifths was the creation of their increased industry, may be inferred from the satisfaction with which M. Leclaire uniformly speaks of his experiment. In 1848, he assured M. Chevalier that the increased zeal of his workpeople afforded him full compensation for his pecuniary concession to them; and in 1857, M. Villaumé reported of him that, notwithstanding the abandonment of so large a proportion of his profits, he was in the habitual receipt of a liberal revenue, thanks to the unusual diligence of his men, and to the vigilant supervision they exercised over each other. Alluding to this last point, M. Leclaire, in one of his pamphlets, intimates that he feels himself in consequence to a great extent relieved from the burthen of mastership. Of late years he has materially modified the details of his plan, retaining, however, the original principle unimpaired. Besides himself, there are two other partners in the concern—a M. Defournaux, and a Provident Society composed of all the other persons (apparently about two hundred) employed.

Each of the three partners has a capital of 100,000 francs invested in the business. Messrs. Leclaire and Defournaux receive each 6,000 francs (240*l.*) as wages of superintendence, and divide one-half of the net profits equally between themselves. The other half goes to the workpeople, two-fifths of it being paid to the Provident Society, and the other three-fifths being distributed amongst the individual members. M. Leclaire, however, still reserves to himself the right of deciding who shall share in the distribution, and to what amount; only pledging himself never to keep back any part, but to pay to the Provident Society whatever fractions of the workpeople's quota may not have been awarded to individuals.

For having devised this plan, M. Leclaire is entitled to a high place among independent inventors. The merit of absolute originality of design is, however, far from being his. Some years before he thought of organising his business in the manner described, Mr. Babbage had remarked of what importance it would be ' if, in every large establishment, the mode of paying the different persons employed could be so arranged that each should derive advantage from the success of the whole, and the profits of individuals should advance, as the factory itself produced profit, without the necessity of making any change in the wages agreed upon.'* In explanation, Mr. Babbage refers to the way in which part of the work is done in the mines of Cornwall, in the lead-mines of Flintshire, and those at Skipton in Yorkshire, and in some of the Cumberland copper-mines. The ore is raised and dressed by gangs of joint adventurers, who, forming themselves into voluntary partnerships, contract for the working of a portion of a vein for so much in the pound of the sale-proceeds of the ore. ' As the earnings of these gangs depend upon the richness of the vein, and the quantity of merchantable metal extracted, the members naturally become quicksighted in the discovery of ore, and in estimating its value, and eagerly

---

* Babbage, Economy of Machinery and Manufactures, p. 117.

avail themselves of every improvement that can bring it more cheaply to market.' Mr. Mill, who also alludes to the Cornish miners, mentions likewise the cases of American China ships, in which it is usual for every sailor to have an interest in the profits of the voyage ; of British whaling-ships, the payment of whose crews is governed by a similar principle ; and of the sea-fisheries of the south coast of England, where, after one-half of the catch has been taken by the owner of the boat and nets, the other half is divided equally between the boatmen : and to these deserves to be added that of Greek merchant-seamen, of whom, as a rule, everyone, from the captain to the cabin-boy, is usually part-proprietor of the ship he sails in. 'The crew of a Greek merchantman,' says the author of 'Eothen,' 'receive no wages, but have all a share in the venture, and in general, I believe, they are owners of the whole freight. They choose a captain, to whom they entrust just power enough to keep the vessel on her course in fine weather, but not enough for a gale of wind. They also elect a cook, and a mate. The cook whom we had on board was particularly careful about the ship's reckoning, and when, under the influence of the keen sea-breeze, we grew fondly expectant of an instant dinner, the great author of pilafs would be standing on deck, with an ancient quadrant in his hands, calmly affecting to take an observation. But then, to make up for this, the captain would be exercising a controlling influence over the soup, so that all in the end went well.' It is certain, how-ever, that the plan, which Mr. Kinglake thus goodnaturedly quizzes, answers admirably. In the early part of the century, when we were at war with Turkey, and when Greek craft were, consequently, lawful prey for British cruisers, the latter might give chase, but the former, being navigated by co-operative mariners, more interested in escaping than their enemies in pursuing, were seldom or never captured. Since Greece has been independent, if nothing else connected with her has flourished, her mercantile marine has—a very great, if not the greater, part of the carrying trade of the

Mediterranean being now in the hands of Greeks.   One other example is mentioned by Mr. Mill, and must not be omitted here.   Previously to 1840, there were no Chinese shops anywhere in the Philippine Islands outside the walls of Manilla.   Ten years later, Chinese immigrants had dispossessed the Spaniards and Mestizos of the best part of the trade in manufactured goods throughout all the twenty-four islands of the group.   In explaining how they gained this advantage over their predecessors, Mr. Macmicking, in his interesting 'Recollections of Manilla and the Philippines,' observes that, 'in the Chinese shops, the owner usually engages all the activity of his countrymen employed by him in them, by giving each of them a share in the profits of the concern, or, in fact, by making them all small partners in the business, of which he of course takes care to retain the lion's share; so that while doing good for him, by managing it well, they are also benefiting themselves.   To such an extent is this principle carried, that it is usual to give even their coolies a share in the profits of the business in lieu of fixed wages, and the plan appears to suit their temper well; for although in general they are most complete eyeservants when working for a fixed wage, they are found to be most industrious and useful ones when interested even for the smallest share.'

Some of these precedents might have furnished hints to M. Leclaire, but very likely he had never heard of them; and of those to whom they were familiar, Mr. Babbage seems long to have been the only one to regard them otherwise than as exceptional curiosities, or to appreciate their fitness for extensive imitation.   It was M. Leclaire who gave the principle involved in them most of its present prestige, and it is his example that has been followed in some remarkable instances in England, as well as in France. Of two of his French copyists, M. Paul Dupont and M. Gisquet, some particulars are given by M. Villiaumé.   Since March 1847, M. Dupont, who is manager of a printing establishment at Paris, employing 300 workpeople, has distributed among the latter a tithe of the profits. On an average, each man's share is about equal to his wages for a fortnight, but it cannot be drawn until its owner retires from the service of the firm. Until then, it goes on accumulating at compound interest, and if left long enough, becomes a little fortune. M. Dupont and his capitalist partners affirm, that their residue of profit, after deduction of the workpeople's tithe, is greater than the sum-total used to be when they took all of it for themselves. M. Gisquet, proprietor of some extensive oilworks at St. Denis, distributes among the hundred labourers in his employment, in rateable proportion to their wages, 5 per cent. of his net profits. Before he did this, many of his men used to get drunk several times a week, in spite of all that he could say or do to prevent them ; but he has now completely cured them of this bad habit, by making dismissal the punishment of getting drunk on weekdays. On an average, their proportion of profits is equal to six weeks' wages, and this is too large a bonus to be risked, for the pleasure of a single drinking bout. Mr. Julian Fane, in a report to the Foreign office,* speaks of M. Godin Lemaire's iron foundry at Guise, as another French establishment selected from a great number 'the proprietors of which have voluntarily introduced a form of cooperation.' In this instance 'the value of the plant is to be divided into shares of 25 francs, by means of which M. Godin Lemaire aims at associating the whole of his 900 workmen in the industrial enterprise which he directs, and stimulating them by the hope of becoming co-proprietors of the house and foundry.'

It is, however, M. Leclaire's English imitators respecting whom English readers are likely to have most curiosity, and respecting whom I am the more tempted to be somewhat diffuse, because I am able to speak of them with knowledge derived from personal observation or enquiry. Foremost on the list stand Messrs. Henry Briggs, Son, and

* Correspondence with H. M.'s Missions abroad on Industrial Questions and Trades Unions, 1867, pp. 52, 53.

Company, owners of the Whitwood, Haigh Moor, and
Methley Collieries, near Normanton in Yorkshire, of which
the original members of the firm appear to have undertaken
the management in or about 1852. During the next
twelve years, nothing could be more unsatisfactory than
Messrs. Briggs's relations with their men. 'As bad as it
could be would be about the mark' was the reply of one
of the latter, when asked what used to be the state of their
mutual feelings. Once, when party-spirit ran particularly
high, Mr. Briggs (senior) was served with an anonymous
notice that he and his son should be shot within the
fortnight. The letter concluded with a Scriptural allusion :
' My nife is sharp, but my bulits is shurer than my nife,
and if i can, i will by God, if it be at noonday you shall
have the arra, if it be in your charit like old Abe.' By ' old
Abe,' be it understood, King Ahab, not poor President
Lincoln, was meant. The Samaritan despot was not the
worst similitude found for Mr. Briggs. ' I believe,' confesses one of the pitmen, who has since seen reason to
modify materially his former opinion of his master—' I
believe I said he would be the devil if he only had horns.'
Another time the same sentiment was expressed in an am-
plified form, and without any qualification, thus—' All coal-
masters is devils, and Briggs is the prince of devils.' At
that time the miners were continually striking work. In
1853, they were ' out' for five months, and again in 1858, for
thirty-five weeks ; but it must be admitted that in both these
instances their conduct was apparently justified by the
result, for on the first occasion they got an advance of thirty
per cent., which it is quite clear they would not have got without striking, and in the other they prevented a threatened
reduction of fifteen per cent. from going beyond seven and a
half. In general, however, very frivolous pretexts sufficed
them. Once they stopped work for six weeks because required to separate the large coal from the small, and again in
the following year for twenty weeks, because desired to riddle
the coal underground. This riddling would no doubt have

given them some additional trouble, and besides, as has been gravely urged in their excuse, the noise made by it might have disturbed the habitual quiet of the pit, and so have prevented any indication of cracking in the roof from being heard. But the real objection to it seems to have been that it was an innovation, the colliers being in the habit of threatening to 'set down,' as they termed it, any employer who ventured to make a change in the customary mode of working, or otherwise to interfere with their trade regulations. Almost more annoying than the prolonged strikes were the shorter stoppages that were always taking place in the intervals between them. Scarcely a week was suffered to pass without the men leaving their work, on some childish pretext or other. Sometimes, it would be because they fancied the coals were not properly weighed. Though they had appointed their own check-weigher, they would not trust his weighing, but suspected him of understating the quantities they were to be paid for. Often, for no better cause than that some man, complained of the day before for not properly filling his corf, would come on the bank and say, 'Now lads, I have had a corf stopped yesterday;' whereupon it would be put to the vote whether they should have a play-day or not, and generally carried in the affirmative. 'Any lad, almost by holding up his hand could make a play-day.' Or it might be that all the men would go off in a body, to hear a lecturer declaim against coal-kings and tyrants. And what was play to the men was almost death to the masters, who, though productive operations were at a standstill, were not the less obliged to keep all the pumping-engines going and labourers employed in preventing the passages from getting out of order. According to Messrs. Briggs's calculation, for every holiday their men took, they were themselves from 120*l.* to 150*l.* out of pocket. Nor did the men content themselves with striking in a merely negative sense. The police had repeatedly to be called in to protect non-unionists from violence. A block of cottages was shown me at Whitworth, the windows of which it had been found necessary to barricade, for the protection of the 'black sheep' penned in them during a turn-out, on whom, in spite of every precaution, an assault was made of so riotous a character, that for their share in it several of the ringleaders were prosecuted at the assizes and sentenced to nine months' imprisonment.

Such, not long ago, was the condition of society in the three collieries under nctice, and not dissimilar it probably still is in most of those of the West Yorkshire coalfield. In their own immediate neighbourhood, however, steps were taken by Messrs. Briggs three years ago, which have wrought a complete revolution. In 1865 they transferred their business to a 'limited liability' joint-stock company, retaining two-thirds of the shares in their own hands, but offering the remaining third in 10*l.* shares to the public, and specially inviting their own employees to become shareholders. At the same time they arranged, 'that whenever the divisible profits accruing from the business, after a fair and usual reservation for redemption of capital and other legitimate allowances, exceeded ten per cent. on the capital embarked, all those employed by the company as managers, agents, or workpeople, should receive one-half of such excess profit as a bonus, to be distributed amongst them as a percentage on their respective earnings during the year in which such profit should have accrued.' They lay no claim to disinterestedness for having adopted this system, which, on the contrary, they admit to have been taken up by them as a business speculation for considerations of convenience, and in the belief, based on careful calculation of chances, that it would prove a blessing as well to those who gave as to those who took. Among the many years in which they had had so much trouble with strikes and cognate annoyances, there had been only one in which they had made ten per cent. profit on their capital, and there had been two in which they had made only five per cent. The course they were meditating could not possibly, therefore, make their receipts lower than formerly, while it would very probably make them higher. Unless profits rose above ten per cent., the men would not be entitled to bonus—there would be no surplus for them to share in. Their conditional right of participation could not possibly, therefore, make the employers' receipts less than before, and it might easily make them more. For if profits did rise above ten per cent., only half the surplus would be taken as bonus on wages, the other half being added to dividend on capital. And if the men would only try to raise profits above ten per cent., their mere trying, even though it failed, would at least ensure a nearer approximation to ten per cent. Besides, it was clearly in their power both to augment gains and to diminish expense. Of the cost of raising coal, not less than seventy per cent. had hitherto consisted of wages paid for manual labour, which, their working with more regularity, with fewer interruptions, and greater attention, would certainly render more productive. Other fifteen per cent. had consisted of the value of various stores and materials (wood, iron, oil, &c.), of which they were habitually wasteful, and of which it rested with themselves to become proportionately saving. Now, if anything could make them more diligent and painstaking, it was likely to be the promise of bonus ; and if this had the desired effect, whatever bonus became payable in consequence, would be payable out of a fund which, but for the promise, would not have been created, and in which, moreover, the bonus-givers would share equally with the bonus-receivers. True, profits might possibly be raised above ten per cent. by causes unconnected with the workpeople, in which case the latter's bonus would be so much dead loss to the employers ; but of this the risk was too small to deserve to be much regarded in comparison with the more agreeable probabilities on the other side.

Upon some such reasoning as this, with reference to themselves, Messrs. Briggs appear to have acted, though well aware, at the same time, that they were consulting

equally the welfare of their servants.   The event has shown
that they reasoned well.   Up to this time their experiment
has been a brilliant success.   All the expectations based
upon it have been realised, and some unlooked-for advantages have accrued.   It began to be tried on July 1, 1865,
and had, therefore, on the corresponding day of 1868
reached its third anniversary.   At the end of the first
twelvemonth, the total of profits was found to be fourteen
per cent., of which the shareholders took twelve and the
workpeople two per cent.   In the second year the total
was sixteen per cent., the shareholders getting thirteen per
cent. and the workpeople three.   In the third year the corresponding figures were seventeen and three and a half.   The
totals of the workpeople's per centages have been 1,800*l.*,
2,700*l.*, and 3,150*l.*, which, being divided among them rateably in proportion to their respective wages, gave them
bonuses averaging 3*l.* 9*s.* 2*d.* in the first year, 3*l.* 3*s.* 2*d.* in
the second, and 2*l.* 3*s.* 7¼*d.* in the third.   The largest bonus
in the first year was 10*l.* 18*s.* 10½*d.*, obtained by a miner
whose earnings amounted to 109*l.* 8*s.* 9½*d.*; in the second,
it was 9*l.* 17*s.* 10*d.*, paid upon 108*l.* 15*s.* 5½*d.*; and in the
third, 11*l.* 9*s.* 5*d.*, paid upon 106*l.* 4*s.* 11*d.*   Last October,
the total number of shares was 9,767, of which, 6,393 were
held by the original proprietors, 192 by a hundred and
forty-eight pitmen and topmen, 262 by twenty-one agents
and clerks, and the remainder by customers and miscellaneous subscribers.   The market price of a 10*l.* share had
then risen to 14*l.* 10*s.*   These are material results, and they
have been accompanied by moral changes which, 'in different ways, but with equal distinctness, have made themselves felt by the employer, the clergyman, the schoolmaster,
the publican, and the policeman.'   Formerly, the men could
not be depended upon for working two days consecutively,
but in the three last years not more than half-a-dozen play
days have been taken, and not one in the last year of the
three.   Once the men had arranged to have a holiday for
the purpose of attending a public meeting in which they

were interested, when a large order for coal arrived, accompanied by an intimation that it must be executed on that particular day or not at all.   Thereupon, though with considerable hesitation, the manager ventured to represent to the men the importance of their giving up their intended holiday.   Formerly the mere circumstance of the manager's particularly wanting a thing done would have been a sufficient reason with the men for not doing it, so habitual was the notion with them that what was good for their masters must be bad for them; but on this occasion they at once consented to do as they were asked.   Another time some forty of them were directed to remove for a month from one pit to another, in order to do some work of a sort to which they were not accustomed, and in which they would not be able to earn their usual wages.   They did not at all like going, and in the olden days would have refused point-blank, but now, after being reasoned with, and having had the necessity of the thing explained, all except two or three went without further ado.   On a third occasion, the price of coal having fallen, notice was given that wages likewise would be reduced.   The men who, some months before, had had their wages raised because the price of coal had risen, now that circumstances had changed, submitted without remonstrance.   On a fourth, the men at one of the collieries having demanded an advance without any of the usual pretexts for such a proceeding, the question was referred by the directors to the men at the other pits, who unanimously pronounced the claim unreasonable, and recommended that those who had made it should be left to strike if they thought fit, rather than have their application complied with.   Formerly men who had a piece of rail to put in were known to break a rail in two in order to get the right length, and, if they got the wrong length, then to bury the pieces in the dirt and break another new one.   Nothing of the kind occurs now. Everyone understands that the value of every bit of iron or timber wasted is so much deducted from the bonus fund.

A new rector coming to Normanton noticed immediately
the great difference between Messrs. Briggs' men and those
of another firm living in rows of houses immediately adjoining—how much steadier and better the former were.
What the rector observed, every passer-by might infer from
the great difference in the appearance inside and out of
the two sets of dwellings. Bonuses are paid in lump
sums at the end of each year. After the first payment
three men spent their bonuses in drink, but they are the
only three out of nearly a thousand who have been known
to do so, and the ignominious expulsion of those three
took place amidst the acclamations of all those of their
companions, a score or two in number, who happened to be
within hearing when the sentence was pronounced. Money,
which the men would formerly have spent on liquor, they
now spend on the education of their children, the number
of whom at school has of late greatly increased, or in the
purchase of additional articles of furniture, among which
a cottage piano quite commonly figures. An immense
change has taken place in their manner to their employers.
'They used to shout to us,' say the latter, 'now they speak.'
What the manner used to be, those who used to witness
and endure it are best able to say. To what it is, others
may testify. Whoever has, like myself, gone with Mr.
Archibald Briggs over one of the collieries, down the pit,
through the yard, and into the cottages, and has noticed
how heartily 'Mr. Archie' is greeted by all he meets, can
need no further proof that he and they are on the best of
terms. 'Our village,' says Mr. Currer Briggs, 'has been
transformed from a hot-bed of strife and ill-feeling between
employers and employed into a model of peace and good
will.' Whoever has lately been on the spot can vouch for
the accuracy of the latter part of this description.*

* [In a paper read before the Cooperative Congress, held in London
in June last (1869), Mr. Archibald Briggs sketched the outlines of a
plan regarded by him as preferable to the one actually in force, and
differing from it in the following particulars :—

1. Surplus profits—or profits remaining after deduction of initial

Usually classed with Messrs. Briggs in respect of their relations with their employed, are Messrs. Greening & Co.,

interest at the rate of 10 per cent. on capital—would be divided rateably instead of equally between capital and labour. For instance, the capital invested being supposed to be 10,000*l.*, the total of wages 6,000*l.*, total net profits 1,480*l.*, and the divisible surplus, consequently, after deduction of 1,000*l.* for interest on capital, 480*l.* ; labour, instead of half the surplus or 240*l.*, would get only three-eighths or 180*l.*, capital taking the remaining five-eighths or 300*l.* This is a perfectly reasonable condition, and is indeed indispensable to render the plan applicable to a business in which the capital invested is greatly in excess of the amount paid in wages. There would be no sense in assigning to work-men the same proportion of the surplus, whether there were but five or whether there were a hundred of them.

2. Wages, instead of varying with the rates current in the neigh-bourhood, would be fixed, permanently or for a term of years, at medium rates. Provided the rates were equitable, this might be for the ad-vantage of both labour and capital. Both would be secured against embarrassing fluctuations, and labour, becoming in a greater degree dependent for its remuneration on its own efficiency, would be stimu-lated to greater efficiency and productiveness, the surplus profits available for distribution between itself and capital becoming in con-sequence proportionably augmented.

3. Of the surplus divisible in any year, a portion might, at the dis-cretion of the managers, be set aside for the creation or augmentation of a Capital Reserve Fund and a Labour Reserve Fund, the two together constituting a reserve which would be available either for meeting unexpected contingencies, or for extending the business ; initial interest on each fund being in the latter case paid to the class of partners from whose accumulated profits it had been derived. This, if never acted upon without the previous consent of the men, would have the good effect of more closely binding up their interests with those of the concern, and rendering them unwilling to sever their connexion with it by seeking employment elsewhere. The previous consent on each occasion of a decisive majority would, however, seem indispensable, for nothing would be more likely to disgust the men with the whole arrangement, than that money admitted to have become theirs under its provisions should be withheld from them whether they would or not. A similar remark applies equally to the proposal that part of a labourer's profits should be retainable by the manager for the purpose of being converted into share capital for the owner's benefit. Clearly this is a case in which the owner should be left to do as he pleased with his own. If you want to prejudice people against a thing which you think will do them good, there is no surer way than to attempt to force it upon them.

4. If in any year the whole net profits were insufficient to pay full

Limited, of Salford ; Messrs. Fox, Head, & Co., of Middlesborough ; and the Sabden Mills Cotton Company.

Messrs. Greening, who are manufacturers of iron and
wire fencing, undertake, whenever their net profits come to
more than fifteen per cent., to divide the surplus with their
labourers. They thus exhibit a genuine specimen of industrial association, though not, it is to be feared, a very
favourable one. The Company have been in existence for
three years, and in the first of these they paid a bonus of
five per cent. on wages, but they do not appear to have
made any surplus profits since, and they are understood to
have been working during part of the time at a loss. This,
if it be really the fact, is most likely mainly attributable
to the depression of trade generally, but it may also be in
some measure due to depreciation of stock in hand, consequent on recent reductions in the price of iron. The
Company's business, besides, is not perhaps one of those
best suited to industrial partnership. The demand for its

initial interest on invested capital, the deficiency might be made up
out of the surplus profits of subsequent years, in part, that is, out of
what would otherwise have become labour's bonus. A supposed justification of this is that if the men share profits in good years, it is but
fair that they should take their share of loss when trade is bad. To
which argument an answer—to my mind conclusive—is that as in the
best years the men would not receive one farthing more than they had
fairly earned, and had rendered fully equivalent service for, viz. stipulated wages in return for ordinary exertion, and a stipulated proportion
of extra profits in return for extraordinary exertion, these receipts of
theirs could not furnish the smallest pretext for deductions from their
corresponding earnings in subsequent years in order to make good
losses sustained by their employers in certain other years, in which
years, be it recollected, the men would have received nothing but the
bare wages, without which neither their labour nor any other in its
place could have been hired. If indeed both parties agreed, there
might be no reason why in bad years draughts should not be made
upon the Reserved Funds of Capital and Labour alluded to above, in
order to bring up capital's initial interest to its usual complement, and
to furnish at the same time a bonus to labour. The wisdom of making
in fair weather a provision for a rainy day would thus be forcibly
illustrated.]

products is very irregular. Few orders are received except in spring and summer, when chiefly it is that fencing is going on. In the autumn and summer months little is done in that way, and as the sort of fencing depends greatly on individual taste and fancy, it would be rash to manufacture largely in anticipation of orders. Of course the demand for labour is equally irregular. Few of the hands whom Messrs. Greening employ in their busiest period, can be retained throughout the year. Their establishment is on a scale which, I was told, could furnish occupation to fifty men and two hundred boys and girls, but on the occasion of my visit in October last, I counted not more than fifteen persons altogether about the premises. Upon those who had been temporarily engaged earlier in the season, the prospect of sharing in any bonus fund which during their limited service they might be able to create, and their share in which, if created, they might subsequently not be at hand to claim, can scarcely be supposed to have had any sensibly stimulating effect.

Messrs. Fox, Head, & Co. are manufacturers of puddle bars and iron plates, employing about 400 hands. Their firm cannot properly be termed an industrial partnership. It consists of only three members, to whom the whole capital stock belongs, but who offer to take on loan any earnings of their workpeople, for investment in the business at five per cent. interest and a rateable proportion of one half of any annual profit there may be over and above ten per cent. They also engage to divide the residue of any such surplus equally between capital and labour ; but this concession is materially qualified by two conditions. In the first place, none but non-unionists are employed, none who will not sign a paper declaring that they neither do nor will subscribe to any trade's union. In the second, if in any year there be either a loss on the business, or less than five per cent. profit, the loss or deficiency is to be made good out of the surplus profits of future years before labour will be permitted to participate. Both of these conditions are cal-

culated to impair the efficacy of the cooperative principle
to which they are attached; and it is owing, perhaps,
quite as much to them, as to the present depression of the
iron trade, that the principle has hitherto remained apparently inoperative. At the date of the most recent report
respecting the firm, no money had been received by it
on loan from the workpeople, nor, up to this time, has
any bonus been distributed amongst the latter. This
last remark applies equally to the Sabden Mills Cotton
Company, but in their case the general unremunerativeness
of the cotton business for years past affords a sufficient
explanation of it.

A firm with better founded though less known claims to
be placed in the same category with Messrs. Briggs, is that
of Messrs. W. H. Smith & Son, of the Strand, the eminent
news agents, who, in an important department of their business, have for several years been acting upon a plan respecting which they have obligingly furnished me with the
following particulars. At each of their railway book-stalls,
the clerk in charge, in addition to a small regular salary,
varying in amount according to local and personal circumstances, is allowed a percentage on all the receipts at his
stall, so that, in proportion as the traffic there increases, his
income increases also. Of the cases which have been mentioned to me as showing how this arrangement works, and
which I am assured might be multiplied to any extent, it
may suffice to cite three. A., placed the year before last in
charge of a book-stall, on salary and commission calculated
from previous receipts at that stall to yield him 38*s*. a
week, netted last year on an average 62*s*. 6*d*. a week. B.,
in a populous place, and at a stall which was considered to
have been well managed by his predecessor, has succeeded
in raising himself, from 53*s*. 8*d*., to 77*s*. 8*d*. weekly. C.,
at a smaller place, where the business seemed without
life, has by special activity raised his wages and percentage
from 26*s*. 3*d*. to 41*s*. 6*d*. weekly. Some of the clerks have
extended the principle applied to themselves to the boys

employed under them, giving the latter, out of their own commission, a percentage on the money received by the boys from passengers by the trains; and all the clerks who have done this say that they have found their account in it.

Messrs. Smith consider that they have every reason to be satisfied with the system they have adopted. Several years' experience has taught them that besides benefiting those working under it, both pecuniarily and by giving them a higher tone, it is directly profitable to themselves, and they intend to extend it, as far as practicable, throughout their business. Two years ago, they decided with respect to several of their employees occupying responsible situations, that these should share in any surplus profit that might be made in excess of a certain specified rate, and they have also arranged that the remuneration of the managers of their branch houses at Dublin, Manchester, Liverpool, Birmingham, and Torquay shall depend upon the results of the business which those managers respectively superintend.

In the same class a place is often assigned to Messrs. John Crossley & Sons, Limited, the eminent carpet manufacturers of Halifax. After the death of the founder of the firm, the business was for some years in the hands of three of his sons, an illustrious brotherhood, who, if they had been contemporaries of Pope, would probably have been selected by his honest muse, together with the Man of Ross, for a share in those praises which he considered lords should not engross. Local belief credits them with having each, long and systematically, paid tithes to God of their yearly substance in the form of good works; and the number of philanthropic establishments and institutions in and about Halifax which call them authors seems of itself sufficient to confirm the current rumour. A beautiful People's Park, a stately Orphanage, two long ranges of picturesque Almshouses, and a little suburb of commodious workmen's dwellings, are far from exhausting the list. In September 1864, the three brothers joined in a fresh movement of beneficence. The immense manufacturing concern, which had previously been exclusively their own, they then converted into a joint-stock association, which at this moment possesses a paid-up capital of 1,100,000*l.*, in 10*l.* shares, whereof 80,000 are retained by the Crossleys, the rest being held by about 1,130 other shareholders. Their primary object in forming the Company being that of 'receiving the cooperation of parties associated in the business,' not only were their workpeople specially invited to become shareholders, but special facilities for so becoming were afforded to many of them. The capital represented by the shares for which these applied was lent to them at five per cent. interest, payable out of the future profits on those shares, on condition that whatever profits there might be above five per cent. should be applied towards the purchase of the shares, until the latter were fully paid for. Thus, if profits should be fifteen per cent.—and they have never been less since the Company started, and in one year were twenty per cent.—the holder of any of the shares in question would not at first be able to draw out any of his proportion of profit, part of which (in the first year, one third) would be deducted for interest on the capital lent to him, while the balance (in the first year, two thirds) would be credited to him as so much paid-up capital. About 10,000 shares, representing 100,000*l.* of capital, have been taken on these terms, and by about 150 of the Company's servants. The total number of persons employed by the firm is about 5,000, of which 150 may perhaps appear an insignificant fraction ; but the latter number, I was informed, comprises almost everyone from the degree of manager to that of foreman, who is entrusted with any superintending functions. It includes, therefore, almost all those whose activity it is of most importance to stimulate. As far as the arrangement has yet proceeded, it has given satisfaction to all affected by it. The directors declare that they have by its means ' enlisted the active energies of all parties necessary to ensure success, and rejoice in being able to report that it has more than realised their utmost expectation.' The shareholding workpeople, on their side, appear to be equally well pleased. They eagerly avail themselves of the new facilities afforded to them for growing rich, and seem to think there is no reason why they should ever stop growing. The foreman by whom I was escorted through some of the spinning rooms and weaving sheds, dilated exultingly on the advantages of the new system. According to him, now that the business has become nominally 'limited,' its progress promises to defy all bounds. In all the gigantic piles of buildings, covering acres of ground, in which it is carried on, space is with difficulty found for the additional looms which are constantly being required. For the accelerated rate with which affairs were advancing he could only account by the fact, that so many more persons had become interested in pushing them on. Of course he and all his mates were doing their best. They thought they were before, but they had discovered that their best might be sensibly bettered. Even in getting fresh customers their aid was not to be despised. None of their acquaintance, when in want of a new carpet, could well resist their importunate recommendations to buy one of theirs.

Thus the enlightened policy on which Messrs. Crossley have entered, benefits the élite of their servants equally with themselves, and their adoption of it undoubtedly enhances their previous claim to be regarded as public benefactors. Still, though well fitted for securing the zealous cooperation of the best portion of their workpeople, their new system is in no higher sense cooperative. It lacks altogether the first essential of all true industrial cooperation, viz., the participation of the simple labourer in profits. Though excellent as far as it goes or professes to go, it is simply an extended partnership, differing from ordinary partnerships in nothing except in its extent, in the liberality of its fundamental arrangements, and in the fact that several of those whose labour the firm employs are among the partners. And the last of these peculiarities is apparently not destined to be lasting. When the present race of shareholders dies out, unless such of them as are in the company's service are succeeded in their situations as well as in their estates by their heirs, the next generation of shareholders may quite possibly not include one single working man.

Neither, except in a very limited sense, can the epithet 'cooperative' be applied to a system which Professor Cairnes, in a very interesting paper in 'Macmillan's Magazine,'* has described as prevailing in the slate quarries of North Wales. The owners or lessees of these provide, it appears, the larger and more expensive machinery, and retain in their own hands the general direction and superintendence of affairs, but beyond keeping the machinery in order and seeing to the number and quality of the slates turned out, they interfere little with details. The portion of a vein which it is proposed to work is divided into sections, which are let out to as many small copartneries, each consisting of three or four superior quarrymen, who hire about twice as many younger and less experienced labourers to help them, and contract to produce slates at so much per thousand. About a third of the whole quarrying population consists of such petty contractors, the other two-thirds of their assistants or 'germyns.' The plan is said to answer admirably in all respects. Before a copartnery can safely commit itself to an engagement, its members must make good use of their heads, and go through calculations requiring some mathematical as well as arithmetical knowledge, and some practical acquaintance with mineralogy besides. Then the business itself embraces several distinct operations, of a nature to compel those engaged in them to have their wits about them. The detaching of the slate in blocks from the mountain side, the sawing of the blocks into suitable sizes, and the final splitting and dressing of them, are all processes requiring for their economical performance much forethought and attention; and

* In No. 63 for January 1865.

that these requisites are duly forthcoming may be inferred from the pecuniary results. The contractors, though paying their germyns, many of whom are mere boys, from 12*s.* to 20*s.* a week, earn for themselves, on an average, 9*l.* a month. The intelligence which their vocation developes, characterises equally their general conduct. Their frugality and prudence are remarkable. Many of them have laid by 200*l.* or 300*l.*, while others, by investing their savings in building societies, have made themselves owners of the houses they live in, houses often remarkable for style and finish externally, and for exquisite cleanliness and neatness within. They live in harmony both with the quarry owners and with the germyns. With the former they have none of the usual causes of dispute : there can be no question about the fairness of a contract which if one copartnery would not take, another would. Of the latter, everyone looks forwards to becoming himself a contractor, and knows that his doing so depends greatly on his acquiring and maintaining the good opinion of the actual contractors. Still, with all its merits, the system is only partially cooperative. It associates capital with labour only in so far as both belong to the same individuals. It does not give to the whole body of labourers a common interest in their work— for to two-thirds of them it assigns nothing beyond stipulated wages, which remain the same whether their labour be more or less productive. The only real cooperators are the remaining third, and these are so in no other sense than that in which the working partners in any other commercial undertaking whatsoever are equally entitled to the appellation.

In short, unless the news agency of Messrs. W. H. Smith may be regarded as a second, the establishment of Messrs. Briggs is as yet the only English example of an industrial partnership at once complete and flourishing. If the success achieved in this solitary instance continue, it will doubtless be emulated in other quarters, but prophets of evil are not wanting who maintain that it is not destined to last. Hitherto, they say, circumstances have been peculiarly favourable. Since Messrs. Briggs commenced their experiment there has been exceptional activity in the coal trade, without which it would have been impossible for anything the men could do to get up profits, from less than ten, to twelve, fourteen, and seventeen per cent. successively. As long as under the present plan they continue to receive substantial additions to what would otherwise be their earnings, the men may not improbably remain content, though quite possibly, even in that case, they may after a while begin to question the correctness of the accounts, and insist that they are not getting as much as they ought. But if there be a temporary stoppage of the extra payments made to them under the present plan, will not their opinion of it materially change? If they find no bonuses coming to them at the end of a year, will they not be suspicious as to the cause? Will they still be content to be excluded from all share in the management? Will not all the old envy and jealousy revive, and the scarcely cemented alliance be rudely broken up?

Of course all this may happen. What is there that may not happen when great masses of men, changing like the ocean with every wind of doctrine, are prime movers of events? It is not indeed the fact that the coal trade has been exceptionally good throughout the last three years. On the contrary, though up to the middle of 1867 there was great activity in the trade generally, there has ever since been great depression. Yet Messrs. Briggs' business has not merely gone on improving, but has improved more in the last bad year than in either of the two previous good ones, net profits for the twelvemonth ending June 30th last having been seventeen per cent. on the capital, instead of fourteen per cent. as in the preceding year, and the amount paid as bonus on wages 3,150*l.* instead of 2,700*l.* Neighbouring coal-owners, disliking Messrs. Briggs' plan, will scarcely credit the reality of its continued prosperity. Less prejudiced observers, however, especially if they have been permitted to inspect the books of the firm and to see with what minute exactitude the accounts are kept, need have no such mistrust. Rather, seeing industrial partnership coupled with progress and individual employership with decline, they will be disposed to connect antecedence with sequence as cause and effect, and, judging of the future from the past, to hope that a system which has done so well hitherto will not do ill hereafter. And for such anticipation there is the more reason because the system has already weathered a worse storm than it seems likely to have ever again to encounter. The chief obstacle in its way was the initial difficulty of getting the men to believe in it. Most of them at first did not understand it, and of those who did and had no other objection to make, many objected to its authorship. 'The thing itself is good,' said one, 'but you see it comes from Briggs, and I have no faith in Briggs.' Many suspected the whole contrivance to be a dodge for ascertaining how much they were earning; many doubted whether there would be a bonus, and more doubted whether, if there were, it would be paid to them. Doubt on these points was so strong and so general, that in the first year only about 300 out of a total of 900 qualified for bonus, by possessing themselves of the penny books in which they were required to enter their daily earnings for the purpose. This, by the way, may explain how it was that in the first year, though the bonus fund was smaller, the average rate of bonus was higher than it has been since. Now, however, the initial difficulty has been got over. The men have learnt to put faith in Briggs. Last year, out of a total of about 1,200 workmen, no fewer than 1,195—probably all who were employed regularly—received bonus. Sufficient curiosity about the system has now been excited to induce almost everyone to look into it, when the first glance suffices to convince him that it is one by which, while he may gain largely, he cannot possibly lose. If trade were at its worst, all who continued in employment would still get the current rate of wages, whatever that might be ; and if trade were too slack to allow of more than bare wages being given, that would be no reason for their supposing themselves cheated. The accounts are open for inspection by such of them—a hundred and fifty or so—as have become shareholders ; and the others, even if prepared to suspect Messrs. Briggs of foul play, would not similarly suspect a hundred and fifty of their fellow-workmen. They could not imagine that all these had turned traitors, and had joined in a conspiracy to defraud them. As little would the fact of the bonus being temporarily stopped in bad times be a reason for the men's repudiating an arrangement under which they might recover the bonus when times improved. Rather would it be a reason for valuing its privileges more highly, and for labouring more strenuously to turn them to account, in spite of disadvantageous circumstances—a reason for extra industry and economy whereby, even out of reduced prices, some augmentation of profits might possibly be extracted.

Messrs. Briggs, besides, are not mere empirics. What they are doing in England, and M. Leclaire and others in France, is not mere guesswork to be judged of hereafter by its results. They are not taking leaps in the dark, taking their chance as to the sort of ground they may light upon. They are acting upon a principle which, whether correct or not, is at least intelligent and intelligible, and which is this —that labourers may, by the conditional promise of extra remuneration, be stimulated to extra exertion and attention, the material products or moral concomitants of which will be a fully equivalent return for the extra remuneration promised. This is the basis of Messrs. Briggs' policy,* the only security for the duration of their or any similar association of labour with capital, or indeed of almost any form of industrial cooperation. Upon the soundness or unsoundness of this principle the future of cooperation

---

* What originally gave Messrs. Briggs the idea on which they have been acting was an article by Professor Fawcett, on 'Strikes, their Tendencies and Remedies,' in the 'Westminster Review' for July 1860.

mainly depends.   If it be false, cooperation must for the most part be either a born inanity, only not dying a natural death because it never had any vitality, or must turn out a mischief to its authors, which they for their own sakes will speedily extinguish.   The essence of all industrial co-operation is conditional participation of labour in profits. Without such participation cooperation is a complete mis-nomer.   If the promise of such participation cannot make labourers work so as to entitle themselves to participate, the promise is a dead letter, and might as well not have been made.   And even though it make them work thus well, yet if it can neither make them work so much better as to keep their employer's residuary profit as high as his total profit used to be and would still be but for their participation, nor induce them so to demean themselves in other respects as to compensate him in some other way for the reduction of his pecuniary receipts, he cannot be ex-pected to continue a system whose only result is the un-fruitful transfer of money from his pocket to the pockets of his workpeople.   The principle will then be proved to be false, and if it be false, cooperation can have no permanence. However thick its blossoms, a chilling frost is sure to come and nip its root while its greatness seems a ripening.   How-ever fair the fabric rise, it is sure to become a ruin without ever being finished.

But, on the other hand, if the principle be true, then no limit can be assigned to its possible development, no number of cooperative failures can prove more against co-operation than that the principle has been applied unskil-fully or in unsuitable circumstances.   If for the sake of a contingent bonus men will so work as to leave their master's profit, after deduction of the bonus, as high as it would have been but for the bonus system, or even if, with-out raising his profits quite so high, they compensate him for the falling off in his pecuniary receipts by their im-proved general behaviour, there may be no reason why an employer who has once adopted the system should afterwards abandon it.   And if the men go farther, and in their desire for augmented bonus create by extra industry an augmented surplus fund, large enough for their master as well as themselves to share in, there will be excellent reason why their master's example should be followed by other masters, and eventually by all so circumstanced as to be able to apply the same principle with prospect of similar effect.

Now, that the principle is abstractedly sound may be demonstrated quite conclusively beforehand.   There is no doubt that men in general could if they pleased do more and better work than they usually do.   One naturally works more with a will when working for oneself than for a master, and when doing piece-work than when paid by time.   Most men too are willing to work harder for the sake of proportionately better pay.   If they were not, there would not be so much readiness on the part of all workers, except trades' unionists, to take piece-work.   Neither would employers be so ready to give it them unless experience had shown that when earnings are made dependent upon the work done, the work done may generally be depended upon for being of not less value than the earnings.   So much for the principle itself.   Its bearing upon coopera- tion is equally obvious.   All cooperative labour partakes largely of the character of piece-work.   Unless a certain quantity of work of not less than a certain quality be done, the men get nothing but bare wages, while for every addi- tion to the quantity, and every improvement in the quality, they are assured of some bonus in addition.   They are thus directly interested in being diligent and careful.   They have a similar assurance with respect to every saving of material they effect, and they are thus interested in being economical likewise, which in piece-work they are not. What is still more to the purpose is, that every individual is even more interested in seeing that the industrial virtues are practised by his companions than in practising them himself.   The superintending efficacy of the master's eye is proverbial.   There is nothing like it for preventing hands from slurring over toilsome or tedious operations.   But the master's eye cannot be everywhere, and as business is ordinarily conducted, where it is absent there is nothing to supply its place.   But when capital takes labour into partnership, every labourer in becoming a partner becomes also a partaker in a master's motives for vigilance.   The interest which any one such petty partner can have in watching over the prosperity of the common undertaking is not indeed to be compared with the solicitude of a single employer for concerns exclusively his own, but the conjunction of many units produces an aggregate of superintending vigilance more efficacious than that of any single master.   Each one knows that the amount divisible between his companions and himself depends on the manner in which he and they do their work ; and even though this do not induce him to do his best himself, it will at least make him anxious that the others should do theirs.   Thus everyone is watched by everyone else.   Everyone has upon him not one, but hundreds perhaps of pairs of eyes, and every eye the eye of a master.   The consequence of this is well shown in Messrs. Briggs' business.   For one thing, the expense of overlookers is sensibly diminished.   The miners overlook each other of their own accord without requiring to be paid for it ; rating those sharply who are not working properly, and likewise those who are guilty of wastefulness. According to evidence given by one of themselves, it is quite a common thing now for a man in passing through the yard, if he meet with a bolt or a large nail, to pick it up and say, 'this is so much bonus saved.'   And the same with the men in the bottom.   They will sometimes get out a prop that is rather difficult to get out, and might have been left under other circumstances, and then they will turn over the expression, 'that is so much saved towards bonus.'

Clearly then, as an abstract proposition, it is true that labour may, by the expectation of additional reward, be stimulated to increased productiveness, material or moral, sufficient to furnish wherewithal to pay the additional reward. As clear is it, that in the truth of this proposition coopera- tion has a firm foundation whereon to build with justifiable confidence. Here, as it seems to me, is that 'basis of consis- tent and acknowledged principle,' for which Mr. Frederic Harrison very properly enquires.*   Here is 'cooperation's reason for the faith that is in it.' Long might cooperation have sought in vain to recommend itself as a promoter of the interests of labour, if it had not possessed the further recom- mendation of conducing to those of capital likewise. This has happily enabled it to make friends of the mammon of un- righteousness, who, while habitations of its own are getting ready, have volunteered to receive it into their houses. The more advanced forms of cooperation will be spoken of in a subsequent chapter.   In this, we are more immediately con- cerned with it in the stage of industrial partnership, of which the system of Messrs. Briggs is the best English specimen, and of which, as of all cooperation, the principle elucidated above is the vital force and animating spirit. Were such partnership generally applicable, and were there any security for its general adoption, the friends of labour might, if not exactly content with, be at least placidly re- signed to the prospect held out by it, so great would be the improvement upon the present therein foreshown. Though association of labour with capital on terms so unequal would leave much to be desired, it would yet accomplish much.   Though far from establishing complete harmony between the contracting parties, it would greatly moderate their hostility, by placing an object common to both, beside the one that has ever been the cause of their fiercest contention, and in respect of which indeed they could not but continue to be opposed.   For about the rate of wages they would still differ as widely as ever.   It would be as much as ever for the advantage of the one to enforce a low,

* 'Fortnightly Review' for January 1860 ; on 'Industrial Coopera- tion,' p. 482.

and of the other to extort a high rate, but their differences
on that subject, though equally wide, would be less bitter
than before.   Employers, if forced to pay enhanced wages,
might console themselves by reflecting that it was, at any
rate, more energetic labour they were paying dearer for ; as
might the employed, if compelled to submit to a reduction,
by considering that by extra exertion they might recover,
under a different name, the amount reduced.   And when
the main question about wages was settled for the time,
there would be little room for dispute about collateral
matters, and next to none about the application of the
labour hired, for both parties would be equally desirous that
it should be applied in the most efficacious manner.   For
mistrust and dislike or indifference on the one side, and for
envy and jealousy on the other, would be substituted something of that fellow-feeling which can scarcely help growing
up between those who, in serving themselves, are helping
each other.   With those labourers who had taken shares,
some sympathy with capital would tincture the old head-
long passion in favour of labour.   With those who had not
yet become shareholders the possibility of their becoming
so subsequently would have a like effect.   When over the
now seemingly impassable gulf a bridge was thrown, by
which the labourer saw some of his companions rising gradually towards the capitalist's level, the latter's superiority
would be more likely to inspirit him with ambitious ardour,
than to gall him, as at present, with hopeless repinings.

Moreover, there are few if any occupations to which industrial partnership is inapplicable ; in one respect, indeed,
it would seem to be, if anything, better adapted to those in
which the proportion of labour employed to capital invested
is small than to those in which the proportion is great.   To
capital, at least, the benefit would apparently be greater.
The proportion in question varies exceedingly in different
occupations, from 70 or 80 per cent. in coal mining to a mere
fraction per cent. in diamond cutting, but the skilful or
careless cutting of a single workman might easily make as

much difference in the value of 10,000*l.* worth of rough diamonds, as the diligence or negligence of fifty colliers hired to assist in utilising a capital of 10,000*l.* could make in the net profits thereupon. Suppose the difference in both cases to be 500*l.*, and the same amount to be consequently a surplus divisible under the rules of industrial partnership rateably between capital and labour. Suppose too, for convenience sake, the diamond cutter and the colliers to be all receiving the same rate of wages, which we will call 2*l.* a week. Each individual labourer's share of profit would then in both cases be about the same, about 5*l.*, but whereas the share of the capitalist owner of the diamonds would be about 495*l.*, that of the lessee of the coal mine would be only about 250*l.* Nor should it be overlooked that even though industrial partnership were less certain to pay capital pecuniarily, increased or improved production is not the only form in which adequate return may be made by labourers for the privilege of sharing in profits. Doubtless there are employers to whom a dinner of herbs where love is is better than a stalled ox and hatred therewith, and who, for the sake of living in harmony with those with whom they were constantly in contact, would consent to surrender to the latter some percentage of their income. Some such employers might possibly take labour into partnership even in trades, in which, from whatever cause, labour might seem incapable by extra industry of augmenting produce at all perceptibly. There is, however, but little chance of the frequent exhibition of such enlightened liberality. So far as yet is the gratification of the moral sentiments in trade transactions from being generally regarded as furnishing compensation for pecuniary loss, the employing mind must undergo a complete revolution in order to become generally disposed to abandon the prejudices which at present oppose the introduction of the bonus system even into trades in which it would plainly be pecuniarily beneficial still more to the employers than to the employed. Herein lies the chief difficulty of industrial partnership.   Here is what most impairs the reliance that might otherwise be placed upon it as an instrument for the reform of industrial organisation.   Its adoption everywhere requires the consent of capital, and labour, where its most vital interests are concerned, cannot afford to depend upon aught but itself.   With the most rapid development that can possibly be expected for it, the partnership or bonus system cannot for ages affect more than a portion of the labouring population, another portion as large or larger remaining outside its pale.   If the latter are, in the meantime, to become participants in like advantages, it will not be by any arrangement with capitalist employers.   The affair will have to be settled by themselves, as fortunately it may be by means of a higher and better form of cooperation for which they possess or may acquire adequate resources of their own—for which no preparations are requisite but what they themselves can make. Into the nature of that cooperation and into their capacity for establishing it I propose presently, and in conclusion, to enquire.   An intermediate chapter must, however, be devoted to the consideration of a subject which is often confounded with cooperation, without having really any nearer connection with it than that of being admirably calculated to prepare the way for it.

CHAPTER II.

'COOPERATIVE' OR ASSOCIATIVE STORES.

'THE principal necessaries for the support of a workman and his family are few in number, and are usually purchased by him in small quantities weekly. Upon such quantities, sold by the retail dealer, a large profit is generally made, and if the article is one whose quality (like that of tea) is not readily estimated, then a great additional profit is made by the retail dealer selling an inferior article.

'In such circumstances, where the number of workmen living on the same spot is large, it may be thought desirable that they should unite together and have an agent to purchase wholesale such articles as tea, sugar, and bacon, &c., in most demand, and to retail them out at prices which will just repay their wholesale cost, and the expense of the agent they employ. If this be wholly managed by a committee of workmen, and if the agent is paid in such a manner as to be interested in procuring good and reasonable articles, it may be a benefit to the workmen, and may succeed in reducing the cost of articles of necessity to the men.'

When I first came upon these paragraphs in Mr. Babbage's 'Economy of Machinery and Manufactures,'* I was half disposed to fancy that in writing them the author had been unconsciously laying the foundation of one of the earliest of those establishments which, under the title prefixed to this chapter, have latterly become so famous. A

* pp. 253-4.

little before, he had expressed a hope that his 'volume
might fall into the hands of workmen perhaps better qualified than himself to reason on a subject which requires
only plain common sense,' and which they would approach
with ' powers sharpened by its importance to their personal
happiness.'   Mr. Babbage's most instructive little book was
published in 1832, between which year and 1844 there was
plenty of time for it to be studied by some of the ardent
enquirers who, about the latter date, adopted and improved
upon the course recommended in the above-quoted passage.
Very probably the book was seen by one or other of them,
and if so, the passage in question may have given them a
useful hint.   As probably, however, they may have obtained the same hint elsewhere.   For their society, though
the first of a new species, belonged to a genus which dated
from at least a score of years earlier.   So-called ' Cooperative Stores ' existed before the Rochdale Agamemnon,
two of them having even preceded it in the same town ;
nor to these primitive specimens was there lacking a pious
chronicler.   A whole generation before the Manchester
' Cooperator' was started under the able editorship of Mr.
H. Pitman, a Brighton newspaper bore the same name.
The information, however, regarding the earlier stores, obtainable from this and other contemporary records, is instructive less in showing how they temporarily flourished,
than why they finally failed.   ' In some cases,' says Dr.
John Watts, summing up in a few pungent words the causes
of decay, ' managers were appointed who had no sufficient
knowledge, either of goods or of accounts ; in others, men
were appointed who had failed in trade for themselves, and
who repeated their experience for the societies; in others,
again, the moral power was not strong enough to resist
temptation, and the stores would some morning be found
vacant, except of accounts requiring liquidation.   In most
of them, the desire to do a large business led to the fatal
error of giving credit, which brought with it the necessity
of getting credit, and its usual concomitant of having to

pay higher prices for worse material. The trade books were filled with small debts, the ready-money customers were lost through the depreciated quality of the goods, and thus was dissipated the small subscribed capital of many a cooperative concern.' *

The history of the Rochdale Pioneers has been often told, and its hackneyed particulars should not be repeated here but that they are indispensable for the complete treatment of our subject.† Twenty-four years ago, twenty-eight operatives of Rochdale, disgusted, as they well might be, with the villainous qualities and outrageous prices of the provisions and groceries procurable from the petty tradespeople with whom they were in the habit of dealing, resolved to become their own purveyors. With scarcely an exception they were all working journeymen, and most of them flannel weavers, but they were also thoughtful, provident men, who, small as their means were, had resisted the temptation of credit at the 'tally' shop, and had managed to keep out of debt. Being free from encumbrance of that sort, they were able to start clear; and clubbing together, and subscribing each his twopence or threepence a week, they gradually made up amongst them the sum of 28*l.*, with which they bought, at wholesale prices, some sacks of flour, and one of oatmeal, a hundredweight of sugar, and a firkin of butter, hiring, at the same time, a place for the stowage of their purchases. Among the bye-streets in Rochdale, where, in truth, all the streets are bye-streets, is one whose name by successive stages has become corrupted from 'the old' into 'T'old,' 'Towd,' and finally, into 'Toad Lane.' Here they took, for three years, and at an annual rent of 10*l.*, the ground-floor of what had once been a warehouse, but of which the first-floor was then in use as a

* 'Cooperative Societies, Productive and Distributive,' by John Watts, Ph.D.

† In this, and also in the next chapter, I have made considerable use of an article of my own, on 'Strikes and Industrial Cooperation' published in the 'Westminster Review' for April 1864.

chapel, and the second as a schoolroom, and arranged that
one of their number, dignified with the title of salesman,
should attend there for a few hours in the evening, twice a
week.   But though the weavers had now got a place for a
shop, they were half ashamed to open it.   When the day
and hour for commencing business arrived, the little party
assembled within to take part in the ceremony, were
abashed at the largeness of the crowd assembled without
to witness it.   Some delay took place before anyone could
muster up courage to take down the shutters, and when at
last the 'store' and its contents were exposed to public
view, all Toad Lane was in a roar.   Loud and long were
the shouts of derision that rose from a host of 'doffers,' a
species of street-boy peculiar to the clothing districts, who
set on by persons who ought to have known better, stared
through the windows or blocked up the doorway, evincing
their characteristically precocious sense of the ridiculous by
the nature of their comments on the modest display of the
'owd weavers' shop.' *

Those may laugh that win.   The joint tenants of the shop
were very likely, at first, its only customers.   They, however,
resorted to it regularly for whatever it could supply, and as
every one paid for what he carried off in ready money, and
at the prices current in the neighbourhood, they had the
satisfaction of discovering, when the sacks and barrels became empty, that the sale proceeds of the contents, if
divided rateably among them, would give to each a considerable addition to the amount of his original venture.
Of course, a speculation that had turned out so well was
presently repeated.   More flour, oatmeal, sugar, and butter
were ordered, and this time in larger quantities than when,
as at first, the embryo association had been jeeringly told
that their whole stock in trade would not fill a respectable
wheelbarrow.   Fresh candidates were now presenting them-

---

* The same story will be found told in more detail, and with a good
deal of humour, in 'Self Help by the People ; History of Cooperation
in Rochdale,' by George Jacob Holyoake.   London, 1858.

selves for admission, and others besides members were appearing as customers. In 1845, their second year, the associates, already increased in number from twenty-eight to seventy-four, made, upon a capital raised from 28*l.* to 181*l.*, a net profit of 32*l.* In 1846 and 1847, they divided 80*l.* and 72*l.*, and, as the following astonishing table will show, they have ever since been going on as well as they began.

Operations of the Rochdale Equitable Pioneers.

Year	No. of Members	Funds	Business done	Profits
		£	£	£
1844	28	28		
1845	74	181	710	22
1846	80	252	1146	80
1847	110	286	1924	72
1848	140	397	2276	117
1849	390	1193	6611	561
1850	600	2299	13179	880
1851	630	2785	17638	990
1852	680	3471	16352	1206
1853	720	5848	22760	1674
1854	900	7172	33364	1763
1855	1400	11032	44902	3106
1856	1600	12920	63197	3921
1857	1850	15142	79788	5470
1858	1950	18160	71680	6284
1859	2703	27060	104012	10739
1860	3450	37710	152063	15906
1861	3900	42925	176206	18020
1862	3501	38465	141074	17564
1863	4013	49361	158632	19671
1864	4747	62105	174937	22717
1865	5326	78778	196234	25156
1866	6246	99989	249122	31931
1867	6823	128435	284910	41619

These are eloquent figures, but they leave a good deal to be told. In proportion as the Pioneers received accessions of members and capital, a growing consciousness of utility encouraged them to embark in new branches of trade. In 1847, linen and woollen drapery was grafted on to the original grocery business, additional space being hired for the purpose. In 1850, a butcher's shop was set up, and soon afterwards a slaughter-house, in which the number of animals of all kinds—oxen, sheep, pigs, lambs, and calves — killed in the first six months of the past year, was 2,023, the weight of meat sold being 347,881 pounds. In 1852, shoe-making, clog-making, and tailoring were commenced. Coal dealing has since been undertaken, and in 1867 a bakery was established. The headquarters of the society are still in Toad Lane, and, until lately, were still in the old warehouse first occupied. Here, though they soon got possession of the whole building, having indeed purchased it outright, they became after awhile somewhat cramped for space, and the scene which Toad Lane used at that time to present on a Saturday evening is said to have been worth a long journey to Rochdale to see. Operatives and others who had just received their wages, are described as coming in swarms to the stores, either in person, or by deputy, and clustering like bees at favourite counters. The grocery and general store would be as full as it could hold of members and their wives and children, laying in next week's stock of flour, potatoes, rice, sugar and butter, while others were chatting outside, waiting their turn to go in. In the draper's shop there would seldom be less than nine or ten women selecting what they required, and in the butcher's three assistants would have as much as they could do to attend to the constant succession of applicants for the hief material of next day's dinner. The news-room and library would be crowded with men and youths reading the newspapers and magazines, or exchanging and renewing books ; and by eleven o'clock, when the premises were closed, between 400*l.* and 500*l.* would have been taken during the day, and the librarian would have given out about two hundred volumes. A description like this would no longer be strictly accurate, for, though the number of customers is greater now than ever, the enlarged accommodation provided affords ample room and verge enough for all. Ten branch stores, each with its own news-room attached, have been opened in different parts of the town and its neighbourhood, for the convenience of families living at a distance from Toad Lane, in which thoroughfare, moreover, the main business was last year removed from its primitive domicile to a new central store, erected at an expense of 12,000*l.* Of this its founders justly boast as being, after the old parish church and the unfinished town hall, the most imposing structure in their somewhat unromantic town. It is of stone, four stories high, and proportionately wide, with three tiers of pointed windows over the square-headed basement range. Within, besides spacious grocery and drapery shops—in the former of which I saw one night about a dozen women, ranged *en queue* like passengers at a railway booking-office, waiting to be served with butter—are an immense assembly room, a board room furnished in a style with which Indian councillors, or Bank of England directors, might be well content, a news-room provided with most English reviews and magazines, and with most of the metropolitan and local newspapers, and a library which bids fair to rival, some of these days, that of the most literary of London clubs. It possesses already 9,000 volumes, and the Educational Committee, who have charge of it, have at their disposal, for the purchase of books and other purposes, two-and-a-half per cent. of the net profits of the society— a percentage at present exceeding 1,000*l.* a-year. Besides the new central store, two other houses in Toad Lane are the freehold property of the society. So also, I believe, are several of the branch stores, and so certainly are a number of cottages which they have built, or are building, on pieces of land belonging to them in different situations. And besides the real property wholly theirs, they have large shares in that of the Rochdale Flour Mill Society, and that of the Rochdale Cooperative Manufacturing Society, two offshoots from their own body, of whom the former possess a corn mill and malt kilns, constructed at an expense of 20,000*l.*, and the latter a cotton mill that cost them

at least 50,000*l.* So has the germ, deposited only five-and-
twenty years ago in the 'owd weavers' shop,' already increased and multiplied.   Such are the sheaves over which
those, who then went forth weeping, bearing precious seed,
are now, with good cause, rejoicing.

It was not without prophetic instinct that the title of
'Pioneers' was assumed at the outset, by the Rochdale
adventurers.   After they had cleared the way, others were
not slow to follow, and associations like theirs, scattered
over all parts of the kingdom, are now to be counted by
hundreds.   In 1867 the number of 'Cooperative' Store
Societies in England and Wales, registered under the Industrial and Provident Societies Act, was 577, comprising
171,897 members, possessing an aggregate share capital of
1,473,199*l.*, doing business to the amount of more than
6,000,000 sterling annually, and realising thereon an annual
net profit of nearly 400,000*l.* The character of their transactions is very varied.   Almost all are grocers, and most
of them are, in addition, provision dealers, or drapers, or
tailors, or hatters, or shoe or clog-makers, or butchers, or
bakers; and many combine several, and some all, of these
trades.   A few are corn millers only, and two or three
bakers only.   By one or two coal only is sold, and by one,
only snuff and tobacco.   There is one store at which beer
is dispensed, and cooperators of the straiter sort shake their
heads when they speak of it, instead of rather regretting
that there should be one place only, affording so much
security that the liquor to be had there will be good
of its kind.*   One society entitled to a few words of spe-

---

* 'If all cooperative stores would adopt the practice of that at
Assington, and sell wholesome homebrewed beer at a moderate price,
to be consumed off the premises, a great step would have been made
towards the extinction of drunkenness.   Men would then buy no more
beer than they wanted, and would drink it at their supper and with
their family at home.   They would get a better article at 25 per cent.
less cost.' . . . .   Of beer-houses and beer-selling cooperative
stores 'it is easy to see which, in the interests of society, most deserves

cial notice, is the 'North of England Cooperative Wholesale,' the idea of which originated with Mr. Abraham
Greenwood, of Rochdale, a veteran 'Equitable Pioneer,'
and the only customers of which are retail Store societies,
its professed office being to purchase for such societies, on
better terms than they would obtain for themselves, if they
entered the market separately. According to a balance
sheet, dated July 11 last, the amount of business done by it
with 207 societies, during the quarter ending that day, was
102,342*l.*, and the profit made was at the rate of twenty
per cent. on its capital of 27,250*l.** Of the retail societies,
some are doing much better than others. The Rochdale
Pioneers have for years been making considerably more
than thirty per cent. profit, but some infant societies may
perhaps have made little if any profit as yet. As however,
of the whole 577 taken together, the average annual rate
of profit is nearly twenty-seven per cent., it is not likely that
many of them are doing at all badly.

The secret of their success is to be found in their mode
of doing business, which, in the cases of such as adopt, as
most of them do more or less, the pattern of the Rochdale Pioneers, possesses some very decided advantages.
They make all their purchases wholesale, and paying
always ready money, they are allowed discount on all they
buy. Never selling on credit, they have no bad debts.
Never permitting any article to be removed from their
shops without being replaced by cash, they are able to
turn over their money many times in the course of a
twelvemonth, and thus to do with it as much as would be
possible with many times the amount under the usual
system of slower returns. Possessing in their own shareholders a large body of assured customers, they have no
necessity for any of those heavy expenses which ordinary

encouragement.'—Rev. James Fraser, in Appendix to First Report of
Agricultural Commissioners, 1867.

* A somewhat fuller account of the Wholesale Society will be given,
further on, in a supplementary chapter.

tradesmen are obliged to incur in order to make themselves and their pretensions known. Their expenses of management are in consequence extraordinarily small, sometimes not exceeding one or two per cent. on the amount of business done. For attracting outsiders their 'equitable' distribution of profits is a device far more efficacious than claptrap advertisements or showy shop fronts. At the Rochdale, Leeds, and most other stores, whenever anyone, whether a member or not, makes a purchase, he receives a tin ticket, denoting the sum he has paid. At the end of every quarter, when profits are declared, a deduction is first made, sufficient to pay interest at five per cent. per annum on capital; a certain percentage (at Rochdale two-and-a-half) is generally next appropriated to an education fund; and the residue is then divided among the holders of the tin tickets. The idea which is at the bottom of this arrangement, may be easily conjectured. A cooperative store is based on the understanding, that all who are parties to its establishment will give it their custom, and after the requisite capital has been supplied, the success of the undertaking, provided it be judiciously conducted, will be proportionate to the custom it obtains. Whatever profit may be made, will be due to the instrumentality partly of the shareholder, partly of the customer, but the former may, not unreasonably, be deemed to be sufficiently recompensed for the use of his capital, if he get the market rate of interest at which capital can be hired. When, therefore, the usual five per cent. has been paid to him out of profit, whatever profit may remain may be looked upon as the product of the customer's operations, and as such to be wholly appropriable to him, if he is to be rewarded in proportion to the share he has taken in the business. Applied consistently, this principle would make no distinction between members and non-members, but would let both share alike in the portion of profits divisible amongst customers. This, however, is never permitted, considerable favour being always shown to members. Nor, in spite of its inconsistency, is there any want of equity in this inequality. Non-members clearly have no claim whatever upon the society, beyond what is conceded to them by the society's regulations. If the regulations conceded them nothing, they would be entitled to nothing. In general the concessions made are very liberal; at Rochdale, for instance, if the financial position of the Pioneers were such as to allow of 2s. 6d. in the pound of what they had spent at the store being returned to members, non-members would probably receive 1s. 8d. in the pound. Customers are not likely to be wanting in shops in which, besides being sure that everything is good of its kind, they are so munificently rewarded for their good sense in coming.

The rapid and continued progress of 'Cooperative Stores' affords matter for unqualified congratulation, for nothing but unalloyed good can proceed from them, and the good they are doing is of various kinds. In the first place, they make a poor man's earnings go further than they ever went before. Whatever he buys at a store, he buys at a lower cost than he could get it at anywhere else, and if he be a shareholder, he gets it at the lowest price at which it could be sold, without loss to the seller; for in the latter case, whatever difference there be between that price and the price charged to him at first, is eventually returned to him.

Secondly, they give to a purchaser the best possible security that whatever he buys will be of good quality, since it is taken from a stock which has been laid in by the purveyors for their own consumption, as well as his. On this point Mr. Holyoake warms into justifiable enthusiasm. 'The whole atmosphere of a store,' says he, 'is honest. In that market there is no distrust and no deception, no adulteration and no second prices. Buyer and seller meet as friends. There is no overreaching on the one side, and no suspicion on the other. Those who serve neither hurry, finesse, nor flatter. They have no interest in chicanery. Their sole duty is to give fair measure, full weight, and pure quality to men who never knew before what it was to have a wholesome meal, whose shoes let in water a month too soon, whose waistcoats shone with devil's dust, and whose wives wore calico that would not wash. These men now buy in the market like millionaires, and, as far as pureness of food goes, live like lords. They make their own shoes, sew their own garments, and grind their own corn. They buy the purest sugar and the best tea, and grind their own coffee. They slaughter their own cattle, and the finest beasts of the land waddle down the streets of Rochdale for the consumption of flannel-weavers and cobblers.' 'When a child,' he adds, 'is sent to a *shop*, it is usual, as children can be put off with anything, to caution him to go to some particular man—the one with grey whiskers and black hair, for instance—and to be sure and ask him for the best butter. But in a *store*, it is as if all the men had grey whiskers and black hair; the child cannot go to the wrong man, and the best butter is sure to be given without being asked for, because no bad is kept.'*

One effect of cooperative stores must obviously be largely to supersede the hucksters' shops, from which the bulk of the labouring population are clothed and fed. But this, instead of being an objection to them, deserves to be placed third among their recommendations. Small shops are great nuisances, and the more they are multiplied in number and diminished in size, the greater nuisances they become. Increased competition between dealers is popularly regarded as a certain pledge for increased cheapness, but the fact is, that excessive increase in the number of competitors infallibly raises prices instead of lowering them. However anxious tradesmen may be to undersell each other, they cannot afford to sell at prices below those on which they can live, and the lowest prices on which they can live must needs be higher when a given amount of business is divided among many than when the sharers in it are few. If anyone's share be too small to maintain

* 'Self Help,' pp. 38–9.

him honestly, the form which competition will take with him will be that, not of reduced prices, but of adulterated quality. The function of mere distribution, for which commodities are so enormously taxed in their passage from the producer to the consumer, might be far better performed than at present, and at a tithe of the present cost, by a tenth part of the host of middlemen at present engaged in it,—by a central store with its eight or nine branches, for instance, than by a hundred of the petty stalls which, until routed out by the Pioneers, used to meet the eye at Rochdale at every turn. Moreover, the petty shops at which the poor are accustomed to deal are a nuisance in other respects than those of dearness and dishonesty. In Lancashire most of them are of the kind termed 'tally-shops,' regular customers at which are furnished with 'strap-books,' wherein their purchases are entered; and these books are balanced weekly or fortnightly, a balance being always suffered to remain on the wrong side of the account, in order that the shopkeeper may retain a hold upon the book-holders. Thus the latter are always in debt, and, as a natural consequence, are recklessly wasteful, since for them to be sparing would be more immediately for their creditors' benefit than their own. It is no small merit of cooperative stores that they are gradually putting an end to all this, drawing to themselves the supporters of the tally-shops, and leaving the latter to perish from consequent exhaustion.

A fourth and kindred merit of theirs is, that shops which they do not supplant, they stimulate to self-amendment. Just as the building of a model lodging-house often causes all the other lodging-houses in the neighbourhood to be remodelled, so may the general establishment of stores, stocked with none but unadulterated goods, eventually leave no choice to ordinary retailers, but either to cease adulterating or to shut up shop. Thus may be closed one prolific source of disease and physical deterioration, against which neither legislative denunciation nor the strenuous

exertions of Dr. Hassall and his colleagues in the 'Lancet
Commission' have hitherto proved of any sensible avail.
Nor might .the moral result in such an event be of less
moment than the sanitary. When it is considered how
almost universal amongst tradespeople is the practice of
adulteration, and how conventional is most people's standard
of morality, few persons questioning the propriety of anything which they see their fellows continually doing—how
apt, too, is the habitual commission of any one species of
dishonesty to prepare the way for kindred transgressions—
it will not seem too much to believe that a great moral
advance might follow a general cessation of the customs
of sanding sugar and watering milk, of whitening bread
with alum and colouring tea with copperas.

In the fifth place, cooperative stores are both great
promoters of prudence, and munificent rewarders of the
prudence they promote. Poverty, particularly English
poverty, is naturally reckless. The scantier its resources,
the less it husbands them. It does not see how the morrow
can be any the better for being thought about; so for the
morrow it takes no thought. What is there, it asks, for those
to put by, who are almost always living from hand to mouth?
and what, if there were anything, would the putting by of
so mere a mite avail? What sort of provision for old age
would be the score or two of pounds which, by systematic
renunciation of beer and skittles, might possibly be at
length scraped together? What compensation would that
be for the long previous years of Lenten abstinence? To
these questions cooperative stores are giving more satisfactory answers than but for them would be possible. They
furnish adequate motives for saving,—furnish also the means
and cherish the habit; nay, if they can once get a poor man
to begin saving, they go on saving for him afterwards,
almost in spite of himself. To frequenters of 'tally' shops
they begin by offering for sale, instead of poisonous trash
and flimsy frippery, good wholesome food and good stout
clothing; and they offer, too, a handsome premium to

buyers, but they permit none to buy who do not come with money in their hands. Whoever, therefore, desires to partake of the proffered advantages, must qualify by first getting, and afterwards keeping out of debt. This rigid enforcement of cash payments is just the sort of discipline required by those to whom it is applied. It holds out intelligible inducements to thrift and foresight. Many a man who now has his 50*l.* or 60*l.* in a store, is ready to acknowledge that before joining he scarcely ever had a penny he could really call his own, and that what made him begin to economise was the desire of gaining access to the store. When one originally so circumstanced has once saved enough to enable him to pay off his shop debts, and to deal regularly with a cooperative store, the latter furnishes him with abundant material for further saving. Out of the money he pays for everything he buys, every piece of bacon and every pound of sugar or tea, a considerable percentage, very nearly as much as a retail dealer would have taken as profit, is set apart for the purpose of being subsequently returned to him. Now almost everything that a working man wants, for the daily use of himself or his family, may be obtained at a cooperative store. He may buy there bread, meat, cheese, butter, sugar, tea, coffee, all sorts of provisions and condiments, and perhaps coal; coats and trousers, boots and shoes for himself, and gowns, bonnets and shawls, parasols and pattens for his wife and daughters. The sum total of his annual purchases is, therefore, something considerable; and so in its degree is that of the drawback thereupon, the former often amounting to 100*l.* or so, and the latter to 10*l.* At the end of every quarter, to every good customer at a flourishing store a present of a couple of sovereigns or so is made, in consideration of his having, not produced, but consumed: those, moreover, who have consumed most receiving most; so that, as the process is described in Lancashire phrase, 'the more they eaten the more they geten.' True, they get nothing but what they have previously advanced, nothing is put into one pocket but what has, as it were, been taken out of the other; and it may not be immediately apparent why the equivalent of the drawback finally restored to them might not just as well have been deducted in the first instance from the prices they were called upon to pay. The actual plan is really, however, much better for the purchasers. If they merely got what they buy at a somewhat cheaper rate, the probability is that they would simply buy so much more, and that at the end of the year they would be none the richer. Whereas, as it is, a man who finds a couple of sovereigns coming to him in a lump, is already in a fit frame of mind for investing, and predisposed to accept the offer of investment made him by the store. By leaving untouched two or three of his first quarterly windfalls, and letting them accumulate, he literally eats his way up to the rank of shareholder; after which, as the habit of saving is commonly a growing one, he will probably not rest content with being holder of only a single share, but will leave some more of his dividends and bonuses to fructify as the former had done. If he does, he will often be delightfully surprised at the quantities of fruit that will be borne for him. A., who in 1850 began by depositing 1s. 3d., and afterwards paid in four successive quarterly instalments of 3s. 3d. each, making 14s. 3d. in all, was then able to stop paying in cash, for the drawbacks which had meantime been entered to his credit, had raised his subscriptions to the shareholder's minimum of 5l. Leaving this untouched, he drew out, between January, 1851, and December 1860, a sum of 41l. in all, which he had acquired in the quality, not of shareholder, but of customer. B., having paid in only 15s., gained in ten years 18l. C. in 1850 held one 5l. share. He never afterwards paid in anything; yet in 1860, though he had drawn out 115l. during the interval, he had still 10l. left. D., an old woman, being advised to draw out her money from the store, which she was assured was going to break, replied with magnanimity worthy of a Spartan matron, ' Well, let it break. If it does it will break with its own. I have only paid 1s., and I have 50l. there now.' All these are somewhat antiquated cases, drawn entirely from early Rochdale experience. A reference to more recent records would, in all probability, furnish still more striking illustrations.*

The above are a few of the ways in which cooperative stores exercise their remarkably beneficial influence; but in truth, whatever they do is both good and well done. The only fault to be found with them, is their assuming a title that does not rightly belong to them, and thereby professing to do something which is not within their province, and which they consequently leave undone. They call themselves 'cooperative,' while there is really nothing cooperative about them. Cooperation means working together, but members of a store society do not work, they only trade together. The circumstances of their associating themselves for a commercial purpose, and of their permitting customers to participate in profits, do not constitute cooperation. The first of these things is done by all joint stock companies, and the second by all life assurance companies that give bonuses to policy holders, but which are nevertheless as much mere joint stock companies as any others. So, too, are the trading associations of working men of which we are now speaking, and whose

---

* Associative Stores on the model of those of Britain are spreading fast over some other parts of Europe. In Germany, according to Professor Pfeiffer, there are between 400 and 500 of them, with from 50,000 to 60,000 members, doing business annually to the extent of at least four millions sterling. In France, according to M. Hubert Valleroux, there are 500 ; most of them in the smaller towns, there being but few in Paris, and not more than 25 in Lyons. Their business is chiefly 'in the baking line and in groceries, but some is done also in clothing and household articles, and a little in butcher's meat. Almost all prosper and give good dividends.' In Switzerland they are not numerous as yet, but the one at Zurich, M. Wirth says, 'furnishes bread for nearly the whole city.' In Denmark there are between 40 and 50. In Sweden and Norway there are three or four, and others are in course of formation.—'Proceedings of London Cooperative Congress, 1869.'

chief peculiarities are the class of persons from whom their members are drawn, and the more than ordinary caution with which their business is conducted. And while all cooperation whatsoever means working together, industrial cooperation—if by that newly invented term anything distinctive be implied—means in addition, not simply working together, but working together with a common object, in which all the workers are interested in proportion to the shares they severally take in the work. To industrial cooperation it is indispensable that all the cooperators shall, over and above stipulated wages, be entitled to share in whatever profits they may jointly make. But in no single instance that I am aware of, do store societies, in their employing capacity, differ from ordinary employers in their mode of remunerating their servants. In no single instance are the latter permitted to participate in profits. Even at Rochdale, those serving in the grocer's or draper's shop, or working in the tailor's shop or in the flour mill, get nothing for the work they do but bare wages. If anything additional be paid to them, it is paid to and received by them in their capacity, not of labourers, but of shareholders or customers. What the pattern Rochdale society omits to do, none of the English societies modelled upon it can be expected to do. To one and all, the first essential of industrial cooperation is utterly wanting.* They possess, however, too many intrinsic excellences to have any need to deck -themselves out with borrowed plumes, and it may without offence be suggested to them that they should drop their 'cooperative' designation, and either call themselves instead, 'associative,' or adopt some other epithet less inconsistent with their real character; unless,

---

* Some of the German store societies are considerably in advance of the English in this respect. Those which have accepted the rules laid down by M. Schulze-Delitzch, pay their storekeepers, cashiers and comptrollers by a 'tantième' of from 2 to 3 per cent. on the business done,' Mr. Morier says, though probably he rather means, on the profits realised.

indeed, they prefer to take another, and that by far the best course of all, by paying their employees in proportion to their own gains, and so rendering themselves, in deed as well as name, cooperative.

At the same time, it must in justice be conceded to them, that, though not themselves cooperative, they are among the most efficient harbingers and auxiliaries of cooperation; and this, though as yet only a collateral recommendation, may come hereafter to be considered their chiefest claim to praise. It is, at any rate, the chief reason why so much space is devoted to them here. There are two ways in which they are performing the important office with which they are thus credited. Working men, in order to be qualified to engage in independent cooperation, must be provided with two things—capital and special training— and associative stores contribute something of each. With every one of the bank notes with which a flourishing store is annually presenting its customers, a whole or half-share in a really cooperative productive association may be purchased; and every one, from manager to shopboy, who is taking any part in the conduct of an 'associative' store, is qualifying himself thereby for taking corresponding part in the conduct of a really cooperative association. No such association can succeed until the members have, by first deserving it, acquired each other's confidence, and membership in an associative store calls forth and fosters precisely those qualities—patience, self-denial, conscientiousness, and public spirit—on which mutual confidence most firmly rests. True, the most advanced of store societies are as yet far from having made all desirable progress in the acquisition of these virtues. Even of the Rochdale Pioneers I have heard it more than hinted that sectarian and partisan jealousies sometimes disturb the harmony of their proceedings; that greed of gain sometimes dictates very shortsighted counsels, and that consciousness on the part of their employees of zealous and faithful service is systematically left by them to be its own chief reward. On this last point there is, indeed, no room for doubt. Though labourers by profession ought to be among the last men requiring to be taught that superior labour deserves superior pay, they not unnaturally grudge paying their own servants better than they themselves are paid, and the most liberal of store societies has yet to learn that a prosperous mechanic's wages are not sufficient acknowledgment of mercantile talents, which, if not employed in making the society's fortune, might have made their owner's ten times over. But whatever in this or any other direction is required to be learnt by store societies, will assuredly be learnt for this if for no other reason, that the knowledge is essential to them. The career upon which the societies in question have entered is one of too general and extended utility not to be persevered in; whatever equipments, therefore, are necessary for its continued prosecution will certainly be ultimately forthcoming. The societies will educate their members into fitness for the duties which are involved in their own association, and in so fitting them, will fit them simultaneously for the requirements of another and superior association.

On the educational appliances possessed by store societies there is at present no time to dwell. To some, which are as it were inherent in their organization, and also to the libraries and news-rooms which they all establish as soon as they can afford it, brief reference has already been made, and equally brief allusion must suffice to their periodical business assemblies and social gatherings. At the former, it is, if not formally ordained, tacitly understood that every member shall have 'full liberty to speak his sentiments on all subjects, if brought forward at a proper time and in a proper manner,' all subjects being further declared with significant tautology to be 'legitimate when properly proposed.' Accordingly whatever is uppermost in men's minds is freely brought forward, and specially the state and prospects of their own affairs, questions respecting the past and future of which often give rise to animated debate.

Observations and reflections are compared, lessons learnt from books are illustrated and tested by the results of experience, and opiniative angularities and crudities are rubbed down and moulded into shape by mutual friction. At the social gatherings, which usually take the form of tea parties, and at which temperate feasting is combined with reasoning, and flowing cups help to open the heart as well as to invigorate the brain, it is a real treat to a stranger to be present. No one, as Mr. Harrison says, who has 'seen Lancashire or Yorkshire workmen with their wives and children meet in their own hall, surrounded by their own property, to consider their own affairs—has heard them join in singing, sometimes a psalm, sometimes a chorus—has listened to the homely wit, the prudent advice, the stirring appeal, and felt the spirit of goodwill, conviction, and resolution with which they celebrate their escape as it were from Egyptian bondage, can fail to perceive that the agency which brings them together, if not itself a moral and social movement, possesses many high moral and social tendencies.'

There remains only to be shown in what grand cooperative conclusions the tendencies thus spoken of may be expected to culminate.

CHAPTER III.

COOPERATIVE SOCIETIES.

'WHEN I speak,' says Mr. Mill, 'of the labouring classes, or of labourers as a class, I use those phrases in compliance with custom, and as descriptive of an existing but by no means a necessary or permanent state of social relations. I do not recognise as either just or salutary a state of society in which there s any class which is not labouring, any human beings exempt from bearing their share of the necessary burdens of human life, except those unable to labour, or who have fairly earned rest by previous toil . . . I cannot think that the working classes will be permanently contented with the condition of labouring for wages as their ultimate state. They may be willing to pass through the class of servants in their way to that of employers, but not to remain in it all their lives . . . In the present state of human progress, when ideas of equality are daily spreading more widely among the poorer classes, and can no longer be checked, except by the entire suppression of printed discussion, and even of freedom of speech, it is not to be expected that the division of the human race into two hereditary classes, employers and employed, can be permanently maintained.' *

Heartily concurring in much of the sentiment thus expressed, I nevertheless presume to take exception to the mode of expression. To me it appears clear that, however objectionable in other respects may be the social state re-

* 'Political Economy,' vol. ii. pp. 333 and 342.

ferred to, there is nothing in it in the slightest degree unjust. If there were, force, under the guise of law, might justifiably step in to alter it. Justice would suggest, would indeed insist upon a new partition of the property whose actual distribution alone it is that permits one class to live without working, and condemns another class to work for the maintenance of both. But all property really entitled to be so called, all property that has been honestly come by, belongs to its owner absolutely, and to all intents and purposes. It must be the product either of his own industry, or of that of others who or whose representatives have bequeathed or otherwise transferred it to him, and in either case his rights over it are complete, for the simple reason that no other human being can possibly have any right in connection with it. He may, therefore, make of it any use he pleases that does not interfere with other people's rights; and among other things he may, if he pleases, live upon it in idleness, live upon the fruits of past labour whether of himself or others which it embodies, instead of by further labour of his own. It may be very undesirable that he should so live. Undoubtedly if he be capable of useful work, it would be better that he should do some sort of work; but forcibly to interfere with the privilege of idleness which the possession of property confers on him and on others situated like him, would itself be a gross injustice, and one not more high-handed than short-sighted, for it would strike at the very root of industry. The world is not to be set right by wrong-doing.

Neither is it quite certain that the existence of a class of men privileged, if they think fit, to live in idleness is an absolutely unmitigated evil. Possibly it may even serve to mitigate still worse evils. Would it not of the two be preferable that there should be many wasting their whole lives in doing nothing, than that there should be none at liberty to choose work that will not pay pecuniarily, and to do it solely because they love it? What to me appears really deplorable, is not so much that there should be a class exempt from the necessity of labour, as that there should be one to whom it is necessary to be incessantly labouring. It is the violence of the contrast between the non-working and the working population—all the wealth on one side, little but toil on the other—yet even in this I maintain there is nothing necessarily unjust, though I have nothing to urge in behalf of its salutariness. As long as it can be said,—

> That the two parties still divide the world
> Of those that want, and those that have,—

so long can there be no merry world for you, my masters ; so long will still

> The same old sore break out from age to age
> With much the same result.

One-half of mankind will never submit quietly to have their maintenance dependent on the other half's caprice, to be mere instruments of production, worked mainly for the benefit of privileged consumers. With such a state of things they cannot be expected to be content. While it endures there can be no social peace, and it would be humiliating to human nature if there could be. How to end it is the most pressing of social problems. Trades' unionism may, as we have seen, do much towards alleviating its enormities, but can only alleviate them, leaving the cause untouched. There are but two ways in which a fundamental change can be wrought : either employers must take the employed into partnership, or the employed must become their own employers. How much the former expedient may do, and how much it must leave undone, have likewise already been considered. It has been seen to be a plan applicable indeed to most if not all occupations, but to be without any security for its adoption in any. What it can do for the employed depends on the will of the employers, and may therefore be indefinitely postponed ; and if all that it can do were done, there would still be much left to do which can only be done by the employed themselves. If these are ever to be completely relieved from their immemorial causes of discontent, they must work out by far the greater part of their own deliverance.   There is no hope of an entirely and universally satisfactory settlement of the conditions of employment unless they can become their own employers.   What ability have they then of providing themselves with the requisites for self-employment ?   At this, the crowning and most interesting stage of our inquiry, we have now arrived.

In prosecuting it, we have fortunately some results of experience to assist us. The idea of industrial cooperation in its highest and purest sense—in the sense, not of partnership between a capitalist employer retaining in his own hands the entire management of his business, and workpeople admitted by him to an interest in the concern in a degree limited, and on terms dictated by himself, but of the association of workpeople, who themselves providing all requisites for their own employment, naturally arrange also entirely among themselves on what conditions they are to work—appears to have originated, or at least to have first become practically embodied, in France soon after the Revolution of 1830.   It was then that what had previously floated loosely about as ' a simple hypothesis, a system, a theory, passed into the domain of practice, became a fact.' For the complete realization of this idea certain things are essential.   A number of workmen having contrived to procure the needful tools and raw material, must agree to work together at the same trade, under directors chosen by themselves from amongst themselves, and must further agree that the entire net proceeds of their industry shall be divided in some pre-arranged proportion among all who have contributed, whether by their labour or their capital, or by both, to the joint production.   Only when, or only in so far as all these conditions are fulfilled, is the higher range of cooperation attained.   Unless of the invested capital a sufficient portion belong to the associated workmen to entitle them to choose their managers, the associa-

tion falls within the category of industrial partnerships.
But wherever capitalist workmen work together under
chiefs of their own election, and divide amongst themselves,
and amongst any non-working shareholders, and any non-
capitalist workmen associated with them, the whole profits
of their undertaking, there is a genuine cooperative
society.*

Of such societies, France, which exhibited the earliest,
still exhibits the most satisfactory, specimens. At one time
there were upwards of a hundred in Paris alone, besides a
considerable number in the departments, and though several
have since failed—as of early attempts in any new field of
activity several invariably do—there are actually about
forty in Paris and about eighty in other towns, and of these,
many have decidedly, and some signally, succeeded. On
the causes of both failure and success some light may be
thrown by the following abridgment of an historical episode
given by M. Feugueray.

Cooperation is one of those things that seldom advance
steadily except by their own momentum. In 1848, however, the Constituent Assembly voted 3,000,000 of francs
for its artificial promotion, and M. Feugueray was named
member of a commission appointed to superintend the
distribution of the grant. In that capacity he had an
interview with two delegates from some hundreds of journeymen pianoforte-makers, who were thinking of forming
themselves into a grand manufacturing association, and
were applying to Government for a subvention of 300,000
francs, or one-tenth of the entire sum voted. For two
mortal hours, M. Feugueray says, he 'prolonged the discourse,' striving in vain to convince the deputies of the
exorbitance of their demand. Their imperturbability was
a match for his eloquence. All his arguments were met by
the reiterated reply that their trade was a peculiar one,
that 300,000 francs was the minimum capital on which
they could possibly commence, and that, in short, they

* See Feugueray, ' L'Association Ouvrière,' p. 2.

would not take one sou less. Fortunately for them, their
application was too unreasonable to be complied with, or
they would doubtless have broken down, just as all others
did that leant too hard on State aid. On its being refused,
the idea of so grand a pianoforte-making association fell
to the ground, but out of the hundreds who had been
parties to it, fourteen—including, by the way, one of the
two previously inflexible deputies—agreed to constitute a
smaller union. This was rather a rash project for men
without either cash or credit; 'but faith,' says Feugueray,
'does not reason: it acts.' Some of them—who had, it
seems, though one does not very well see how, been working
on their own account — came forward with 2,000 francs'
worth of tools and materials; and each of the fourteen contrived, by hook or by crook, to pay up a subscription of 10
francs towards the creation of a floating capital, to which
some trifling additions were made by a few workmen unconnected with the enterprise except by sympathy. Altogether a sum of 229 francs 50 centimes was collected, and
on March 10, 1849, the association was formally constituted.

   There were not, however, funds enough to cover even
those current expenses without which a workshop cannot
possibly be kept open; and as for wages, two months
elapsed before any one of the associates touched a sou.
How then, one naturally asks, did they exist during the
interval? 'In the way,' M. Feugueray replies, 'in which all
workmen live when out of work—that is to say, by sharing
the meals of comrades in work, and by selling piece after
piece the few things they possessed. Thus bravely persevering, they got in due course some saleable work finished,
and on May 4 the sale proceeds were divided amongst
them, at the rate of 6 francs 61 centimes each, out of which
it was arranged that 5 francs should be taken in cash, and
the balance devoted to a 'fraternal repast.' Accordingly
the fourteen associates, most of whom had not tasted wine
for a twelvemonth, sat down with their wives and children
to a table at which the meagreness of cheer, provided at

the rate of about 3*d.* per family, was so abundantly supplemented by the cheerfulness of the guests, that the little festival continued long afterwards to be spoken of in the workshop with contagious emotion.

'For another month wages remained at 5 francs weekly per head, but in the course of June a baker—whether speculative or music-mad does not appear—arranged for the purchase of a piano at 480 francs, on condition of the price being taken out in bread.   This provided the indispensable for seven weeks more, and thenceforward prospects went on gradually brightening.   In August weekly wages had risen to 10 francs; subsequently they advanced to 15 and 20 francs, which latter sum, moreover, represented much less than half of each man's real share of profit, every one having left in the concern a good deal more of his own than he had drawn out.   On the last day of 1850 the society, which less than ten months before had commenced with next to nothing, had accumulated a capital stock of 32,930 francs.'   At this point M. Feugueray's narrative stops; but Mr. Mill, on the authority of M. Cherbuliez, states that subsequently the association became divided into two, one of which in 1854 possessed a capital of 56,000 francs, or 2,240*l.*, and in 1863 had increased the amount to 6,520*l.* Since then, Mr. Fane tells us, the amount has become between 7,000*l.* and 8,000*l.* The little story is full of instruction, but the mode of procedure it describes is not to be held up for exact imitation.   As a rule, out of nothing not anything can be made, certainly not pianofortes; and any of Broadwood or Erard's men who, without more of the miscellaneous wherewithal than our adventurous fourteen were provided with, should undertake to manufacture the same complex musical instruments, would scarcely find unreasoning faith sufficient to carry them through the enterprise.

Some details regarding four or five others of the Parisian societies may be of use in illustrating remarks presently to be made on their general organisation.

One, the Association Remquet, is so called after its founder, foreman in a printing establishment which in 1848 became forced to wind up its affairs. Remquet thereupon proposed to his fellow-workmen that they should join with him for the purpose of carrying on the business on their own account. Fifteen consented, and, obtaining a loan of 80,000 francs from the State for needful preliminary purchases, formed themselves into a society, with Remquet at its head, and under regulations which fixed the rate of wage for every description of work, and provided for the gradual formation of a working capital by a deduction of one-fourth part of every man's wages. This capital was to pay no dividends or interest until the expiration of the ten years for which the society was intended to last, but at the end of that term was to be divided among all the associates in the ratio of their contributions—that is to say, in the exact proportion of the work each had done. When the ten years had expired, the net capital remaining after repayment of the Government loan, amounted to 155,000 francs, which, being divided, gave on an average between 10,000 and 11,000 francs to each member—7,000 francs to him who got least, and 18,000 francs to him who got most.

A 'Fraternal Society of Operative Whitesmiths and Lampmakers' had been founded in March 1848, by a body of 500 workmen, comprising very nearly all who were engaged in that branch of industry. It soon broke down, however, under a numerical weight so disproportionate to its infant strength, but was succeeded in the following year by a more modest assemblage of forty journeymen, who, without any borrowing, raised what capital was immediately needed by subscriptions amongst themselves. After undergoing many vicissitudes, which at one time reduced the number of members to three, anon raised it to fourteen, and again reduced it to three, this second society at length felt itself consolidated with a constituency of forty-six. It proceeded then to reform its statutes in those respects in which they had proved defective, and in 1858, by which time it had by successive recruiting increased the number of its members to a hundred, it possessed a capital of 50,000 francs, and made 20,000 francs of profit. In 1864 the capital had increased to 90,000 francs and the business done to 120,000.

The most ancient cooperative society in existence is that of the jewellers, formed in Paris in 1831 by eight workmen, with a capital of no more than 200 francs, arising from their scanty savings. A Government loan of 24,000 francs enabled them in 1849 considerably to extend their operations, and in 1858 they were doing business to the value of 140,000 francs, and making thereon a profit large enough to give to each member a dividend equal to twice his wages. According to the latest account, they have now a capital of 100,000 francs, and divide upon it nearly 20 per cent. yearly.

In June 1848 an operative association of cabinet-makers was begun in a small way by nine journeymen, possessed of 369 francs' worth of tools and 135 francs in cash. Their good taste, however, and their good faith in the execution of orders rapidly obtained for them a great deal of custom, and before long the original nine had multiplied to 109. They received from the State, at three and three-quarters per cent. interest, a subvention of 25,000 francs, repayable in fourteen years. In the third year of their existence their capital had grown from 504 to nearly 30,000 francs, and in 1855 it was 123,000 francs. In 1857 the concern was the most important of its kind in Paris, and was doing a business of more than 400,000 francs a year. The total number of associates and 'auxiliaries' had then become 165. Among them work is paid for according to a settled scale, which allows of from three to seven francs being earned daily, according to the zeal and ability of the workmen. The weekly average is 25 francs, but there are few who earn less than 20, while many get 40, and some of artistic pretensions 50 francs a week.

But of all the French societies the most considerable is

that of the Paris masons, begun in August 1848, by seventeen of them, with a joint-stock capital of 362 francs, or 14*l.* 10*s.* In 1858 it consisted of 85 members, and from 300 to 400 auxiliaries, its capital at the same time being apparently 180,000 francs, or 7,200*l.*, upon which the profits for the year were equal to fifty-six per cent. It had then just finished the construction of three or four of the finest mansions in the metropolis. In 1860 its capital was 14,500*l.*, that is to say had more than doubled in two years. In 1867 it got a contract for building, for about 80,000*l.*, the Paris Station of the Orleans Railway. In the preceding year every shareholder, according to an authority quoted by Mr. Axon, ('Notes on Cooperation Abroad' in 'Companion to the Almanack for 1870,') 'received in addition to his wages a bonus of 5*s.* 9*d.* for each day he had worked, and 28 per cent. on the capital he had invested.' Previously to their becoming associated, these masons, says M. Villiaumé, were poorly clad in vest and blouse, because they never had at their disposal the 60 francs needed for a frock coat, but now most of them are as well dressed as the bourgeois, and sometimes with better taste.

Regarding fourteen Parisian societies, including apparently two of those just noticed, a tabular statement, the result of careful personal investigation, was drawn up in 1863, and kindly placed in my hands by my lamented friend, the late Max Kyllmann of Manchester. The occupations pursued by them are those of jewellers, chairmakers, masons, tanners, turners, file-makers, last-makers, spectacle-makers, locksmiths, carriage-frame-makers, and house painters. At the end of 1862 the total number of members was 340, and the number of hired workmen employed by and working with them 618. In eight of the fourteen societies wages are paid by the piece, in the others by the day, according to capacity, the wages of individuals being represented as ranging from 48*l.* or 50*l.* to 60*l.* per annum. In all, in addition to wages, the workmen get a larger or smaller share of the profits. In some cases all the profits are divided amongst them in the ratio of their wages, and in others three-sevenths, or six or nine-tenths, are similarly distributed. Three societies divide equally among the workers without reference to wages ; one divides in proportion to capital and wages added together, and one, in which none but members are employed, on capital only. The aggregate amount of capital of all the fourteen is stated by Mr. Kyllmann at 36,122*l.*, with which the amount of business done in the last year recorded by him was 106,678*l.*, and on which the profit realised during the same period was 8,298*l.*, or very nearly twenty-three per cent.

At Lyons there are three great cooperative societies, of which the largest, the 'Société des Tisseurs,' comprises 1,800 members, and the 'Association des Rubaniers' counts 1,200 members, and possesses a capital of 1,200,000 francs or 48,000*l.*

My information respecting French cooperative societies is, I am sorry to say, derived entirely from reading and conversation ; but of those which have as yet sprung up in England, there are a few of which I am able to speak with more or less of personal knowledge. Foremost among them—foremost in infamy and fame—stands the Iscariot of the tribe—one that bade fair to be their glory, but has become their shame. The 'Rochdale Cooperative Manufacturing Society,' one of the colonies thrown off by the Equitable Pioneers, embarked in 1854 in the cotton trade, with funds too limited to allow of its hiring more than a single room, in which of course mechanical appliances could be only sparingly adopted. It started, however, as genuinely cooperative, announcing that of whatever net profits should be realized, after enough had been taken to pay interest at five per cent. on capital, the balance should be divided rateably between capital and labour, the portion assigned to labour being divided amongst all the labourers, in proportion to the wages they severally earned. Thereupon all the workpeople engaged, whether sharehold-

ing or not, set to work with the will natural to those who
were working for themselves ; and the interest they all took
in their common business, and the skill and care displayed
by them, produced in the very first year a substantial net
return. This attracted many new members, by whose
subscriptions the capital was raised to 5,000*l.* Part of an
old mill was then hired and stocked with looms, and by
the end of another year or two the accession of fresh
subscribers, and the accumulation of profits, were such as
to enable the society to purchase a site for a new cotton-
factory, and to place upon it, at a cost of 50,000*l.*, one
better built, better looking, and better arranged than any
other in the town, and fitted up with steam engines of 120-
horse power, and with other machinery of the very best
description. The cooperators were their own architects,
purchased all the materials, and contracted for the building
at so much a foot, paying ready money for everything.
Here, in 1861, 300 operatives of a noticeably superior
description, and almost all of them English — a rare
thing in the midst of a population containing so large an
Irish element—were doing an amount of business which,
notwithstanding the derangement of the cotton trade consequent on the American civil war, was yielding a profit of
between seven and eight per cent. on the capital employed.
There was thus every encouragement to the association to
persevere in the course on which it had entered. A grand
career was open to it. It was, as has been said, an offshoot
from the Equitable Pioneers, and many of the members no
doubt retained much of the original enthusiasm which
had made the parent society, at its outset, announce among
its ulterior projects the magnificent one of 'arranging
as soon as practicable the powers of production, distribution, education, and government; or, in other words, of
establishing a self-supporting home colony of united interests, or assisting other societies in establishing such
colonies.' In the ambitious direction thus indicated the
younger association had made some important steps.

Apparently it had only to proceed as it had begun, in order gradually to fulfil its honourable mission, when it was observed first to falter irresolutely, and then after some hesitation to turn back. Of the numerous members who had recently come in, a large proportion had been attracted solely by the prospect of large returns, and had entered without any higher view than that of their own personal gain, and with too much of the penny wisdom habitual to petty speculators to be able to appreciate the superior wisdom of a politic liberality. These after a while began to regard the extra payments made to the operatives, under the name of bonuses, as so much waste of money. They did not consider that the fund from which those payments were made might not have existed but for the extra efficiency to which industry had been stimulated by the prospect of obtaining them, and that the same fund, beside providing for the bonuses, provided also a surplus wherewith to swell the dividends on capital. It seemed to them, on the contrary, self-evident that the dividends would necessarily be augmented, if all profits were declared to belong exclusively to capital, and accordingly a resolution to that effect was moved at a general meeting, and though successfully resisted on two or three occasions by the more farseeing few, was eventually carried by a decisive majority. From that moment the society ceased to be cooperative in everything but a name, which it still retains in self-complacent unconsciousness of the reproach therein implied. The society still exists, and in truth may be said still to flourish, for at the beginning of this year * its capital had increased to 120,000*l.*, it had two well-built mills containing 50,000 spindles, and a new loom-shed furnished with 870 looms, and after having worked for three years at a loss, it was expecting to be able shortly again to declare a dividend. But in losing the one feature by which it was origi-

* It may be as well to remind the reader that all these statements are to be understood as having been written in December, 1868.

nally distinguished from other manufacturing associations of Lancashire operatives, it has lost also most of the interest which once belonged to it in connection with the subject of a work like the present. Let us reason no more concerning it therefore, but, having given it a look, pass on to industrial confederacies of smaller dimensions but sounder material.

In Bridge Street, Manchester, is a house rented and occupied conjointly by two little communities, one of six tailors, the other of nine hatters, distinct in their organisation, but residing side by side in brotherly harmony. When I first visited them, towards the end of 1863, I was informed, with regard to the tailors, that in the first half of that year, their capital being then 173*l.*, their sales had amounted to 495*l.*, the wages divided amongst them to 169*l.*, and their net profit to something less than 16*l.* These are not high figures, yet taken by themselves they might suggest too favourable a notion of the state of affairs, for the tailors had not work enough to keep them fully employed, and the most that could be said of them was that they had kept their heads well above water. Their average annual earnings were not much short of 50*l.* per head, but they had never received any dividend or other addition to bare wages, whatever profit they had made having apparently been applied to the augmentation of their capital. The hatters, though they likewise had reason to complain of want of custom, were doing better. Their capital, which, when they started in 1851 was only 38*l.*, was then more than 600*l.*, the difference having been made up entirely by appropriations from profits, which in one instance within the previous three years had been 67*l.*, and in another 39*l.* in six months. During the twelvemonth ending with June 1863, however, in consequence of poor's rates having doubled, and the price of raw materials having greatly advanced, their net profits had been only 20*l.*, but more than 300*l.* had been distributed as wages among the four members who alone were regularly engaged in the business, and the three or four extra hands occasionally employed.

All those employed, whether members or not, shared rateably in proportion to their wages, in any surplus profits remaining after payment of interest at five per cent. on capital.
On paying the twin establishments a second visit five years
later—about three months ago—I was disappointed to
learn how little progress had been made during the interval.
The hatters indeed had raised their capital from 600*l.* to
750*l.*, and there is work enough to keep five members and
one auxiliary regularly employed, but the tailors had been
rather unfortunate.   They had conformed to the custom
universal in their trade of giving credit, and little less than
300*l.* of what ought to be their available assets are now in
consequence represented by bad debts.   This for a while
threw them back a good deal, but they have latterly made
up most of the way they had lost.   What most keeps both
hatters and tailors back is want of custom, a circumstance
as it seems to me not particularly creditable to the large
number of persons at Manchester who pride themselves on
their connection with its 'cooperative' stores.

In Rochdale, a small society was formed last spring for
the purpose, as their prospectus states, of 'carrying on the
wire-drawing and card-manufacturing business on the
bonus on labour principle,' the cards manufactured by them
being those used in the carding rooms of textile factories.
In October last there were thirty members holding altogether 435 one-pound shares, on which 280*l.* had been paid
up, and a loan of 250*l.* more had been obtained from the
Pioneers at five per cent. per annum.   The society are
settled in premises held by them on lease, at a net annual
cost of 35*l.*, and there I lately found busily at work a
manager at 35*s.* a week, two other men at 30*s.* each, and a
boy at 5*s.*, the labour of all of whom is entitled to share
equally with capital in any profits that may remain after
deduction of interest at the rate of 7½ per cent. on capital.
The experiment is too new to warrant any confident prediction as to its result.   The cotton manufacture, too, to
which chiefly it has to look for encouragement, is itself in

too depressed a state to be just now a good customer for 'cards.' As far, however, as I could judge from a hasty glance at the accounts, the concern appeared to be doing a fair amount of business.

At Wolverhampton is to be seen another genuine specimen of productive cooperation—one whose existence may even now be trembling in the balance, but whose survival until now, in spite of the unscrupulous persecution to which it has been subjected, says a good deal for the strong vitality of the cooperative principle. Plate-lock-making is a branch of business almost confined to Wolverhampton, where four or five years ago it was entirely in the hands of four large and three small masters, employing altogether about 250 men, all of whom were somewhat loosely connected together in a trades' union very ill provided with funds. A score or two of the workmen were in receipt of good wages, as either 'forgers' or 'finishers,' but the bulk of them were either 'stockers' or 'filers,' and miserably paid. In 1864 the union applied for an advance of wages, which, according to my information, was prospectively promised by the masters, on condition that the actual rates should remain unaltered for a specified time; but when that time had elapsed, and the men who had agreed to the proposed terms, and had fulfilled their part of the engagement, called upon the masters to fulfil theirs, the latter refused on some pretext or other to redeem their pledge. Thereupon the union, after giving due notice to the masters of their intention, and being defied to do their utmost, formed an independent lock-making association, composed at first of only seven men, with a capital of 13*l.*, raised gradually by weekly subscriptions of 3*d.* a head. Before long, however, the number of members had increased to 100, and the capital more than proportionably; and the masters then discovering that the petty upstarts whom they had at first so much despised were becoming dangerous rivals, endeavoured to crush them by underselling them, and lowered their own prices, first by seven and a half, and afterwards by fifteen per cent. These moves, however, the associated workmen partially counteracted by reducing their own wages, subjecting themselves to extreme privations in consequence for the space of two years. Another measure, to which as I was informed the masters had recourse, was that of buying up the whole stock in the town of the particular sort of wood required for plate-locks, and of endeavouring to dissuade the iron merchants from supplying the cooperators with the requisite metal; and when this plan also failed, they next insisted on reducing the wages of those workmen who had till then remained with them, and thereby drove most of them too into the bosom of the association. The present position of affairs, as I understand it, is as follows. The larger masters—for the sympathies of the three smaller ones are with the association—have brought their own business to a stand-still, while the association have their warehouse full of articles which they have been manufacturing for 'stock,' and which they cannot dispose of because they are standing out for the prices of a year or two back, while the factors, whom they are hoping to have as customers, are holding back in hopes of being able to purchase at the reduced rates adopted by the masters. Thus the fate of cooperation in this instance, seems to depend on whether sellers or buyers will be able to hold out longest. If the former can continue to maintain themselves until the latter consent to pay remunerative prices, their desperate struggle will be crowned with complete success ; they will be able to pay off all their debts, and will have the greater part of the trade in their hands. Otherwise the masters who have been contending with them, will have the satisfaction of feeling that, while half-ruining themselves, they have completely ruined their opponents. In the meantime the association have appealed to the public for pecuniary aid on loan, and have placed their accounts in the hands of Professor Fawcett, to enable him to judge whether their financial condition is such as to offer adequate security to lenders. The

reader will observe that I do not profess to have heard
more than one side of the story ; but unless that side be
completely contradicted by the other, and if a cooperative
society can ever be a fitting subject for external support,
the persecuted Wolverhampton plate-lock makers would
appear to furnish a case in which such support may be
temporarily rendered with permanently beneficial effect.*

In London and its neighbourhood there are a few societies which must not be left quite unnoticed here.   That of
the ' Framemakers and Gilders ' has a capital of 2,667*l.*
held by twenty-three members, of whom six besides the
three managing directors are workmen employed in the
business.   The average number of men employed is forty-
two.   The business done in 1868 amounted to 5,415*l.*
The ' London Cooperative Cabinet Makers' Society ' consists of eighty-three members with a share capital of 263*l.*,
and a loan capital of 104*l.*   It employs nine men, all members, and in 1868 did business to the amount of 1,205*l.*
The ' Perseverance Boiler Makers' Society ' at Deptford,
consisting of nine members, ' undertakes boiler-making and
iron ship work in general.'   It had in December 1868 only
11*l.* of share and 20*l.* of loan capital, yet had done 545*l.* of
business during the year, against 192*l.* in the previous
year.

Of similar societies, ' productive ' as they are called on the
Continent, to distinguish them from societies of consumption

[* The account given in the text applies to the latter end of 1868.
The reader will be pleased to learn that these Wolverhampton cooperators have pretty well weathered the storm against which they were
then struggling.   According to intelligence with which I have just
(January 1870) been favoured by Mr. Kettle, ' they may now be con-
gratulated on having surmounted their preliminary difficulties.   Their
manager speaks most satisfactorily of their present state and prospects.
The master who was their most active and persistent opponent has
advertised his business for sale, and the second in command of the
opposition is understood to be heartily tired of the contest.   Prices are
not yet sufficiently remunerative, but the associated workmen look
forward with hope to the improvement of trade, which now seems to
have set in, to bring up prices to their normal level.']

or store societies, there seem to be in Germany between twenty and thirty, the most ambitious being that of the machine-makers at Chemnitz, who began with 400 members and a capital of 6,000*l.*, but whose property became subsequently heavily mortgaged; the most prosperous, that of the watchmakers of Freiburg, begun by fourteen journeymen with a capital of 400*l.*, upon which in the first year they divided 60 per cent.

Of all these associations, French, English, and German, it may be observed generally, that those of the first-named nationality might have effected more if they had attempted less, as might those of the two others likewise, if they also had not been in too great a hurry, although in a different way. One difference between them is the origin of their animating idea, which in the one case was cradled in the philosopher's study, in the other on the workman's bench, and whose idiosyncrasy in each case smacks strongly of its birthplace. The speculative philanthropists who in France first devised the theory of what is there termed 'operative association,' and have ever since been its chief expounders and propagandists, designed it from the beginning to be a means of elevating the entire labouring population, and have uniformly insisted on the necessity of arranging all its details with a view to that end. Let it, they say, before all things be understood that no operative association is created for the sole benefit of the original associates, whose primary duty on the contrary it is to take the earliest opportunity of bringing in fresh associates to partake, without money and without price, of the advantages which they will find to have been prepared for them. The firstfruits of all profits are to be devoted to the formation or augmentation of a 'social capital,' one and indivisible, of which the society are to be collectively owners, but which they must never, even though about to dissolve their union, distribute among themselves, and from which no individual, even when separating from the society, can be allowed to withdraw his share. The object of the social capital is to insure the perpetuity and the perpetual growth of the society, so that the latter may become a means whereby an ever-increasing number of those who must otherwise have remained bondsmen of capital may be raised to industrial independence, until at length such independence be made the lot of all labourers.* Doubtless a magnificent project, of which, moreover, it would be disparagement to say that the noble sentiments it involves are noble in spite of their fallacy. There is nothing false about them. They are perfectly true, and in suitable circumstances would be perfectly practicable. Their only defect is, that the key they are pitched in is of a mood too high for ordinary human nature. Men, in general, are not yet prepared to moil and toil, and then voluntarily to give up out of their hard earnings for the benefit of those who, being equally able, might fairly be left to moil and toil as they themselves have done, for the sake of a similar reward. Here and there may be found a few of public spirit sufficiently advanced to induce them to undertake such disinterested labour, and the number of French workmen who have shown themselves so endowed is large enough to prove that France is capable of doing other things for an idea besides going to war for it. Still the idea in this instance would have been much more efficacious if it had been less ambitious, and would have reached further if it had not aimed so high. The theories of French apostles of cooperation have seldom, if ever, been attempted to be carried out in practice without considerable alterations, yet the amount of deference paid to their more premature particulars may not improbably be one reason why French cooperative societies have hitherto been of such comparatively slow growth. It may have been noticed that all the fourteen societies together, whose statistics were tabulated by Mr. Kyllmann, were not in 1862 doing much more than two-thirds of the amount of business done in the same year by the Rochdale Pioneers alone.

* See Feugueray, pp. 3, 9, 12, and 13.

In England, cooperation has been started with less ambitious aims. In every instance the sole motive for its adoption has been the desire of its adopters to benefit themselves, without any more enlarged or elevated views. In aspirations so limited, if there be nothing undeserving of commendation, neither is there anything particularly admirable; yet it may be questioned whether, if the advantage of labourers generally, instead of that of only a small fraction of them, were the object proposed, the course followed by English common sense would not be better calculated to accomplish it than the one selected by French generosity. English cooperators make no parade of comprehensive sympathy; they profess no solicitude about their unassociated brethren, and do not offer to assist them in associating; yet, if they succeed in their own purposes, they will really have been affording the best possible kind of assistance, by setting an example of success, which it is as easy for their brethren to imitate as it was for themselves to set. At the same time, it must be owned that in their mode of procedure they might easily have set a better example. All the difficulties they have encountered, all the risks they have run, have been owing mainly to their having commenced action prematurely. They would not wait until they had scraped together adequate preparatory funds, and so they have been obliged to have recourse to credit, or to get otherwise into debt. These are the rocks on which the Manchester tailors and Wolverhampton plate-lock-makers have grounded, and the dangers of which it will require careful steering on the part of the Rochdale card manufacturers to avoid. A cooperative society can never make a prudent start unless it have previously possessed itself of resources of its own sufficient for its maintenance until it becomes firmly established.

Past errors of cooperative societies must not, however, be mistaken for omens of an evil future. Rather it is to be hoped they will serve as beacons to warn off from perilous paths. They could not properly be styled errors if there were a necessity for their being repeated. The real question is whether there is anything inherent in the nature of cooperative societies to necessitate their failure, or at least to incapacitate them for extensive or permanent success. One eminent thinker, who has given much attention to the subject, is strongly of opinion that there is. He does not deny that certain trades in which, as in those of house painters, shoemakers, and masons, little plant or capital is required, and in which what is of chief consequence is personal skill and care on the part of individual workmen, may be carried on perfectly well by associations consisting solely of workpeople. But success in such cases, he thinks, proves nothing, though it surely does prove that to all the trades in question, and to all the other very numerous trades to which the same conditions apply, industrial cooperation is perfectly well adapted. Though such trades may separately be each but 'a drop in the ocean of industry,' still taken altogether they compose amongst them no insignificant portion of its waters. It must, however, be admitted that what is done in them affords no proof that the same thing could be done in the more extensive developments of industry. It is to a great extent the fact, as Mr. Harrison contends, that the direction of large capital 'demands freedom from other pursuits, devoted attention, professional training, habits of business; that most complex forms of industry demand for their direction some kind of engineering talent, acquaintance with the markets, long familiarity with an involved mass of details, mechanical, monetary, administrative; that the head of a great production must have scientific knowledge, technical knowledge, practical knowledge, presence of mind, dash, courage, zeal, and the habit of command.' Clearly, too, these essentials will never be found diffused throughout a large association of mere workmen. But how then, it is asked, can such an association be competent to manage a large concern? How ridiculous would it not be for the hammermen at a forge to suppose themselves capable of carrying on Whitworth's engineering business, or building the 'Great Eastern.' Imagine the London and North Western Railway managed by its stokers and pokers, or the Peninsular and Oriental Company's affairs managed by the seamen of the several vessels. Is it not clear that all great industrial occupations would come to destruction without those special aptitudes which nothing but long experience can give, and even they can give only to a few ?*

To questions like these but one reply can be made. Let it be at once conceded that no plural number is ever fit to direct or manage anything. Every noun of multitude whatsoever—committee, council, board, parliament, congress—is by nature and constitution disqualified for performing in its collective capacity any executive duties of any kind. Its proper office is to consider what is to be done, and to appoint suitable persons to do it ; but if it attempt, as it almost always does, to interfere with the details of execution, the result of its intermeddling will infallibly be that which proverbially ensues whenever a plurality of cooks exercise their independent theories in the concoction of the same mess of broth. Great as is the hash which has been made by most English railway boards, it would no doubt have been greater still if the whole mass of shareholders had taken upon themselves the immediate conduct of affairs. And that which a numerous body is, by reason of its number, unfitted for doing, it will not be at all the better fitted for doing because it is made up of working men. There is no such magic in this latter name as enables those who bear it to dispense with more substantial qualifications. If number be fatal to good management, however intelligent and instructed be the individual members, it will not be less fatal because the members are drawn from a class comparatively unintelligent and uninstructed. If two masters would be enough, unless one of them acknowledged the other as a master spirit, to ruin

* Mr. F. Harrison on ' Industrial Cooperation,' in ' Fortnightly Review ' for January 1866.

any concern, there can be no question about the ruin that would ensue if all the workmen engaged in the concern divided the mastery amongst them.   And if the workmen would be collectively incompetent to undertake the management, *à fortiori* they would be incompetent to direct a manager.   Let all this be freely conceded, together with all its logical consequences.   Those consequences are of no great moment, amounting to no more than this, that cooperative, equally with all other societies, are incompetent immediately to govern themselves.   But it does not follow that they are not, equally with any other society, competent to provide for their own government.   It does not follow that, because they cannot directly manage their own affairs, they cannot procure or devise proper machinery of management. There is, on the contrary, abundant certainty that they can. Besides the Rochdale specimen already spoken of, there are and have for years been in different parts of Lancashire, at least a dozen large cotton mills owned entirely by associated working men, and managed quite as well and successfully as any private establishments of the kind. One association, the Sun Mill Company at Oldham, was at the end of the cotton famine 15,000*l.* in debt, but latterly, by improved management, it has been brought into a state in which, even in this time of depression, it is able to pay its shareholders twenty per cent. on their capital. Now this company and others like it differ in nothing from cooperative societies except in their not having adopted the cooperative principle of paying labour in proportion to profits.   They consist equally of working men,* destitute for the

* .The Sun Mill Company has now a share capital of 50,000*l.*, and a loan capital of 42,650*l.*, both owned almost exclusively by working men.   It is governed by six directors, all of whom except the president are working men in receipt of weekly wages, as the president himself likewise was for thirty years.   The company's yarn is now so well known that it is no longer necessary to send samples of it to Manchester or other markets—buyers relying on the reputation of the company—and the managers boast that they produce a larger quantity than any other mill in the world employing only the same number of spindles.

most part of all those aptitudes, natural or acquired, which are presumed to be indispensable for directorial functions. Whatever be the disabilities of cooperative societies in these respects are theirs equally, yet in spite of them they contrive to provide very efficiently for their own government, and in spite of the same disabilities cooperative societies could no doubt provide similarly. That the thing is to be done is proved by experience, nor is there any difficulty in understanding how it may be done. The 'commercial genius and the instincts of a skilful trader' are not, we are told, to be hired, any more than 'the inspiring authority and the electric will of a great military or political chief.' But the inspiring and electric qualities aforesaid are to be hired. Some of the greatest captains that ever lived were soldiers of fortune, and one seldom walks up Parliament Street on a summer's afternoon, without meeting considerable choice of statesmen by profession, quite ready to become the instruments of any premier who will give them office. Similarly in the industrial world the special kind of administrative ability there required is a regularly marketable commodity, with which industrial associations, finding that they cannot get on without it, provide themselves by paying its price. Every '*association ouvrière*' in France, every cooperative society in England, appoints a *gérant* or manager, who with regard to all current business is invested with much the same discretionary authority as the admiral of a fleet or the general of an army. Just as one of these, after receiving his instructions from the sovereign or minister, uses his own judgment as to the mode of carrying on the enterprise entrusted to him, so does a *gérant* or manager with respect to the operations on which the ruling council of his society have resolved. With reference to those operations, and also in any sudden emergency, his powers during his tenure of office are, if he have nerve enough for his position, sufficiently near, for all practical purposes, to those of an independent employer. If he be fit for his post, he will watch with all the latter's care the state and prospects of the markets, with a view to the timely contraction or extension of business, and will on all occasions act on his own responsibility with not less of promptitude and decision. With an arrangement which allows him so much discretion, a disciple of Comte ought to be the last to find fault. It ill becomes a Comtist at any rate to object that a cooperative constituency which trusted so much to their manager would place themselves completely in his hands, and completely relinquish the independence attaching to them as owners of the capital invested in their business. In fact, though the manager were not acting immediately under direction, he would be always subject to control ; he would hold office only during good behaviour or during pleasure, and, like an admiral or a general, would be sure to be displaced if he failed to give satisfaction. How can it be said that under this plan the shareholders 'lose all responsibility and all practical power to control the management'? To that blending of republicanism with despotism which seems to be a favourite idea with some leading positivists, what closer approximation could reasonably be expected from raw beginners ?

Another difficulty which has been imagined to lie in the way of cooperation seems to me to be purely imaginary. It being indispensable to cooperation that labour should share with capital in profits, how, it is asked, shall the share to which it is entitled be determined ? A very short answer to this question may suffice to disentangle its perplexities. If, as we ascertained a long way back, labour be not entitled even to any wages, except what capital has agreed to give, *à fortiori*, it cannot, except by similar agreement, be entitled to any share of profits. If capital have not agreed to give any profits, labour cannot be entitled to any. Whatever, therefore, be the share of profits which capital has agreed to give, that share, however small it be, and neither more nor less, is labour's due share, though it behoves capital for its own sake to take care that the share is not too small to have the desired effect of stimulating labour to extra exertion. But though capital may thus decide in the matter arbitrarily, and cannot possibly decide otherwise than equitably, still if some principle upon which to decide be sought for, there need be no difficulty in finding three or four to select from. If, for instance, it be proposed to remunerate labour and capital in proportion to the relative values of the quantities of each engaged in joint production, those values may be easily determined. As things which are equal to the same thing are equal to each other, the quantity of labour represented by 100*l*. of wages, must be pecuniarily equal to 100*l*. of capital, and if the whole joint produce of labour and capital were divided between them in accordance with this pecuniary valuation, there would be an intelligible reason for so dividing them. Or if capital should propose to deduct from profits for its own behoof five per cent., or whatever else might be the current rate of interest, on its own amount, before dividing the residuum with labour, for that also an intelligible reason might be assigned. For the current rate of interest, whatever it be, may always be obtained by the capitalist on good security, and without his having anything himself to do with the employment of labour. Very plausibly, therefore, he might decline to share with labour more than that surplus over and above current interest, which alone the labour employed by him had, in combination with capital belonging to him, contributed to produce. Yet with equal plausibility, where both the capital and labour were supplied by the same individuals, might it be urged in behalf of labour, that capital would be sufficiently remunerated if it received as much as it could be hired for, and that therefore the whole of any profit made in excess of current interest on capital should be taken by labour. And yet, again, capitalist employers might, without any semblance of injustice, begin by deducting the current rate not simply of interest but of profit, arguing that the rate in question was obtainable by employers who gave nothing but stipulated wages, and that it was therefore only the surplus beyond that rate that was entitled to be treated as the result of labour's extraordinary exertions. Here are principles in plenty, if principles be desired. Whichever of them in any given circumstances answers its purpose best, or gives most satisfaction to all concerned, is the best ; but in respect to justice all are upon a par, for all equally respect every right with which they come in contact.

Another difficulty that has been imagined is of an opposite kind. It has been suggested that if labourers be permitted to participate in profits, they may in fairness be required to take their shares likewise in any losses that may be incurred, and we are invited to reflect on the straits to which workpeople, engaged in a business that for years together might be worked at a dead loss, would be reduced. Here again, as it seems to me, a mere phantasm is quite needlessly evoked. How little pretext there can ever be for requiring cooperative labourers to assist in making good out of their wages the losses of their employers will be readily seen on reference once again to the reason why they are permitted to share in profits. In forming industrial partnerships, the employer's motive always is his expectation that labourers will be thereby stimulated to such extra exertion as will add at least as much to profits as the share assigned to them will take away. If this expectation be more than realised, the employer has made a good bargain : the additional sum paid by him to his men is earned beforehand by the additional productiveness of their labour. If the expectation be not realised, the worst that can be said is, that he has made a bad bargain, but in no conceivable case can he be warranted in claiming the suggested amends. How can the fact of labourers having on one occasion received extraordinary pay for extraordinary exertion disentitle them on another to ordinary pay for ordinary exertion ? Or how can the fact of their not having been stimulated, as was expected, by the promise of bonus in addition to customary wages, disentitle them

subsequently to customary wages ?   These remarks apply
just as much to labourers in the employment of a multitudinous cooperative society, as to those engaged in industrial
partnership with an individual employer or private firm,
in so far, that is, as they are mere labourers.   If they be
capitalists in addition, then of course the case is materially
altered.   Then whatever losses their business may sustain
they are bound in their quality of capitalists to make good
out of their subsequent earnings, of whatever description—
out of wages, if need be, and if profits will not suffice.

Perhaps it may be thought with respect to labour's proper
share of profit, that the difficulty of determining its amount
is not the only difficulty in connection with that particular
point, and that, even when the labourers were content with
the aggregate sum, they might disagree about its mode of
partition among themselves.   Apparently the fairest plan
would be the usual one of dividing in the ratio of wages ;
but might not this tend to aggravate the discontent natural
to those in receipt of the lower rates of wages ?   Hired
servants of a master with whose supremacy within his own
domain trades' unionism has not interfered, must accept
without murmuring the tasks he assigns to them, for they
are not in a position to dispute his right to judge for himself
how the employment afforded by him shall be distributed.
But members of an association which all have joined on
equal terms may not be so submissive to the decrees of
one of their peers, and may be disposed to accuse the
manager of favouritism, and to take themselves off in
disgust, if a worse paid description of work be allotted to
them than to others whom they consider no abler than
themselves.   Possibly there may always be some little risk
of this kind, but there are two reasons why there is never
likely to be much.   For, firstly, as the manager's income,
like that of every other member, depends upon the productiveness of the labour under his direction, he is interested in assigning to every man the kind of work for
which that man is best fitted ; and, secondly, the members

collectively are interested in seeing that he does so. In general, he will honestly try to put the right men in the right places, and if, by mistake or otherwise, he fail in this part of his duty, the parties aggrieved will certainly not fail to appeal to their fellows, who, being well acquainted with each other's characters and abilities, will be able to decide at once whether anyone has been unjustly treated, and, if so, will for their own sakes, as well as his, insist on his having redress. If, on the other hand, a complainant cannot persuade his comrades to accept his estimate of himself, he will have cause to suspect that he has overrated his value, and to acquiesce in a sentence confirmed by the general voice. In practice little, if any, of the apprehended inconvenience is found to arise. 'It is very remarkable,' says Feugueray, speaking of the French *associations ouvrières*, 'that their rules, though more severe and more exacting than those of ordinary workshops, are much more strictly attended to. Good-will and mutual emulation are found to answer better for the repression of idleness and disorder than the fear of a master with unlimited powers of scolding and dismissing. So true is it that one obeys no laws so well as those which one has oneself had a hand in enacting, and that when people are in earnest they will submit to any regulation, however irksome, whose utility they recognise.'*

But even though all the difficulties besetting cooperative societies in their earlier stages were surmounted, there is another ground on which it may and has been questioned whether they could have any permanent existence. It is not unreasonably apprehended that the shares would naturally aggregate into a few hands. To declare them inalienable, as in France, would be to confine them to highminded philanthropists, to that 'small tally of the singular few' whose chief motive for taking them would be love of the brethren. To require that all shareholders should likewise be employés of the society, and to insist that anyone withdraw-

* 'L'Association Ouvrière,' pp. 7, 8.

ing from the society's employment should sell out, would
most probably deter anyone from investing on terms so
likely to result in his having to sell out at a loss.   To limit
the number of shares capable of being held by single individuals would limit proportionably the utility of the societies as fields of investment.   But unless recourse were had
to the first or the third of these expedients, and if the shares
rose in value, there would be nothing to prevent their being
bought up by capitalists as promising speculations—nothing,
at least, except the natural unwillingness of the original
holders to part with such profitable investments—and of
those holders some might be improvident or unfortunate,
and all would certainly die off in time.   In a variety of ways,
shares would be sure to change hands, and a large proportion
might easily become accumulated in the hands of a few, and
at any rate individual shareholders, if prudent and economical, would acquire what to them would be wealth.   If trade
continued good and profits high, many a man who had
begun with 5*l.* or 10*l.* might before long find himself in possession of 500*l.* or 1,000*l.*, when it is taken for granted that
he would not consent to abide at the loom or spindle, but
that, separating himself from the ranks of the employed, he
would set himself up as an independent employer.   It is not
at all clear, however, why he should do anything of the kind.
His original atom of capital had multiplied in the manner
supposed because it had been invested coöperatively, and,
if left so invested, it might go on so multiplying indefinitely.
Why, then, should it be withdrawn ?   Its owner could scarcely
expect that his few hundreds of pounds would do nearly so
well as the entire capital of a small concern, as they were
actually doing as part of the capital of a large one, and
having shown so much good sense previously, he would
scarcely now show so little as to make the change merely
for the pleasure of taking rank as a master.   As long as
wages continued to be an object to him, it would clearly be
wiser for him to continue to earn them as a simple operative, receiving in addition continually increasing profits on

his continually accumulating capital, than to pay himself wages out of his own pocket, and out of his own diminished profits.   But even if he did resolve to set up as a master, and even though all of his companions similarly circumstanced did the same, and though the whole share capital got in consequence into the hands of men having no connection with the concern except as holding shares, still that would be no reason why the society should cease to be cooperative.   For, as can scarcely be too often repeated, the one thing and the only thing indispensable to cooperation is the participation of labour in profits.   This is the one essential principle, in the absence of which there can never be cooperation, and the presence of which always constitutes cooperation ; and although, on the one hand, the principle cannot be expected to be adopted except in so far as it is believed in, yet, on the other, wherever it is believed in and has been adopted, and has by its results justified the faith reposed in it, there it will surely be persevered in.   Speculators who had bought up the shares of a cooperative society because the society had shown itself commercially successful, and who perceived that its success was due to its adoption of cooperation, would for their own sakes, and in pursuance of their own speculative views, retain cooperation.   If they did so, there would, notwithstanding the total change in the individual constituents, be no essential change in the cooperative character of the constituency, which would remain for all practical purposes as truly cooperative after every one of its members had ceased to be a working man, as it had been when it was composed exclusively of working men.

From this examination of the various theoretical objections urged against cooperative societies, there would appear to be nothing in their nature or circumstances to prevent the higher form of cooperation which they exemplify from succeeding perfectly, while there are facts enough bearing on the subject to show conclusively that it may. And since it may succeed, it most assuredly will.   The

working classes who have devised it as an engine for their
own regeneration may be safely trusted to discover eventually proper modes of utilising it, though, probably enough,
not until after many abortive trials.   The brilliant future
which cooperative societies have before them may, probably
enough, be one of very gradual development.   Many of
those whose acquaintance with cooperation, and whose zeal
for its propagation are greatest, often betray but imperfect
perception of its true principle ; and when the teachers
and missionaries are at fault, where shall the pupils and
proselytes be ?   Many obstacles beset their path, many
disappointments and failures are doubtless in store to
dishearten them and for sceptical observers to exult in.
Cooperation of the higher kind cannot advance except in
proportion as the true cooperative spirit becomes diffused
amongst those cooperatively disposed.   What Mackin-
tosh said of political constitutions, is equally true of cooperative societies.   They cannot be made, they must
grow, and to grow vigorously they must be left to grow
naturally.   To attempt to force or bolster them up, as was
done by the state in France during the shortlived rule of
democracy after 1848, would be far more likely to stifle
them in the birth.   Under the sunshine of patrician patronage, they may possibly shoot up into gourdlike luxu-
riance ; but if so, they are pretty sure to wither as soon as
the artificial fostering is withdrawn, if not sooner.   Both
the legislature and private well-wishers had much better
stand aloof, the former after removing any anti-cooperative
obstructions which bad legislation may have created, the
latter not presuming at the most to do more than offer a
few hints as to precautions to be taken and dangers to be
avoided.   The best, and, indeed, only suitable auxiliaries
of cooperative societies are the store societies which in
England preceded them, and imitations of which are
rapidly spreading over France and Germany.   These,
which, in modes already once or twice referred to, have
been rendering valuable preparatory service to real ' coope-

rative societies, are now in many cases in a position to furnish them with well trained and well equipped recruits, and may besides indirectly render not less useful service by means of the edifying and encouraging example which their history sets.   It is chiefly because store societies have always been left to get on as they could, that they have always got on so well.   It is because there was no aid from without for them to look to, that they have looked so well after their own affairs, taking good heed to their path, picking their steps carefully, and specially shunning the treacherous quicksands of credit.   And as it was thus that the self-control and force of character were developed within them, without which it would have been impossible for them to raise or to maintain themselves, so while they have been moved forward collectively by their own sole endeavours, they have at the same time been educating their individual associates for greater achievements of self-elevation.   In now furnishing from their own ranks fully qualified volunteers for cooperative societies, they will be simply pursuing the course with which they began, and fulfilling further purposes of their self-appointed mission. But as the only safe dependence for pure working class cooperation is in self-help and mutual help, so can there be little chance for its permanence, if it be taken up by others than those previously prepared by character and habit to help themselves and each other.   It is not enough to get together a heterogeneous levy of labouring men and women, and to persuade them to combine their savings and their industry in some joint business as a promising specula-tion.   If commercial gain be the chief motive for combin-ing, the moral requisites of success are almost certain to be deficient.

For a mere joint-stock company the prime necessity is sufficient funds, but much of the capital of which a coope-rative society stands in need must be of more precious material.   The individual associates undertake one of the most difficult of tasks — that of collective self-discipline.

They undertake to maintain order among independent equals, which can be done only by these same equals rendering to chiefs of their own appointment—who were yesterday the companions of all and may to-morrow be the subordinates of some—the same unhesitating and unmurmuring obedience as would be exacted by a master invested with absolute authority. They must be their own taskmasters and overseers, setting themselves of their own accord whatever portions of work the interests of the commonweal would assign to them, and executing those portions with as much strictness as they would themselves require from workmen whom they were set to superintend. But for this it is necessary that they should possess an active devotedness, a sense of duty and of honour, a fervour of public spirit, not more rarely met with perhaps among working than among other men, but of rare occurrence among men of any class. Nor is this the whole. That capacity for industrial administration, which Mr. Harrison assumes to be necessarily absent from mere working men, I do not myself conceive to be at all frequent amongst them. I go no farther than to affirm that its germs are there as elsewhere, and that as its want becomes felt the germs will be gradually developed, as in numerous instances they have actually been already. I have little doubt that if the men employed in an extensive colliery were, with only their present education, to attempt the conduct of the concern, through the medium of directors or managers chosen from amongst themselves, 'the whole thing would,' as Mr. Henry Currer Briggs says, 'break down in a month;' but I have as little doubt that, as the same gentleman adds, the same men 'are quite capable of being educated up to the requisite mark.' As long, however, as so many things essential to the success of cooperative societies remain exceptional, successful cooperative societies must needs be exceptional likewise. Nay, it is desirable that such societies should at first be both few and small, for on no other condition can they be so constituted

as subsequently to increase and multiply.   Common honesty
is but one of the things without which continuous cooperation is impossible, and when the poet exclaims, 'common
honesty!' and bids us 'say in what time hath honesty
been common,' we are constrained to reply that the time
has not come yet.   It is coming though, if cooperation is.
The latter must for its own sake help it on.   The rule respecting the adaptation of supply to demand holds good in
morals as in economics, to this extent at least, that when
an object which large bodies of men have greatly at heart
cannot be accomplished without the presence of certain
virtues, those virtues will generally be forthcoming.   Even
among thieves there is honour, because unless thieves were
true to each other, there could be little successful thieving.
Surely, then, as the desire for cooperation spreads among
working people, the qualities necessary for its manifestation
will spread too.   The very desire for them will suffice to
create most of them.   Integrity, zeal, loyalty, administrative capacity, will all exhibit themselves in full measure
in time.   The process, however, must necessarily be slow.
For a while it were to be wished that none but the *élite*
of working men should attempt cooperation, associating
themselves in the first instance only with men whom by
sufficient previous intercourse they had learnt to know, and
whom by knowing they had learnt to trust, and admitting
none afterwards, except on probation, whose previous reputation was not itself a strong guarantee of fitness.   Better,
as M. Feugueray says, 'advance slowly for the sake of advancing surely : better recruit slowly than recruit badly:
better wait till the fruit ripen naturally than run the risk of
spoiling it by forcing :' better, as I may add by way of
illustration, begin with half a dozen well-assorted operatives
in a weaving shed than with an indiscriminate half-thousand
in a factory.

Beginning, then, on a small scale, as in prudence they
ought to do, cooperative societies must needs take time to
grow ; yet with moderate care and judgment to what

gigantic stature may they not attain at last? On this point, those who have any faith in the system are warranted in having unbounded faith. M. Feugueray speaks of co-operative societies as destined to go on extending and enrolling in their ranks an ever-increasing number, until the day, 'too remote but certain,' when in the world of industry there shall be none but cooperators; and I am not at all ashamed to own that I share largely in M. Feugueray's anticipations. Regarding the subject as soberly as I can, it seems to me impossible that the day should not arrive when almost all productive industry, and most of all other industry, will be in one sense or other cooperative, when the bulk of the employed will be their own employers, and when, of the portion who have other employers, most will be participators in those employers' profits. The reader, perhaps, laughs derisively. So did the doffers in Toad Lane laugh, when the first detachment of Pioneers broke ground there. So might all the shopkeepers in Rochdale have mocked anyone who had then ventured to predict that, within a quarter of a century, the petty store just opened would be metamorphosed into an establishment carrying on by far the largest retail business in the town. They would laugh less confidently now, however, even if they heard some one prophesying that, before the century is over, there will be no retail business carried on in Rochdale, except by the Pioneers, and that in another century or so, most towns in England will have followed the example of Rochdale in substituting for private shops 'cooperative stores.' Yet private enterprise has a better chance of holding its own against associations of operatives in retail trade than against genuine cooperation in productive industry. There may be no sufficient reason why, after the small fry of shopkeepers have been altogether superseded, retail houses, on the scale of Ridgway's or Shoolbred's, should not continue to flourish, however large the associative stores which have risen by their side. But in the fact that all persons working for cooperative societies have special motives for doing the most instead of the least work possible, there is sufficient reason for believing that those societies, when more matured, will possess, over all competitors that are not wise enough betimes to adopt the cooperative principle, an immense advantage, which will enable them to go on extending until they occupy the greater part of the field of industry. Something like the following may be imagined as the fashion in which their eventual predominance will be established.

Irrespectively of the many other classifications of which industrial occupations are susceptible, they may be arranged in three divisions, according to the proportion which the cost of the labour engaged in them bears to the whole current expenditure. First may be placed those businesses in which the proportion is very large, and which have already been proved by experiment to be well adapted for industrial partnerships; but wherever these latter are suitable, cooperative societies proper are equally suitable. Such businesses therefore may be expected to be wholly divided between industrial partnerships and cooperative societies. Secondly, there are occupations in which the proportion in question may be too small to appear to allow of very much being saved or produced by extra pains on the part of the employed; and in these the inducement either to individual employers to form industrial partnerships, or to associated capitalist workmen to allow conditional bonuses on wages to non-shareholding workmen in their employment, may not be sufficiently apparent to have much immediate effect. In many of such occupations, however, the quantity of labour needed absolutely as well as relatively is comparatively small, not more than, if the capital were subdivided among several shareholders, the latter might themselves contribute. Such shareholders, associating themselves for the purpose of carrying on business without other manual agency than their own, and agreeing to divide the entire net profits among themselves, partly as wages and partly as dividends, would constitute a society purely cooperative, and containing within itself, moreover, elements of success which no uncooperative establishment would possess. Societies constituted on this plan might therefore get into their hands many of the occupations of the second order. So constituted, it may indeed perhaps be thought that they could not be lasting, because whenever a shareholder died, or for other reason ceased to assist in the business with his labour, it would be necessary that his capital should be either withdrawn or transferred to some one prepared to take his place as a labourer. In general, however, the capital of a seceding shareholder would be voluntarily so transferred. According to the hypothesis, the success of the undertaking would be evidently contingent on all its shareholders being engaged in it as workmen. When a shareholder, therefore, either withdrew or died, he himself in the one case, or his heir in the other, would perceive that for him to remain as a sleeping partner in the concern would be to cause it to be conducted on unsound principles on which it could not prosper, and he would consequently look out for a purchaser willing to enter the business as a workman. Nor would there be any lack of suitable purchasers when the great majority of the labouring class, being cooperatively employed and correspondingly remunerated, were in positions to accumulate money for investment. Thirdly, there are a few occupations in which the expenditure on labour is comparatively very small indeed, and very greatly exceeded by the value of the materials to which the labour is applied ; and in these the amount of capital required might be much too great to be provided by the few labourers whom the same capital would furnish with full employment. Possibly such exceptional employments may always, or as long as the race of large capitalists subsists, be monopolised by large capitalists remunerating their labourers with wages only. Such exceptional employments are not, however, numerous ; neither, in the circumstances supposed, would superior workmen be likely to enter them unless attracted by extraordinarily high wages, together perhaps with the privilege in addition of investing in the business any savings they might make; while, in all other employments, cooperation in one form or other seems destined to become hereafter the rule. In all other employments labourers will apparently either become their own employers, or when not owners of the capital that employs them, will be admitted by its owners to participation in its fruits. To this state we seem to be surely though slowly tending. It will be reached only by gradual steps, but arrival at it finally is to all appearance certain, and may perhaps be earlier than the most sanguine expectants venture as yet to hope. The world has sensibly quickened its rate of movement since Galileo first discovered it to be moving.

There remains now little but to note some of the particulars implied in the consummation thus treated as inevitable, provided only that the world last for a sufficient number of centuries to allow of its being brought about. In the first place, there will be an end of epidemic poverty. When labour has undergone the anticipated reorganisation; when all, whose livelihood depends on their obtaining adequate employment, are assured of employment sufficient for their maintenance—though those who come after us may still have poor amongst them, though the poor, even then, may not have ceased out of the land—what poverty may remain will be only a sporadic malady. For, be it observed parenthetically, there will be an end at the same time to the over population, which is the most prolific cause of epidemic poverty—and is indeed almost another name for it. When people in general are well-to-do, there will be small risk of excessive multiplication of the species. There will be at least as much danger of the world becoming depopulated through excess of Malthusian prudence.

Further, as M. Feugueray says, 'what elevation, what dignity, what independence will not the labourer acquire under the new *régime!* No longer a servant depending on a master; an inferior, subject in the execution of his tasks to the harassing superintendence of a superior extraneously imposed ; the son of a slave still bearing the relics of his father's chains and ever hesitating betwixt cringing and revolt ; he will become a freeman, subject to no laws but those which, having contributed to frame them, he cordially accepts, working with none but equals, owing obedience only within the prescribed limits of his service, and only to elected functionaries whom a majority of the community have invested with temporary authority. What changes in character, in ideas, in habits, will not then be witnessed, what development of intellectual activity and functional aptitude, what disclosure of hidden talent, what penetration of the operative mind with sentiments of loyalty and forethought! Then will the taste for intellectual pleasure become diffused, then will manners be softened and polished, then will finally disappear the worn-out prejudices of barbarism. Man appreciating his own dignity will acquire more respect for that of others, and from the intercourse of life all those odious distinctions of class will be effaced, which, even where proscribed by the letter of the law, and even in the midst of democracy, have always hitherto been retained in practice.'* Then, as the same results are summed up by Mr. Mill, will have taken place 'a change in society, which will combine the freedom and independence of the individual with the moral, intellectual, and economical advantages of aggregate production ; which without violence or spoliation, or even any sudden disturbance of existing habits and expectations, will realise, in the industrial department at least, the best aspirations of the democratic spirit;' and which is, in short, the 'most beneficial ordering of industrial affairs for the universal good which it is at present possible to foresee.'

From the blessings of the social transformation thus spoken of, the principal drawback is the difficulty of looking forward to anything of a similar sort beyond, for to

---

* Feugueray, pp. 71, 72.

human perversity to have nothing to desire is almost as incompatible with perfect satisfaction and content as not to have what one does desire.   What cannot be distinctly foreseen, however, may sometimes be not obscurely fancied, and among the readers who have accompanied me thus far there may perhaps be a few not so disdainful of imaginative pictures as to refuse to glance at the one drawn in the next chapter.

CHAPTER IV.

LABOUR'S UTOPIA.

I STOOD in spirit upon Pisgah's brow,
    And ranged, with ravished eye, the Promised Land,
    The good land and the large that lay below,
Basking in genial sunniness, and fanned
    By vernal Zephyr's odoriferous wing,
    From floral censer wafting incense bland,
And with the mingled music echoing,
    Of purling brook, and warbling bird, and glee
    Of pastoral pipe the dance companioning
Of youths and maidens under greenwood tree,
    And measured sound, withal, of axe and flail
    And stricken anvil ringing merrily.
For not — as poets of Arcadian vale
    Have feigned—had idlesse here unruffled sway,
    Bidding who would, on joy unearned regale,
Nestle to sleep, and rise again to play,
    Knowing no interchange but sport and rest,
    While Life flew by like summer holiday.
Here, pleasure won from toil more poignant zest.
    With cheerful zeal all emulously strove.
    Each, daily, to allotted task addressed,
Through yielding loam the easy furrow drove,
    Or tilled the terraced side of vine-clad hill,
    Or delved for ore, or quarried marble clove,
Or plied the craftsman's or mechanic's skill
    With awl or needle, or at bench or loom,
    Or forge or furnace, or in textile mill,

Or with gay tint bade pictured fancies bloom,
　Or sculptured life on animated stone
　Bestowed,—or, pacing slow through forest gloom,
Pondered or mused in meditation lone,
　Wooing coy Truth, and what her glance revealed,
　Clothing in speech or song of varying tone.
And grateful Earth, the while, rejoiced to yield
　Her increase, and with milk and honey flowed,
　And with her corn and wine the garners filled.
And many a garden-girdled city showed
　Her pillared piles and streets of palaces,
　Wherein, in social fellowship, abode
Brethren, unjostled by the envious press
　Of competition's rivalry, for all
　Shared equally, none coveting excess.
Each in such office laboured as might fall
　To him most fitly,—such as several taste
　Or special talent made congenial :
Laboured assiduous—howsoe'er were traced
　His duty's limit,—and his gathering brought
　And at the Commonweal's disposal placed :
Nor larger meed for larger service sought :
　Who gathered much had nothing over, nor
　To him who gathered little lacked there aught.
Weakly or strong, with equal effort bore
　Each one his due proportion, nor did they
　Who added largelier to the general store
More merit therefore claim, nor aught betray
　Save gratitude for ampler strength bestowed,
　Wherewith in ampler measure to purvey.

Sufficed it to the richliest endowed
　Their gifts to exercise, more liberal
　Subservience rendering to the mutual load.
Nor was the burthen grievous, which to all
　Was meted fairly—from which none refrained.
　All laboured—wherefore none was labour's thrall.

None were there who, with galling fetter chained,
　　Cowered beneath the driver's lash, and spent
　　With noontide fervour, newly goaded, strained.
None were there, who in crowded garret pent,
　　Where fevered breath clung round them like a shroud,
　　With spinning brain o'er midnight travail bent.
None, who with sullen resignation bowed
　　Beneath the yoke of hopeless helotry ;
　　Pariahs, by their own kindred disavowed,
Incessant moiled, as though alone might be
　　The Many's calling for a haughty Few
　　To drudge, and pander to their luxury.
Albeit many were content to hew
　　Wood and draw water,—for that menial care
　　Claimed not entire existence as its due.
E'en might the lowliest means of life prepare,
　　Nor for life's sake the cause of living lose,*
　　Nor from life's holier purposes forbear.
Leisure was theirs, with privilege to use
　　For inward culture, and to think and feel,
　　And nature's book and their own heart peruse :
And leisure, too, for pastime versatile,
　　To join the jocund throng, on village green,
　　In course or game athlete, or giddy reel :
Or, if more pleased the quiet joy serene
　　Of contemplated beauty,—then to stray
　　'Mid bright parterres of variegated shene,
Where rainbow hues the panelled earth inlay,
　　And list some hidden choir's concerted strain
　　In mood obedient to the music's sway :
Or, freely visitant in Art's domain,
　　To wander, curious, through Palladian halls,
　　Or Grecian gallery, or Gothic fane,
Scanning the carved reliefs and capitals,
　　And breathing miracles of Phidian mould,
　　And glowing fulgence of the pictured walls :

* Et propter vitam, vivendi perdere causas.

While, as they gazed, within them would unfold
   Germs undeveloped of a finer sense,
   Loosed from the cumbrous clay's relaxing hold,
And quickened by the nurturing influence
   Of just proportion, grace and dignity,—
   Perceptions of a new intelligence.
So potent is the tranquil energy
   Of Art to stimulate the fallow mind:
   So eloquent its silent poetry.
Wherefore, to no exclusive grade confined,
   Its softening and ennobling sentiment
   All ranks and every order disciplined,
The clownish gait remodelled, and unbent
   The knitted frown of snarling churlishness,
   And courtesy with homely candour blent.
Wherefore, content, nor checked by rude address,
   Could every class, in liberal intercourse
   Each with the other freely coalesce.
And in that free enchange was fresh resource
   Found of example's unobtruded aid,
   Inward æsthetic prompting to enforce.

Pleasant it was to watch, when day decayed,
   The ploughman, homeward wending wearily,
   Halt to remark the play of light and shade
In forest glade's perspective greenery,
   Or stoop to cull a herb or mineral,
   Or look up wistful to the western sky:
Pleasant to note the concourse cordial
   Of sage and bard with artisan and hind,
   In porch or garden, or at festival,
Where converse eloquent and wit refined
   United with the banquet's jovial cheer
   The feast of reason and the flow of mind.

Nor was there lacking, for the calmer sphere
   And even tenor of domestic life,

Aught that its tranquil joyance might endear.
No mere attendant in monotonous strife
    With want, nor follower in a dull routine,
    Nor drudging housemate, was the gentle wife,
Whose simple elegance of form and mien,
    And taste in whatsoe'er her hand arrayed
    Betokened purity enshrined within,
Contagious, and effectual to persuade
    To emulous and imitative love
    Of the divine ideal so portrayed.
Not rivals were the ardent youth who throve
    By manhood's side, nor eager to forestall
    Their heritage, nor seeming to reprove
Their elders' lingering, but habitual
    Rebuke, in watchful reason's sobering tone,
    Opposing to impetuous passion's call:
Not ignorant that self-restraint alone
    Upheld the fabric of their social state
    Unmoved upon self-poised foundation-stone:
Nor unreluctant, therefore, to abate
    Nature's instinctive flame, whence purer light
    Rose, to more pure devotion dedicate.

Such was the vision—in such colours dight,
    Of Labour's promised land of happiness,
    Which, when in spirit raised to Pisgah's height
'Twas given me to behold, with not the less
    Of prescient rapture, that no hope was mine
    Myself to enter in and to possess.
Not less in peace may I my part resign
    Whose eyes have seen millennium drawing nigh,
    Tutored its distant tokens to divine.
For 'twas no vain mirage that mocked my eye,
    Like to what dweller on Catanian shore
    Sees, when Fay Morgan paints the peopled sky.
My vision was of shadows thrown before
    Coming events, things that shall surely be,

Nor now delayed but until man, no more
Wholly on blinding lust intent, shall see
That his own interest and his kind's are one,
Blended in individual destiny.

Here the volume originally ended, and I have been repeatedly twitted, with more or less, or with no goodnature,
for introducing an attempt at verse into a staid treatise on
economics.   The step may have been ill-judged, but it was
taken advisedly, and for reasons into which, if I know myself,
no particle of affectation entered.   The higher stage of social
improvement towards which industrial cooperation and the
other beneficent influences specially referred to in the foregoing dissertations can be distinctly perceived to be tending,
would, if attained, be still very far below social perfection :
and desiring to show what is my own ideal of that perfection, I preferred describing it in metre, first, because I
happened to have a metrical description ready to my hand,
and secondly, because I felt that the aspirations therein
expressed would be more likely to be tolerated in juxta-
position with the licence of verse than with the sobriety of
prose.   Not that I am prepared to acknowledge any
extravagance in the vision with which my eyes have been
indulged.   Rather, am I persuaded that it must needs come
true sooner or later, provided only that chaos do not come
again first.   No doubt all past attempts, from the time of
the apostles downwards, to found a social republic, have
proved utter failures, owing to the inadequacy, either in
steadiness or in number, of those who have tried the experiment.   No doubt complete success must be preceded
by a world-wide diffusion of brotherly love, of which there
is as yet little enough among the nearest blood relations ;
and for the whole human family to become composed of
members loving each other as brethren will no doubt take
some time.   Still, time and time enough is the one thing

wanted for all consummations not absolutely impossible, and, among the rest, even for this. Already here and there may be found a few individuals who would be quite prepared to have all things in common, if only they could be joined by a sufficient number of similarly prepared associates. Some of us could readily point to some half-dozen or so of such among our personal acquaintance. Very estimable persons these are, occupying deservedly high places on our lists of friends, but by no means extorting from us any extraordinary homage. They by no means appear to us to have reached a pitch of moral elevation inaccessible to the multitude; after all, the most that need be said in their praise is that they have learnt to love their neighbours as themselves; and to do this would not have been so repeatedly given to us as a commandment if obedience of it were utterly beyond the power of average human beings. Mankind have never yet had a chance of showing of what intellectual, nor consequently of what moral advances they are capable. It is but a disjointed, piecemeal education, that the best instructed individuals have ever received, and the masses—'ignorant masses,' as we with proud consciousness of the difference between darkness and dusk, are in the habit of calling them—were for ages left without any, as indeed, for the most part, they are still. How should those who were never taught to distinguish between good and evil, know how to escape the evil and pursue the good? What else, without elevating precepts that they could understand or appreciate to guide them, could they do but follow each other's example, and go on perpetually grovelling along the low level congenial to self-seekers? Does it follow that if better light were to dawn upon them they would not endeavour to rise towards the light? And better light is dawning; society is awakening to the conviction that its only hope of safety lies in its furnishing suitable and early training to its dangerous classes; and even England, though still lagging far behind on a path on which it ought to have been her pride to take the lead, has begun to follow, however tardily, the lead of the Continent and of America, in respect to national education. Religiosity will not much longer be suffered to prevent those who are worst off in this world from being taught how to better themselves here, out of spite with itself for not being able to resolve how they should be taught what might better them hereafter : neither will the rights derived from the procreation of children be much longer held to include the right of bringing up children in ignorance of everything but misery and vice. Since rival sects cannot agree how the people are to be taught, an unsectarian legislature must step in to decide the question, providing adequate means of primary instruction for all for whom adequate provision of the same kind is not otherwise made, and insisting on those means being used by all for whom they are provided : insisting, moreover, that the abundant provision made by ancestral piety and munificence for instruction of a higher order shall no longer be misapplied, but be made accessible to all, however poor, who by success at primary schools may prove their capacity for duly profiting by the advantages afforded in superior places of learning.

When these educational appliances have come in aid of industrial unionism and industrial cooperation, and when all public employments are thrown open to merit as freely as private ones, though Labour's Utopia may still be very distant, large strides will have been made towards it. Whatever social inequalities may still continue to exist will be perceived to exist not in consequence of, but in spite of the arrangements of society, and will cease to be causes of social discontent. When all men and all women are adequately provided with artificial facilities for developing whatever talents they have been gifted with by nature, and for using those talents, subsequently, for their own individual advancement, any one's ill-success in life will plainly be the result either of his own fault or his own ill-luck, and for which, if he need not blame himself, he will at least have no pretext for blaming others ; neither is it easy to see how, in other than very exceptional cases, it will then be possible for ill-success to go far beyond keeping men in those conditions of life for which their relative capacities or incapacities best qualify them. Well, then, with the sense of social injustice, that mainspring of social hatred, thus dried up, with cooperative organization under various forms drawing men closer together and habituating them to look, not every one on his own things only, but every one also on the things of others, and with other agencies more strictly educational combining to promote intellectual, and with intellectual, moral growth, what stoppage of moral growth need there be, short of that development of which universal fraternity would be the outward and visible sign ? Truly I can see none, unless, as I said, chaos return prematurely—unless our social Utopia be forestalled by one of those physical catastrophes on which philosophers of a cheerful turn of mind are now-a-days so fond of speculating — a dispersion of solar heat into infinite space, mayhap, or a glacial *débâcle*, which would reinstate the earth as it was while without form and void, and before the Spirit of God had begun to move upon the face of the waters.

CHAPTER V.

SUPPLEMENTARY.

COOPERATIVE PROGRESS AND PROSPECTS. 'BREAKERS AHEAD.'

'COOPERATIVE' store societies with the 'Equitable Pioneers' at their head, have by this time had quite as much praise—I will not say as they deserve, but as is at all likely to do them good. After the long course of cloying commendation to which they have been subjected, a little outspoken criticism may prove a salutary alterative. Many of them are exhibiting symptoms of that rarest of diseases, pecuniary plethora. As all their shareholders may reckon pretty confidently on five per cent. dividends, and as to each of their customers is assigned periodically a separate percentage on the aggregate amount of his purchases, which has only to be left in the hands of the society, in order at once to become or gradually to accumulate into a share or shares, there is very considerable inducement to customers to become shareholders, and to shareholders to increase their shares; and the consequence is that the share capital of the store societies is at present increasing at an average rate of forty per cent. per annum. It is not possible, however, for the business of any of the societies to go on long increasing at anything like the same rate. Their sales are transacted almost exclusively with members of the labouring class, and those of any particular society with the labouring population of the immediate neighbourhood. In the conduct of business of such limited extensibility, only a proportionably limited quantity of capital can be profitably

employed, and the larger the proportion of customers that
become shareholders, the smaller on an average must be
each one's share in that quantity. If all the customers
were shareholders, the sellers would be equally numerous
and identical with the buyers; each of them would be as it
were dealing with himself alone, and no one could hold
more than the very small share of capital necessary for
that purpose without either preventing some of his associates from holding even so much, or making to the aggregate capital an addition for which the aggregate business
could not furnish employment; the necessary effect of such
an addition being to cause the same total of profits to be
distributed over a larger capital and thus to bring down the
rate of dividend. Now, this is an inconvenience of which
some of the larger societies—although there are none as
yet that have not many more customers than shareholders—
are already becoming painfully sensible, and those of
Rochdale and Halifax have in consequence and in self-
defence, been lately paying off non-purchasing shareholders,
and refusing to retain several thousand pounds of accumulations which purchasing shareholders were desirous of
leaving in their hands. Their capital, however, in spite of
these efforts to keep it down, is still a good deal above
what they have occasion for, and how to utilise the surplus and the additional funds which their constituents, if
permitted, would gladly commit to their charge, is a problem that is seriously embarrassing them. Several suggestions for its solution have been under consideration, and
one or two have been made the subject of experiment.
During the first twenty years or so of their existence, all
the store societies confined themselves almost exclusively
to retail trade; but in 1863, forty-four of them combined
to form the 'North of England Wholesale Agency and
Depôt.' This is an association standing to the societies by
which it is constituted in the same relation as that in which
each of them stands towards its individual constituents. It
undertakes to purchase for them the stores of various kinds

which they require, and in its subsequent sales to them, gives them in a roundabout fashion, imitated from their own practice, the benefit of the cheapness at which the comparative magnitude of its transactions has enabled it to purchase. It charges them probably the same price at which they could themselves have bought wholesale, but the net profits arising from the difference between that price and the still lower price itself has paid, are, after deduction of five per cent. on capital, divided rateably among its customers, in the proportion of the varying amounts of their purchases. Only store societies are accepted by it as customers, and, according to the original programme, these were to give it the whole of their custom; but this stipulation has not been adhered to. Few of the societies can be got to understand that it may be for their interest to supply themselves, even from a wholesale firm in which they are themselves partners, with articles which they can buy cheaper elsewhere, and party and personal feeling and local jealousies and suspicion not improbably sometimes prevent them from supplying themselves from it even with articles which they can nowhere else get on better terms. Still, though it has not received all the support it might fairly have counted upon, the wholesale establishment has done extremely well. By the end of 1868 the number of its constituent societies had increased from forty-four to ninety-one, exclusive of fifty-three others which were dealing with it, though they had not joined it as members. Its total of annual sales, too, which in 1864 was 9,400*l.* had risen to 423,000*l.*, and that its business is not less lucrative than extensive may be inferred from the fact that finding itself cramped in the premises it originally rented, it has been able out of its reserve fund to spare 9,000*l.* for building itself a mansion at Manchester, where its headquarters are.* There is a second association of the same class, denominated the ' Scottish Cooperative Wholesale,' with a capital

---

* Report by Mr. W. Nuttall, in Proceedings of Cooperative Congress, pp. 39-42.

of 1,208*l.* held by forty-one affiliating store societies, and having Glasgow as its central station ; and a third, the 'Metropolitan and Home Counties,' which, however, has scarcely yet emerged from the embryo stage.

It is easy to understand what manifold advantages retail store societies may derive from their connexion with one of these wholesale establishments. It places the smallest of them on a level, in many respects, with the largest, enabling all equally, without sending separate agents of their own to distant markets, to avail themselves of the experience and skill of practised buyers, and to provide themselves with goods of the best description on the lowest terms. It relieves them from the necessity of locking up capital in large stocks of goods, and from the risk of large loss on goods that might eventually prove unsaleable, enabling them also to do with less warehouse room. In these several ways it lessens their outlay, and permits them, at their choice, either to lower their selling prices proportionately, or to make proportionately larger profits for subsequent division among their customers. A higher utility of the wholesale machinery consists in its linking together numerous separate societies in federal bonds, and giving them common objects to be interested in, to discuss, and at first, no doubt, to dispute about. By dint of disputing on subjects on which all are personally interested in getting at the truth, those who begin by differing often end by agreeing, and agreement on small matters is one of the best preparations for concord on larger.

It is, however, the financial success of the wholesale undertakings which is chiefly to be noted here, for it is probably owing to this that some of the leading store societies are just now turning their thoughts to greatly enlarged undertakings of a similar kind. Why, it is asked, should their foraging operations be confined to the United Kingdom ? Why should not the 'North of England Wholesale,' or some analogous association, start as shipowners and foreign merchants, and import grain, groceries, draperies, and sundries direct from the producing countries? Of capital there is enough and to spare for a good commencement of these or any other feasible schemes, and there is no overweening conceit in assuming that the management which has shown itself so efficient at home will not lose its cunning by going abroad. And in truth there would seem to be few branches of commercial or industrial enterprise in which working men's associations may not advantageously engage, provided only they go the right way to work. Before, however, engaging in either of the two just alluded to, it may be well for them to consider what special risks they will thereby encounter, and what special precautions it may behove them in consequence to adopt. They will do well to recollect that ordinary shipowners and merchants, whether individuals, private firms, or joint-stock companies, meet with very various experiences, scarcely less often marring than making their fortunes ; and a trading league of working men following the same vocation, with no more than ordinary heedfulness, would no doubt have its full share of similar reverses, which moreover in its case would be more certainly and more immediately fatal. For there is no one respect in which a league of this novel sort would possess any peculiar advantages over its old-fashioned competitors in the commercial arena, and there are several in which it would labour under great comparative disadvantage. Even though it confined itself, as in common prudence it would, to purveying for the store societies out of which it had sprung, it could not, with more certainty than the existing 'North of England Wholesale Agency,' reckon upon having those societies as regular customers. Confining itself too to export trade, as in its capacity of mere purveyor it would be obliged to do, it would generally have to send out its ships in ballast, thereby virtually doubling the freight of its homeward-bound cargoes. Its agents, again, having to conform to the conflicting views and fickle policy of a plurality of masters, could not venture to act with the

same promptitude and decision as the correspondent or
deputy of a single merchant or of a firm directed by one
master mind, and would, in consequence, be continually
neglecting to avail themselves of favourable conditions of
the market.   The final result could scarcely fail to be that
the association would find the cost of importing greater
than that at which it might have purchased from other
importers.   Its imports would either therefore remain unpurchased by the societies on whose account they were
ordered, or if purchased by the latter at not less than cost
price, would place them at a disadvantage in their capacity
of retailers.   Profit on the federal capital invested in the
foreign venture would, of course, in such circumstances be
out of the question ; and the investing confederate societies
would be fortunate if they had not cause to regret that
they had not let their spare capital lie at home idle, and
gone on resignedly paying to its individual owners interest
upon it out of the profits of their domestic business.

Store societies must not deceive themselves as to the
secret of their past commercial success, which is mainly
this, that hitherto they have wisely refrained from con-
fronting any of the more serious of commercial dangers.
They have scrupulously avoided the quicksands of credit
and the whirlwinds of speculation.   They have had none
but ready money dealings, and have been their own chief
customers, and they have besides had among their servants
an unusually large proportion zealous of good works, devoted assistants whose freshness of enthusiasm for a new-
born cause was of itself a sufficient pledge for diligence and
fidelity, and might almost have exempted them from
supervision, yet who have nevertheless been generally sufficiently within the view of their employers to allow of all
their proceedings being closely watched.   With so many
safeguards it was scarcely possible to incur any serious dis-
aster, but equal immunities must not be expected by any
association of working men that may venture to challenge
the ordinary perils of trade with only the usual equipment

of ordinary traders. Rather would the uncertainty of success, which always attends a speculative career, be then
converted into certainty of failure. Even though the society's enlarged operations were in no other sense rash than
as being carried on beyond the range of the society's
supervision, the society would have but a poor chance, if
engaging in them with only its present organisation, and
without some improved principle of action. But to engage
in distant commerce is almost necessarily to become involved in a game of hazard, and if this game is to be
played for a working class association by agents whose zeal
has lost the edge of novelty, and to whom no fresh stimulants are applied, the odds will be too great against the
society in competition with energies more concentrated,
better directed, and more practised than its own.

Circumstances would indeed be materially changed if
store and other societies, styling themselves 'cooperative,'
were prepared to act up to their pretensions and to become
in reality what hitherto they have been only in name. Let
them fairly adopt the cooperative principle, let them—the
Rochdale Pioneers, for very shame, setting the example
and leading the way—take, in their capacity of employers,
their own employed into industrial partnership, increasing
the remuneration of all service rendered to them in proportion to every increase in the pecuniary value of the produce
of that service. Let their managers, secretaries, and
cashiers, their shopmen and shopwomen, their shoemaking,
clogmaking and tailoring hands, the labourers in their
cornmills and the operatives in their cotton mills be paid,
either in lieu of or in augmentation of fixed wages, by commission on the business they severally assist in, and let the
same plan be observed in any new branches of business
that may hereafter be undertaken, and it will matter comparatively little what those new branches are. So far as
adherence to their golden rule of exclusively ready money
dealings would permit, societies really cooperative might
become agriculturists, manufacturers, shipowners, and mer-

chants.   True, until they had learnt to commit themselves
with confidence to the guidance of selected leaders of ascertained competence, they would labour under the serious
disadvantage which always belongs to the divided counsels
of a plurality of masters in comparison with the singleness of
purpose of an individual chief.   But the superior efficiency
of subordinate agency would go far towards compensating
for inferiority of management, and it may be presumed
that the intelligent activity of Manilla shopmen and Greek
sailors, of M. Leclaire's artizans and Messrs. Brigg's pitmen, would be more than equalled in still more genuinely
cooperative shops, and ships and workplaces ; nor is it too
much to suppose that similar qualities would be displayed
little less decidedly by foreign deputies of a cooperative
mercantile society than by a partner in a mercantile firm
despatched on mercantile errands abroad.

But though on condition of their honestly adopting the
principle indicated, there may be few commercial or industrial pursuits on which associations of working men need
fear to enter, on no other condition will it be safe for them
to leave the beaten path with which alone they are at present familiar.   If prepared to exhibit the enlightened
liberality, which is the soul of all genuine cooperation, they
may prudently advance in almost any direction, thereby
promoting at once their own separate interests and the
general interest of universal labour.*   But until so prepared
they had better restrain their commercial ambition, which
will otherwise too surely hurry them to a destination, the
very opposite of that which they are proposing for themselves.

Moreover, although having the greater part of the commercial world before them where to choose, there is yet
one corner of it from which the associations in question,

---

* A paper by Dr. John Watts, printed in the ' Proceedings of the
Cooperative Congress,' pp. 43, 44, contains some judicious remarks on
the order of succession most suitable for different kinds of cooperative
enterprise.

however cooperatively disposed, cannot too heedfully stand aloof. There is one profession, and that unfortunately one for which English store societies are evincing a peculiar predilection, against which they and all similar societies cannot be too earnestly warned. To judge from the proceedings of the London Cooperative Congress of 1869, of the temper of the various bodies there represented, no scheme finds more favour in their sight than one for the formation of a 'Cooperative Bank,' the sole partners or shareholders in which, and also its sole customers, would be cooperative societies, real or nominal, and trades unions. These would deposit in it their spare capital, which would be employed in making, to such of them as might from time to time require such aid, loans at 5 per cent., which interest, if the bank had anything like the average business of ordinary joint-stock banks, would, it is expected, return to the constituent associations 10 or 15 per cent. upon their investments, instead of the paltry $1\frac{1}{2}$ or $2\frac{1}{2}$ per cent. at present paid to them upon their deposits with private bankers. A supposed recommendation of this plan is that of the financial condition of the borrowing societies much more might easily be known than a private bank commonly knows of the circumstances of its customers. A fatal objection to it seems to me to be that the so-called cooperative societies could not become customers in the manner expected, without casting adrift their sheet anchor. It is, I believe, a fact that every store society that has prospered has traded exclusively on its own capital, and that every productive society that has failed has operated with partially borrowed capital. Apparently, therefore, societies of either of these two kinds either would not become customers or would be very objectionable ones, and trades' unions plainly would be infinitely worse. A trades' union would seldom have occasion to borrow except when its members were on strike, but most certainly a bank undertaking to find funds for unionists on strike would presently have no alternative but to follow unionist example and to strike likewise. Nevertheless, suppose store or other industrial associations other than trades' unions to deal with the bank as borrowers as well as depositors, thereby becoming its debtors as well as its creditors, and suppose too, as we needs must, that having abandoned the course to which their solvency had previously been due, one or other of them should every now and then become bankrupt in consequence—its irrecoverable loans would then be so much abstracted from the sum total of cooperative capital, a circumstance but ill-conducive to the interests of general cooperation. So far as those are concerned, it would seem that if an industrial society must needs borrow it had better borrow from uncooperative than from cooperative lenders. Or suppose again that the bank, not confining itself to dealing with industrial associations, should engage in general banking business. For that occupation, neither have industrial associations any special aptitude naturally, nor could even cooperation give them any. The prospect of getting a percentage on profits might indeed tend to make the clerks more active, but it would also tend to make the managers more venturesome, and in the conduct of a bank, discretion is of still more account than activity. One thing general banking business would be likely enough to do for the associations that engaged in it: it would cure them of the surfeit of wealth of which some are complaining. They could hit upon few expedients better calculated to turn pecuniary plethora into atrophy.

What as much as anything seems to have made most of the parties to the late Cooperative Congress so enamoured of their great banking scheme is misconception with respect to the Credit Banks established in Germany under the auspices of M. Schulze Delitzsch. Of these, of which though in 1852 there was but one, there are now 1,200, with at least 500,000 members, a share capital of about two millions sterling, and a yearly business of about twenty millions, the best and clearest English account is that given by Mr. B. R. Morier,* Her Majesty's Chargé d'Affaires at Darmstadt, of whom according to far better judges than I can pretend to be, it is little to say that for thorough knowledge and understanding of things German, political or politico-economic, he is probably without a rival among Englishmen. Credit Banks may be described as coalitions of artizans or handicraftsmen formed for the purpose of borrowing on their aggregate credit money to be subsequently lent to individuals amongst themselves. Each associate is required to be an able workman, and in employment sufficiently regular to ensure his being able to contribute by periodical subscriptions a prescribed share of the requisite capital. Each associate, too, renders himself liable for the debts of the association to the full extent of his private property, and though of such property no single associate may possess more than a very small quantity, almost every one possesses some little, and many mickles making a muckle, a sensible amount is the result, upon the joint security of which amount, and of the share and reserve capital of the bank, whatever sum is obtained on loan, becomes available for distribution on loan among the separate shareholders. No loans, however, are made except to shareholders, or to any even of these excepting such as are of recognised worth, moral and industrial, or even to them except for the purposes of their several occupations, and that only on a scale commensurate with their ascertained requirements, or in general for periods of more than three months, or, if the loan be more than half as much again as the borrower's share in the capital, without material security or personal sureties. Then, the entire net profits of the first year and a certain percentage of those of succeeding years are set apart in order to form, together with the entrance fees of members, a reserve fund to meet emergencies. In this way the risk

* In two reports of marked ability, printed in ' Correspondence with H. M.'s Missions abroad, regarding Industrial Questions and Trades' Unions,' 1867 ; and in a paper read before the Cooperative Congress in 1869.

is rendered exceedingly small, and in comparison with the security so small that in practice capitalists are found ready enough to lend ten times the amount of the paid-up capital, which is the utmost that Credit Banks can borrow without breaking their own laws. The interest they have to pay does not usually exceed 4½ per cent. The rates at which they lend vary from 6½ to 14½ per cent., the highest of which may seem moderate to men among whom, according to M. Morier, before they joined the association, 60 per cent. was a common borrowing rate, and 700 per cent. one not unheard of.

These are the outlines of a system the conception and elaboration of which are due solely to M. Schulze Delitzsch, and do high honour to their distinguished author. Not the least among its many merits is the provision it makes for the solidification and amplification of its own basis. It is ordained that the amount for which credit is pledged shall from the outset not exceed a certain proportion to capital, and a course is marked out, continued adherence to which will gradually lessen and eventually obliterate that proportion, and do away entirely with the necessity for resort to credit. According to rule, the realised capital of one of M. Schulze's banks is never to be less than 10 per cent. of the whole trading capital, is to be raised as rapidly as possible to 20 or 25 per cent., and is ultimately to reach a maximum of at least 50 per cent. There is, however, no reason for its stopping there. It might be left to go on increasing until it became cent. per cent., when realised capital and trading capital would become one and the same thing. In regard to solidity, the system would then approach very nearly to perfection. Neither for this would it be necessary for the shareholders to make any extraordinary efforts or sacrifices. They would not have to increase their subscriptions proper beyond what might otherwise have been requisite. They would simply have to content themselves for a time with dividends at the current rate of interest on their paid-up shares, and to allow all surplus profits to go towards augmentation of the reserve fund. Neither would they have to do this for a very lengthened period. The profits of the business done with the share capital would suffice of themselves to pay ordinary interest on that share capital, so that the entire net profits of the borrowed capital would remain available for other appropriation. These latter profits, it may be presumed, would be at least 3 per cent., and increasing, as if applied in the manner supposed they would do, at the rate of arithmetical progression with compound interest super-added, they would require little more than twenty years in order to accumulate into a sinking fund of equal amount with the loan from which they had been originally derived. When this was done all danger of insolvency would be absolutely eliminated. What had begun as a credit bank would have been converted into an institution whose business would consist in making loans to its shareholders out of their own money, and which would possess consequently a stability that no imaginable defalcations on the part of individual customers could jeopardise : while at the same time the bank's constituent shareholders, in return for their temporary abstinence and self-denial in allowing the bank's capital to attain full development, would be abundantly rewarded by the regular and largely enhanced dividends on which they might thenceforward reckon with absolute certainty.

It is needless to insist on the value of a system which, ' in an incredibly short space of time has spread its ramifications over the whole face of Germany,' and which is already placing at the command of labour twenty millions sterling worth of material aids to self-employment. Such rapid progress, and such visibly beneficent efficacy are its best and sufficing eulogists. It is important, however, to note distinctly both in what the utility of the system consists, and what local peculiarities of circumstances have favoured its development. In Germany, the industrial ascendency of large over small capitals is much less decided than in this country. Factory labour has not there, nearly to the same extent as here, supplanted domestic labour. In every department of production, Germany still retains a considerable number of independent workmen doing business on their own account. These are the chief constituents and chief customers of the credit banks, and almost the sole customers also of what in Germany are called 'raw material associations;' the object of which, as may be inferred from their name, is to purchase materials in large quantities for distribution at low prices among small producers. From each of these classes of institutions they derive assistance of the kind which they most need, the former permitting a poor artisan or handicraftsman to borrow, on nearly as good terms as the largest manufacturer, as much money as he can be safely trusted with for the purposes of his calling ; the latter offering to him equal facilities with his richest rivals for providing himself with industrial necessaries in the cheapest market. The benefit hence accruing would be very great if it consisted simply in enabling small masters and master workmen somewhat to prolong the contest in which they are engaged with large employers, and gradually to prepare for succumbing eventually to their antagonists instead of being crushed suddenly ; but the benefit will be incalculably greater if they avail themselves of the respite allowed to them individually to combine together in genuinely cooperative societies, and so to qualify themselves for maintaining the contest indefinitely, and retaining their industrial independence permanently. Now it is in the opportunities which it affords for doing this that the great merit of M. Schulze's system seems to me to consist. In Germany, as elsewhere, the ultimate doom of small production is perhaps irrevocably sealed. There, no more than elsewhere, will it be possible for industry on a small scale to make a permanent stand, at least in the majority of manufacturing operations, against the advantages which the possession of superior machinery, more minute division of labour, and more economy of superintendence give to the large capitalist. Opposed by such odds, it must needs be overpowered at last, and unless it enlarge its own dimensions, the utmost that M. Schulze's or any other system can do for it is to break, by postponing, its inevitable fall. But with the help of M. Schulze's system, it may have both time and means for enlarging itself—for growing by aggregation from small to large production, and what is more essential than all else, into larger production invigorated by the exceptional energy which belongs to cooperation ; for though the immediate object of credit banks be to assist the shareholders in separately maintaining their industrial positions, it affords them at the same time much of the particular education required to fit them for industrial association. By being brought together for a common purpose, the shareholders acquire something of the fellow-feeling and public spirit which fellowship for worthy ends seldom fails to engender. From the profits of their banking ventures they obtain, both in their collective and individual capacities, the funds indispensable for their engaging in further collective enterprise. The share they are called upon to take in administration elicits their administrative talents. Referring to this last point, Mr. Morier describes the German credit societies as ' small democratic republics, in which the entirety of the citizens not merely control the management of their affairs, but themselves manage them,' ' business knowledge and business habits becoming thus generally diffused, and a body of business men being trained up within the association,' ready either to take the places of vacating managers, or to occupy corresponding places in any class of industrial association.

Of the perfect suitableness of arrangements like these to the industrial circumstances of Germany, there can be little question, but it by no means follows that they would be equally well adapted to the very different circumstances of the British Islands. Very few of our workmen are independent in the sense of being their own employers, and the few that are would not greatly improve their industrial prospects, by borrowing, if they should be able so to borrow, on their collective credit, for the purpose of extending their respective undertakings. The number of large employers, and also the disparity between their resources and those of independent workmen, are already too great and are too rapidly increasing to leave to the latter any chance in direct competition with them. What enables small masters and petty dealers temporarily to hold their ground amongst us is the share they retain of the custom of the comparatively poor, and even this custom is being continually encroached upon by the operations of large traders. The ascendency of large capitalists besides being firmly fixed, is too far advanced not to go on advancing. If small capitalists would not be overborne, the only resource open to them is one already frequently adverted to. They must make their capitals great by association, and reinforce association by cooperation. But even then, and however many cooperative societies had sprung up in consequence, there would still be little more place in this country than before for credit banks analogous to those of Germany. Such of the cooperative societies as had thriven would not require the aid of the banks, and to such as were still in their infancy it could not be prudently given; neither could the latter, which alone would have any motive for establishing credit banks, be able to provide the requisite means. Requiring all and more than all the money of their own which they could scrape together for the prosecution of their own proper business, they would have none to spare for investment in banking business. There would therefore be no paid-up shares to serve as securities for loans, neither would a cautious capitalist be likely to regard the collective credit of many penniless societies, all equally eager to borrow, as much better security than that of any one of them separately. Nor again, even if this preliminary difficulty were got over, and a bank were actually established, could there be much doubt as to its fate, which indeed has been recently foreshadowed by the sudden decease, after a brilliant but brief career, of the 'Crédit au Travail' of Paris?* No very different end could well be in store for a bank, without other customers than industrial associations that could not become customers, without violating one of the most vital of their constitutional principles.

Some English industrial associations have latterly given part of their attention to building operations. At Rochdale, the Equitable Pioneers have constructed five or six rows of six or eight-roomed dwellings for the purpose of letting or selling them to working-class families. The store societies of Bacup and some other places have been acting similarly, and there and elsewhere more of the same kind would have been done, but for the obstacles to the conveyance and acquisition of real property which are presented by our land laws, and which are daily rendering those laws more and more intolerable nuisances. Being intolerable, however, they will not much longer be suffered to impede a movement which at once affords a perfectly safe

---

* The history of the 'Crédit au Travail' is full of instruction, and deserves to be carefully studied by ardent cooperators. It was founded in 1864, and in the early part of 1868 was spoken of by M. Rieder as follows : 'This is to my eyes the establishment which best responds to the general wishes, the only one whose laws may be copied literally by every friend of cooperation who wishes to lead the workmen to unite for their mutual benefit.' In December following it failed, and in June last its funeral oration was thus pronounced by the Rev. Mr. Molesworth : 'It was in the hands of excellent and admirable men. I do not think I ever in my life met with any, more generous or single-hearted, or more anxious to do good. They were also men of remarkable literary ability, but they were theorists and politicians, not men of practical business knowledge and habits ; admirable for turning out a grand scheme of operations, but quite unfitted to carry it into effect. The institution which they formed was rather a loan society than a bank, and as they were animated by a spirit of the most enthusiastic and generous propagandism, I have no doubt they made their loans very liberally, but somewhat too rashly : that they established societies where the elements of success did not exist, and led others to lean on their assistance which could not be sustained, or which would have done better without such support.'

investment for the spare funds of those who engage in it,
and supplies, as far as it goes, one of the most crying of
working-class wants, that of suitable habitations.   Such a
movement the law might be content to at least let alone,
for it is one from which nothing but good can proceed,
provided only that it do not lead to the premature adoption
of schemes resembling it a little in name but differing
widely from it in essentials.   So far as it has hitherto proceeded, it has had no other visible effect than that of
reproducing at Rochdale and elsewhere the excellent idea
embodied in the *cités ouvrières* of Mulhouse, but it has also
given rise to aspirations very far ahead of itself, and to
frequent talk about 'home colonies,' 'associated homes,' and
' cooperative villages.'   In these, according to the programme, 'supply is to be systematically adapted to
demand, and demand is to be determined by the extent of
the reasonable wants of the population.'   The colonists are
to consider beforehand what quantities of different articles
they will require, and having thus ascertained demand, are
to make arrangements for supplying, as nearly as may
be, just it and no more, producing cooperatively certain
articles, and obtaining others by equitable exchange with
the external competitive world, wherein, although, ' owing
to the immense powers of production which now exist,'
there is believed to be always more produce on sale than
there are customers for, it is still not doubted that the
excellence of cooperative products will ensure for them a
ready market.   The goods thus ' cooperatively obtained,'
are to be 'cooperatively possessed and distributed, so
that all may be able to enjoy the products of the united
industry of all,' the influence of a special education being
so directed as to prevent the numbers or wants of the
community from exceeding their self-supporting ability.
Every one will then be assured of a fair share of employment and of adequate remuneration for his labour.   With
a view to all which, a limited liability company is to be

formed to supply on loan 'funds for the practical initiation of the new order of things.'*

Of projects like these, whatever others may think, the worst that I am myself disposed to say is that their time is not yet; the world is not yet ripe for them. It is needless to point to the palpable anachronism involved in arrangements designed for purposes transcendentally disinterested, yet depending for execution on a joint-stock company, caring for nothing but for interest on its money, yet content to rely for that interest on the productive industry of a community predetermined on principle to be only moderately industrious. Some day or other mankind may be prepared, though scarcely in the mode suggested, to convert Blithedale romances into realities, but that day is still a long way off, and the surest sign of its having at length dawned will be that fitting instruments for effecting the romantic realisation in question will offer themselves spontaneously, without requiring to be coaxed or subsidised. Meanwhile, cooperative zeal may find abundance of preparatory occupation in attempts of a much humbler character. Agricultural cooperation, for instance, must make considerable progress before cooperative colonisation can be at all hopefully commenced ; and agricultural cooperation has rather receded than advanced from the stage to which, in some parts of Europe, it had reached during the middle ages. In one of his later chapters M. Feugueray gives an interesting account of certain *colonies agricoles*, which he imagines to have been peculiar to France, but to which parallels may probably be found in most countries that retain much of the impress of mediævalism. Wherever a great territorial lord, whether sovereign or subject, possessing sufficient despotic authority for the purpose, chooses to hold the entire population of one of his villages collectively and severally responsible for the entire rent of the lands occupied by them, the entire population naturally assume collective rights corresponding with their collective liabilities.

* 'Proceedings of Cooperative Congress.' Paper by Dr. Travis.

Their modes of exercising these rights vary considerably. In Russia, unemancipated serfs holding lands in common, usually divide either the whole or the cultivated portions of those lands amongst themselves, each family receiving a certain share to be held for a certain period, at the end of which a new general partition takes place. This is the usual custom in India also, where, however, sometimes, village lands are cultivated as well as held in common by the whole village population, among whom is shared the net produce, after deduction of the Government due, and this seems to have been the ordinary practice in the French 'colonies' of which Feugueray speaks. Late in the last century several of these were still extant in full vigour in Auvergne and the Nivernois, and a picture of one drawn from the life, in 1788, by M. Legrand d'Aussy, presents some singular features. The example selected from some half-dozen in the same neighbourhood was that of Pinon, near Thiers, in Auvergne. This was a little hamlet composed of four households, numbering nineteen men, women, and children of the same name (Guittard), and, with the addition of thirteen servants, forming a population of thirty-two in all. The origin of the community was hidden in the depths of antiquity, but was supposed to date from the twelfth century. The form of government was an elective patriarchate. By a majority of votes in full general assembly were chosen a 'master' and a 'mistress,' who however, were never permitted to belong to the same household, and between whom were divided all administrative functions—the one superintending sales and purchases, directing repairs, apportioning fieldwork, and regulating the higher domestic economy ; the other looking after the poultry-yard, the kitchen, the laundry, and clothing department. The other members of the family stood to these in the relation of children to parents. All worked together so far as the nature of their several occupations would permit, were lodged and boarded together, ate at the same table, dressed in the same style, and did all at the general expense. For everything belonged to everybody ; all property remained in mass ; no one inherited, no one bequeathed; nothing was divided, unless one of the young women married out of the society, when 600 francs were assigned to her as dowry. Besides dwellings and out-houses, their real property consisted of rye-land, vineyards, a wood, a garden, and a great many chestnut trees, on the produce of which they lived, consuming it all themselves, and seldom having any left for sale. What money they had was derived from the sale of articles of cutlery, in the manufacture of which part of them were employed. On the whole they must have been well enough off, for they were famous for their charity, no beggar being suffered to pass their doors without being offered bread and soup, and, if it were winter, a bed in a room fitted up on purpose, with a brazier in it. So late as 1840, another specimen of the same species—that of the Jaults, which had existed from time immemorial, had weathered the storms of the Revolu-tion, and was still flourishing—was discovered by M. Dupin in a corner of the Nivernois. This consisted of thirty-eight persons, forming one single household, and holding in fee simple a domain, the value of which had by their industry been raised to more than 200,000 francs. When one of their maidens married a stranger, the dowry she carried off with her was 1,350 francs. The conditions of membership are summed up by M. Dupin as those of living with, work-ing with and for the community, and having it for sole heir, so that the society became perpetuated by the substi-tution of persons, without any change in its constitution, its mode of being, or its property. The morality of the Jaults was a rule proved by its having had only one recorded exception; and even then, we are told, the scandal of which one young person inconsiderately allowed herself to become the subject, an opportune marriage almost im-mediately repaired. Their sanitary condition was perfect ; the men were strong and tall, and the women robust, and some of them not bad-looking—*quelques-unes assez bien—*

and their material well-being was the more striking from
the contrast presented to it by the village of Les Garriots,
where, until dissolved by the Revolution, a similar community had similarly flourished. There, the principal
building was still standing, and still sheltered some of its
former inmates, but its spacious apartments had been
divided, a partition wall cut the fireplace of the old kitchen
and refectory in half, and from their separate kennels a
few squalid creatures peeped out suspiciously on their
strange visitors, but slunk back as soon as spoken to.
Among the Jaults there were plenty, health, gaiety ; among
the Garriots penury and gloom.*

Jaults and Guittards, interesting not more as relics of
the past than as earnests of a possible future, have now
followed in the wake of the Garriots. All have passed
utterly away, leaving no specimens of the same class behind ;
and in France nothing has yet sprung up to supply their
places—neither industrial partnerships between farmers
and labourers, nor associations of small landowners, though
no expedient would seem better calculated than this last
to remedy the evils resulting from excessive subdivision of
the land. Unfortunately, long moral preparation is requisite to enable French peasants to accept a change so opposed to all their previous modes of thought. Before they
can comprehend and appreciate its bearings, they must be
so far metamorphosed as to rid themselves of that passion
for land as an individual possession which has become to
them a second nature, and as yet there are no signs of
such a transformation having even commenced. For industrial partnership between farmers and labourers, indeed,
there is more call, as there are also greater facilities, on the
English than on the French side of the Channel, but everywhere its adoption will be impeded by powerful obstacles
—plentiful lack of good-will on the part of the masters,
plenty of positive ill-will on that of the men—greed, pride,
hardness among the former, envious spite and jealous dis-

* Feugueray, 'L'Association ouvrière,' pp. 160–166.

trust among the latter—indisposition to make advances on the side from which alone they can be made, as much indisposition or more to meet them on the other. There is little exaggeration in the description once given by a Saturday Reviewer of the two great divisions of our agricultural population : employers, considering themselves to have a sort of property in those to whom or for whom they are always paying either wages or poor rates ; employed, recognising, without at all relishing, the destiny assigned to them of drudges to the lucky folk, grand enough to get leases and to do their ploughing and mowing by proxy. Here doubtless are strong mutually-repelling influences, not, however, hopelessly unappeasable. Among the educated men who, in many Scotch and some English counties, have now taken to farming as a profession, there must be not a few to whom the ever-smouldering feud between themselves and their retainers would be an unceasing source of discomfort, even if it did not occasionally break out into flames, not always metaphorical, and who would gladly see their way to the establishment of more mutually satisfactory relations, on a basis of mutual interdependence and mutual interest. It would not be surprising, therefore, if, before long, some Lothian or Northumbrian farmer were to attempt an agrarian imitation of the example set by Messrs. Briggs, nor need we doubt that the experiment, if tried with equal tact and judgment, would prove as successful in the fields as in the colliery. Whoever should make such a move would, after all, be only following, and at a humble distance, the lead given a good while back in a remarkable instance by an English country squire.

Considering how little disposed even now are any persons similarly circumstanced to go and do likewise, one would like to know exactly how it was that fourteen years before the first enrolment of Rochdale Pioneers, Mr. Gurdon, of Assington Hall, in Suffolk, came to conceive, and became emboldened to act upon, an idea which class prejudices might have been expected to make him regard as very

objectionably revolutionary. Early in 1830, having a farm
that would become vacant at Michaelmas, he called together
the labourers of the parish, and offered to let it to a limited
number of them on condition of each of the number subscribing 3*l.* towards providing the requisite stock, he himself engaging, in that case, to lend them, without interest,
what additional money might be needed. Only fifteen
accepted the offer, the 3*l.* subscription proving an insuper-
able bar to the rest, as it might have done to all, if Mr.
Gurdon had not helped the respondents to his invitation by
letting them have for the season some waste land, which
they dug up and planted with potatoes and oats. At Michaelmas the fifteen took possession of their farm, consisting at first of 66 acres, with a rude but decent homestead
upon it, and received from the landlord, according to promise, a loan of 400*l.* The rent agreed upon was about
36*s.* per acre, inclusive of rates and taxes, or about 30*s.*
net, and this and all other dues they boast of having always
paid with unvarying punctuality. In about ten years and
a half they had restored the 400*l.* In 1855, Mr. Gurdon,
finding, as he says, that he had ' no other land so well
farmed as theirs,' added 47 acres to it, and in 1867 he
added 16 or 17 acres more, making in all 130 acres ; which
are now held on a fourteen years' lease at a net rent of
197*l.* 10*s.*, *exclusive* of rates and taxes, by twenty-one joint
tenants, an accession of six having been made to the
original fifteen. Having paid off their landlord's loan,
they are now complete owners of all the stock and implements on the farm. They have six horses, four cows, 110
sheep, and from 30 to 40 pigs ; and they are in possession
also of a first-class thrashing machine. The original 3*l.*
shares are now worth 50*l.* each, and the accumulated savings
thus invested do not represent all that has been gained, for
though ' all years have not been equally remunerative,
there has not been one without some little matter to divide.'

In 1854 Mr. Gurdon made over to a similar copartnership

of 36 members, each of whom had to subscribe 3*l.* 10*s.*, a farm which at first consisted of only 70 acres, but which has since been more than trebled in size. Here again he lent without interest 400*l.*, the whole of which was paid back in the course of a few years; and the little society, now occupying 212 acres, at a rent of 325*l.*, exclusive of 50*l.* of tithes, rates, and taxes, are not only out of debt, but are in possession of farming stock to the value of 1,200*l.*, their original seventy-shilling shares being in consequence worth 30*l.* each.

By most people these results may be deemed eminently satisfactory, but they will rather disappoint those who, duly appreciating the powerful efficacy of the cooperative principle, may not be aware that the principle has been but imperfectly applied at Assington. The two farms together do not afford regular work for more than ten or twelve out of the fifty or so of able-bodied shareholding labourers, and few of the others accept even occasional jobs on their own fields, their excellent characters ensuring them constant employment elsewhere. These others, therefore, are little more than passive capitalists, sleeping partners in the concern; while the ten or twelve active members receive as wages only the rates current in the neighbourhood, all profits being divided equally among all the shareholders, each of whom is restricted to a single share. The actual cultivators, therefore, would be benefited only in the proportion of about one-sixth of any addition which extra exertion on their part might make to the net produce, and their motives for extra diligence are weakened proportionally; whereas, if after deduction of five per cent. interest on capital, the balance of profits, instead of being wholly appropriated by capital, were shared rateably with labour as represented by wages, capital itself might not improbably be a sensible gainer by reason of the increased productiveness to which labour so stimulated might attain. The augmented produce might very possibly be enough, after covering the bonus to which labour had become entitled, to leave something more than before for capital. The profits actually realised have been, on one of the farms, 1,000*l.* in forty years ; on the other, 1,200*l.* in five years, or at the annual rates of 25*l.* and 80*l.* respectively ; no very extraordinary returns to be made by farms of 131 and 212 acres. Still, in spite of every drawback, the experiment has been a decided success. The heads of fifty labouring families have, by the acquisition of 30*l.* or of 50*l.* worth of property, been made rich beyond any dream of avarice the most sanguine of them could previously have formed. To the dry bread which used to be the staple of their food, home-brewed beer, milk, pork, bacon, have been added as habitual articles of diet. From recipients of relief as paupers, they have become payers of poor's rates. Though some of them cannot write or read, they can all afford to send their children to school, and ' there is not one of us,' writes one of them, ' who has not endeavoured to make each of his children a better scholar than himself.' Their landlord also has good reason to be satisfied. His land is better cultivated than it ever was before, and the rent for it is regularly paid and with sensibly diminished deductions on account of poor's rates.* When the example set by him comes to be generally known, it will scarcely remain long without imitators. He has shown how gentlemen in his position may, at considerably less than no expense, indulge in the luxury of doing good, of a kind nearly akin to one for which members of their favoured class often display considerable aptitude. They are in general fond of experimenting on live stock. Whenever one of us other unfortunates, whose doom it is to be for six days out of seven in populous city pent, manages to escape into the country from Saturday till Monday on a visit to some compassionating squire, he is almost sure, if supposed to have any turn that way, to be led after church on Sunday

* Rev. James Fraser's Report to Agricultural Commission, 1867 ; also ' Cooperator' for February 1863, and January 16, 1869.

through the cowhouses and piggeries, and be called upon to admire the sleekness and snugness of the inmates. But the host would get quite as much credit as a breeder, both in his visitor's eyes and his own, if he were to pay as much attention to the human as to the bovine and porcine stock on his estate, and had equally fine specimens of the former to exhibit. True wealth, as Carlyle somewhere says, consists in the abundance, not of the things which you possess, but of those which you take an interest in, and there are few English villages in which the raw material of such wealth does not abound for owners of the soil, capable of taking as much pride in the men as in the cattle that help to till it, and willing to learn from Mr. Gurdon one of the ways in which, with little trouble and no risk, the material may be suitably fashioned.

What under Mr. Gurdon's auspices has been done at Assington, will, however, be all the more likely to be done elsewhere if other landlords are not left to take the initiative quite so completely as he has been. There are many more gentlemen having land to let than money to lend with it, but if a score or so of ploughmen and the like were to come forward with money of their own in their hands sufficient to stock a farm, there would be little need for hesitation in letting them have a lease of it. Their having managed to scrape together the requisite preliminary capital would of itself be a tolerable pledge for their continued good management. Now, among other useful lessons which experience at Assington teaches, is how farm labourers aspiring to the rank of farm tenants may furnish themselves with the needful pecuniary equipment. The parish is not a large one, covering about 3,000 acres, with a population of about 700; but it is large enough to maintain an associative store, established seven years ago mainly through the instrumentality of a retired butler, quite a paragon, one fancies, in his way. Many of the working men who have taken shares in the concern are already in the habit of saying that they need no longer trouble themselves about their house-rent, for that the store pays it for them, intimating thereby that their aggregate dividends on shares and purchases amount, on an average, to 4*l.* or 5*l.* a-head annually. If so, a dozen members might in half-a-dozen years put together 400*l.*, so having, to begin with, as much money of their own as the earlier of Mr. Gurdon's copartneries had to borrow at starting, together with a scarcely less valuable amount of associative training, which the copartnery had to spend some years in subsequently acquiring. That would be a very timid landlord who should fear to accept such candidates as tenants, unless indeed he disliked the prospect of their subsequently raising themselves still nearer to his own social level, for probably enough their ambition would not rest content at their first elevation.   Probably enough, from tenants in common they would desire to become proprietors in common, and with time and patience they might find means and opportunities of purchasing either the lands they were occupying or others equally suitable. By many, perhaps, the creation of a new peasant proprietary by a process like this would be regarded as a decided retrogression.   For myself, as I need scarcely say, the idea is the very reverse of terrible, nor in truth can I think of anything which, to the most hopelessly depressed section of our labouring population, would be more practically edifying than the sight of it in full operation. This is, however, not the place for obtrusion of my favourite hobby, nor indeed does space remain for the introduction of any fresh topic. With a few passages of somewhat diffuse moral, corresponding with the heterogeneous preamble out of which it arises, this, perhaps, too discursive chapter shall therefore conclude.

Self-helpfulness is the life-blood of industral cooperation, and the purer the blood and the freer from adventitious stimulants, the stronger and firmer will be the tissues. Naturally enough, ardent sympathisers in the cooperative cause are eager to promote it ; but movement, they should recollect, is not always the steadier or more direct for being pushed, particularly if the push be given at the wrong end. Associative stores as in England, mutual credit banks as in Germany and France, sound 'provident' societies everywhere, are forms of association well fitted to qualify their members for subsequent association of a higher order, and philanthropy unattached might usefully expend itself in encouraging their adoption, provided that, in opposition to the usual precept, it were content to do so by word instead of deed, by suggestion chiefly, and by offering instead of obtruding even that. In this way there is work to be done everywhere, and in rural parishes more especially, resident gentry, laic or cleric, might do much. But it should never be forgotten that whatever is done on behalf of working men that tends in any degree to impair their self-reliance, tends in the same degree to the defeat of its own purpose. Neither is there much less danger in urging towards any species of association any who do not, by readily undertaking it, show themselves to be consciously fit for it. On these points all evidence is concurrent. Of fifty-six societies which participated in the 3,000,000 francs voted by the French Constituent Assembly in 1848 for distribution on loan amongst cooperative associations, eighteen collapsed in the first year; only nine survived until 1855; only four were in existence in 1864. 'Our societies,' says M. Valleroux, 'vary greatly as to their capital. Some have abundance ; others nothing but debts. These are the young ones that have borrowed to make a start. Recent misfortunes have, however, taught us that in order to maintain themselves, societies must start with their own resources. Those to which money has been lent have almost always brought loss upon the lenders without themselves succeeding.' 'One fault,' says Mr. Fane, 'in the organisation of French societies has been too much faith in the combination of skill and labour, and too little regard for the cooperation of capital. . . . Another great mistake has been the preference of societies of production to building societies, loan societies, and societies of consumption. The latter should come first, for they enable the workmen to effect savings, and to learn providence. Their tendency is to endow him with the capital and the prudence without which his participation in the productive form of association is seldom satisfactory.' 'Our mutual credit societies,' says M. Valleroux, consisting of 'working men accustomed to see each other and to choose each other to conduct business matters, are almost all progressing, because the members, being careful in selecting each other, no unworthy ones are received, and each makes a point of honouring his engagement.' German workmen, says Mr. Axom, 'have become gradually convinced that to found a manufacturing society, and to conduct it to prosperity, it is necessary, not only to unite the capital needful for the making and sale of the goods, but to be able also to count upon business knowledge, upon the true spirit of co-operation, and honesty of management. So they do not hasten to open such establishments, but wait for a favourable opportunity.' In a word, cooperators are being taught by experience that self-dependence and self-discipline are first essentials of success, and it would ill become friends of cooperation to dissuade them from acting up to the lesson. Quite laudably these latter may, in accordance with a resolution come to at the late Cooperative Congress, proceed to the establishment of 'a propaganda for extending the cooperative system to agricultural and other districts where at present it is not in operation.' Hereby they will at least obtain safety-valves for the escape of their own superabundant fervour, and not improbably may substantially further the good cause they have at heart. But there or thereabouts the friends of cooperation, unless prepared like Messrs. Briggs or Mr. Gurdon to become themselves cooperators, had better stop, without, at all events, attempting to devise financial apparatus for the artificial incubation of cooperative eggs. Whatever eggs are not addled in the laying will have a much better chance of being properly hatched if left under the care of their parents.   My own full assurance of faith in the future of cooperation has already perhaps been more than sufficiently stated.   Yet one additional prediction regarding it shall be hazarded.   'The child of Socialism,' as Mr. Morier styles it, 'rescued from the dangerous custody of its parent, and brought up in the orthodox tenets of the economic faith,' it is, I am persuaded, destined to beget, at however remote a date, a healthy Socialism as superior to itself in all its best attributes as itself is to its parent.   But for the forthcoming of such offspring it is indispensable that there be no violent shortening of the natural period of gestation.   Or, if I might venture on one more simile, and liken cooperation to a plant which unaided labour, having first raised as a seedling, has ever since trained and tended, I would say that it is destined to grow into a mighty tree, beneath whose branches universal labour shall one day find shelter, and take alternately its exercise and rest.   But for this the tree must have room to spread, and exposure to harden it.   To enclose it in a hot-house, or to seat it on a hot-bed, would only be to stunt or stifle it.

LONDON: PRINTED BY
SPOTTISWOODE AND CO., NEW-STREET SQUARE
AND PARLIAMENT STREET